Bicycling the Louisville Metropolitan Area

Michael W. Thompson

ISBN: 0-692-94343-9
ISBN-13: 978-0-692-94343-4

DEDICATION

This book is dedicated to my smart, lovely, and talented daughter, Laurel G. Thompson.

CONTENTS

ACKNOWLEDGMENTS

Of the many people without whom this book would not have been possible, I would like to personally thank my daughter Laurel Thompson, my father Gary Thompson, my mother Faye Thompson, and my sister Jennifer Thompson, all of whom have encouraged me over the past few years and have endured my many projects, hobbies, and interests. Finally, I wish to thank the Comets, my riding companions whose company and stimulating conversations have helped while away many long miles over the past few years. The beer and hot wings didn't hurt, either.

Sunset over the Ohio River

FOREWORD

From a cyclist's perspective, the state of Kentucky has something to offer for almost everyone. There are many regions with flat terrain and well-maintained roads that are ideal for novices, as well as areas with steep, challenging hills and exhilarating descents for the more advanced or adventurous rider. Kentucky has a bit of everything, including wide-open rural areas with scenic views, majestic rivers, thriving urban environments, and many sites of interest to explore. With many recent improvements to the road system and efforts to ensure the safety of cyclists, there has never been a better time to take up the sport and explore the many treasures that the state of Kentucky has to offer.

Most of the cycling guides covering Kentucky have traditionally focused on the state's larger urban centers: Louisville and Lexington. The first guide in this series, *Pedaling Paducah and the Jackson Purchase*, covered the western edge of the state. The second book in this series covers the Louisville Metropolitan area, which is within an easy driving distance for most Kentuckians and many residents of neighboring states. The Louisville area offers a mixture of all the features about Kentucky that make it great for cycling: areas of flat, easy terrain; challenging hills; numerous parks and green spaces; and a thriving urban core with a rich history and many points of interest to explore. Metro Louisville also features the Louisville Loop, an ongoing civic project that will eventually encircle the entire city with more than 100 miles of bike paths, bike lanes, and shared-use roadways. In the Louisville area, there is something for cyclists of every interest and skill level to enjoy.

What sets this guide apart from others is that while previous guides have focused primarily on the many rural areas outside of the city and/or outside of Jefferson County, this guide focuses primarily on routes that explore the city's urban core and suburbs. In contrast to other guides, the route

1

descriptions in this guide also describe the history of the areas along the route and highlight points of interest. A special effort has been made to emphasize many interesting places and objects that may be a little off the beaten path or that are seldom noticed.

Many of the routes outlined in this guide explore the diverse neighborhoods that comprise the city's urban core and suburbs, areas that even many lifelong residents have never explored. Instead of simply coming and going from their own homes and neighborhoods and passing familiar scenery along the major arteries without ever slowing down to notice the passing scenery, this guide encourages people to slow down, take a few detours, and discover the many interesting things there are to be found, whether they are traveling by bicycle, by foot, or even in a car or motorcycle.

To that end, this guide was created to encourage visitors and residents of Metro Louisville to slow down a bit, explore their surroundings, and perhaps utilize alternative modes of transportation in the process. Have fun exploring!

GEOGRAPHY, GEOLOGY, AND CLIMATE OF THE LOUISVILLE METROPOLITAN AREA

The Louisville metropolitan area refers to the city of Louisville and the entirety of Jefferson County, Kentucky (now incorporated as Louisville Metro), in addition to the seven surrounding counties in Kentucky and Floyd and Clark Counties in Indiana. Often referred to as "Kentuckiana," the Louisville metropolitan area is listed as the 44th largest metropolitan area in the United States. According to the 2010 U.S. Census, the population of the Louisville metropolitan area was 1,307,647. Since 2003, Louisville has had a combined city and county government, referred to as the Louisville/Jefferson County Metro Government, or Louisville Metro. The population of Louisville Metro was 756,832 according to the latest census.

Like most major cities in the United States, Louisville has many distinct and unique neighborhoods that have their own histories and characteristics. The city's oldest neighborhoods are located along the Ohio River and include the Downtown district and the Portland neighborhood immediately to the west. As the city grew, new arrivals settled in the areas just outside of the city's core to form the Russell, Phoenix Hill, Butchertown, and Smoketown neighborhoods. By the end of the 19th century, population growth and improvements in public transportation allowed citizens to move even farther away from downtown. With the outward migration away from the city's crowded core, the Beechmont, Wilder Park, Old Louisville, and Shawnee neighborhoods began to grow. Commuter trains, introduced around the turn of the 20th century, fueled further growth in outlying suburbs, including Anchorage, Okolona, Prospect, and Pewee Valley.

Many smaller towns and cities developed within Jefferson County during the 19th and 20th century, such as Jeffersontown, Prospect, Middletown, Indian Hills, and Shively. As the city of Louisville grew, some of them incorporated in fear of being annexed and incorporated into the rapidly growing city of Louisville. By the end of the 20th century, many of these smaller municipalities found themselves nearly or completely surrounded by the city of Louisville to the point where their boundaries were indistinct from those of the surrounding city. Government officials pushed for further annexations, but they were met with vehement resistance by residents who feared losing their sovereignty to the larger city despite the appeal of reducing duplication of services and gaining additional municipal services.

By the turn of the 21st century, the argument over city and county government consolidation had reached its peak. The city of Louisville and Jefferson County finally achieved consolidation in 2003, combining the city and county governments to form Louisville Metro. Independently incorporated municipalities within Jefferson County also became a part of Louisville Metro, but in deference to resistance from suburbanites, many of them were able to retain their small city governments.

Falls of the Ohio

The Ohio River is located along the western and northern borders of Jefferson County and has played a major role in the area's history and settlement pattern. In particular, the Falls of the Ohio, a series of discontinuous rapids and shallow areas stretching for nearly two miles over a 26-foot drop in elevation, shaped a large part of the city's early history. Created by the relatively recent erosion of hard Devonian limestone, the Falls of the Ohio was the only major obstacle to navigation over the Ohio River's 983-mile course. The exposed fossil beds of the falls have served as a major boon to paleontologists and biologists, giving a rare glimpse of life on the bed of the shallow seas that once covered large parts of North America hundreds of millions of years ago.

The river has also shaped the geology of the area, which varies greatly from west to east. Most of the northern and western portions of Jefferson County are a vast floodplain with rich, alluvial soils and mostly flat terrain. This region encompasses most of the city's urban core, including downtown, Old Louisville, and the neighborhoods immediately west of downtown. This floodplain stretches southward to the Valley Station neighborhood, which is situated in the southwestern corner of Jefferson County. In fact, most of Jefferson County could be considered part of the Ohio River floodplain,

4

although the soils and underlying rock in many areas are more similar to that of the Outer Bluegrass region of the state. The Outer Bluegrass is generally characterized as a plateau of rolling hills with exposed Ordovician limestone and shale covered with rich, fertile soils. Most of Jefferson County lies between the plateau of the Outer Bluegrass to the east, the Mississippian Plateau to the southwest, and the Mitchell Plateau to the north. Elevations in the area drop off from these three geologic formations into the river valley. To the north and west, elevations are approximately 800 to 900 feet; to the east, the elevations are approximately 600 to 750 feet, rising slowly to 900 feet toward Frankfort. The river valley in between these interior low plateaus can often trap heat, moisture, and pollutants into the city during the hot summer months. This phenomenon, compounded by Louisville's urban heat island problem, contributes greatly to the oppressive heat and humidity that generally characterize Louisville summers.

Areas west of 1st Street, and especially those nearest to the river on Louisville's western edge, are at the lowest elevations. At about 460 feet elevation, these areas tend to be more flood-prone than areas to the east and south. Periodic flooding along the river has greatly affected settlement patterns, especially after the great 1937 Ohio River flood that sent many residents seeking higher ground to the east and south.

East of 1st Street, the soils are composed of loess made from loosely cemented sand and silt blown by the wind. Loess soils are highly porous and may cave in from time to time when they become saturated with water. This contributes greatly to the pothole problem that plagues some sections of Louisville, especially around the Eastern Parkway area. For example, a water main break in 2014 created a massive sinkhole that flooded the nearby Tyler Park area.

The southernmost portion of Jefferson County between Fairdale and Valley Station lies within the Knobs Region of Kentucky. This region of the state begins just southwest of Louisville at the edge of the Mississippian Plateau and extends through portions of Hardin, Jefferson, and Bullitt Counties. From here, the uplift continues southeast toward Lincoln County and the Cumberland Plateau. The knobs are small hills that are the result of erosion of the edges of the two plateaus, leaving a series of hills with a limestone capstone and shale-rich slopes. Jefferson Memorial Forest, a 6,500-acre portion of the land in southern Jefferson County within the Knobs Region, has been set aside as the country's largest urban forest.

Far eastern Jefferson County is within the Eden Shale Hills, considered by many geologists to be a part of Kentucky's Outer Bluegrass. These small, steep hills separate the Outer and Inner Bluegrass regions of the state. From Jefferson County, the hills extend north of Lexington and continue eastward, eventually ending near Flemingsburg. The shale hills of eastern Jefferson County are generally steeper, but not as tall, as those in southwestern

5

Jefferson County or in Clark County, Indiana.

Although the landforms in the area can greatly affect the weather at times, Louisville's climate is classified as humid subtropical, or Cfa, according to the Koppen climate classification system. This climate type is characterized by moderate average temperatures, moderate amounts of precipitation, and four distinct seasons. Spring-like weather typically begins in mid-March, with frequent rains and occasional violent thunderstorms. The area begins to experience summer-like conditions by mid-to-late May, although streaks of cool weather may occasionally occur through the early part of June.

Summers in the Louisville area, like most of the state of Kentucky, tend to be characterized by considerable heat and humidity. During the summer, high temperatures frequently exceed 90 degrees Fahrenheit and the humidity level usually exceeds 70%, making for uncomfortable dew points above 63 degrees Fahrenheit for most of the day. Thus, light-weight moisture-wicking jerseys are a must when cycling during the summer months. On average, the high temperature in Louisville exceeds 90 degrees about 30 days per year. Heat waves of 7 days straight or longer with high temperatures of 90 or more are not uncommon. Dry spells during the summer are also common, especially after mid-August.

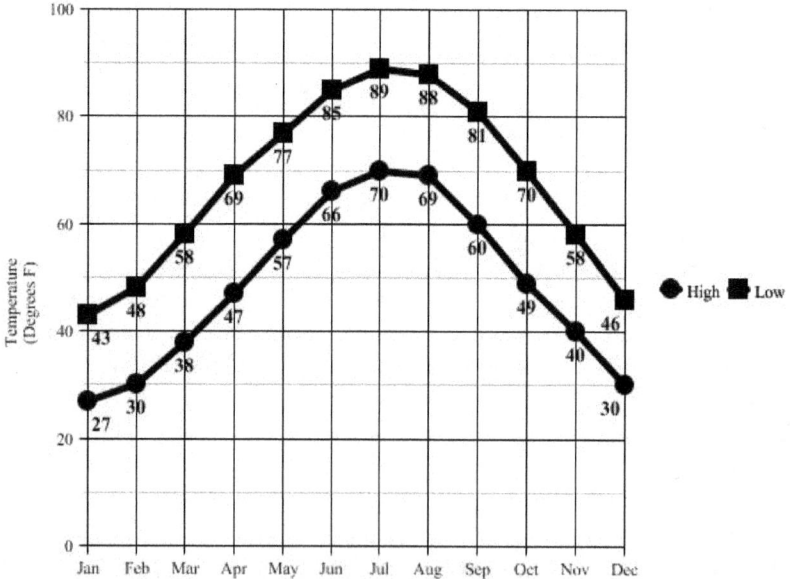

Average Monthly Temperatures for Louisville, Kentucky

Although rain chances are highest between March and June and lowest between September and February, precipitation may occur any time of the year. Thus, it is incumbent upon cyclists to check the weather forecast before riding, especially when riding longer distances or farther away from home. During the spring, it may be necessary to pack a poncho or light rain jacket on longer rides if rain is anticipated. During the summer, spotty thunderstorms may occasionally occur during the heat of the afternoon, particularly if the temperature is very hot. Otherwise, unless rain is specifically in the forecast, the chances of a sudden rain shower spoiling a ride are actually quite low.

The heat and humidity of summer usually relent by mid-September, with fall weather setting in by the end of the month. Fall temperatures are typically very pleasant and rain is infrequent. For these reasons, many local cyclists consider September, October, and November as the best months of the year to ride. Winter temperatures typically arrive by late November, along with an increase in precipitation. High temperatures during December and January are usually in the low or mid-40s with a brisk wind, but a quick afternoon ride is easily possible with the right winter riding gear. As long as you dress for the weather and are prepared for unexpected weather events, it is quite easy to cycle year-round in the Louisville area.

Wind speeds in the Louisville Metropolitan area average around 5-10 miles per hour and typically come out of the south or west. Wind speeds are usually the calmest during the morning hours and increase during the heat of the afternoon, but seldom exceed 15 miles per hour. Kentucky typically experiences higher wind speeds between January and March, with the lightest winds occurring from August to October. Thus, winds are seldom a factor when riding here, although they may be significantly stronger in the areas next to the Ohio River. Downtown Louisville may be particularly windy during the winter and early spring months, as the winds from the Ohio River are seemingly amplified as they pass between tall buildings.

Overall, Louisville Metro has a pleasant climate that makes year-round cycling possible with a little preparation. The area's varied geography means that there are vast areas of flat, easy terrain, as well as hillier regions that provide a decent challenge for more advanced or adventurous cyclists. Louisville truly does have something for nearly everyone.

HISTORY OF LOUISVILLE

The greater Louisville area has seen multiple civilizations appear and disappear over the past several thousand years. The first settlements in the Louisville area were built by the Adena and Hopewell cultures of the Early Woodland Period, between 1000 BC and 200 AD. Later settlements were built by the Fort Ancient and Mississippian cultures during the Woodland Period, between 1000 and 1650 AD.

Despite a long history of human occupation, the area was largely uninhabited by the time European settlers arrived in the 18th century. The Beaver Wars, a series of conflicts between the Iroquois and other native tribes in the area, had largely resulted in the depopulation of the Ohio Valley after the end of the Woodland Period. Following the Woodland Period, the land was largely claimed as a hunting ground by multiple tribes, including the Shawnee and Cherokee. Few settlers entered the area before 1751 when France relinquished control of the area to Britain at the end of the French and Indian War.

Much of the area's early history was shaped by the Falls of the Ohio, the only natural barrier to travel on the Ohio River. The rapids at the falls necessitated the movement of goods and passengers over land to ships on the other side of the falls, making the area a natural stopping point along the waterway. As a result, several permanent settlements, including Louisville, arose along the Ohio River around the falls.

The first permanent settlement was founded in 1778 when General George Rogers Clark led a group of 80 settlers and 150 soldiers from the Illinois Regiment to the Falls of the Ohio. The settlers cleared land for agriculture on an island at the Falls, which became known as Corn Island. General Clark and his soldiers soon left the area to fight the British in the territories north of the Ohio River, and the settlers moved across the river to the Kentucky side of the river to establish a more permanent settlement. At

Clark's request, the town was named Louisville in honor of King Louis XVI of France for his assistance during the Revolutionary War.

Many native tribes, however, still claimed the area around the Falls of the Ohio as tribal hunting grounds and resented the presence of the settlers. They frequently raided the new settlements that they saw as encroaching on their tribal lands. The settlers built a fort on the bank of the river near modern day 12th Street to protect themselves. The fear of raids further increased in 1780 after Bird's invasion of Kentucky, a series of bloody conflicts along the Licking River led by Captain Henry Bird and a band of more than 1000 British and Native American soldiers. In response, the settlers at Louisville built a more secure fort, known as Fort Nelson, beside the river between modern day 7th and 8th Streets. Later that year, the Virginia General Assembly and Governor Thomas Jefferson approved the town charter for Louisville and established Jefferson County, one of three counties carved out of Kentucky County, Virginia. Louisville was named as its county seat.

Monument to Fort Nelson

Within a few years, settlers began moving out of the forts and into the surrounding area. By 1783, a general store, a courthouse, a hotel, and a post office had been established in Louisville. In 1785, a second town was formed at the lower side of the falls and incorporated as Shippingport. Neither town grew very quickly, however, due to the continued threat of Indian attacks. That problem diminished after a decisive victory in the Northwest Indian Wars at the Battle of Fallen Timbers in 1794. The victory, which ended the war, forced the British and Indian troops to fully withdraw from the area. With the threat of raids gone, the pioneers ventured further away from the fortified settlements and spread out throughout the area. By the end of the 18th century, Louisville had a recorded population of 359 inhabitants.

Louisville grew greatly in size, population, and influence during the 19th century. As the United States grew to the west and south, the volume of goods being shipped down the Ohio River increased greatly. Since the boats moving these goods were unable to traverse the falls, the cargo had to be unloaded and transported over land to the lower side of the falls. The need to move goods over land around the falls triggered massive population growth in the area. By 1810, there were 1,357 people living in Louisville.

Steamboats soon made their debut on the nation's waterways. In 1811, the *New Orleans* arrived in Louisville from Pittsburgh, and within a few years, steamboats had become powerful enough to ply upstream. This made the shipment of goods up and down the Ohio River even more economical, and the movement of goods through Louisville accelerated. To meet the increased demand, many mills and factories were built. Several rival settlements, including Shippingport and Portland in Kentucky, and New Albany, Jeffersonville, and Clarksville in Indiana, all began to develop along the river at this time and threatened to outgrow Louisville in both population and influence.

During the first two decades of the 19th century, the numerous settlements along the Ohio River around the Falls of the Ohio vied to become the dominant city in the region. Each settlement drew up plans to build a canal to bypass the Falls of the Ohio, but none of those plans ever came close to completion. The only effort that came close to succeeding was an 1818 effort by the Indiana Canal Company to build a canal on the northern side of the river. Work on the canal was initiated, but the failure of a key dam and the Panic of 1819 soon ended that effort.

In the early 1820s, Charles Thurston of Louisville proposed a canal on the Kentucky side of the river from Louisville to Portland. The Louisville

Louisville and Portland Canal

and Portland Canal Company, chartered in 1825, raised funds from both private and public sources, and work on the project commenced later that year. After numerous setbacks and the near depletion of funding, the project was completed in 1833, six years behind schedule and nearly $700,000 over budget. Even though the canal was nearly obsolete by the time its construction was completed, the project eventually proved to be profitable, and the business that it drove to the Kentucky side of the falls caused the city of Louisville to outgrow its neighbors. Eventually, Shippingport and Portland were annexed into the city of Louisville, and the city's rapid growth soon made it the largest city in the state of Kentucky. The canal was eventually purchased and taken over by the federal government in 1855 amid complaints about high tolls and the canal's inability to handle the larger steamboats in use by this time. Despite the canal's problems, the heavy traffic it brought and the businesses that it supported fueled rapid economic and population growth in 19th century Louisville.

In addition to economic expansion and population growth, the 19th century also witnessed many major improvements in science, technology, education, and health care. In 1803, Meriwether Lewis and William Clark, the younger brother of General George Rogers Clark, set out from Clarksville, Indiana on their

Lewis and Clark monument in Clarksville

famous expedition to explore the Louisiana Purchase. The Lewis and Clark Expedition described and documented over 300 animal and plant species, many of them new, and documented the weather and geography of the American West. Their journey of exploration also cemented the U.S. Government's claim to the lands west of the Mississippi River, leading to the westward expansion of the country.

In 1816, Louisville Library Company opened the city's first library. The city soon opened its first public schools in 1829, which educated children up to the age of sixteen. The school, under Edward Mann Butler, was first housed in the upper level of a church at the corner of 5th and Liberty Streets and later moved to a building near 5th Street and modern-day Muhammad Ali Boulevard. By 1851, Male and Female High Schools opened their doors, with more than 17 high schools open their doors all across the city and surrounding county over the next two decades. The Kentucky School for the Blind opened in 1839, with the American Printing House for the Blind opening up nearby when the school moved its campus to the eastern edge of town in 1855. By 1870, the city's first schools for African-American children opened, and by 1873 the two schools were merged to form Central Colored School, which opened in a building located at 6th and Kentucky Streets.

Improvements in health care and the introduction of higher education were also made during the early 19th century. In 1825, the Louisville Marine Hospital opened, helping to address the rash of epidemics occurring throughout the area during the early 1820s. Today, the land it once occupied along Chestnut Street is home to Louisville Medical Center. The University of Louisville was organized between 1798 and 1846 from the consolidation of Jefferson Seminary, Louisville Medical Institute, and the Louisville Collegiate Institute.

Improvements in transportation and infrastructure also helped to spur economic development. By the middle of the 19th century, the railroad industry began to develop around Louisville, with the Louisville and Nashville Railroad opening a line in 1859. Strategically located at the Falls of the Ohio, the new railroad was poised to make Louisville prosper as a major shipping hub. Coupled with improvements in other sectors of the economy, these developments spurred additional population growth and made many residents wealthy. In each decade between 1800 and 1850, the city's population more than doubled. By 1850, Louisville had a population of 43,194 and was the 14th largest city in the United States.

Despite a rapidly growing population and expanding economy, racial strife and the looming threat of civil war would soon threaten to derail the city's progress and throw it into chaos. Much of the city's early growth was due to its strategic location at the Falls of Ohio as a major hub for the shipment of goods up and down the river, and the slave trade readily took advantage of it. Between the 1820s and 1850s, up to 5,000 slaves were sold in Louisville and transported down the Ohio River. Louisville's seedy slave trade gave rise to the phrase "sold down the river" as many families were split up at the slave auctions held downtown. From Louisville, slaves were shipped downriver to New Orleans, where they were then auctioned off to sugar and cotton plantation owners.

Town Clock Church

On the other hand, the Ohio River also represented a glimmer of hope to escaping slaves who sometimes referred to it as the "River Jordan" because it was the last obstacle to the free states of the North. The large numbers of escaped slaves attempting to cross the river in Kentucky led to a cottage industry for bounty hunters, but many area residents also assisted escaped slaves by providing stops on the Underground Railroad. One of the Underground Railroad's more notable stops was the Town Clock Church in New Albany, Indiana, situated directly across the Ohio River from western Louisville.

Prior to the outbreak of the U.S. Civil War, Kentucky was regarded as a border area between the slave states of the South and the free states of the North. Although Kentucky never officially seceded from the Union, slavery was well established in many parts of the state. As a major transportation hub, Louisville was poised at the center of the state's slave trade and the epicenter of the controversy over the practice. Consistent with its border state location, the people of Louisville were fairly evenly split over the issue of slavery, although Louisville's unscrupulous slave traders were generally shunned by most of the city's residents regardless of their opinions on the issue. Some of the city's merchants did extensive business with the south and likewise supported the Confederacy, but most professionals and blue-collar workers supported the Union and were opposed to slavery. In the 1860 election, Kentucky voters equally rejected both Abraham Lincoln and John C. Breckenridge, essentially sending the message that Kentuckians wished to remain within the Union, but also that they wanted to leave the institution of slavery intact.

With the outbreak of the U.S. Civil War in 1861, Kentucky's neutrality in the matter was challenged. Supporters of the Confederacy began sending supplies to the armies of the south by rail and by steamboat from the lower side of the falls. In July 1861, a federal judge stepped in and asserted the right to stop the shipment of supplies on the L&N Railroad. A few days later, the U.S. War Department established numerous training camps across the state, and a major Union garrison was established across the river in Jeffersonville, Indiana. In the election of August 1861, Unionists won a majority in both houses of the Kentucky General Assembly, further emboldening President Lincoln and strengthening the state as a Union stronghold despite the protests of Governor Beriah Magoffin, a notorious Confederate sympathizer.

After numerous Confederate raids and incursions into Kentucky, Union General Ulysses S. Grant established a presence in Paducah. In response, Confederate President Jefferson Davis ordered troops under Confederate Generals Albert Sidney Johnston, Simon Bolivar Buckner, and Felix Zollicoffer to establish a presence stretching from Columbus in the west to Cumberland Gap in the east. In response to the looming threat, Union General Robert Anderson established a garrison in Louisville. Anderson soon stepped down, and General William Tecumseh Sherman took charge. Sherman requested 200,000 troops to take care of Johnston and Bolivar's Confederate troops, and Louisville soon became a major staging ground for Union soldiers from Indiana, Pennsylvania, and Wisconsin as they headed south toward the front lines.

The heavy Union presence in Louisville thwarted most of the Confederacy's attempts to capture the city, largely sparing it from the heavy tolls of death and destruction that befell many cities further south. Only two attempts were made to seize the city. In 1862, Confederate General Braxton Bragg made plans to invade Louisville, but the heavy Union presence in the city and lack of support from the Confederate Army convinced him to abandon those plans. In June 1863, Brigadier General John Hunt Morgan threatened to sack the city during Morgan's Raid. Departing Sparta, Tennessee with 2,460 cavalrymen, Morgan rode north toward Union territory through Springfield and Bardstown, Kentucky. A detachment was sent to Louisville across the Ohio River near Twelve Mile Island, but they were soon captured. Rather than face the Union Army at Louisville, Morgan traveled west to Brandenburg, seized two steamboats, and then transported his remaining forces across the river to Mauckport, Indiana. Morgan's forces quickly overwhelmed the small Union force stationed nearby at the Battle of Corydon, the only Civil War battle fought in the state of Indiana. Morgan's forces then moved through Ohio and West Virginia, raiding other nearby towns along the way. Morgan was eventually captured in the battle of Salineville by Brigadier General James M. Shackleford. He was killed less than a year later in the aftermath of a raid near Greenville, Tennessee.

Following the war, many returning Confederate veterans, feeling betrayed by the Republican Party and its abolitionist policies, took control of the city's political machinery. The political environment in Louisville between 1865 and 1900 leaned toward the Democratic Party. Many Confederate cemeteries and war memorials were established throughout the area, particularly between 1890 and 1900. A Confederate cemetery was established in Pewee Valley, Kentucky, a Confederate veterans' retirement home was built nearby, and a monument honoring Confederate soldiers killed during the Civil War was erected on a small plot of land on Third Street near the modern-day campus of the University of Louisville. For more than a century, the monument served as a controversial reminder of the war to many of the city's residents, who mostly sided with the Union cause and opposed slavery.

Following the Civil War, Louisville continued to experience growth both economic and population growth. Although the city didn't experience explosive growth as it had during the early 19th century, the city's population continued to increase, reaching 100,753 by 1870 and 204,731 in 1900. The construction of railroads on the city's eastern side, as well as other infrastructure improvements, led to growth in the city's eastern suburbs, a trend that has continued well into the 21st century.

In 1876, Louisville became home to a minor league baseball team, the Louisville Grays. Although the Grays only played for two seasons, Louisville attracted a major league baseball team, the Louisville Eclipse, in 1882. In 1885, the Louisville Eclipse became known as the Louisville Colonels. The Colonels played in the American Association until the National League absorbed it in 1892. The Colonels continued to play in Louisville until 1899.

Louisville's baseball obsession ultimately led to the creation of one of the city's iconic products. In 1883, John Hillerich provided a custom wooden baseball bat to the Eclipse's Pete "The Gladiator" Browning. Hillerich's fine wooden bats, which iwere constructed from white ash, soon became a hot commodity. The bats were dubbed as the Louisville Slugger, and the name became synonymous with the sport. Hillerich & Bradsby soon became a major manufacturer of baseball bats, and the Louisville Slugger factory soon produced more than 2 out of 3 of the wooden baseball bats sold nationwide.

Louisville's preoccupation with sports was also bolstered by the horse racing industry. The first Kentucky Derby was held at Churchill Downs (then known as the Louisville Jockey Club) on May 17, 1875, where more than 10,000 spectators witnessed Aristides win the race. This tradition continues every year on the first Saturday in May when more than 100,000 fans from across the world pour into the city for a weekend of revelry and tradition.

Science and innovation were very much alive in Louisville during the late 19th century. In 1883, the first Southern Exposition, a series of World's Fairs that ran for five years, opened in Central Park in present-day Old Louisville. The exposition attracted millions of visitors, providing an opportunity for Louisville to showcase its progress and industry to the world. The show introduced Thomas

Louisville's Central Park

Edison's incandescent light bulb to the world, with more than 5,000 of the bulbs used to illuminate the exhibition hall.

The city also underwent a period of major construction and modernization during this era. The Columbia Building, Louisville's second skyscraper, was completed at the corner of Fourth and Main Streets in 1890. In 1891, Frederick Law Olmstead was commissioned to create a system of three major parks along the city's edge, connected by shaded parkways. Passenger trains made their debut in 1891, and soon Louisville boasted the largest train station and network in the entire southern United States.

Industry also flourished in Louisville during the late 19th century. In particular, the bourbon industry underwent a major expansion. Distilling had always been a major industry in Kentucky since its initial settlement, but whiskey pioneer Elijah Craig invented the process of charring the oak barrels in which the whiskey was aged, creating a fine whiskey that was superior in flavor. Dubbed bourbon, either for the French Bourbon dynasty, for Bourbon Street in New Orleans, or for Bourbon County, Kentucky, the whiskey was soon in high demand, and Kentucky was at the epicenter of its production. Although the term bourbon can be traced to the early 19th century, it was consistently used by 1870 to describe Kentucky's native whiskey.

At the time, the Ohio and Mississippi Rivers served as the primary routes in and out of Kentucky, thus placing Louisville and the Falls of the Ohio at

Bourbon rickhouses

a crucial point in the distribution of the fine liquor. Prior to the arrival of the railroads, most of the bourbon produced was shipped to Louisville and loaded onto flatboats for distribution to New Orleans down the Ohio and Mississippi Rivers. Even after the arrival of the railroads and other infrastructure improvements, many bourbon distillers found Louisville to be an ideal location for their distilleries because of its status as a major transportation hub. Several distillers set up operations in the city during the late 1800s, most notably George Garvin Brown, who began distilling bourbon under the Old Forester label in 1870. Brown later partnered with George Forman, forming Brown-Forman and Company, and by the 1890s, business boomed.

By the close of the 19th century, Louisville had a booming economy, a burgeoning population, and a rapidly improving infrastructure. The good times, however, would not last as the city entered the 20th century. Louisville's fortunes soon gave way to a new set of challenges that would forever change the city and her people.

By the early 1900s, political corruption had become a major problem across the country, and it was particularly acute in the city of Louisville. Between the late 19th and early 20th century, the political machine era had arisen in many of the country's large cities, in which a political party was organized under a single powerful boss with authoritative control of all or most political offices in a city or county. In Louisville, the powerful Democratic Party political machine was controlled by John Henry Whallen, the owner of the Buckingham Theater, a burlesque theater located near Third and Jefferson Streets. Whallen was often referred to as the "Buckingham Boss," and had a seedy reputation. In order to protect his financial interests he engineered the election of P. Booker Reed as mayor in 1885; in turn, Reed named Whallen as the Chief of Police. Whallen was now well positioned to control many of the city's municipal jobs, and he ruthlessly influenced local elections through bribery, vote buying, voter intimidation, and threats of reprisals.

The age of the political machines had reached its height by 1900, and many efforts were made to rid the political system of the corruption that held the city hostage. One such effort was the formation of the Fusionist Party, an anti-corruption party that had the support of Republicans and many of the city's liberals. Joseph T. O'Neal ran as a Fusionist in the 1905 mayoral election against Paul C. Barth, the Whallen-backed Democratic candidate, but lost in a hotly contested election. The results were challenged in court, and in 1907, the Kentucky Court of Appeals overturned the election. The overturned mayoral election marked the beginning of the decline of the political machine era in Louisville. Although Whallen still managed to influence the 1909 and 1913 elections through the use of race-baiting tactics, his political machine continued to decline in influence, particularly after his death in 1913.

The early 20th century in Louisville also witnessed the emergence of tuberculosis as a major public health menace. Although tuberculosis has been known historically for many thousands of years and was regarded as a disease of the urban poor, it was widespread throughout the United States by the late 19th and early 20th centuries. By the 1880s, *Mycobacterium tuberculosis* was identified as the disease's causative agent, and it was determined to be contagious. Heavy disease tolls in the large, crowded cities of Europe and the east coast of the United States led to a movement to encourage infected individuals to seek treatment in isolated sanatoria, where infected individuals could benefit from constant medical supervision, fresh air, and concentrated labor. Louisville's Waverly Hills Sanatorium opened in 1910 to help address the public health threat and operated until 1961 when new advances in treatment rendered the facility obsolete.

The threats of disease and corruption took a back seat to the country's entry into World War I in 1917. Soon, Camp Taylor was established on the city's south central side as a major military training camp, housing nearly 50,000 soldiers at one point. Author F. Scott Fitzgerald was stationed at Camp Taylor during the war, and he later featured it in his novel *The Great Gatsby*. The base was dismantled after the war's conclusion, and returning soldiers quickly stripped the barracks of lumber to build a large number of small bungalows and cottages in the area.

Following the post-war economic expansion of the 1920s, the Great Depression brought its own brand of misery to Louisville. With little economic growth and sky-high unemployment, the city's population faced many difficulties on a daily basis. After a long period of growth, the city's population leveled off in the 1930s as many families put off having children. Many of the city's younger residents left in search of scarce jobs as the unemployment rate soared to more than 26%. But just as the city was beginning to mount a meager economic recovery, the city's troubles were compounded by the Great Flood of 1937.

Between January 9 and 23, 1937, constant heavy rain showers caused the Ohio River to overflow its banks. The river crested on January 27 at a record 57 feet, inundating nearly 75% of the city. The flooding killed 90 people and displaced hundreds of thousands of residents, forcing many people to seek higher ground. Later, the city installed concrete floodwalls along the riverfront to help prevent widespread damage in the future from the river's frequent floods. The memory of the Great Flood of 1937 forever changed the city's settlement pattern, favoring the higher ground of the southern and eastern suburbs.

Despite the enormous economic and human toll exacted by the Great Flood, it had a silver lining-the reconstruction efforts began to chip away at the city's unemployment rate. By 1940, the unemployment rate had dropped to 11%, and the rate dropped even further with the expansion of manufacturing that accompanied the outbreak of World War II. Soon, the city snapped out of its economic doldrums, and manufacturing began expanding in order to help supply the war effort.

Like many other major American cities, Louisville experienced a major decline around the middle of the 20th century. In particular, improvements in transportation infrastructure, state laws aimed at limiting annexation, and the recent memory of the devastating 1937 flood together spurred a mass migration of the city's residents away from the city's core toward its outer suburbs, a trend that has continued well into the 21st century. Many of the city's outer suburbs, particularly in the eastern portion of Jefferson County, quickly incorporated in order to prevent annexation by the city of Louisville. As the city's population leveled off and then declined, downtown Louisville experienced a devastating economic decline that left once vibrant portions of the city in virtual ruins. By 1971, the city's iconic Brown Hotel had closed, the Fontaine Ferry Park amusement park had closed due to racial tensions on the city's west side, and Haymarket, Louisville's premier farmer's market, had closed due to the construction of Interstate 65. Many areas of downtown became sparsely inhabited, and with the neglect came blight and crime. From the 1950s through the 1980s, most Louisvillians considered downtown unsafe and unsightly.

Despite these and other challenges, the arts flourished during the 20th century. The Speed Art Museum opened in 1927, the Louisville Orchestra was founded in 1937, and the Kentucky Opera and Louisville Ballet were established in 1952. Actors Theater of Louisville opened its doors in 1964 and quickly became a major regional theater.

Despite the pessimism and gloom of the mid-to-late 20th century, the closing of the 20th century and the dawning of the 21st century brought a major renaissance and revival to the city. The city and county governments were merged in 2003 to create Metro Louisville, streamlining government services and providing a voice for many disaffected citizens that has created a more cohesive sense of community. With the improving economy, plentiful jobs, declining crime rates, and reduction in urban blight, people began moving into Louisville's older neighborhoods and downtown district again.

Many older homes were renovated and spruced up. Businesses, restaurants, and bars sprang up, fed by the influx of urban professionals. The many attractions in downtown Louisville have also proven to be a strong draw for tourists and locals alike.

Concomitant with economic development, Louisville has made a major investment in the city's livability with improvements in infrastructure for alternative modes of transportation, renovation and improvement of its many parks, and the development of new parks and green spaces. Louisville's Olmstead Parks have received much-needed repairs and upgrades. New parks and projects, such as the Parklands of Floyds Fork and the Louisville Loop, have greatly improved the city's livability by providing additional green spaces and recreational opportunities for Metro Louisville's growing population.

Despite the many challenges and difficulties that Louisville has faced, her spirit has endured. And as the 21st century progresses, Louisville's future looks bright.

CYCLING IN METRO LOUISVILLE

Most local and state laws in the area treat bicycles as motor vehicles. A bicyclist is entitled to use the road equally as much as a car except where they are otherwise prohibited by signage. Cyclists must ride as close to the right-hand side of the road as practically possible and in the same direction as the flow of traffic. This is meant to allow faster moving vehicles to pass safely, but bicyclists are not required to ride on the shoulder of the road. Cyclists are allowed to fully enter the roadway when there are obstacles in the road, or when riding at the very right-hand edge of the road would endanger the cyclist. If a bicycle lane is present, cyclists are required to use the lane whenever possible. Excursions from a bicycle lane are permitted when avoiding obstacles in the roadway or making turns. On two-lane roadways, bicyclists are permitted to ride no more than two abreast.

Many urban cycling experts discourage riding at the extreme right-hand edge of the road and instead recommend that cyclists ride about three feet into the lane. This is to discourage vehicles from remaining in the lane when passing, possibly coming too close to the cyclist. On streets where there are parked cars, it is also recommended that cyclists ride a few feet into the lane to avoid car doors opening suddenly. Cyclists are allowed to move fully into the lane when preparing to make a left turn, or when allowed by signage. In most cases, Kentucky's laws are widely seen to protect cyclists' right to take the lane when necessary.

Although Kentucky lacks an official 3-foot law that requires motorists to allow cyclists sufficient room to maneuver when being passed, most driving regulations in Kentucky state that motorists should allow cyclists and pedestrians 3 feet when passing. The Kentucky Driving Manual also states this, although there is no clear indication that this recommendation is enforceable in a court of law. An attempt to pass a 3-foot law in Kentucky was mounted in the Kentucky General Assembly's 2016 regular session.

Although the bill was passed in the Senate, it was not voted on by the House.

Riding on sidewalks is not only dangerous but also it is illegal within the city of Louisville for cyclists over the age of 11. Motorists at intersections are usually looking for other vehicles in the roadway in the direction of travel, and seldom pay attention to pedestrians or cyclists on the sidewalk. Furthermore, riding on sidewalks is dangerous at crosswalks, where turning vehicles may not notice bicycles attempting to cross the road. Studies have shown that cyclists riding on sidewalks are several times more likely to be involved in accidents than cyclists who are riding on the road, in the correct lane, and in the direction of traffic. Furthermore, bicycles on the sidewalk can pose a danger to pedestrians, especially in crosswalks.

Like motorists, cyclists are required to signal when stopping or turning. From the perspective of a motorist, a cyclists who is riding within the lane with the flow of traffic and indicating his or her intentions using the proper hand signals is much easier to deal with and predict than one who is riding against traffic, on the sidewalk, and/or making sudden, unpredictable maneuvers. Cyclists observing traffic regulations are also much less likely to be involved in an accident, and numerous studies of bicycle-car collisions support this assertion.

Bicycling safety is not only highly recommended in all cases, it is required by law. Safety is especially crucial when riding at night, as nearly 40% of accidents involving bicycles occur between 6:00 PM and midnight. Cyclists riding after dark are required to have a white light in front and a red light in the back. Lights may be attached to the bicycle, or to the back of the rider's jersey. Brightly colored or reflective clothing, while not required by law, is extremely helpful in ensuring that bicyclists can be seen clearly by motorists. And although Louisville Metro does not require cyclists over the age of 18 to wear helmets when riding, helmets save lives and are HIGHLY recommended. Nearly all studies indicate that helmets save lives and prevent many serious injuries in the event of a crash.

Cyclists should always be prepared for emergencies, especially when riding alone, in unfamiliar places, or in areas where they will be more than a few miles from home. Most experts recommend that every cyclist carry at least a small emergency pack with them at all times in a small underseat bag or in a container attached to the frame. The pack should contain tire levers, a CO_2 cartridge for inflating tires, a tire patch kit or spare inner tube, and a few first aid essentials, such as adhesive bandages, gauze, and a small amount of antiseptic wound cream. It is also highly recommended that cyclists carry identification with them at all times, such as a driver's license or ID bracelet. A cellular telephone can be especially helpful in case of an accident or mechanical failure, but it is always wise to enclose the phone inside a case or plastic bag to ensure that the device is not exposed to moisture from sweat or sudden rain showers. Finally, many cyclists recommend carrying a small canister of pepper spray for emergencies.

Although many cyclists may feel uncomfortable sharing the road with vehicles, bicycle accidents in Louisville are actually quite rare. Although Louisville drivers can be impatient and rude at times, the vast majority of motorists in the area are courteous and friendly. In fact, many of them will even give a nod or wave as they pass by.

Sojourn Community Church, formerly St. Vincent de Paul Church, in Shelby Park

THE TOURS

Many new cyclists, visitors, and new residents have experienced difficulty in identifying fun, safe places to ride in the area. This guide contains 25 tours of the Louisville metropolitan area that vary between 8 and 50 miles in length, with the majority between 10 and 25 miles. Most of these tours are designed to be completed in 1-3 hours while still allowing time for riders to stop and enjoy points of interest along the way. They also cover a full range of difficulty levels, ranging from flat and easy to hilly and difficult.

All of the tours described in the guide are on paved roads and/or bicycle paths and are thus accessible to any type of bicycle. Each tour includes parking information, as well as descriptions of places along the route where provisions, such as water or snacks, are available. Other than carrying a water bottle (or two) and any appropriate snacks for longer trips, no additional equipment is necessary other than the essential safety equipment described earlier.

The tours described in this guide also attempt to highlight some of the history and points of interest along the way. The Louisville area has many hidden treasures along and near these routes, and this guide attempts to explore as many of them as possible. A few alternative routes and side trips, when available, are also described. Although every attempt has been made to be thorough, there are still many great routes and points of interest that were omitted from this guide simply due to the lack of space and time.

Now, let's get out there and ride!

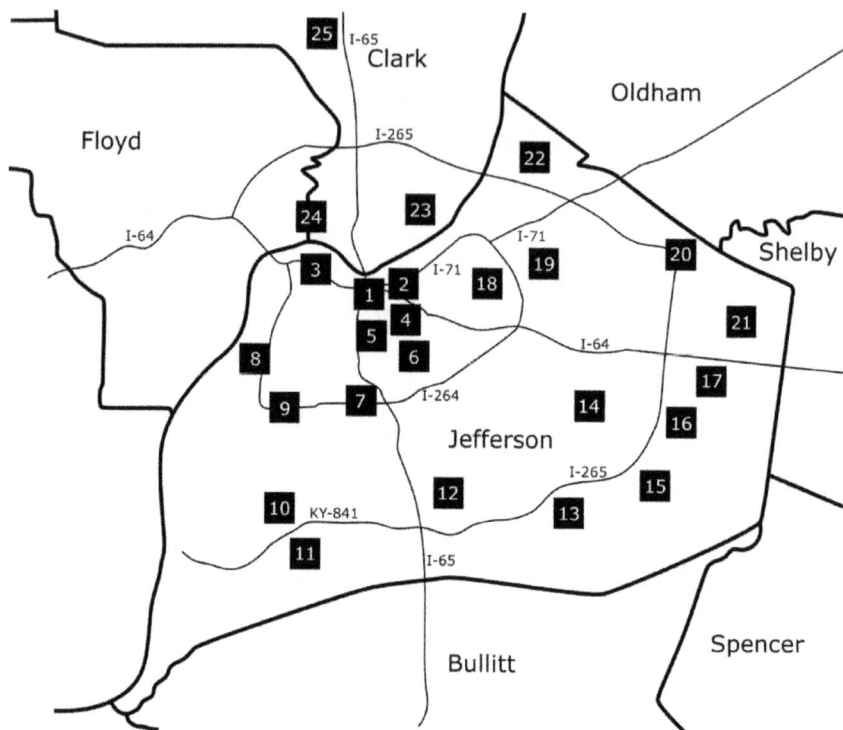

Recommended routes for beginners:

1 – Downtown, Old Louisville, St. Joseph, Shelby Park, and Smoketown - 13.8 miles, easy
2 – Irish Hill, Butchertown, Phoenix Hill, Clifton, and Crescent Hill – 9.1 miles, easy
6 – Cherokee and Seneca Parks – 8.2 miles, moderate
9 – Shively – 9.5 miles, easy
24 – Clarksville and New Albany – 13.7 miles, easy

Recommended routes for sightseeing:

1 – Downtown, Old Louisville, St. Joseph, Shelby Park, and Smoketown - 13.8 miles, easy
2 – Irish Hill, Butchertown, Phoenix Hill, Clifton, and Crescent Hill – 9.1 miles, easy
3 – Western Louisville – 17.0 miles, easy
4 – The Highlands – 11.6 miles, moderate
24 – Clarksville and New Albany – 13.7 miles, easy

Recommended routes for scenery:

11 – Fairdale and Jefferson Memorial Forest – 18.7 miles, moderate
13 – Fern Creek – 17.4 miles, moderate
15 – Seatonville – 20.0 miles, difficult
16 – Parklands of Floyds Fork – 38.8 miles, moderate
21 – Long Run and Simpsonville – 22.6 miles, moderate
22 – Prospect and Western Oldham County – 23.0 miles, difficult

Recommended routes for advanced cyclists looking for a challenge:

10 – Waverly Hills – 13.2 miles, difficult
15 – Seatonville – 20.0 miles, difficult
17 – Fisherville and Eastwood – 15.5 miles, difficult
22 – Prospect and Western Oldham County – 23.0 miles, difficult

Recommended routes for exploring Louisville's history:

1 – Downtown, Old Louisville, St. Joseph, Shelby Park, and Smoketown –
      13.8 miles, easy
2 – Irish Hill, Butchertown, Phoenix Hill, Clifton, and Crescent Hill – 9.1
      miles, easy
3 – Western Louisville, 17.0 miles, easy
7 – Southern Louisville, 15.0 miles, moderate
8 – Louisville Loop, 50.5 miles, easy

	Tour	Distance	Difficulty
1	Downtown, Old Louisville, St. Joseph, Shelby Park and Smoketown	13.8 mi	Easy
2	Irish Hill, Butchertown, Phoenix Hill, Clifton, and Crescent Hill	9.1 mi	Easy
3	Western Louisville	17.0 mi	Easy
4	The Highlands	11.6 mi	Moderate
5	Audubon Park, Schnitzelburg, and Germantown	9.4 mi	Easy
6	Cherokee and Seneca Parks	8.2 mi	Moderate
7	Southern Louisville	15.0 mi	Moderate
8	Louisville Loop	50.5 mi	Easy
9	Shively	9.5 mi	Easy
10	Waverly Hills	13.2 mi	Difficult
11	Fairdale and Jefferson Memorial Forest	18.7 mi	Moderate
12	Okolona	8.7 mi	Moderate
13	Fern Creek	17.4 mi	Moderate
14	Jeffersontown	15.9 mi	Moderate
15	Seatonville	20.0 mi	Difficult
16	Parklands of Floyds Fork	38.8 mi	Moderate
17	Fisherville and Eastwood	15.5 mi	Difficult
18	St. Matthews and Indian Hills	14.2 mi	Moderate
19	Anchorage and Middletown	19.0 mi	Moderate
20	Berrytown and Pewee Valley	15.5 mi	Moderate
21	Long Run and Simpsonville	22.6 mi	Moderate
22	Prospect and Western Oldham County	23.0 mi	Difficult
23	Big Four Bridge, Utica, and Jeffersonville	27.5 mi	Moderate
24	Clarksville and New Albany	13.7 mi	Easy
25	Memphis and Henryville	21.3 mi	Moderate

Louisville Slugger Museum on Main Street

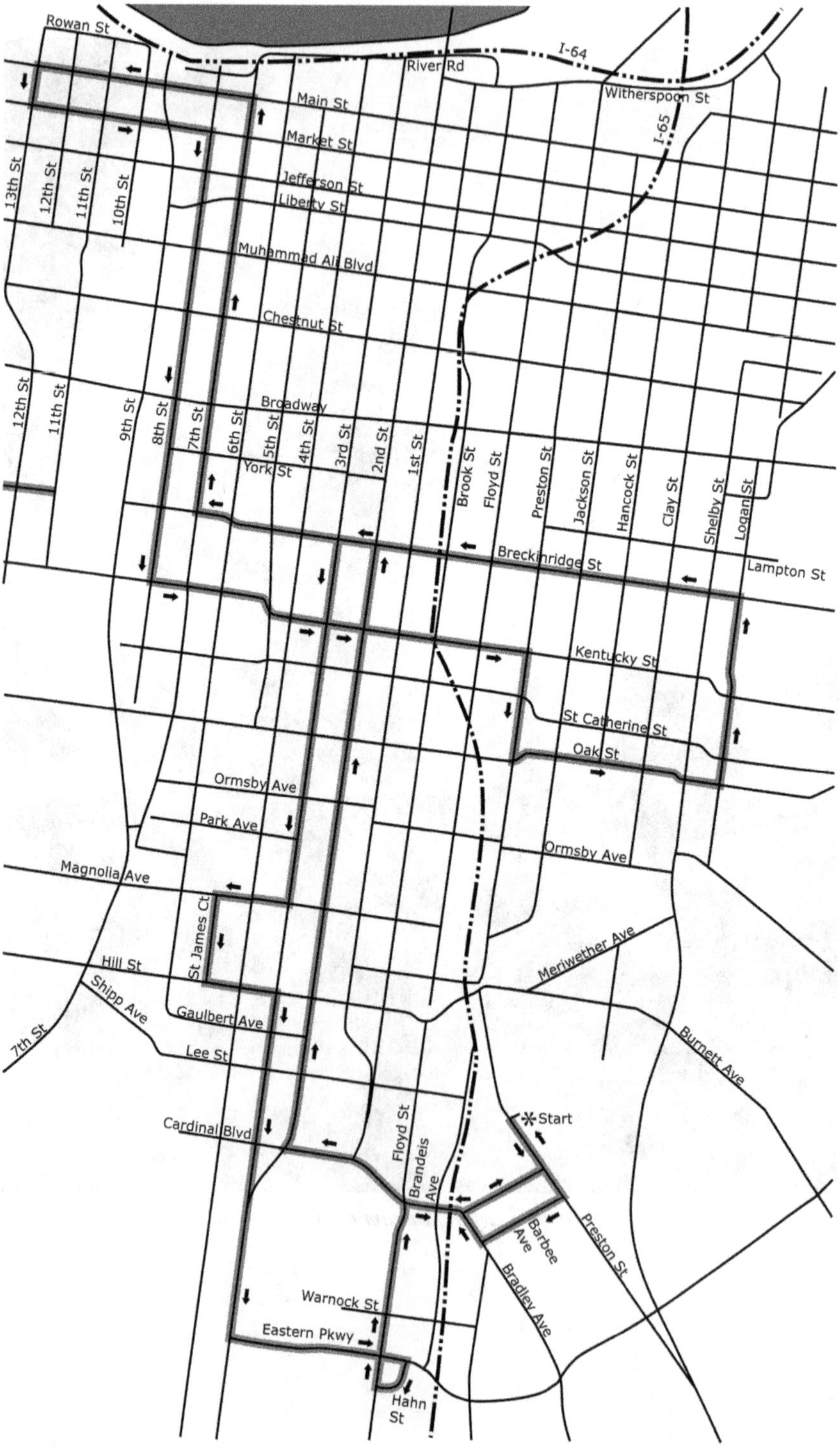

Rowan St
I-64
River Rd
Main St
Witherspoon St
I-65
Market St
Jefferson St
Liberty St
13th St
12th St
11th St
10th St
Muhammad Ali Blvd
Chestnut St
Broadway
12th St
11th St
9th St
8th St
7th St
6th St
5th St
4th St
3rd St
2nd St
1st St
York St
Brook St
Floyd St
Preston St
Jackson St
Hancock St
Clay St
Shelby St
Logan St
Breckinridge St
Lampton St
Kentucky St
St Catherine St
Oak St
Ormsby Ave
Park Ave
Ormsby Ave
Magnolia Ave
St James Ct
Meriwether Ave
Hill St
Shipp Ave
Gaulbert Ave
7th St
Lee St
Burnett Ave
Start
Cardinal Blvd
Floyd St
Brandeis Ave
Barbee Ave
Preston St
Bradley Ave
Warnock St
Eastern Pkwy
Hahn St

1 DOWNTOWN, OLD LOUISVILLE, ST. JOSEPH, SHELBY PARK, AND SMOKETOWN

Distance: 13.8 miles

Difficulty: Easy. Traffic may be heavy at times on downtown streets and in portions of Old Louisville. On many streets, cyclists should be cautious of traffic at intersections due to visibility concerns, such as parked cars.

Points of Interest: Museum Row; Conrad-Caldwell House; Old Louisville; St. James-Belgravia Historic District; St. Joseph, Shelby Park, Smoketown, and Limerick neighborhoods; Shelby Park; University of Louisville; Freedom Park

This first tour explores the streets of Louisville's downtown and the Old Louisville, Shelby Park, and Smoketown neighborhoods, highlighting many of the city's most prominent points of interests along the way. Louisville's downtown roughly encompasses the area between the Ohio River and 9th Street to the west, Hancock Street to the east, and York and Jacob Streets to the south. Although there are only 3,000 residents who call this area home, the downtown district is home to Kentucky's major business and financial districts, its tallest buildings, and many of the state's major museums and tourist attractions. Downtown is also home to most of Louisville's local governmental offices, and to several colleges and universities as well. As the state's major economic engine, the economic health of Louisville's downtown district is generally considered to be a bellwether for the rest of the state.

Downtown Louisville has witnessed many changes since the city's founding in the late 18th century. In its early days, downtown Louisville was

29

an important stop for riverboats that had to navigate around the Falls of the Ohio. By the late 19th century, downtown Louisville had become a booming manufacturing district, strategically poised along the river and several major railroads. But by the mid-20th century, a decline in manufacturing caused downtown Louisville to undergo a major decline as well. At the turn of the 21st century, a major renaissance took root as residents began to take pride in the area, cleaning away most of the blight and crime. With the revival of economic activity, many businesses, young professionals, and longtime residents returned, and numerous museums, parks, and other attractions have opened up. Likewise, improvements in infrastructure and accessibility have made the city much more bicycle-friendly, enabling residents and visitors alike to explore the city's major historic sites on two wheels. Today, downtown Louisville is a great place to live, work, and conduct business, and the many festivals and events held downtown attract throngs of visitors and tourists.

Old Louisville

Situated due south of the downtown district, Old Louisville is a historic neighborhood that extends from York and Jacob Streets southward to the University of Louisville's northern border at Cardinal Boulevard and Brandeis Avenue. The neighborhood encompasses 48 city blocks and was first developed as a suburb of Louisville in the 1870s. With the introduction of horse-drawn trolleys as public transportation at this time, the area attracted many of the city's wealthier citizens, who built large, stately homes that largely remain intact today. Most of the area was fully developed by the 1890s, and the neighborhood became the major social and political center of the city.

Old Louisville is nationally known for the beautiful architecture of its many stately, well-maintained homes. Most of the homes in Old Louisville were built from brick or stone, and consist of beautiful Victorian styles such as Romanesque and Queen Anne. Few buildings in Old Louisville have been demolished; with the exception of a few modern high-rise buildings, the numerous vehicles plying its streets, and a few other modern conveniences, the neighborhood appears much as it would have in the late 19th century.

Like most of Louisville's urban core, Old Louisville also experienced a major decline in the 1950s and 1960 as the exodus of its residents to the newer neighborhoods being built in eastern Jefferson County accelerated. It was around this time that the neighborhood came to be known as Old Louisville. By the 1980s, Old Louisville's crime rate had skyrocketed, and the neighborhood was in danger of becoming blighted like some of the city's western neighborhoods. Beginning in the 1990s, however, Old Louisville experienced a major renaissance as faculty, staff, and students from the University of Louisville, as well as many young professionals, began flocking to the area and renovating many of its beautiful old buildings and apartments. By the turn of the 21st century, Old Louisville was well regarded as a hip place to live and do business. Numerous bars, restaurants, and small shops sprang up to serve the population, and there are many significant cultural events that take place in the area, such as the annual St. James Art Fair.

Lying due east of Old Louisville is the Smoketown neighborhood, roughly defined as the area between Broadway and Kentucky Street, Interstate 65, and the CSX railroad tracks just east of Logan Street. It lies immediately west of the Highlands, and north of the Shelby Park neighborhood. Smoketown got its name from the many brick kilns that operated in the area in the early 19th century and produced a large volume of smoke from processing the ample clay deposits in the area. Most of Smoketown's numerous kilns had ceased operation by the 1880s, and there are few traces of the kilns left in the area today. What does remain of Smoketown, however, is the typical tale of boom, bust, and urban renewal that has characterized many large cities along the Ohio River.

Smoketown was first settled in the 1850s by German immigrants arriving in Louisville via the Ohio River. Its character soon changed with the arrival of thousands of newly-freed African-American slaves from rural areas in Kentucky in 1866. With improvements in transportation, streetcars were extended into the area in the late 1860s, spurring further population growth. The area soon boomed, with narrow shotgun houses lining labyrinths of crowded streets. By 1880, over 15,000 residents called Smoketown home.

Smoketown experienced a major decline over the early 20th century as many of its residents left for outlying suburbs to the east. Despite the rapid depopulation, Smoketown remained a solidly working class neighborhood with many tightly knit families well into the 1960s. But Smoketown's depopulation accelerated in the 1970s, with heavy crime and urban blight evident by 1980. Many of Smoketown's homes fell into disrepair, and the area's many small shops were replaced with bars and liquor stores.

Accentuating the crime and blight was the decline of Sheppard Square, a public housing project that was built in the neighborhood during the 1940s. By the 1980s, Sheppard Square became an infamous hotbed of crime, drugs, poverty, and neglect, and this reputation persisted well into the 21st century. With the increase in crime, Smoketown's depopulation accelerated. During the 1990s, nearly two-thirds of the neighborhood's residents left, and its population dropped to barely 2,100 residents by 2000. Smoketown's population has since stabilized around 2,250, but it is hoped that this will change with the many urban renewal efforts of the last decade. Among these efforts is the ongoing redevelopment of Sheppard Square as a mixed income housing project.

The tour begins in the heart of Louisville's St. Joseph neighborhood. St. Joseph is situated immediately east of Interstate 65 and the University of Louisville and is named for the former St. Joseph's Infirmary that relocated to the corner of Preston Street and Eastern Parkway in 1926. The Infirmary was sold to Humana in 1970 and closed in 1980 when the company moved the bulk of its operations to Audubon Hospital on Poplar Level Road. Most of the former hospital was demolished, and the land was sold to a developer who built the University Park Apartments at the corner of Preston Street and Eastern Parkway. All that remains of the infirmary today is Lourdes Hall, which was renovated by the Louisville Housing Authority into a retirement home.

Most of the St. Joseph neighborhood consists of simple bungalows and shotgun houses, and was settled primarily by German immigrants who arrived in the area around the turn of the 20th century. Preston Street is also home to several iconic Louisville bars and restaurants, including Nord's Bakery, which is famous for their delicious maple-bacon donuts that make an excellent reward for an afternoon of cycling. The tour begins at the entrance to Preston Park at the corner of Preston and Augustus Streets. Parking is available in several areas of the park, or along Preston Street.

Route Directions – Downtown, Old Louisville, Shelby Park, and Smoketown

0.0 Left onto KY-61/Preston Street
0.2 Right onto Barbee Avenue
0.4 Right onto Bradley Avenue
0.5 Left onto E Brandeis Avenue
0.8 Continue onto Cardinal Boulevard
1.0 Right onto S 2nd Street
2.5 Left onto W Breckenridge Street
3.0 Right onto S 7th Street
4.0 Left onto W Main Street
4.5 Left onto N 13th Street
4.6 Left onto W Market Street
5.1 Right onto S 8th Street
6.2 Left onto W Kentucky Street
7.2 Right onto S Preston Street
7.4 Left onto E Oak Street
7.9 Left onto Logan Street
8.6 Left onto Finzer Street
8.7 Left onto S Shelby Street
9.0 Right onto E Breckenridge Street
9.9 Left onto S 3rd Street
10.8 Right onto W Magnolia Avenue
11.0 Left onto St. James Court
11.2 Left onto W Hill Street
11.4 Right onto S 3rd Street
12.2 Left onto Eastern Parkway
12.6 Right onto Hahn Street
12.7 Right onto S Floyd Street
13.2 Right at roundabout onto E Brandeis Avenue
13.4 Left to continue on E Brandeis Avenue
13.5 Left onto KY-61/Preston Street
13.8 Right onto Augustus Avenue and Preston Park

Route Description – Downtown, Old Louisville, St. Joseph, Shelby Park, and Smoketown

0.0 Left onto KY-61/Preston Street

The ride begins at the entrance to Preston Park in the heart of Louisville's St. Joseph neighborhood. This neighborhood was developed in the 1890s by David Meriwether and consists mostly of shotgun houses and bungalows. Many of the original homes are still standing, although many have been converted into apartments and rentals that serve the nearby University of Louisville.

0.2 Right onto Barbee Avenue

Most of the homes here don't have driveways, so there are always many cars parked along the streets in this area. Although bicycles are a popular mode of transportation here, cyclists should always be wary of car doors opening suddenly and vehicles entering and exiting the lane of traffic.

0.4 Right onto Bradley Avenue

Bradley Avenue heads northwest, ending at its intersection with Brandeis Avenue. The next turn on the route may be confusing to people who are not familiar with the area's traffic patterns. To the right, Brandeis Avenue is one-way, carrying eastbound traffic toward Preston Street. To the left, the street carries two-way traffic. Directly ahead, there is a guard rail that separates eastbound traffic entering Brandeis Avenue from Arthur Street, which carries traffic exiting Interstate 65. The route turns left here, heading westbound on Brandeis Avenue toward the University of Louisville.

0.5 Left onto E Brandeis Avenue

Traveling west on Brandeis Avenue will feel strange to many cyclists, with eastbound traffic on the left and more eastbound traffic to the right that is separated from the lane by a guard rail. Brandeis Avenue passes underneath Interstate 65 and comes to a 4-way stop at its intersection with Arthur Street. This intersection and the roundabout at Floyd Street carry a considerable amount of traffic. Cyclists should exercise the utmost caution in these locations and pay strict attention to the traffic lights and signs. There are many cyclists who commute to and from the university in this area, so most motorists are at least attentive and aware of bicycles.

West of Floyd Street, a bike lane arises as the road heads downhill under the railroad tracks. The underpass floods frequently after heavy rains;

afterward, there is often mud, sand, and other debris present in the bike lane that may force cyclists into the lane with traffic. As the road heads back uphill, the University of Louisville appears on the left side of the road.

0.8 Continue onto Cardinal Boulevard

Brandeis Avenue becomes Cardinal Boulevard as the road passes west of South 1st Street. The University of Louisville's Belknap Campus, its main campus, sprawls southward past Eastern Parkway from this location. The University of Louisville traces its origins to 1798 when the Kentucky General Assembly chartered the institution as Jefferson Seminary. The school opened in 1813 but closed in 1829. Its assets were obtained by the Louisville Collegiate Institute and Louisville Medical Institute. In 1846, the General Assembly combined the schools' resources and chartered the University of Louisville, combining the medical school, the college, and a law school.

The 20th century brought change and progress to the university. Many new programs and schools were added, and the university transitioned to more full-time faculty rather than relying on part-time faculty drawn from the ranks of the city's professionals. By 1951, the university was desegregated. But with the mass migration of Louisville's population toward the suburbs, the school experienced a severe decline in its funding with the erosion of the city's tax base. As a result, the school was brought into the state's public higher education system in 1970. Today, the University of Louisville enrolls approximately 22,500 students across three campuses.

A dormitory and classroom buildings for the School of Education can be seen on the left side of the road here, and there are athletic fields belonging to DuPont Manual High School across the road on the right. The dormitory, Unitas Tower, was built in 1971 and named for pro football Hall-of-Famer Johnny Unitas (1933-2002), quarterback for the University of Louisville Cardinals from 1951 to 1954. After graduation, Unitas was drafted by the Pittsburgh Steelers but soon cut from the squad. In 1956, Unitas joined the Baltimore Colts and became their starting quarterback by the 1957 season. That year, he led them to a 7-5 record and their first ever winning season. The very next season, Unitas led the Colts to the NFL championship on December 28, 1958, defeating the

Johnny Unitas Tower

New York Giants 23-17 in what has since been billed as the "greatest game ever played."

Unitas played for the Colts until 1972, racking up MVP honors in 1957, 1959, 1964, and 1967, and starting for the Colts in the 1971 Super Bowl, which the team won 16-13 over the Dallas Cowboys. After 1972, however, Unitas had declined considerably, was benched, and subsequently traded to the San Diego Chargers. He played the 1973 season in San Diego but retired at the end of the year due to numerous health concerns. Over his career, Unitas completed over 2,800 passes for more than 40,000 yards, setting many records in the process. His jerseys, number 16 at the University of Louisville and number 19 at Baltimore, were eventually retired.

Later in life, Unitas became an advocate for safety in football, bringing attention to the many physical injuries and disabilities he sustained during his 18 years in the NFL during an era in which the heavy padding and other essential safety equipment used today were virtually unheard of. Late in his NFL career, he suffered from arm and hand problems that severely hampered his abilities as a quarterback. Later in life, his right arm and hand were virtually unusable, and he was plagued by knee problems.

Just past the University of Louisville's campus, the route turns right onto S 2nd Street, heading into Old Louisville.

1.0 Right onto S 2nd Street

DuPont Manual High School

Heading away from the University of Louisville, the route enters the beautiful Old Louisville neighborhood. South 2nd Street is one-way heading north, and has two lanes of traffic with cars parked on both the left and right sides of the street. The right lane is a combined bicycle and traffic lane, as indicated by the shared use lane signage painted on the road. The speed limit here is 25 mph and there are often other bicycles on the road, so aggressive drivers are seldom a problem although cyclist should be wary of motorists who frequently disregard red lights throughout Old Louisville.

At the intersection of 2nd and Lee Streets is DuPont Manual High School, one of Louisville's original public high schools. Founded in 1892 as DuPont Manual Training High School, the school offered a three-year curriculum of industrial and mechanical training classes interspersed with general academic subjects. The school's original building located at the corner of Brook and Oak Streets has since been converted into apartments. After briefly merging with Louisville Male High School between 1915 and 1919, the school returned to its original building and became Male's chief athletic rival, especially during football season.

The Gothic revival-style building seen here was built in 1934 to house Louisville Girls High School. Originally opened as Louisville Female High School in 1856, the school was renamed in 1911 and moved to a facility located at 5th and Hill Streets. Louisville Girls High School moved to this building in 1934. In 1950, DuPont Manual Training High School and Louisville Girls High Schools merged due to budget concerns. The new school was housed in the Girls High School building located here, and the campus of the new school has remained at this location ever since. Over the past half-century, the campus was gradually expanded to include nearly two full city blocks.

A little farther, across from Gaulbert Street, is Louisville Youth Performing Arts School, affectionately known to locals as "YPAS." The school is one of only two schools in

4th Street in Old Louisville

Kentucky allowing students to major in performing arts in high school, and one of only 100 or so in the country. The school's students take most of their general education courses at Manual High School while studying the arts at YPAS. Admission is competitive, and most of the school's graduates go on to attend major performing arts colleges.

As 2nd Street continues northward through Old Louisville, a full bike lane appears north of Oak Street at the right-hand side of the road. There is a parking lane to the right of the bike lane, so cyclists should be alert for cars pulling in and out of traffic, or for car doors opening suddenly. Past Kentucky Street, there is a grocery store on the left side of the road, and traffic congestion picks up slightly. The next turn on the route is at the end of this block, onto W Breckenridge Street. The bike lane on Breckenridge Street is on the left side of the road, so it will be necessary to fully take the left lane of

2nd Street just ahead of the intersection.

2.5 Left onto W Breckenridge Street

Immediately after turning onto Breckenridge Street, a protected bike lane appears on the left-hand side of the road. Breckenridge Street is one-way, carrying only westbound traffic. At intersections, the bike lane is shared with turning vehicles, so cyclists should keep track of motorists moving into and out of the lane of travel.

There are two notable Old Louisville landmarks on Breckenridge Street. The first of these is Spalding University, one of Louisville's many independent colleges and universities. Spalding was founded by the Sisters of Charity in Nazareth in Louisville in 1920 as Nazareth College, a four-year Catholic college for women. At that time, the college was housed in the Tompkins-Buchanan-Rankin house on S 4th Street, which still serves as the university's administration building. Built in 1871, it is a good example of Italianate architecture. The north and south sides of the building still appear largely as they did when the structure was first built.

Nazareth College was renamed as Spalding College in 1969 for Mother Catherine Spalding, the Sisters' founder. In 1971, the college was merged with Nazareth Academy in Nelson County, which was also run by the Sisters. The college became coeducational in 1973, at which time admission was opened to students of all faiths. The college was reorganized as a university in 1984. Today, the university offers programs that are primarily geared toward allied health occupations, the humanities, and education.

At the corner of Breckenridge and 4th Street there is a large, beautiful stone church on the right-hand side of the road. Built in 1910, this magnificent building is one of the city's treasured landmarks, and it has been home to Lampton Baptist Church since the early 1970s. With severely declining attendance, however, the building fell into disrepair. In 2014, a building swap deal saw Lampton trade facilities with the rapidly-growing Immanuel Baptist Church near Shelby Park. With this deal, this architectural treasure will hopefully be restored for generations to come.

Past S 6th Street, the route enters a light industrial area. The next turn on the route, onto S 7th Street, occurs very soon afterward. To make the turn, it will be necessary to leave the bike lane west of 6th Street and fully take the right lane.

3.0 Right onto S 7th Street

Upon turning onto 7th Street, another bicycle lane appears, this time on the right-hand side of the road. A large post office facility on the right side of the road serves much of Old Louisville and downtown. Soon, traffic on

7th Street must cross Broadway; the traffic light here may take a minute or two to change, and the weight sensor usually doesn't pick up bicycles at the intersection.

Across the street is the Gene Snyder U.S. Courthouse and Custom House, a Louisville landmark that is on the National Register of Historic Places. Built in 1931, the building is an excellent example of Classic Revival architecture. Its impressive Corinthian columns and rounded windows are reminiscent of the United States Treasury Department Building in Washington, D.C. The courthouse is impressive as it looms over Broadway and is well worth an afternoon tour.

Gene Snyder U.S. Courthouse and Custom House

The building's interior is just as impressive as its exterior. The expansive lobby has an impressively inlaid marble floor. The elevators still have their original bronze doors and are decorated with intricate moldings. The walls are decorated with a series of ten paintings by Kentucky artist Frank Weathers Long that was commissioned by the Public Works Act in 1935.

In 1986, the building was renamed for former Kentucky congressman Marion Eugene "Gene" Snyder (1928-2007), who represented Kentucky's third congressional district (which includes the city of Louisville and most of Jefferson County) in the U.S. House of Representatives from 1963-1965 and Kentucky's redistricted fourth district (which includes neighboring Oldham County and northeastern Kentucky) from 1967-1987. A portion of Interstate 265 is named for Snyder.

One block north of the federal courthouse is the Romano L. Mazzoli Federal Building, named for the former U.S. Representative who served as the representative for Kentucky's third congressional district from 1971 to 1995.

One block to the east, at 6th and Broadway, is the building housing the *Courier-Journal*, Louisville's primary newspaper and Kentucky's largest. The newspaper was formed from the 1868 merger of the *Louisville Daily Journal*, a house organ of the Whig Party founded by George Prentice, and the *Louisville Morning Courier*, founded by Walter Newman Haldeman. During the U.S. Civil War, the two media outlets were largely at odds with each other; the staunchly pro-Union *Daily Journal* opposed slavery and secession, while the *Courier* was pro-Confederacy. With Kentucky occupied by Union forces for much of the war, the *Courier* moved to Nashville briefly but returned after the war's conclusion.

In 1868, the Courier and the Journal merged. Henry Watterson, the son of a Tennessee congressman and a former Confederate soldier who served under General Nathan Bedford Forrest, was appointed as the new media outlet's editor. Watterson advocated for the industrialization of the southern states and was instrumental in attracting the Southern Exposition to Louisville in 1883. In 1876, he was elected to serve out the remainder of U. S. Representative Edward Parsons' term after Parsons died in office.

During his career at the Courier-Journal, Watterson published many controversial and thought-provoking editorials, eventually winning the Pulitzer Prize in 1918 for his editorials supporting the entry of the United States into World War I. He finally retired in 1919 after numerous policy clashes with the liberal Robert Bingham, who had recently purchased a controlling share of the paper. Kentucky's portion of Interstate 264 is named for Watterson.

Bingham served as the paper's editor until 1933, when the position was passed on to his son Barry Bingham, Sr. In 1971, Barry Bingham, Jr. assumed the editor's position, and remained in the position until the paper was sold to the Gannett Company in 1986. During the Bingham era, Robert, Barry, and Barry Jr. continued Watterson's obsession with high-quality journalism but instituted a change in editorial position. The Binghams largely advocated for improvements in education, race relations, and the alleviation of poverty in the Kentucky's Appalachian counties. The Bingham family is generally well regarded among Louisvillians and once

owned other media outlets, including WHAS-TV and WHAS-AM.

By 2008, the Gannett Company experienced heavy financial losses amid a decade-long decline in print newspaper circulation that was primarily due to competition from online news outlets. As a result, most of Gannett's newspapers, including the Courier-Journal, experienced massive layoffs, shedding nearly 20% of its workforce. The Courier-Journal's circulation, however, has stabilized and even increased since the layoffs were announced. The Courier-Journal now appears to be well poised to continue as Kentucky's largest and most important news outlet for many years to come.

As 7th Street continues north of Liberty Street, the bicycle lane disappears and is replaced with a shared use lane. During normal business hours, there are many vehicles parked along the right side of the road, making it necessary for cyclists to ride clear of the parking lane to avoid vehicles moving suddenly or car doors opening. Just north of Liberty Street is the Jefferson County District Court and Judicial Center. The Louisville Metropolitan Police Department's headquarters is located one block north of the courthouse at 7th and Jefferson Streets. There are many parking garages in this area, and cyclists must be vigilant in looking for cars that may be pulling in and out of them.

As the route approaches the next turn at 7th and Main Streets, Louisville's Museum Row comes into view. The intersection is usually busy, and cyclists will need to move into the left turn lane to avoid vehicles continuing north on 7th Street.

4.0 Left onto W Main Street

Main Street is one-way, carrying only westbound traffic. Like 7th Street, this area of downtown is often very busy, especially during normal weekday business hours and the morning and afternoon commutes. Caution should be observed here due to the large number of vehicles in this area, especially since many of them are busy looking off to the side at the many shops, restaurants, bars, and museums. The road consists of three traffic lanes, with a parking lane on the far right-hand side of the road and occasional cut-outs on the left side with parking meters. There is a shared bike lane in the far right traffic lane. Cyclists should take the entire lane here to avoid the many parked cars suddenly entering the lane of travel or opening their doors.

Museum Row begins at the corner of 7th and Main Streets, with the 21c Museum and Hotel at the corner. The 21c is a unique boutique hotel with a contemporary art gallery that is open to the public. Its unusual men's restroom has

Main Street in downtown Louisville

won awards, coming second only to the men's room in Nashville's Hermitage Hotel. Men at the urinals in the restroom can see out through a one-way mirror into the adjacent hallway. There is also a very large gold-colored replica of Michelangelo's naked David statue adorning the corner, which is apparently very popular with the throngs of tourists who constantly pose for pictures next to it. There are many historic offices and storefronts along Main Street, and it is a wonderful area to explore on foot or by bike. To the right, between 6th and 7th Streets, are the Evan Williams Bourbon Experience and the Kentucky Center for the Performing Arts. To the left are the Kentucky Science Center, the Louisville Slugger Museum, and the Frazier History Museum, all of which are well worth an afternoon exploring. Between April and November, this area is teeming with tourists walking up and down the sidewalks, exploring the museums, and visiting the many shops, restaurants, and bars that line the street. Louisville's downtown area has made a huge rebound from its virtual desolation in the 1980s and nowhere is this more evident than along this stretch of Main Street.

At the corner of 8th and Main Streets immediately west of the Kentucky Science Center is a curious memorial that most locals pass without notice. The oddly-shaped tornado sculpture commemorates the massive F4 tornado that destroyed much of the California and Russell neighborhoods to the west on March 27, 1890. The tornado then tore through the downtown business district, collapsing the Falls City Hall at 1124 West Market Street, killing 44 people. The tornado continued eastward, damaged the water tower at the end of Zorn Avenue and left a wide swath of destruction in its wake. In all, 90 people lost their lives, more than 200 were injured, and tens of millions of dollars' worth of damage was done to the city, making it the 25th most deadly (26th after 2011) tornado in recorded history. The oddly-shaped memorial located here serves as a constant reminder of how the Ohio Valley's mild spring weather can quickly turn deadly.

After crossing 9th Street, the road passes under a mass of freeway ramps and then emerges back into the sunlight as it crosses 10th Street. At the corner of Main and 10th Streets is Caufield's, a costume and novelty shop that is a long-time Louisville tradition. Caufield's was founded in 1920 by photographer Keran Caulfield, who found that his true calling was selling practical jokes to the customers in his waiting room rather than his photography business. Today, Caufield's manufactures and sells costumes and novelties nationwide, and is well known for hosting an annual Halloween parade through downtown Louisville.

On the right side of Main Street, between 10th and 11th Streets, is a historical marker commemorating the Election Day riots of August 6, 1855, marking a very dark and violent period of Louisville's history. The incident, later referred to as "Bloody Monday", was clash between members of the American Party (commonly referred to as the "Know Nothing" Party) and the mostly Irish Catholic immigrants that inhabited the Quinn's Row neighborhood that once stood here.

The Know-Nothings were an offshoot of the disintegrating Whig Party, which existed in the United States between 1833 and 1854. Presidents Zachary Taylor and William Henry Harrison were elected president as members of the Whig Party; however, the party was divided by issues such as prohibition, immigration, and slavery by the 1850s. The deaths of party stalwarts Henry Clay and Daniel Webster in 1852 caused the party to splinter, with most former Whigs in the north joining the newly-formed Republican Party. A number of southern Whigs formed the American Party, a short-lived political party that primarily sought to greatly reduce the immigration of Irish and German Catholics into the United States and limit their influence on politics. The party had few effective leaders and was still strongly divided over the issue of slavery. Louisville Mayor John Barbee, elected in early 1855 after former mayor James Speed was ousted by the Kentucky Supreme Court, was a Know-Nothing.

On August 6, 1855, armed gangs of Know-Nothings surrounded several polling places around Louisville during the state's gubernatorial election. As the polls closed, rioting erupted and quickly spread throughout the Butchertown area and in Quinn's Row, the neighborhood that once stood at this site. Homes and businesses were destroyed and looted, and citizens were

Bloody Monday historical marker

dragged from their homes and workplaces and killed. Later that evening, all of the homes on Quinn's Row were set ablaze, and the violence escalated. It was only after direct intervention by Mayor Barbee that the destruction and bloodshed stopped.

Nobody was ever held accountable for the violence and killings of Bloody Monday. Official estimates were that 20 people were killed, although the Catholic Church has maintained that the actual death toll was well over 100, as entire families perished in the fires. Dozens of empty buildings and storefronts, as well as the charred remains of Quinn's Row, remained untouched for years. The event spurred tens of thousands of citizens to pack up and leave for other cities in the Midwest, most never to return. The large emigration depopulated large areas of the city and caused major financial losses.

As Main Street leaves the downtown area, the route turns left from Main Street onto N 13th Street.

4.5 Left onto N 13th Street

Two-way traffic returns on 13th Street. The next turn of the route occurs one block later, onto Market Street.

4.6 Left onto W Market Street

Market Street has one lane of traffic with a bike lane on the right-hand side of the road. There is a parking lane to the right of the bike lane, and since parked cars may occasionally block the bike lane here, cyclists should pay close attention to road conditions. As the road passes east of the freeway on-ramps and off-ramps, the road becomes one-way, carrying only eastbound traffic.

To the left, along 10th Street between Main and Market Streets is a building housing the Old 502 Winery and Falls City Brewing Company. The brewery is the reincarnation of the legendary Falls City Brewing Company, formed in 1905 by a number of local grocers to break the monopoly of the Central Consumers Company. Despite a hiatus in production during Prohibition, the brewery operated continuously until 1978, when Heileman Brewing Company purchased the brand and moved production to a facility in Evansville, Indiana. Many older Louisville residents swore off the beer forever because of that unforgivable sin, but the brand had been in serious decline since the early 1970s due to competition with Budweiser, Pabst Blue Ribbon, and other major brands.

Despite the company's decline and downfall in the 1970s, Falls City was the first beer to introduce the familiar Sta-Tab, which could be used to open the can and was then folded back against the can's lid. Falls City also introduced Billy Beer to the nation in 1977 in honor of President Jimmy Carter's beer-swilling brother Billy Carter, who was a fan of Pabst Blue Ribbon beer. Falls City discontinued Billy Beer in 1978, citing lackluster sales.

The Falls City brand was later sold to the Pittsburg Brewing Company, who produced the brand until 2007. Falls City Beer was revived in 2010 as a craft beer producer. Although many of Louisville's older residents remember the Falls City Beer of their youth as a watered down, flavorless, cheaply produced product, Falls City's new owners have sworn off the reviled formulas of the late 1970s and now produce six varieties of craft beer in their new facility on 10th Street.

East of the freeway ramps, the Snead Manufacturing building sits on the left side of the Market Street. The building dates back to 1910 and is on the National Register of Historic Places. This building replaced the Snead and Company Iron Works, which produced much of the ornamental iron works that once graced buildings throughout the city. The original facility burned in 1898 and was replaced by the building that currently stands here. The new building has hosted numerous offices and manufacturing firms over the past century. Today, the building houses numerous apartments and condominiums, art galleries, and glass blowing studios.

5.1 Right onto S 8th Street

Within a block of the turn onto 8th Street, a bike lane appears on the right side of the road. There is a parking lane to the right of the bike lane, so cyclists must stay aware of car doors opening and to vehicles moving across the bike lane. The bike lane ends south of Magazine Street and is replaced with a shared use lane. Otherwise, the traffic on 8th Street is much calmer than on Main and Market Streets.

At the corner of 8th and Chestnut Streets is the Technical Campus of Jefferson Community and Technical College (JCTC). It is the largest of 16 colleges that operate under the umbrella of Kentucky's Community and Technical College System (KCTCS), headquartered in Versailles. KCTCS was formed in 1997 under the Patton administration, which stripped the state's community colleges from the University of Kentucky and merged them with the state's technical schools. JCTC's main campus is located along Broadway between Brook and 2nd Streets on the west side of Interstate 65.

Soon, 8th Street crosses Broadway at a busy intersection. At the corner of 8th and Broadway is a large building that houses offices of the Louisville Gas and Electric Company. Farther off to the right there is a large 11-story building visible from the intersection of Broadway and 9th Street that is adorned with large "L & N" neon lights on its eastern side. Completed in 1907, the edifice once housed the headquarters for the Louisville & Nashville Railroad, which operated from 1850 until 1970. The building replaced the company's previous headquarters at 2nd and Main Streets and was moved here adjacent to Union Station. It was purchased by the state of Kentucky in 1984 and currently

L&N Building

houses offices of the Kentucky Cabinet for Health and Family Services. Union Station, just to the west of the L&N building, currently serves as the headquarters for the Transit Authority of River City (TARC), which runs the city's public transportation system.

South of Breckenridge Street, 8th Street enters the Limerick neighborhood, spanning 5th and 9th Streets between Breckenridge and Oak Streets. Limerick was developed in the 1860s and settled by a large number of Irish immigrants from Limerick County, Ireland, most of whom took jobs with the Louisville & Nashville Railroad. The new arrivals built modest shotgun houses throughout the area, and a few of the more wealthy arrivals built large mansions along St. Catherine Street. A large number of African-Americans soon moved into the area's backstreets and alleys, and by 1900, had moved into many of the shotgun houses and cottages in the area as some of the Irish railroad workers moved southward toward Wilder Park and Beechmont. Historically, both ethnic groups in this area of town cooperated and lived peacefully together, a tradition that still continues in the neighborhood today.

Today, Limerick is a designated Historic Preservation District. Portions of Limerick have been profoundly affected by the renewal of Old Louisville, which many residents consider the neighborhood part of. Other portions of Limerick, such as this area along 8th Street, are still affected by urban blight, with numerous brownfields located to the west.

6.2 Left onto W Kentucky Street

Kentucky Street continues through the Limerick neighborhood. The road was recently reconfigured to include a single lane of traffic, a protected bike lane to the left, and a parking lane on the far left-hand side of the road. As Kentucky Street meets 7th Street, there is a historic school building on the right that currently houses Simmons College, another of Louisville's many private colleges and universities. Simmons College was founded as State College in 1879 by Pastor Henry Adams and the Convention of Colored Baptist Churches to provide higher education for Kentucky's African-American population. The college was first known as Kentucky Normal Theological Institute but was later renamed as Simmons College in honor of Rev. Dr. William J. Simmons, a well-educated former slave who held several degrees from Howard University. Under Dr. Simmons' tenure between 1880 and 1890, the college flourished and became a full-fledged university offering a broad curriculum. By 1900, the university offered professional degrees in law, nursing, and medicine in conjunction with Louisville National Medical College, Central Law School, and the University of Louisville. Thus, it was fitting to name the college for the man who helped develop it into a nationally recognized institution.

By 1930, however, the university had become insolvent. The facility at 7th and Kentucky Streets was purchased by the University of Louisville, which continued Simmons' operations, but eventually absorbed most of it and renamed it as Louisville Municipal College. The college served as a segregated branch of the University of Louisville until desegregation in the 1950s rendered it obsolete. Simmons College, however, was allowed to continue its mission of educating and preparing men and women for Christian ministry. The college was eventually renamed Simmons Bible College and its operations moved to a location at 18th and Dumesnil Streets.

Since the mid-2000s, Simmons College has undergone a major revival. Under the leadership of Dr. Kevin Cosby, the college was renamed Simmons College to reinforce the school's mission of liberal arts education with an emphasis on faith and community service. After a major fundraising effort, the college purchased its original facility at 7th and Kentucky Streets. In 2006, Simmons College reintroduced athletics, sponsoring men's and women's basketball teams for the first time since 1930. Today, Simmons College is thriving and its future looks bright.

Simmons College

The other side of Kentucky Street was once home to Eclipse Park, where the minor league Louisville Colonels baseball team once played. The facility that once stood here was the third baseball stadium built in Louisville; the first one was built in 1871 at 28th and Elliott Streets and was rebuilt at 28th Street and Broadway in 1892 in what is now the city's Parkland neighborhood after the original structure was demolished in a fire. The minor league Colonels team played here from 1902 until 1922, when Eclipse Park was again destroyed by fire. The lot remained vacant until 1938 when a government housing project was built here.

On the right side of the street, at the corner of 6th and Kentucky Streets, is a building that once housed the Central Colored School. Dedicated in 1873, this building housed the first school dedicated to the education of the city's African-American children. Grades one through eight were taught at the facility, with high school classes added in 1882. At that time, the school's name was changed to Central Colored High School. The school soon outgrew the building at this location and moved to a building at 9th and Magazine Streets in 1894.

A little farther down Kentucky Street, between 6th and 5th Streets, is Ben Washer Park, one of Louisville's many small pocket parks. As Kentucky Street continues east of 5th Street, a small side street

Memorial Auditorium

47

called Baseball Alley branches off to the left as Kentucky Street makes an S-curve to the south before continuing eastward. Baseball Alley was used as a shortcut in the early 1900s for fans to make their way from the 4th Street trolley over to Eclipse Park to watch the Colonels play.

On the left side of the street past the S-curve is Memorial Auditorium, a Greek Revival concert hall that opened in 1929 and was dedicated to the city's World War I veterans. Although the facility is used primarily for graduations, recitals, and other smaller events today, it has hosted many large concerts during its history, including many rock concerts during the 1960s and 1970s. The building has excellent acoustics and is also home to the world's largest Pilcher pipe organ. Across 4th Street from Memorial Auditorium is Memorial Park, another one of Louisville's many pocket parks, which has a Greek theme complementing the beautiful building across the street.

Beyond 4th Street, Kentucky Street continues through the eastern portion of Old Louisville and past a building that houses the Kentucky Derby Festival's corporate headquarters. It then passes the 17-story Baptist Towers retirement apartments as it heads toward Interstate 65. Near the interstate, the scenery changes as the area becomes more residential in character.

As the road emerges from underneath the interstate and passes east of Floyd Street, it enters the Smoketown neighborhood. In a dramatic contrast to the neatly maintained Victorian buildings and manicured lawns of Old Louisville, Smoketown is filled with narrow shotgun houses and bungalows, interspersed with blocks of vacant storefronts and abandoned industrial properties.

Ohio Valley Bag and Burlap Building

7.2 Right onto S Preston Street

The turn onto Preston Street briefly leaves Smoketown, heading into the Shelby Park neighborhood that lies just to the south. Less than one block after turning onto Preston Street, there is a large historic brick factory building on the right side of the road with faded paint that identifies it as the former home of the Ohio Valley Bag and Burlap Company. Built sometime during the late 19th century, the building was originally home to the Falls City Jeans and Woolen Mills factory. The facility has hosted several other businesses throughout the years and is currently occupied by a locally owned woodworking company.

The next turn of the route occurs roughly a quarter mile later, onto Oak Street, which lies at an oblique angle to Preston Street.

7.4 Left onto E Oak Street

Oak Street makes a shallow S-curve to the north and then continues into the Shelby Park neighborhood. Between Jackson and Clay Streets, Shelby Park lies on the right side of the road. A historical marker on the side of the road commemorates the neighborhood's founding in the mid-1800s when working class German immigrants settled in this area. In 1907, Louisville Mayor Paul Barth purchased a 17-acre parcel to the south of this site for construction of a modern park designed by the Olmstead Parks firm. The park is named for Isaac Shelby, the first governor of the state of Kentucky.

During the 1980s Shelby Park was suffering from many of the same problems as Smoketown, with many dilapidated homes, vacant storefronts, and general urban blight due to the mass exodus of its residents to the suburbs. Without government support for redevelopment of the neighborhood, most of the dilapidated properties remained in the hands of private owners and

Shelby Park Neighborhood

landlords who had little incentive to properly maintain the homes. Today, Shelby Park has a very active and influential neighborhood association. The association's "Save Our Shotguns" program has offered workshops and expositions on home renovation, offered home improvement seminars and demonstrations, and promoted the revitalization of the neighborhood. And unlike many suburban neighborhood associations, neighborhood leaders have promoted the idea of improving the neighborhood's walkability and have taken steps to preserve Shelby Park. With time and persistence, the Shelby Park neighborhood will nicely complement Old Louisville with its historic preservation efforts.

The building along Oak Street facing Shelby Park was once the home of the Shelby Park Branch Library. In 1911, neighbors around Shelby Park each donated $2 toward the construction of a Carnegie endowed library. The library was closed in 1993 and combined with the Highlands library branch, currently housed in the Mid City Mall along Bardstown Road. In recent years, a number of Shelby Park residents have made an effort to revive the neighborhood's branch library.

One block beyond Shelby Park, at the intersection of Oak Street with Shelby Street, is a large majestic church building. Dating to 1884, the building was originally home to St. Vincent de Paul Catholic Church. The church was once a thriving institution, but with the rapid depopulation of the Smoketown and Shelby Park neighborhoods in the late 20th century, the magnificent cathedral fell into disrepair as the church's attendance and funding underwent a serious decline. The building was abandoned in 1990, but in recent years has seen new life as the home of Sojourn Community Church.

7.9 Left onto Logan Street

Logan Street in Smoketown

Logan Street is one way, heading northward out of the Shelby Park neighborhood toward Smoketown. Near the border of the two neighborhoods, at the corner of Logan and Mary Streets, is the Keswick Democratic Club, an interesting building with an antique neon sign that currently serves as a social club and meeting place independent of one's political leanings. The building was home to Louisville's punk rock scene during the mid-2000s, but today hosts luncheons and is available to rent for private events. Although the building has been on Logan Street since the 1930s, not much information on the building's history can be found.

As Logan Street re-enters Smoketown, there are numerous brownfields visible on the right side of the road bordering Beargrass Creek, as well as a few businesses still operating on the left side of the road. Smoketown experienced a massive exodus of its residents beginning in the early 1990s that is particularly evident along Logan Street. There is very little traffic in the area, as there are few people that work or live here. The few cars passing through here use Logan Street as a shortcut between Schnitzelburg and East Broadway.

Further adding to the area's desolation are two large crumbling, abandoned factory buildings on the right side of the road: a tall one near Lampton Street, and another one further up the street near the next turn on the route at Finzer Street. Just prior to the next turn on the route, the markings on the road direct traffic turning onto Finzer Street to move into the left lane. Cyclists should be cautious in this area and watch for vehicles suddenly moving into their lane of travel here, as the lane restriction comes very suddenly and drivers unfamiliar with the area's traffic flow usually fail to anticipate it.

8.6 Left onto Finzer Street

8.7 Left onto S Shelby Street

Shelby Street heads back toward the heart of Smoketown. Even though the neighborhood has fallen on extremely hard times, there are glimmers of hope present. The first two blocks of Shelby Street have suddenly sprung to life, with many of the few residents remaining here renovating and restoring their historic shotgun houses and bungalows. Within a few years, revitalization of the Sheppard Square housing project should be complete, attracting residents back to the area with a mixed income housing development, new green spaces and parks, and a more pedestrian-friendly feel. It is hoped that it will breathe new life into Smoketown while still preserving the neighborhood's proud history.

9.0 Right onto E Breckenridge Street

Breckenridge Street carries westbound traffic back toward Old Louisville. There is a protected bike lane along the street on the left side of the road, a single lane of traffic, and a parking lane on the right side of the road. Along the way, there are more signs of renewal. Many of the street's shotgun houses have been renovated and restored, and a few businesses have even opened.

As the street passes underneath Interstate 65, it once again enters Old Louisville. One block west of here, at the corner of Breckenridge and 1st Streets, is the Family Scholar House. The charity that runs this apartment building seeks to end the cycle of poverty by providing support to single parent students seeking to earn a college degree and move toward self-sufficiency.

The route retraces itself a short distance between 2nd and 3rd Streets, passing Spalding University again, before turning left onto 3rd Street.

9.9 Left onto S 3rd Street

Third Street heads back through the heart of Old Louisville. There is a bike lane on the right side of the road, with two lanes of traffic and parking lanes on either side. Cars may enter or leave traffic suddenly from the parking lanes, so cyclists should pay close attention to their surroundings through this area.

Third Street is also one of the more scenic areas of Old Louisville, with many beautifully maintained and restored Victorian homes on both sides of the street and mature trees that shade the road from the hot summer sun. Among the many historic homes along the street, the mansion at 1366 S 3rd Street stands out as a beautifully restored single-family residence that is an excellent example of the homes of the time.

10.8 Right onto W Magnolia Avenue

Magnolia Avenue is narrow and has a parking lane on both sides, but there is a shared use lane here. Motorists here are accustomed to seeing many cyclists through this area, and thankfully there is not as much traffic here to contend with.

On the right side of the road west of 4th Street is Central Park. The park was originally part of the DuPont estate and was known as DuPont Square. The land was developed as a park in the 1870s and subsequently opened to the public. By the early 1900s, the entire DuPont family had relocated to Delaware, and the city officially purchased the property. The park is lined with large mature shade trees and pedestrian pathways. It is often a welcome diversion from the city's hot, humid summers.

Between 1883 and 1887, the Southern Exposition was held in Central Park and on some of the land extending to the south. The Southern Exposition was a five-year series of World's Fairs held for 100 days each year from August through October, and this was Louisville's chance to show the world the progress and technology being developed in the south. Of particular interest to visitors at the Southern Exposition was a large display of Thomas Edison's incandescent light bulbs. Most of Central Park was boxed in for the display in 1883 and 1884, with more than 5,000 light bulbs illuminating the building's interior. The display at the Southern Exposition is largely credited for introducing the idea of using Edison's light bulbs for interior home lighting.

11.0 Left onto St. James Court

The next turn on the route enters the St. James-Belgravia Historic District, one of Louisville's treasures and a must-see for visitors. The neighborhood was placed on the National Register of Historic Places in 1972 and is the home of the annual St. James Court Art Show that is held in early October. The event has been running since 1957 and annually draws more than 300,000 visitors from all over the country. In recent years the event has grown so large that many booths now spill out onto 3rd and 4th Streets during the event.

The neighborhood was established at the end of the Southern Exposition when the land used to host the event was sold off in lots for home sites. Numerous expensive homes were built in the new exclusive neighborhood. Although there are many beautiful Victorian homes in the historic district, there are two homes that stand out: The Conrad-Caldwell House, located at the west corner of St. James Court and Magnolia Street; and the notorious Pink Palace, located at the corner of St. James and Belgravia Courts.

The Conrad-Caldwell House was built in 1893 for Theophile and Mary Conrad by famed architect Arthur Loomis of the Clark & Loomis firm. The Conrads made a fortune in the tanning industry and spared no expense in having a lavish home built on a premium lot across the street from Central Park. The home, often called "Conrad's Castle" by local residents, incorporated all the latest innovations and technology, including interior electric lighting and indoor plumbing. The home is famed for its intricate parquet flooring that highlights the woodwork in each room.

The home was built using $35,000 worth of Bedford limestone, quarried in southern Indiana, and widely considered

Conrad-Caldwell House

to be the highest quality limestone in the country. Limestone from the same quarries is much sought after and has been used in the construction of many prominent buildings. The home's architectural style is known as Richardsonian-Romanesque, a revival style that freely incorporates 12th century Italian, southern French, and Spanish elements. Buildings in this style exhibit capped cylindrical towers or turrets at the corners of the building, many intricate gargoyles and other carvings, and carved archways between interior rooms. Other buildings in this style include the main building of the American Museum of Natural History in New York, Cincinnati City Hall, and the courthouses in Barbour County, West Virginia, McCulloch County, Texas, and Wayne County, Indiana.

After Theophile Conrad's death in 1905, the home was sold to William E. Caldwell, who made his fortune building elevated water tanks like those seen on New York City rooftops. The company is still in business and is headquartered in Louisville. The home remained in the Caldwell family until

1947, when it was sold to the local Presbyterian Church for a retirement home. In 1987, the St. James Court foundation purchased the home. The home was lovingly restored to its former Edwardian era glory and now houses a museum. The facility is also available for weddings, gatherings, and other events. It is the best example of the grandeur of Louisville's historic homes and is a must-see destination for visitors and local residents alike.

The Pink Palace on St. James Ct.

A little farther down St. James Court is a magnificent fountain, and there are many other magnificent homes on either side of the street. Near the end of the block is the second significant home in the neighborhood. Colloquially known as the Pink Palace, the home was built in 1891 and was originally made of red brick. It first housed a gentlemen's club and casino where the men in the neighborhood would gather to drink alcohol, smoke cigars, and play cards. Upstairs, the building had large closets that were rumored to contain beds where ladies of the evening would entertain the club's guests. Sometime during the early 20th century, the home was sold to the Women's Christian Temperance Union, who painted the building its distinctive shade of pink. Today, the home is owned by a group of investors who rent the home out for special events, especially during the Kentucky Derby. The home is said by many to be haunted.

11.2 Left onto W Hill Street

Hill Street serves as a major thoroughfare connecting Shelby Park, Old Louisville and the Park Hill neighborhood west of here. Traffic may be heavy during rush hour, so patience and caution may be needed. At the corner of 4th and Hill Streets is a cluster of homes constructed in the chateauesque architectural style, one of the many architectural styles found in Old Louisville. Homes in this style have characteristically high-pitched gables and pointed roofs, and were generally built in the 1890s in Louisville.

11.4 Right onto S 3rd Street

The next turn of the route is back onto 3rd Street, where there is a bike lane available. A few blocks farther south, across Cardinal Boulevard, the road passes by the western edge of the University of Louisville campus. The intersection of 3rd Street and Cardinal Boulevard is extremely busy, and vehicles frequently run the red light. Extreme caution is advised at this intersection, and likewise through the university to Eastern Parkway.

On the left side of the street is the bulk of the University of Louisville's main campus, known as the Belknap Campus. The property was originally developed as a site for a cemetery but was later sold to an organization in 1860 for use as a reformatory for juvenile delinquents. The organization moved to a site in Lyndon in 1920; in 1923, the land was sold to the University of Louisville. There are four historic buildings that remain on the university's campus: Ford, Gardiner, Gottschalk, and Jouett Halls, that already existed on the site when the university purchased it. The buildings have been renovated and remain in use today.

Just past Cardinal Boulevard, on the left side of the road, is Freedom Park. Completed in 2012, the park commemorates the civil rights movement in Louisville and highlights the city's African-American history. The white building within the park is the Playhouse, the oldest building at the University of Louisville's Belknap Campus. The edifice was built in 1874 and originally

U of L's Freedom Park

served as the chapel for the juvenile reformatory that once operated at the site. In 1925, the building was repurposed as a theater. Today, the university's African-American Theater program hosts events in the building.

Beyond the Playhouse, the bike lane disappears as 3rd Street continues past Brandeis Avenue, forcing cyclists into the right lane of traffic. Speeding vehicles on 3rd Street may pose a hazard to cyclists in this location, so extreme caution should be used when merging into the lane with cars. Just to the left of the road in this location is the southernmost point of the strip of land between 2nd and 3rd Streets that houses Freedom Park. At the tip of the point of land is the former site of a 70-foot memorial to Confederate soldiers killed during the U. S. Civil War that has been an ongoing source of controversy over the years. The monument was constructed in 1895 with funding from the Kentucky Women's Confederate Monument Association and was originally located at the intersection of 3rd and Shipp Streets. It was moved to this location in 1954 when the Eastern Parkway viaduct over the

University of Louisville's campus was constructed. There have been numerous protests at the site ever since. In 2002, the university's board of trustees approved a plan to develop the rest of the strip of land surrounding the Playhouse, creating Freedom Park. The monument, however, remained in place.

In 2016, amidst popular opinion and political pressure, the monument was finally dismantled and relocated to a site in Brandenburg, about 40 miles to the west. Brandenburg was the site of Confederate General John Hunt Morgan's raid into Indiana on July 8, 1863. After its removal, the monument was placed among other monuments and historic sites in downtown Brandenburg.

Speed Art Museum at the University of Louisville

South of Freedom Park, the two lanes of the street curve sharply to the left, and then to the right, The street is very rough in this area, so cyclists should watch road conditions closely in this area. On the left side of the road is the Speed Art Museum. Named for prominent Louisville businessman John Breckinridge Speed, the museum's original building opened in 1927 and was very recently expanded and renovated. To the right of the museum, the University of Louisville's main library can be seen. Just beyond the library is the Brandeis School of Law and the university's southern entrance. From this point, Grawemeyer Hall and the university's iconic Thinker statue can be seen in the distance.

12.2 Left onto Eastern Parkway

Eastern Parkway leads past many classroom buildings on the University of Louisville's Belknap Campus. A bike lane opens up immediately after making the turn and ascends a small hill, but cyclists should pay close attention to the crosswalks and be wary of pedestrians on both sides of the street that may run out in front of traffic without warning. Beyond the classroom buildings, a viaduct carries traffic over the railroad tracks below.

As the viaduct begins to descend back toward the ground, the next turn on the route onto Hahn Street appears suddenly. Cyclists should be alert for inattentive motorists who may cross the bike lane to move into the turn lane without first checking for oncoming cyclists.

12.6 Right onto Hahn Street

Hahn Street curves back to the right and descends back toward the university, ending at Floyd Street.

12.7 Right onto Floyd Street

Floyd Street leads past the eastern edge of the University of Louisville's campus, passing numerous athletic training facilities, the natatorium, a large parking garage, and the university's student center. The right lane, once a parking lane, was recently opened to traffic, so it is acceptable for cyclists to ride in the right lane through this area. There are often many vehicles entering and exiting the parking garage, so cyclists should be cautious and look for vehicles suddenly entering or leaving the roadway. Fortunately, plans appear to be in the works to install a bicycle lane along Floyd Street in this location.

13.2 Right at roundabout onto E Brandeis Avenue

Brandeis Avenue comes to a 4-way intersection with Arthur Street as it ascends a small hill and approaches the underpass at Interstate 65. Beyond the 4-way intersection, there is a guard rail that separates eastbound traffic heading from Arthur Street toward Preston Street. Traffic in this lane merges into the left lane of Brandeis Avenue. As the guard rail ends, Brandeis Avenue branches, becoming Bradley Avenue to the right and continuing as Brandeis Avenue to the left. Cyclists should remain in the right lane and then turn left to continue onto Brandeis Avenue. Oncoming traffic turning left onto Brandeis Avenue from Bradley Avenue must stop, but drivers frequently disregard the stop sign, so caution is advised.

13.4 Left to continue on E Brandeis Avenue

13.5 Left onto KY-61/Preston Street

13.8 Right onto Augustus Avenue and Preston Park

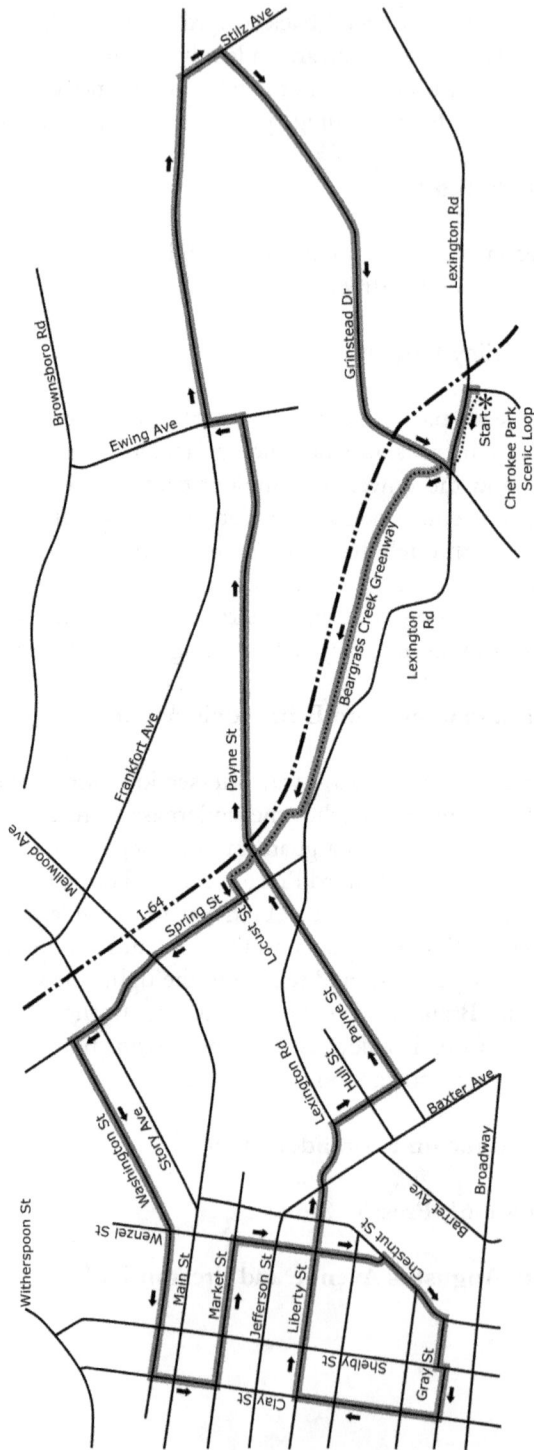

2 IRISH HILL, BUTCHERTOWN, PHOENIX HILL, CLIFTON, AND CRESCENT HILL

Distance: 9.1 miles

Difficulty: Easy. Mostly flat terrain, but moderate to heavy traffic on some roads, particularly during morning and evening commute hours.

Points of Interest: Beargrass Creek Greenway, Irish Hill neighborhood, Butchertown neighborhood, Thomas Edison House, St. Martin of Tours Church, Phoenix Hill neighborhood, NuLu (East Market) district, Crescent Hill neighborhood

This tour explores many of the older established neighborhoods of the city's urban core that lie east of downtown and Interstate 65. These neighborhoods were once referred to as Louisville's east end, or uptown, long before the suburban development of eastern Jefferson County began in the late 1940s. As Louisville's downtown district has experienced a rebirth since the beginning of the 21st century, so have many of its historic uptown neighborhoods.

Like many of the neighborhoods surrounding Louisville's downtown core, the Irish Hill neighborhood was first established around the time of the U.S. Civil War on higher ground lying between the middle and south forks of Beargrass Creek. The development was originally referred to as Billy Goat Hill due to the large number of goats that a nearby farmer allowed to graze on the hillside, but it soon came to be known as Irish Hill due to the influx of Irish Catholic immigrants to the area.

Life in 19th century Irish Hill centered around the church, and as the area's population grew, several large churches were established to serve the population. In 1873, St. Brigid Catholic Church was established in the neighborhood. In 1890, St. Aloysius Church was established in the same building when St. Brigid moved to a new location nearby.

Although Irish Hill is a small neighborhood, it is a significant part of Louisville's history and boasts many important historical structures and sites, including Eastern Cemetery; the site of the former Beargrass Pork Slaughterhouse; the Kentucky Distillery and Warehouse, once the largest whiskey warehouse in the world; and the City Workhouse, which operated between 1878 and 1954 at the corner of Lexington Road and Payne Street. Although the City Workhouse was demolished in 1966, many older Louisvillians still remember the prisoners who were brought in every morning on a paddy wagon to break up enormous limestone blocks at the site. Today, Breslin Park, one of the city's many pocket green spaces, sits at the site where commoners convicted of relatively minor offenses, such as public drunkenness, loitering, or vagrancy, did hard labor for their crimes.

Butchertown was originally developed in the 1820s along the Lexington and Louisville turnpike, along what is now Story Avenue. Beargrass Creek was later re-routed to the east, passing through Butchertown. By the 1830s, many stockyards and butchers moved their businesses into the area because of the ease of using the creek for the disposal of animal remains, a practice that was prohibited downtown by the city's health codes. The stockyards, butchers, and associated businesses in the area prospered, but with them came many bars. Soon, the neighborhood developed a reputation for drunkenness and violence.

Butchertown remained a mixed residential and industrial area through most of the rest of the 19th century. By 1900, however, Butchertown experienced a slow, steady decline, as several meat packing plants moved into the area and seriously changed the neighborhood's culture. In 1931, the neighborhood was zoned industrial. In 1937, the Ohio River flood destroyed many of the area's homes and initiated a mass depopulation of the area that continued through the rest of the 20th century. The development of new suburbs in eastern Jefferson compounded Butchertown's depopulation. The construction of Interstates 64, 65, and 71 put further pressure on Butchertown's few

Butchertown neighborhood

remaining residents, many of whom lost their homes to eminent domain. The ensuing traffic, with the noise pollution that it brought coupled with the stench from the stockyards and slaughterhouses, continued to drive residents away.

But as many neighborhoods in Louisville have experienced a rebirth in the 21st century, so has Butchertown. With the construction of Waterfront Park, the Big Four pedestrian bridge, and Louisville Extreme Park, Butchertown suddenly became a fashionable area to live and attracted many young professionals and other urbanites.

The Phoenix Hill neighborhood of Louisville encompasses the area roughly bounded by Market Street, Preston Street, Broadway, and Baxter Avenue. Wedged between downtown and the Highlands, Phoenix Hill is home to the large cluster of hospitals and medical research buildings that can be seen from Interstate 65, several historic churches, and the famed Phoenix Hill Tavern, a famous Louisville nightclub and landmark that closed its doors for good in 2015.

The area is part of a large tract of land that was granted to Colonel William Preston in 1774 and was annexed by the city of Louisville in 1827. As Louisville's population grew in the 19th century, Phoenix Hill grew as well. By the 1850s, the neighborhood was very densely populated with newly arrived German immigrants. The overcrowding, compounded with the rise of the anti-immigration Know-Nothing Party in the 1850s, served as kindling that fed the fire of hatred that exploded in 1855 with the Bloody Monday riots. It is thought that the riots actually began in Phoenix Hill near the St. Martin of Tours church. In the aftermath of the riots, more than 10,000 residents left for other cities throughout the Midwest.

After the violence of the U.S. Civil War, peace ensured and Phoenix Hill began to grow again. A park was added, along with the Phoenix Hill Brewery. Life in Phoenix Hill soon revolved around recreational pursuits, and the brewery added a skating rink, bowling alley, and a dance floor. Patrons of the brewery were treated to beautiful views of downtown and entertainment such as bicycle races and stage shows.

The good times didn't last, however. The brewery closed in 1919 with the ratification of the Eighteenth Amendment. The building and recreational areas soon fell into decay, and the large brick building it once occupied was finally dismantled in 1938. By 1939, Phoenix Hill's overcrowding problem was compounded by the construction of the Clarksdale Housing Complex. Clarksdale was the first government-subsidized housing development in the state of Kentucky and was originally developed to assist in the resettlement of veterans and their families during and after World War II. The development consisted of 58 buildings and soon proved to be costly to maintain. By the late 1960s, the development had become a hotbed of drugs, crime, and misery. Longtime residents voted with their feet and joined the many city residents fleeing toward Louisville's bustling eastern suburbs while the few remaining businesses in the neighborhood closed their doors or moved elsewhere.

Phoenix Hill's decline finally reversed itself in the 1970s. In 1975, the neighborhood's remaining businesses formed the Phoenix Hill Association. Two years later, Mayor Harvey Sloane declared the area as a model revitalization area, and federal revitalization funds flowed into the neighborhood to fix up dilapidated properties. In 1988, a major road project led to the construction of the Chestnut Street Corridor, connecting Jefferson Street and Baxter Avenue to Gray and Campbell Streets. This project diverted much of the heavy traffic that once passed through Phoenix Hill to the east, reducing congestion and spurring further revitalization of the neighborhood. Recently announced plans to convert open some of the area's one-way streets to two-way traffic have been widely lauded by the area's businesses, who stand to benefit from the increase in accessibility.

East Market (NuLu) District

The 21st century has brought further progress to Phoenix Hill. In 2005, the Clarksdale Housing Complex was completely demolished, although not without controversy, as part of the city's Hope VI program that was modeled after the redevelopment of government housing projects in Chicago. It was replaced with the Liberty Green development, a mixed-income housing development. Despite the controversy, the demolition and redevelopment of Clarksdale led to a major renaissance in Phoenix Hill and in adjacent downtown. No longer afraid of crime, many people have moved back into the area and refurbished many of the neighborhood's historic shotgun houses. New condominiums and apartments have appeared at the neighborhood's northern edge, and broken and buckling sidewalks in the area have been repaired. The East Market district, lying between Phoenix Hill to the south and Butchertown to the north, has undergone a complete transformation and now boasts trendy bars and nightclubs, restaurants, boutiques, and antique shops. Along with Butchertown, Phoenix Hill has become a desirable neighborhood for many young professionals and other urban dwellers.

The Clifton neighborhood lies at the top of a ridge overlooking the Ohio River, deriving its name from the surrounding landscape. Many also believe that Clifton's name may have been derived from the sheer hillsides that were left from the extensive limestone quarrying that occurred in the area during the middle of the 19th century. The cliff from which Clifton probably derives its name can be seen along the descent on Ewing Avenue heading north from Frankfort Avenue toward U.S. 42/Brownsboro Road.

Like many of the neighborhoods that lie east of downtown, Clifton developed around the Lexington and Louisville turnpike, which encompasses much of present-day Frankfort Avenue. U.S. 42/Brownsboro Road, Interstate 64, and Ewing and Mellwood Avenues form the neighborhood's boundaries. Clifton is well known for its many diverse churches but is best known as the location of the Kentucky School for the Blind, which relocated to a site in the neighborhood in 1853. Clifton was chartered as a town in 1875 but subsequently annexed between 1895 and 1897.

The last part of the tour passes through the Crescent Hill neighborhood just east of Irish Hill and about four miles from the center of downtown. Like many of Louisville's neighborhoods surrounding downtown, it was developed around 1850, and like Butchertown grew along the Louisville and Lexington Turnpike. Frankfort Avenue, a popular dining and shopping destination, lies at the site where the turnpike led through Crescent Hill. Crescent Hill was initially incorporated as a city in 1884, but most of it was annexed by the city of Louisville in 1897 along with the Clifton neighborhood. The neighborhood boasts many of Louisville's important historical sites, including the Peterson-Dumesnil House, the Louisville Water Company's Crescent Hill Reservoir, and the Southern Baptist Theological Seminary.

Many of Crescent Hill's earliest homes served as summer homes for wealthy residents. A large fairground was established in 1853 near where Crescent Avenue lies today. The facility hosted many local, state, and national events for nearly two decades. The land was eventually purchased by the St. Joseph Catholic Orphan Society, which established the St. Joseph Children's Home at the site in 1885.

The tour begins at the edge of Cherokee Park at a small parking lot near the park's northern entrance along Lexington Road. From this location, the Crescent Hill neighborhood lies due north on the opposite side of Interstate 64, and the Irish Hill neighborhood lies due west across Grinstead Drive about 1/4 mile to the west. The first portion of the route follows a short greenway that runs along Beargrass Creek and emerges near the border of the Irish Hill and Butchertown neighborhoods.

Route Directions – Irish Hill, Butchertown, Phoenix Hill, Clifton, and Crescent Hill

0.0 Left onto Ledge Road
0.1 Left onto Lexington Road
0.2 Right onto Beargrass Creek Greenway at intersection
1.3 Continue onto Locust Street
1.4 Right onto Spring Street
1.8 Continue onto Adams Street
1.9 Left onto E Washington Street
2.7 Left onto N Clay Street
2.9 Left onto E Market Street
3.2 Right onto S Wenzel Street
3.6 Right onto E Chestnut Street
3.7 Continue onto Chestnut Street Connector
3.8 Right onto E Gray Street
3.9 Left onto S Shelby Street
3.9 Right onto E Gray Street
4.0 Right onto S Clay Street
4.3 Right onto E Liberty Street
5.0 Right onto Cooper Street
5.1 Left onto Payne Street
6.8 Left onto Ewing Avenue
6.9 Right onto Frankfort Avenue
7.6 Right onto Stilz Avenue
7.8 Right onto Grinstead Drive
8.9 Left onto Lexington Road
9.0 Right onto Ledge Road
9.1 Right into parking lot

Route Description – Irish Hill, Butchertown, Phoenix Hill, Clifton, and Crescent Hill

0.0 Left onto Ledge Road

At the east side of the parking lot, Ledge Road leads into Cherokee Park. It is often labeled incorrectly as Cherokee Park Scenic Loop on your GPS or map. From this location, cyclists should turn left onto Ledge Road and then immediately left onto Lexington Road to head toward the Beargrass Creek Trail. Alternatively, there is a narrow greenway that begins at the west side of the parking lot near an informational sign and leads to the intersection of Lexington Road and Grinstead Drive. From here, the entrance to the Beargrass Creek Trail is located diagonally from the street corner.

0.1 Left onto Lexington Road

There is a short bike lane on westbound Lexington Road that ends at its intersection with Grinstead Drive. This is an extremely busy intersection, so extreme caution is advised. Many cyclists will choose to take the right lane at the traffic light, follow the vehicles through the intersection, and then immediately pull over to the curb at the opposite corner to enter the Beargrass Creek Trail that begins on the street corner on the other side of Grinstead Drive. When choosing this course of action, it is <u>highly</u> advised to take the entire lane instead of riding along the very right edge of the lane in order to prevent right-turning vehicles from colliding with bicycles traveling straight through the intersection. The easiest course of action, however, is for cyclists to pull up to the corner to the right and press the pedestrian crossing button, and then walk their bicycles in the crosswalk to the opposite side to enter the Beargrass Creek Trail.

0.2 Right onto Beargrass Creek Greenway at intersection

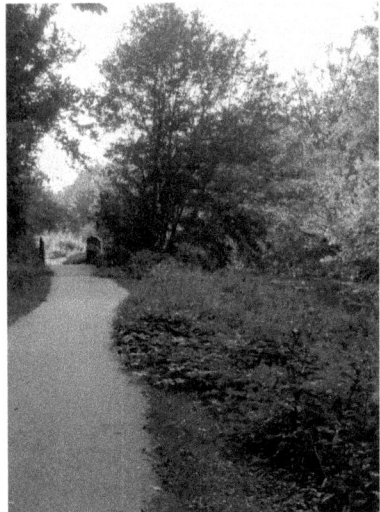

Beargrass Creek Greenway

The greenway descends a small hill and then curves sharply to the left, so it is advisable to be ready with the brakes, especially if the pavement is wet. After this curve, the greenway is mostly straight and flat, but there is always the possibility of encountering wet pavement and/or mud through this location after heavy rains or when the creek floods the greenway.

The greenway runs parallel to the Middle Fork of Beargrass Creek, which flows through Seneca and Cherokee Parks as it heads toward the Ohio River. The Middle Fork merges with the South Fork just south of Main Street between Irish Hill and Butchertown. Interstate 64 lies just on the other side of the creek from the greenway. Beargrass Creek is among the most polluted waterways in the state of Kentucky due to the large population and the urban environment surrounding it. After heavy rains, sewage overflows are common, and contact with the water in the creek should be avoided.

About one mile later, the greenway turns to the northwest and crosses the creek over a bridge that may be slippery after rain events or early in the morning on humid days. The greenway then ascends a small hill, runs adjacent to Interstate 64, and then ends at Locust Street.

1.3 Continue onto Locust Street

Locust Street intersects with Spring Street a few hundred feet to the west of the end of the greenway. Traffic on Spring Street does not stop, so caution should be used when making the next turn on the route onto Spring Street.

1.4 Right onto Spring Street

A shared-use lane begins on Spring Street as it skirts the edge of the Irish Hill neighborhood. The route soon crosses Mellwood Avenue, where there is a bike box that allows bicycles to get ahead of traffic at the intersection and ensures visibility. It is hoped that with time, the city will adopt more of these at high-traffic and problematic intersections to reduce bicycle-car accidents. Past this intersection, the road crosses the South Fork of Beargrass Creek and then becomes Adams Street as the road crosses Story Avenue and enters the Butchertown neighborhood.

1.8 Continue onto Adams Street

The next turn on the route is onto Washington Street, several hundred feet north of Story Avenue.

1.9 Left onto E Washington Street

Washington Street passes through the heart of Butchertown, with its many historic homes, storefronts, and churches. With the urban renewal that has begun throughout Butchertown, many of the historic homes and buildings have been restored and repainted, and a thriving urban population now lives here.

There are several important historical sites along the Washington Street corridor, including the St. Joseph Catholic Church, built in 1866, which lies along the left side of the street between Adams and Webster Streets. The church was home to a mixed German/Irish congregation until 1877, when a separate church for the area's Irish Catholic population opened a little farther to the west.

The homes in Butchertown are a seemingly random mixture of styles, with stately brick Queen Anne or Greek Revival style homes intermixed with wood frame shotgun houses. At its height, Butchertown was a primarily working class neighborhood, but its proximity to downtown, the railroad, and the Ohio River made it equally attractive to a number of more affluent residents. The eclectic mixture of architectural styles and sizes of the homes here reflect the diversity of the neighborhood's residents.

On the right side of Washington Street is the Thomas Edison house, a small cottage that was once home to inventor Thomas Alva Edison. Edison came to Louisville in 1866 to work for Western Union. He left briefly, heading to South America, but was turned back at New Orleans. He returned later that year and took up residence in Butchertown at this small home on Washington Street.

Thomas Edison House on Washington Street

In 1867, Edison spilled sulfuric acid onto his boss's desk, was promptly fired, and left town for good. Edison had the last word, however, when his incandescent light bulb was demonstrated at Louisville's Southern Exposition in 1883. Today, the small house that Edison lived in during his time in Louisville hosts a small museum that showcases many of his inventions.

2.7 Left onto N Clay Street

2.9 Left onto E Market Street

East Market Street is the heart of Louisville's East Market district, known to locals as NuLu. Although it is formally part of the Phoenix Hill neighborhood, NuLu is a good example of much of the urban renewal that has swept across Louisville's urban core. The area is now home to many art galleries, specialty shops, restaurants, and bars, and prides itself on its commitment to sustainability. Area restaurants offer locally sourced and organic foods and a few businesses boast energy-efficient commercial buildings as well.

NuLu District

The area is also home to the NuLu Bock Beer Festival, which was revived in March 2016 for the first time in nearly a century. Bock beer is a rich, dark malt-heavy lager that was once extremely popular with Louisville's large German population. It requires a much lower brewing temperature than other styles and must be fermented for several months instead of

just a few weeks. In Louisville, bock beer was brewed over the winter and released in March during Lent. When the beer was released, the German community would hold a huge festival that featured goat racing ("bock" is German for goat) and, of course, plenty of the hearty bock beer. These festivals date back to 1858 in Louisville and continued until 1919 when the eighteenth amendment went into effect.

3.2 Right onto S Wenzel Street

Following the next turn, the route enters the heart of the Phoenix Hill neighborhood. The densely packed frame homes and shotgun houses that can be seen in various places through this area are typical of the neighborhood. Evidence of ongoing urban renewal is more visible at the southern end of the neighborhood, near the end of the street. At the corner of Wenzel Street and Muhammad Ali Boulevard is Webb's Market, one of Louisville's many small hidden gems and a favorite among locals. The small grocery is also home to a deli and lunch counter that offers good, inexpensive plate lunches featuring southern cuisine. The wonderful smells wafting from the store often make a compelling reason to stop and enjoy a quick lunch.

3.6 Right onto E Chestnut Street

Wenzel Street ends at East Chestnut Street. One block to the southwest, the road continues straight ahead as the Chestnut Street Connector, connecting the road to Broadway, as East Chestnut Street branches off as a one-way street (eastbound) to the west. The Chestnut Street Connector, built in 1988 to reroute traffic away from the center of the Phoenix Hill neighborhood, was a major factor that has helped to fuel the neighborhood's appeal as a desirable place to live.

3.7 Continue onto Chestnut Street Connector

3.8 Right onto E Gray Street

At the corner of Gray and Shelby Streets is St. Martin of Tours Catholic Church, one of Louisville's many historic churches. Built between 1853 and 1854, it is one of the oldest remaining large buildings in the city. In 1861, the church's enormous pipe organ was installed. In the 1890s, the church's large stained-glass windows were imported from Germany and installed. In 1901, the church acquired the remains of Magnus and Bonosa, two early Christian martyrs. The church experienced a large decline in the 1970s, but like much of Louisville experienced a revival in the 1990s under the leadership of Friars Vernon Robertson and Dennis Cousens. The building across Gray Street from the church, with "St. Martinus Pfarrschule 1898" inscribed on the side, is the former St. Martin Catholic School.

St. Martin of Tours Church

3.9 Left onto S Shelby Street

A short distance later, Gray Street continues on the right. Traffic on Shelby Street is one way, heading south.

3.9 Right onto E Gray Street

4.0 Right onto S Clay Street

After crossing Muhammad Ali Boulevard, the street divides to form a traffic circle as it enters Liberty Green. The street here is brick, making it necessary for cars and bicycles alike to slow down and pay close attention to the road. The apartments, condos, and townhomes here were built on the land formerly occupied by the Clarksdale Housing Complex. The design of the new development is similar to the design of new public housing developments in Chicago and is a template for the ongoing redevelopment of Sheppard Square in Smoketown. Beecher Terrace, located just west of downtown in the Russell neighborhood, has also been targeted for similar redevelopment in the near future.

4.3 Right onto E Liberty Street

From here, the route heads eastward, leaving the Phoenix Hill neighborhood and heading back toward Irish Hill. Liberty Street crosses East Chestnut Street at the edge of the neighborhood. As it approaches Baxter Avenue, the three lanes of travel divide, with the rightmost lane restricted to right turns onto Baxter Avenue. Cyclists following the route here should ensure that they are in one of the two left lanes in order to continue straight ahead on Liberty Street.

Across Baxter Avenue, Liberty Street becomes a two-way road and passes under a railroad bridge that divides the two lanes of travel. At this point, cyclists should occupy the rightmost lane to ensure that they are in the correct lane to facilitate the next turn on the route onto Cooper Street, which lies just beyond the triangular traffic island formed where Liberty Street merges onto Lexington Road. Eastbound traffic heading from Liberty Street onto Lexington Road has the right of way, but cyclists should be wary of westbound traffic turning left to continue onto the remaining block of Lexington Road, which becomes Hamilton Avenue as it crosses Baxter Avenue just to the west of this location.

On the left side of the road between Liberty Street and the South Fork of Beargrass Creek is Irish Hill Park, one of Louisville's many pocket green spaces.

Nicholas Finzer House

5.0 Right onto Cooper Street

Just to the left of the route, at 1212 Hull Street, is the Nicholas Finzer house. The large Italianate edifice, dating to 1868, seems out of place among the small bungalows and shotgun houses of Irish Hill. However, it was one of the first homes built in the area.

Today, the home has been divided into apartments.

5.1 Left onto Payne Street

Payne Street leads through the heart of Irish Hill, past densely packed shotgun houses, and then emerges near Eastern Cemetery. Eastern Cemetery was built in 1840 on the city's outskirts and was originally owned by the 4th Street Methodist Church. Keeping with Methodist tradition, the cemetery united people from all walks of life, from rich to poor, and buried people of all races on the same property. A crematorium was opened in 1920. The building still stands near the cemetery's Baxter Avenue entrance but has since been converted into apartments.

Eastern Cemetery made national news in 1989 when a whistleblower alerted the media to the facility's practice of burying multiple people in the same grave, an abuse that apparently began as early as the 1920s and continued well into the 1980s. Multiple maps of the cemetery contain inconsistencies regarding the placement of graves at the site. The Louisville Crematories and Cemetery Corporation, which owned Eastern Cemetery and two other properties at the time, was later dissolved, leaving the cemetery abandoned and vulnerable to vandals. It is also said that the cemetery is haunted due to the company's past abuses. Due to the chronic mismanagement and abandonment of the cemetery, many of the statues and headstones have been damaged. In recent years, a volunteer group known as the Friends of Eastern Cemetery has been maintaining the property.

On the left side of the road is Breckinridge Franklin Elementary School, and just beyond the school is Distillery Commons, the former site of the Old Kentucky Distillery, which was once the largest whiskey-making facility in the state. Today, the facility's former warehouses have been converted into a mixture of commercial and retail spaces.

Distillery Commons

On the right side of the road, just east of Eastern Cemetery, is Breslin Park, a pocket green space that was built on the former site of the City Workhouse. The facilities at the park were recently refurbished or replaced, and it now boasts a children's playground, a walking path, and a fountain that is popular with Irish Hill residents during the summer. Few traces remain of the human misery that

once existed here

At the end of Breslin Park, Payne Street crosses Lexington Avenue and then soon climbs a hill to cross Interstate 64 and enter the Clifton neighborhood. The Clifton neighborhood is named for the cliff overlooking the Ohio River on which the neighborhood sits. Much of Frankfort Avenue, with its many boutiques, restaurants, and other attractions, lies within this neighborhood.

Clifton Center

Clifton's settlement pattern was somewhat different than Irish Hill, Butchertown, and Phoenix Hill in that the neighborhood was not as densely populated. Clifton was settled in multiple waves between 1860 and 1930, so there are many diverse architectural styles in the neighborhood. The homes also differ greatly in size and affluence. The diverse home styles, the many churches of all denominations, and the metropolitan feel of Frankfort Avenue combine to give Clifton a hip, urban vibe.

A little further down Payne Street, on the left side of the road, is the Clifton Center. The beautiful building that houses the center was built in 1929 and originally housed the St. Frances of Rome Catholic Elementary School. The school closed in 1975. The theater was lovingly restored in the late 1980s, and later the non-profit Clifton Center took over operations. Today, the Clifton Center serves as a gathering place for the arts and cultural events that further enrich this thriving neighborhood.

6.8 Left onto Ewing Avenue

The intersection of Ewing Avenue and Frankfort Avenue, one block north of the end of Payne Street, is a busy intersection with a limited line of sight. Unless traffic is unusually light, it is best to wait at the intersection for the traffic light to change before turning right onto Frankfort Avenue.

6.9 Right onto Frankfort Avenue

Frankfort Avenue passes through the heart of the Clifton neighborhood and has a hip big city feel to it. The road is lined with numerous shops, boutiques, restaurants, and other independent businesses. There are usually many pedestrians walking up and down the sidewalks and cars parked along the side of the road, so caution should be observed. On the other hand, the many bistros and coffee shops in the area make a compelling reason to stop for a while and enjoy the afternoon.

7.6 Right onto Stilz Avenue

Just beyond the turn, the Louisville Water Company filtration facility sits off to the right. The water company also owns a large reservoir just north of Frankfort Avenue, a little to the east of this location. The next turn of the route, onto Grinstead Drive, lies directly across the street from the entrance into the water filtration facility, one block south of Frankfort Avenue.

7.8 Right onto Grinstead Drive

For the first block, the road is a shared use bicycle lane. Soon, the parking lane on the right side of the road disappears and becomes a bike lane, so cyclists should use the lane whenever possible. Prior to 2015, most of Grinstead Drive between here and U.S. 125/Bardstown Road was a four-lane road with cars parked on both sides of the road. Many vehicles exceeded the speed limit, and there were frequent accidents due to motorists failing to notice stopped cars attempting to turn left across traffic. Now, the thoroughfare has undergone a so-called road diet, which reduced the number of lanes to three and added bike lanes on both sides. Despite early complaints, the road diet has made the road safer and reduced commute times by moving turning traffic into a center lane away from through traffic.

Grinstead Drive is mostly downhill from here, so it is easy to gain speed through this section of the route. About one-half mile along the road near the bottom of the descent lies the Southern Baptist Theological Seminary. Some of the seminary's classroom and administrative buildings can be seen from here, atop a small hill on the left side of the road, although the campus may be difficult to see due to the tree cover between April and November. The seminary, founded in South Carolina in 1859, relocated to Louisville in 1877. The present campus, situated between Grinstead Drive and Lexington Road, was designed by Fredrick Law Olmstead and opened in 1926. At the time, it was the largest theological seminary in the world. The institution was also the first seminary in the United States to offer doctoral level studies. Today, Southern Baptist Theological Seminary consists of Boyce College, an undergraduate institution dedicated to teaching ministry, and two graduate schools that offer master's and doctoral degrees in numerous fields.

A little farther down Grinstead Drive is a stately building atop a large hill. Built between 1930 and 1932, the building houses Barret Traditional Middle School. Formerly Barret Junior High School, the institution was renovated in the 1970s and 1980s to repair and update the building and to add air conditioning. During the great flood of 1937, Barret served as a relief center for Louisville residents fleeing the rising waters of the Ohio River.

Barrett Traditional Middle School

Past Barret, the road begins to rise in elevation slightly as it widens to four lanes and passes underneath Interstate 64. The bike lane at this point merges with the right lane and becomes a shared use lane. Cyclists should be wary of traffic exiting and entering the freeway in this area. Past Interstate 64, cyclists should move into the left lane and then into the left turn lane when approaching the intersection with Lexington Road. Less experienced cyclists, or those extremely wary of vehicular traffic, can walk their bicycles across the intersection at the pedestrian crosswalk. Vehicles commonly run red lights at this intersection, so cyclists are advised to be very cautious when turning.

8.9 Left onto Lexington Road

A very narrow bike lane leads the way from the intersection to the entrance into Cherokee Park.

9.0 Right onto Ledge Road

9.1 Right into parking lot

Butchertown Neighborhood

3 WESTERN LOUISVILLE

Distance: 17.0 miles

Difficulty: Easy. Mostly flat terrain with light to moderate traffic in most areas.

Points of Interest: Waterfront Park, Shippingport Island, Louisville and Portland Canal, McAlpin Locks and Dam, Portland neighborhood, Shawnee neighborhood, Russell neighborhood, Parkland neighborhood, Muhammad Ali's boyhood home, California neighborhood, Brown-Forman distillery

Louisville's west end, generally regarded as the area west of 10th Street and north of KY-2054/Algonquin Parkway, encompasses a large number of neighborhoods that have garnered a reputation for crime and blight since the 1960s. Although many area residents avoid the area because of this reputation, their fears are misplaced. Louisville's western neighborhoods are rich in history and have contributed a great deal to the city's culture over the past two centuries.

Although the west end certainly faces a number of challenges, such as poverty, crime, and blight, signs of urban renewal have appeared and instilled hope into the residents of these neighborhoods. Most notably, the renewal of the Portland neighborhood has led to a large decrease in crime in the area and the opening of several businesses. Likewise, there are plans to encourage economic redevelopment of the Russell neighborhood to the south of Portland. Although there is much consternation among media outlets and certain activists regarding the increase in shootings and murders in 2016 and 2017, it is important to remember that even with these increases, these crime rates are far below the crime rates experienced here and in other sectors of the city during the 1960s and 1970s. There are many important historic and cultural points of interest in the area, and irrational fears should never prevent anyone from exploring these neighborhoods.

A large part of what is considered as Louisville's west end today is composed of smaller cities and towns that developed around the Falls of the Ohio during the late 18th and early 19th centuries and were later annexed into the city. The Falls of the Ohio refers to a large series of shallow rapids caused by a 26-foot drop in elevation over a two mile stretch of the Ohio River. The series of rapids are created by an exposed Devonian fossil bed that did not erode as rapidly as the surrounding area. Historically, the Falls were the only major obstacle to river traffic along the river's entire 981-mile course, making it necessary to unload cargo and move it over land before reloading it on the other side of the falls.

27th Street on Shippingport Island

One of the first cities to develop in the area was Shippingport, Kentucky, which was incorporated in 1785 on a small peninsula jutting into the Ohio River. The town was originally named Campbell Town for John Campbell, a Revolutionary War soldier who obtained the land for his service in the war. The land was sold in 1802, and renamed Shippingport. At the time, a warehouse and flour mill were located at the site. Shippingport's population soon swelled, numbering more than 500 residents by 1820. During this era, Shippingport, Portland, and Louisville along the Kentucky side of the river competed with the towns of New Albany, Clarksville, and Jeffersonville on the Indiana side of the river for the business of merchants shipping goods down the Ohio River. Because of the barrier that the falls posed to the shipping industry, many businesses and warehouses began appearing up and down the Ohio River on both the Kentucky and Indiana sides to supply materials and labor needed for moving cargo around the falls.

Portland, Kentucky was founded in 1811 on land owned by General William Lytle of Cincinnati. Situated just below the falls, the town was well situated to load goods transported over land to ships on the lower side of the falls. A wharf was built at the site of the new town, and business boomed. Portland's population swelled with new arrivals, and by 1817, the town was expanded to accommodate its rapid growth. Soon, Portland rivaled Louisville as the area's major settlement.

The many merchants shipping goods down the Ohio River between

Pennsylvania and New Orleans, however, set their eyes on digging a canal to bypass the falls to eliminate the expense of shipping goods over land. Many efforts to fund construction of a canal came and went between the late 1700s and early 1800s, but a private company was finally chartered in 1825 to build the canal. The Kentucky side of the river was chosen as the site for the canal, and construction began in 1826. The route that was chosen cut through the low-lying land at the southern end of Shippingport, isolating it as an island. As construction continued, many of the warehouses in Portland and Shippingport closed, increasing the influence of Louisville over them and other area towns. By 1828, the town of Louisville incorporated as a city, and Shippingport was included within the city's boundaries. Eventually, a hydroelectric plant was built on the island, and its population waned. In 1958, the federal government bought the rights to the rest of the land, and Shippingport's last remaining families finally left the town.

The city of Portland remained after the canal opened, but it lost much of its influence and prosperity to the city of Louisville. Portland incorporated as a city in 1834, but it was annexed by Louisville in 1837 when a new rail line running from Lexington to Portland's wharf was built. After the new rail line went bankrupt, Portland again incorporated in 1842; however, its independence would be short-lived. Portland was again annexed by the city of Louisville in 1852. After annexation, Portland persisted as a working class neighborhood of Louisville until the floods of 1937 and 1945 destroyed the wharf and many of the area's original homes, driving most of the working class families out of the area. By 1950, the mass exodus created blight and attracted crime, and the neighborhood underwent a serious decline. Many of Portland's displaced residents moved to Louisville's southern neighborhoods, transforming the Wilder Park, Oakdale, and Beechmont neighborhoods with a the rapid influx of new residents.

In 2006, Portland began a renaissance with its designation as a Preserve America community. Portland's warehouse district, only a few blocks from Louisville's museum row, has begun to develop into a museum and arts district. Developers working on Portland Wharf Park have envisioned a large park to rival Louisville's Waterfront Park, although flooding in 2012 destroyed portions of the park and forced city officials to detour the Louisville Loop through Portland away from the park. Despite this setback, Portland's revival has continued. A local brewery opened a new production facility in Portland's warehouse district in 2015, and several other local companies have announced their intentions to follow suit. Just as her residents have worked hard, persevered, and adapted to change over the past two centuries, Portland appears poised to enjoy a much-deserved revival.

This tour also explores portions of Louisville's other western neighborhoods, including Russell, Shawnee, Parkland, and California. The Russell neighborhood is partially wedged between Portland and Louisville's downtown. Characterized by its many remaining examples of 19th-century architecture, the Russell neighborhood is listed in the *National Register of Historic Places*. It stretches from 9th to 31st Streets between Market Street and Broadway, and the area is easy to explore by bicycle.

Russell was named in honor of African-American educator Harvey

Russell neighborhood

Clarence Russell, Sr. (1883-1949), in 1926. Originally from Bloomfield, Kentucky, Russell had a very prominent career, serving as Dean of Kentucky State College in Frankfort (now Kentucky State University), and later as president of West Kentucky Industrial College (now West Kentucky Community and Technical College). He was the founder of the state's first Parent-Teacher

Association and later served as president of the Kentucky Education Association and as a specialist in the United States Office of Education.

The area was first settled in the 1830s by free African Americans who bought parcels of land west of 9th Street. The area grew quickly in the 1870s when a newly-constructed streetcar line enabled people to commute from the neighborhood into Louisville's downtown. The new arrivals built many beautiful Victorian homes, churches, and schools. Many wealthy black professionals moved here during this period, and the arts and culture flourished. In contrast to many other neighborhoods, most of the new arrivals also owned their homes, and there was a strong sense of community among residents. For many decades, the Russell neighborhood prospered and served as the heart of African-American culture in Louisville, earning it the nickname "Harlem of the South."

The good times, however, did not last. Russell began a steady decline in the late 1940s when residents began moving to newly-integrated neighborhoods on Louisville's south and east sides. Urban decay and blight soon ensued. By the 1960s, many of the neighborhood's magnificent homes and shops were left vacant and dilapidated. Many of them were razed to make way for warehouses, industrial sites, and public housing complexes. The most prominent of these housing complexes, Beecher Terrace, became notorious as a hotbed for crime. But Russell's residents, long weary of government neglect and broken promises, now have a reason for cautious optimism with the announcement of a large government grant to raze Beecher Terrace and replace it with a mixed-income housing development.

Little is known of the founding of Louisville's California neighborhood, which lies due south of Russell. Its original name was thought to be Henderson, but it soon became known as California because it was considered Louisville's far-west. The area was first settled in the 1850s by German immigrants. After the conclusion of the U.S. Civil War, the German settlers were joined by a large number of freed African-Americans. By the end of the 19th century, California was a thriving, integrated working class neighborhood.

Like nearby Russell, California experienced a mass exodus beginning in the 1950s as many residents began leaving for the new suburbs in eastern Jefferson County. By 1985, the neighborhood had lost nearly half its population, and it soon experienced extreme urban decay. Property values dropped sharply, and many properties sat abandoned, attracting drugs, crime, and despair.

California has since become the target of many urban renewal efforts. In 1968, Brown-Forman moved its corporate headquarters to the California neighborhood on Dixie Highway between Garland Avenue and Howard Street. Since 1989, the company has provided funds to renovate homes and establish housing projects in the California neighborhood. Although the various urban

California Neighborhood

renewal efforts have helped to alleviate blight in the neighborhood, progress has been slow.

This tour begins at the base of the Big Four Bridge in Waterfront Park, where parking is available. From here, the route follows the Louisville Loop past downtown, before turning onto N 26th Street toward Shippingport Island and the McAlpin Locks and Dam. From here, the route returns to the Louisville Loop in the Portland neighborhood and then explores several sites of interest within the Russell and California neighborhoods before returning to the Louisville Loop for the return trip.

Michael W. Thompson

Route Directions – Western Louisville

0.0 Right onto E River Road
0.4 Right onto E Witherspoon Street
0.7 Right onto Bingham Way
0.8 Left onto Louisville Loop
3.4 Right onto N 26th Street/Marine Street
3.5 Left to continue on N 26th Street
3.8 Continue onto N 27th Street
4.1 Turn around on N 27th Street
4.4 Continue onto N 26th Street
4.6 Right onto N 26th Street/Marine Street
4.7 Right onto Lannan Park Access Road
4.8 Right onto Lannan Park Road
4.9 Left onto N 27th Street
4.9 Right onto Northwestern Parkway
5.0 Left onto N 27th Street
5.1 Right onto Portland Avenue
5.7 Left onto Northwestern Parkway
7.2 Continue onto Southwestern Parkway
7.3 Left onto W Market Street
8.9 Right onto S 28th Street
10.4 Right onto Virginia Avenue
11.0 Right onto Louis Coleman Jr. Drive
11.2 Right onto Grand Avenue
11.3 Left onto S 32nd Street
11.4 Right onto Greenwood Avenue
11.9 Right onto S 26th Street
12.0 Left onto Greenwood Avenue
12.6 Left onto U.S. 60/Dixie Highway
12.9 Right onto W Breckinridge Street
13.2 Left onto S 15th Street
14.6 Right onto N 16th Street
14.7 Continue through floodwall pedestrian tunnel
14.8 Right onto Louisville Loop
16.1 Right onto Bingham Way
16.1 Left to continue on Bingham Way
16.2 Left onto Bingham Way
16.3 Left onto E Witherspoon Street
16.6 Left onto E River Road
17.0 Left into Waterfront Park parking lot

Route Description – Western Louisville

0.0 Right onto E River Road

The Louisville Loop begins at the base of the Big Four Bridge and runs along the sidewalk on E River Road and E Witherspoon Street. This section of the Louisville Loop is extremely popular among walkers and runners. At most times of the day, it is far safer and easier for cyclists to ride directly on the adjacent roads to avoid weaving in and out of the pedestrian traffic on the Louisville Loop. There are often cars parked along the side of the road, so cyclists should be careful to stay far enough into the lane of traffic to avoid car doors opening suddenly.

0.4 Right onto E Witherspoon Street

The intersection of E River Road and E Witherspoon Street is often very busy. Cars often run through red lights here and are not always looking for bicycles, so caution is advised in this area. Traffic here increases greatly when there are events occurring in Waterfront Park or at the stadium nearby.

0.7 Right onto Bingham Way

Bingham Way is a short thoroughfare that leads from E Witherspoon Street to W River Road. The Louisville Loop follows the sidewalk along Bingham Way, and there is a large curb that prevents bicycles from easily hopping on and off of the Louisville Loop here.

As Bingham Way ends it curves sharply to the west, passes under Interstate 64, and becomes W River Road. A small cul-de-sac branches off as the road curves, and it also serves a drop-off point for people patronizing the many businesses and restaurants nearby. There is a small guard shack at the entrance to the cul-de-sac that serves as a valet station. At this point, cyclists should turn right into the cul-de-sac at the end of Bingham Way and pull up directly onto the sidewalk at the end of it. The Louisville Loop intersects with this sidewalk as it continues on along the riverfront toward the west end, and there are loop trail and mileage markers along the sidewalk here that mark the route. Although it is generally illegal for cyclists to operate on the sidewalk in the city, it is permitted here because the Louisville Loop follows this sidewalk through the riverfront area.

0.8 Left onto Louisville Loop

The Louisville Loop continues past the restaurants and through a few parking lots as it continues under Interstate 64. The loop soon emerges into the light again near the site where the Belle of Louisville is docked on the Ohio River. Cyclists riding the Louisville Loop should look closely for signs and markings on the pavement that mark the bike route because they are difficult to see amidst the hustle and bustle through this area. Slowing down is also recommended due to the heavy pedestrian traffic in the area.

West of the busy wharf area, the trail forks. The right-hand fork descends a small knoll and heads down toward the river bank, where there is often heavy pedestrian traffic and rough pavement. The left-hand fork heads away from the river, heading through a barren-looking field. The pavement here is smoother and there is less pedestrian traffic to contend with, so it is the preferred route. The two forks converge approximately 0.3 miles to the west.

At the 3.0-mile mark, the trail ascends the levee as the trail crosses the railroad tracks and makes several switchback turns as it enters Lannan Park. Just past Lannan Park, the trail crosses N 26th Street. At this point, the route turns right onto N 26th Street as it heads toward Shippingport Island.

3.4 Right onto N 26th Street/Marine Street

N 26th Street curves sharply to the left, and Marine Street branches off to the right. The route continues to the left on N 26th Street, heading toward the bridge over the canal.

McAlpin Locks and Dam

3.5 Left to continue on N 26th Street

After Marine Street branches to the right, N 26th Street continues straight ahead, then curves sharply to the right and ascends a bridge over the McAlpine Locks and Dam that is situated at the end of the Louisville and Portland Canal. The canal first opened in 1830 and greatly eased shipping delays and expenses on the Ohio River by bypassing the Falls of the Ohio. Two locks were added to the end of the canal in 1872. In the 1920s, the locks were expanded and a dam was added at the end of the canal for generating hydroelectric power. In 1962, the canal was widened to accommodate larger barges. After the canal was widened, the facility was renamed as the McAlpin Locks and Dam after William McAlpin, who served as the District Engineer for the Army Corps of Engineers. The bridge provides excellent views of the canal and locks.

3.8 Continue onto N 27th Street

As the road crosses the canal, it becomes N 27th Street.

4.1 Turn around on N 27th Street

The road ends at a fenced off area shortly past the descent from the bridge. The McAlpin Dam is situated further down N 27th Street beyond the fences, and public access is not permitted. There are no homes in the area now; the last homeowners in Shippingport left in 1958, and ownership of the land reverted to the government. The warehouses and facilities that can be seen in the area are used for operations of the canal, locks, and dam.

To the left, a small access road leads to a parking lot for the Angler Foot Path, a trail that leads down to the river. The parking lot is a convenient place to turn around, to stop for a break, or to hike down to the river bank.

4.4 Continue onto N 26th Street

4.6 Right onto N 26th Street/Marine Street

At the end of the bridge, cyclists should bear right at the fork to remain on N 26th Street. The road again crosses the railroad tracks, heading back toward the Louisville Loop. The route, however, continues along N 26th Street past the trail, through the floodwall, and into Lannan Park as it enters the Portland neighborhood.

4.7 Right onto Lannan Park Access Road

Beyond the floodwall, the road seems to fork three ways. The access road to Lannan Park is the rightmost road that curves sharply to the right as it heads toward the park's exit. This road ends shortly at Lannan Park Road.

4.8 Right onto Lannan Park Road

Lannan Park Road travels out of Lannan Park, passes underneath Interstate 64, and then ends at N 27th Street.

4.9 Left onto N 27th Street

4.9 Right onto Northwestern Parkway

5.0 Left onto N 27th Street

5.1 Right onto Portland Avenue

Portland Avenue was one of the original roads in the area, connecting the towns of Louisville, Portland, and Shippingport. The road was constructed in 1818 and originally named the Louisville and Portland Turnpike. Today, Portland Avenue is a one-way street that carries westbound traffic toward Northwestern Parkway. Most of the street is lined with working class single-family homes, but Portland Avenue between N 25th and 27th Streets still contains a few historic storefronts that recall a more prosperous time. Shaheen's Department Store, located on Portland Avenue near N 26th Street, has operated here continuously since 1922, selling work clothing and children's school clothing.

Shaheen's on Portland Avenue

Beyond N 30th Street, Portland Avenue passes underneath a low railroad trestle. The supports of the trestle divide each lane into two sections, and it will be necessary to move to the left or right within the lane of travel. In general, it is safer for cyclists to move to the right, although debris in the roadway may preclude this.

Portland Avenue ends at a somewhat confusing intersection with Northwestern Parkway and N 33rd Street. Although it appears that Portland Avenue simply feeds into Northwestern Parkway heading west, traffic on Portland Avenue must wait for the traffic light here before veering leftward onto Northwestern Parkway. Vehicles sometimes fail to yield at this intersection, so caution should be observed.

5.7 Left onto Northwestern Parkway

Northwestern Parkway is lined with many stately Victorian homes and tall, majestic oak trees that provide much-needed shade during the summertime. The road is wide, with four lanes of travel and parking lanes on both sides of the road. It is generally safest for cyclists to remain in the rightmost lane of travel, but Northwestern Parkway doesn't carry a large amount of traffic. There are few traffic lights to contend with, so it is possible for cyclists to pick up speed through this area without much difficulty. The well-manicured homes here are reminiscent of Eastern and Southern Parkways. Many of the city's residents are unaware of the beauty and rich history of this hidden pocket of the city.

The parkway passes underneath Interstate 264/Watterson Expressway and then enters the Shawnee neighborhood just beyond its intersection with Bank Street. The Shawnee neighborhood was developed after the completion of Shawnee Park in 1895. As more homes were built in the area, the neighborhood was annexed by the city of Louisville and streetcar lines were extended

Northwestern Parkway

into the area. Many wealthy families bought land and built homes in the neighborhood, with the larger, more stately homes located adjacent to the park and to Shawnee Golf Course.

Between the early 1970s and the mid-2000s, the Shawnee neighborhood experienced a decline in prosperity as many of its wealthier residents left for newly-developed neighborhoods in Louisville's east end. Soon, many people viewed the neighborhood as being unsafe, and blight and poverty followed. But Shawnee's residents have endured. Spurred by a rash of murders in the area in 2005, residents took action to reduce crime and fight poverty in the area. In 2007, many area residents lobbied local officials to deny liquor licenses to stores along Market Street, citing a rise in crime surrounding stores that sold liquor. Later that year, four precincts voted to ban alcohol sales after a rather contentious campaign during the election season. Since 2007, crime in the Shawnee neighborhood has declined significantly. Whether it is a direct result of the 2007 ballot measures, an indirect result of the effort, or a totally unrelated phenomenon, Shawnee's future is looking much brighter. Shawnee residents are proud of their neighborhood and are actively engaged in efforts to improve the quality of life in west Louisville.

7.2 Continue onto Southwestern Parkway

A little beyond the 7-mile mark, Northwestern Parkway becomes Southwestern Parkway.

7.3 Left onto W Market Street

West Market Street begins as a shared use lane and passes through a residential area consisting mostly of small single-family homes. To the right, W Market Street ends at the Louisville Riverwalk, which continues along the Ohio River and leads into Shawnee Park.

Fontaine Ferry Park, an amusement park that operated from 1905 until 1969, once stood near this location along the river. During the era of segregation in the early 20th century, the park was mostly off-limits to African-American patrons except for a few days per year. After the neighborhood was integrated in the 1960s, Fontaine Ferry Park was opened to all patrons, but to many in the African-American community the park still represented the legacy of the Jim Crow era. In the spring of 1969, the park was severely damaged during a period of racial unrest in Louisville's west end, resulting in its closure. The park reopened briefly during the early 1970s under new ownership but quickly closed in 1975 due to poor attendance. The facility was eventually purchased in 1981 by the city of Louisville, which sold the few remaining rides to other amusement parks.

Also along W Market Street is the Academy @ Shawnee, a magnet high school in west Louisville that is geared toward preparing students for careers in technology.

East of S 33rd Street, Market Street passes under Interstate 264 as it enters the Russell neighborhood. At certain times of the day it may be sufficiently dark underneath the overpass that cyclists may need to turn on a front and/or rear light to ensure that they can be clearly seen by motorists.

8.9 Right onto S 28th Street

South of Market Street, 28th Street passes through the heart of the Russell neighborhood. Although most of the neighborhood's more stately and interesting homes are located to the east of this location, some of Russell's former grandeur can be seen in a few locations. At the intersection of 28th and Chestnut Streets, for example, some of the neighborhood's original homes and shops can be seen to the east along Chestnut Street. Many of Russell's original homes, however, have fallen into disrepair or have been replaced by smaller single-family homes.

On the right side of 28th Street between Magazine Street and Elliott Avenue is Elliott Park, one of Louisville's many small pocket green spaces. The area here between Magazine Streets and Broadway has a very rich history, although there are few traces of it that remain. About one block to the west on Magazine Street was the site of the kidnapping and murder of Alberta Jones, an important local civil rights pioneer. Jones graduated from Central High School and attended the University of Louisville on scholarship.

A prosecutor by trade, Jones attended law school at Howard University and graduated fourth in her class. In 1959, she became the first African-American woman to pass the Kentucky Bar. Jones served as the first attorney for Muhammad Ali (then known as Cassius Clay) in the 1960s. Most notably, Jones created the Independent Voters League and was an influential figure in the civil rights movement in Louisville during the turbulent 1960s.

On August 5, 1965, Jones was beaten and her body thrown into the Ohio River. Officially, her murder has not been solved, and the case remains open. Recently, the FBI matched a fingerprint found in Jones' car to a man who was 17 years old at the time of the murder. However, the Commonwealth's Attorney declined to prosecute the case, citing the loss of evidence and the deaths of key witnesses. A call to reopen the case was made in 2016, refuting many of the Commonwealth's Attorney's assertions and citing both the availability of the lead detective on the case and the availability of the last witness to have seen Jones alive, who lived near her last known location in the 2900 block of Magazine Street.

Elliott Park

The area between Elliott Avenue and Broadway that lies south of Elliott Park was once the home of Eclipse Park, the home of Louisville's major league team from 1882 and 1893. Louisville has a long and proud baseball tradition, hosting many major and minor league teams for well over 100 years. From 1882 to 1884, the city's major league team was known as the Louisville Eclipse. In 1885, the team was renamed as the Louisville Colonels. The Colonels played at Eclipse Park at this site until it was destroyed by fire in 1893. Eclipse Park was rebuilt at a site across Broadway, and the team continued to play at the new Eclipse Park until it too was destroyed by fire in 1899. In 1900, the team's owner purchased a controlling interest in the Pittsburgh Pirates and took 14 of Louisville's players with him, including legendary shortstop Honus Wagner and outfielder Fred Clarke, both of whom are members of baseball's Hall of Fame.

The Louisville Eclipse was founded in the 1870s. The Eclipse (later known as the Louisville Colonels) joined the newly formed American Association (AA) in 1882 and remained a member of the league until it folded in 1891. The AA often challenged the National League for dominance, even participating in an early World Series during part of the league's existence. During the team's years with the AA, Louisville made a complete turnaround from a league worst last-place finish at 27-111 in 1889 to a pennant and an 88-44 record in 1890 under new ownership. The Colonels played in the 1890 World Series against the Brooklyn Bridegrooms (later known as the Brooklyn Dodgers), which ended in a 3-3-1 tie as the weather worsened during late October. Plans were made to hold a final game in the spring of 1891 to resolve the series, but that game never happened due to a dispute between the two leagues.

When the AA folded in 1891, the Colonels joined the National League and continued playing through the 1899 season. In 1900, the team's owner purchased a controlling interest in the Pittsburgh Pirates and took 14 of Louisville's players with him, including legendary shortstop Honus Wagner and outfielder Fred Clarke, both of whom are members of baseball's Hall of Fame. Although several minor league teams played under the Colonels name during the 20th century, 1899 marks the end of Louisville's status as a major league baseball host city.

As 28th Street passes Broadway, it enters the Parkland neighborhood. Farther south, the intersection of 28th Street and Greenwood Avenue marks the site of Louisville's 1968 riots. The local NAACP had located its Louisville headquarters to this location, and on the night of May 27, 1968 a large crowd of several hundred people gathered here to protest the assassination of Martin Luther King, Jr. in Memphis and to the impending reinstatement of a white police officer who had badly beaten a black man. In response, Mayor Kenneth Schmied issued a curfew and called for nearly 700 National Guard troops to quell the riots and restore peace. By May 29th, the riots had subsided, but not before two protesters were dead and nearly 500 had been arrested. The riots caused a panic among many Parkland and Russell residents, who subsequently fled the area, closed businesses, and left their homes abandoned and in disrepair. It was the 1968 riots that gave many residents of Louisville the perception that the city's west end neighborhoods were unsafe, a sentiment that has unfortunately persisted until the present day.

10.4 Right onto Virginia Avenue

11.0 Right onto Louis Coleman Jr. Drive

S 34th Street was renamed for Rev. Louis Coleman, Jr. (1945-2008), a prominent community activist and civil rights pioneer. A graduate of Louisville Central High School, Kentucky State University, and Presbyterian Theological Seminary, Coleman headed the Justice Resource Center. Among his many accomplishments, Coleman is credited with heading an effort to increase the recruitment and retention of African-American coaches in Kentucky.

11.2 Right onto Grand Avenue

A quick right turn onto Grand Avenue leads to the boyhood home of Louisville's most famous native son, Muhammad Ali, which is tucked away on a quiet side street here in Louisville's west end. The modest two bedroom house at 3302 Grand Avenue was home to the Clay family from 1947 until 1961. A historical marker sits in front of the home that once housed the famous boxer's family. The home sat empty for most of the 1990s and 2000s, but was lovingly restored in 2016 and opened as a museum to the boxing legend.

Muhammad Ali's boyhood home

Born Cassius Marcellus Clay, Jr. in 1942, Ali is one of boxing's most recognized and respected competitors and was named as the "Sportsman of the Century" by *Sports Illustrated*. Ali began training as a boxer in 1953 when he met police officer and boxing trainer Joe Martin, who encouraged Ali to learn to defend himself and confront the thief who had stolen his beloved red and white Schwinn bicycle.

Ali soon won three Kentucky Golden Gloves titles and later went on to win a gold medal at the 1960 Summer Olympics in Rome. After turning professional, Ali went on to win the world heavyweight world title in 1964 by defeating heavily favored Sonny Liston. Later that year, Ali, joined the Nation of Islam and changed his name.

In 1967, Ali applied as a conscientious objector to avoid conscription into the military during the Vietnam. His application was denied, and the boxing great was arrested, convicted as a draft evader, and subsequently stripped of his heavyweight title. Ali appealed immediately and remained free on bond, but from 1967 to 1970 he was unable to obtain a boxing license and unable to fight.

In 1970, a victory in federal court allowed Ali to have his boxing license reinstated, and Ali wasted no time in mounting a comeback. He soon became a contender to face heavyweight champion Joe Frazier, and the two fought in March 1971 in what became billed as the "Fight of the Century." Despite a valiant fight that went back and forth all night, Frazier won the fight by unanimous decision.

Following his first official loss, Ali won six fights over the next year, but lost to Ken Norton in 1973, suffering a broken jaw in the process. He initially considered retirement from boxing after the defeat, but then won rematches with Norton and Frazier in 1974. Since Joe Frazier had recently lost his title to George Foreman, this set up a fight between Ali and Foreman in Kinshasha, Zaire later that year in what was billed as the "Rumble in the Jungle." Ali won the fight by knockout in the eighth round in a match that attracted over 60,000 spectators and is considered to be one of the greatest sports events of the 20th century.

Ali lost the heavyweight boxing title in 1978 to Leon Spinks in a split decision, but he regained it later that year in an epic rematch that made him the first heavyweight boxer to win the world title three separate times. Muhammad Ali came in and out of retirement several times between 1979 and 1981, but retired for good in late 1981 to focus on his charitable and religious work. In 1984, Ali was diagnosed with Parkinson's, widely blamed on the many hits he endured during his prestigious boxing career

During his later years, Ali's public appearances become less and less frequent due to his deteriorating health. When Ali died in 2016, it is said that the entire city came out to pay their respects as the funeral procession made its way through the city, ending at Cave Hill Cemetery on Baxter Avenue, where he was interred in a private ceremony. The modest single-family home here lies testimony to the humble upbringing of Louisville's native son and one of professional sports' greatest champions.

11.3 Left onto S 32nd Street

11.4 Right onto Greenwood Avenue

11.9 Right onto S 26th Street

12.0 Left onto Greenwood Avenue

East of 26th Street, Greenwood Avenue enters the California neighborhood. Victory Park, located along Greenwood Avenue between 22nd and 23rd Streets, was associated with drugs, crime, and gang activity for many years. Beginning in 2008 with the arrests of a number of known gang members, police and community members have made much progress in ridding the park and surrounding neighborhood of the crime that had plagued it for many years.

12.6 Left onto U.S. 60/Dixie Highway

Greenwood Avenue ends at Dixie Highway. Most residents associate Dixie Highway with the congested 6-lane highway that extends southward from Interstate 264/Watterson Expressway deep into southwestern Jefferson County. The road actually begins at W Broadway and extends through the California neighborhood toward Shively where the road widens to accommodate the increase in traffic.

North of Garland Avenue, the corporate headquarters of Brown-Forman is on the left side of Dixie Highway. The Brown-Forman Corporation was founded in 1870 by George Garvin Brown, who began selling high-quality whiskey in brown bottles. Today, Brown-Forman is one of the largest liquor companies in the world, selling high-quality brands such as Woodford Reserve, Old Forester, Early Times, Jack Daniel's, and Chambord. The facility here produces Brown-Forman's popular Old Forester bourbon. The enormous Old Forester bottle mounted on top of the building has been a landmark of the California neighborhood for many years now.

Brown-Forman has maintained their corporate headquarters at this location since 1968. In addition to improving living conditions and fighting blight in the California neighborhood, the company is also a major sponsor of the arts and education in metropolitan Louisville. There are many excellent views of the facility on Breckenridge Street (following the next turn on

Brown-Forman Headquarters

the route), where many of the company's warehouses are located.

12.9 Right onto W Breckinridge Street

In addition to the Brown-Forman warehouses located here, the Heaven Hill Company maintains a facility in this area. Heaven Hill was founded after the end of Prohibition and is one of the largest independent family-owned companies in the United States. The company produces many different spirits, but their premier brands are their Evan Williams and Elijah Craig bourbons. Heaven Hill is headquartered in Bardstown, Kentucky, about 60 miles to the south of Louisville.

13.2 Left onto S 15th Street

South 15th Street is a designated cycling route and has a dedicated bike lane between Breckenridge Street and Broadway. North of Broadway, the bike lane disappears as the road becomes a one-way street heading north, Traffic on the road is generally light. South 15th Street becomes N 15th Street after it crosses Main Street.

N 15th Street ends as it curves sharply to the left, becoming Portland Avenue as it leads into the heart of the Portland warehouse district. To access the Louisville Loop and head back to the start of the route, cyclists should turn right onto N 16th Street, which is the first cross street beyond the curve.

14.6 Right onto N 16th Street

The road continues north toward the floodwall and seemingly ends at Northwestern Parkway. The road beyond this point is extremely rough, but it is passable on a bicycle. Cyclists should slow down and be on the lookout for the many potholes through this area. The road continues a short distance ahead across Northwestern Parkway before narrowing and passing through the floodwall and intersecting with the Louisville Loop.

14.7 Continue through floodwall pedestrian tunnel

On the other side of the floodwall, there is a considerable amount of gravel, dirt, and other debris that is occasionally washed ashore when the river level rises. It will be necessary to proceed very slowly through this area or dismount and walk your bicycle here to avoid falls.

14.8 Right onto Louisville Loop

From this location, the route doubles back to return to the ride start in Waterfront Park.

16.1 Right onto Bingham Way

16.1 Left to continue on Bingham Way

16.2 Left onto Bingham Way

16.3 Left onto E Witherspoon Street

16.6 Left onto E River Road

17.0 Left into Waterfront Park parking lot

Historic home in Portland, built ca. 1900

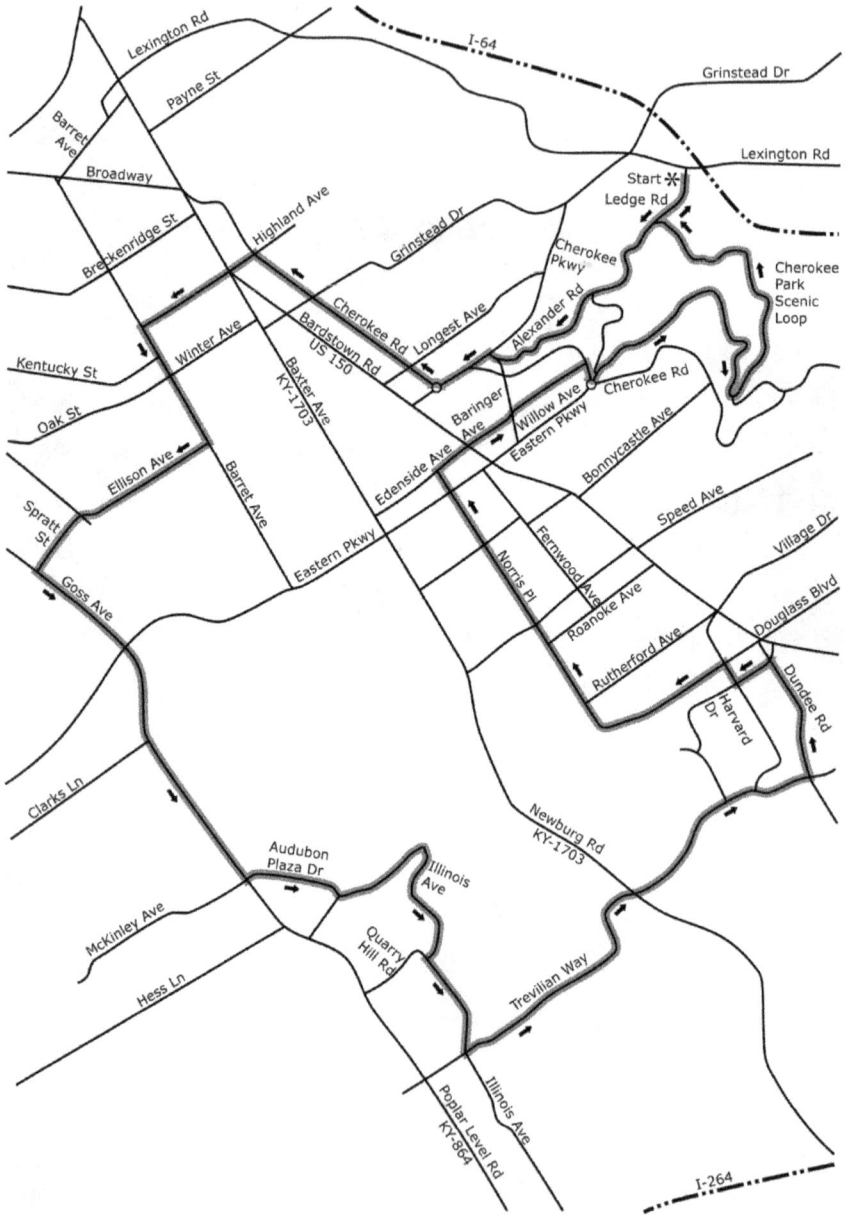

4 THE HIGHLANDS

Distance: 11.6 miles

Difficulty: Moderate. A few hills, but no significant climbs. Traffic may be heavy in some areas and at certain times of day.

Points of Interest: Cherokee Park, Original Highlands neighborhood, Germantown neighborhood, Deer Park neighborhood, Belknap neighborhood, Poplar Level neighborhood, Bellarmine University, Louisville Zoo

Louisville's popular Highlands neighborhood is situated on a series of small hills between the middle and south forks of Beargrass Creek that rise steeply above the Ohio River floodplain. Geographically, it occupies the sector of the city that lies along U.S. Highway 150/Bardstown Road corridor and stretches from East Broadway south to Rufer Avenue, west to Barret Avenue, and east to Cherokee Park. This area bills itself as the Original Highlands, but the Highlands area today encompasses the area along the Bardstown Road corridor southward to Interstate 264/Watterson Expressway. The Highlands neighborhood is well known for its many nightclubs, fine restaurants, art galleries, and independently owned businesses. Friday and Saturday nights usually find the area teeming with large crowds of people enjoying an evening out at the many bars, nightclubs, and fine restaurants located in the area.

The Highlands area was one of the last areas of the city's core to see development. Like other nearby areas, the neighborhoods of the Highlands were built on land that was surveyed by and granted to Colonel William Preston of Fincastle County, Virginia for his service in the French and Indian War and American Revolutionary War. Upon Preston's death in 1781, his son Major William Preston inherited the land and built a plantation called the Briar Patch, where he and his descendants lived for many decades. In 1869, the land was inherited by Susan Christy Preston, who subdivided a portion of the land for development.

While the proximity of Bardstown Turnpike (now Bardstown Road) made the area attractive to many early settlers, a streetcar line was added in 1871 and spurred interest in the area. The development of Cherokee Park in 1891 made the area a highly desirable area in which to live, and many new homes were built around this time. As a result of this settlement pattern, the residential neighborhoods of the Highlands are an eclectic mixture of working class shotgun houses, bungalows, and sprawling Victorian mansions that sometimes seem randomly interspersed along winding tree-lined streets.

Like most other areas of the city's core, the Highlands experienced a period of decline that began with the flight of its wealthier residents toward the eastern suburbs in the 1950s and continued well into the 1970s. By 1975, many of the older buildings along Bardstown Road and Baxter Avenue were in serious need of repair, and rising crime rates threatened the area's economic viability. In particular, the Mid-City Mall on Bardstown Road had become an eyesore and a magnet for crime, prompting a public boycott by residents of the surrounding neighborhoods. By 1976, the boycott and declining economy forced the mall into bankruptcy. The mall was purchased in 1977, and its new owners worked with neighborhood activists to successfully repair and revitalize the facility. Buoyed by their success, many of the activists involved formed the Highlands Commerce Guild that has continued to revitalize the Highlands and promote economic development. As a result of this and other factors, the Bardstown Road corridor has become a thriving commercial and residential area of the city.

The tour begins in Cherokee Park, in the parking lot adjacent to Lexington Road on the north side of the park. In addition to being less crowded than many of the other parking areas in Cherokee Park and in the Highlands, the parking lot is also convenient to Interstate 64 from the Grinstead Drive exit and to the northern portion of the Highlands via Grinstead Drive or Lexington Road.

Route Directions – The Highlands

0.0 Right onto Ledge Road
0.1 Continue onto Cherokee Park Scenic Loop
0.5 Right onto Alexander Road
0.9 Right onto Willow Avenue
0.9 Left onto Cherokee Parkway
1.1 Right onto Cherokee Road at roundabout
1.8 Left onto Highland Avenue
2.2 Left onto Barret Avenue
2.6 Right onto Ellison Avenue
3.0 Left onto Spratt Street
3.3 Left onto Goss Avenue
3.6 Continue onto Poplar Level Road
4.4 Left onto Audubon Plaza Drive
4.7 Left onto Illinois Avenue
5.4 Left to continue onto Illinois Avenue
5.8 Left onto Trevilian Way
7.3 Left onto Dundee Road
7.6 Left onto Harvard Drive
7.8 Right onto Boulevard Napoleon
7.9 Left onto Douglass Boulevard
8.3 Continue onto Norris Place
9.1 Right onto Edenside Drive
9.3 Continue onto Baringer Avenue
9.8 Right onto Cherokee Road
9.9 Right onto Cherokee Park Road at roundabout
10.0 Continue onto Cherokee Park Scenic Loop
11.0 Left to continue onto Cherokee Park Scenic Loop
11.5 Right onto Ledge Road
11.6 Left into parking lot

Route Description – The Highlands

0.0 Right onto Ledge Road

From the parking lot on Ledge Road, the route heads toward the Highlands through the Cherokee Park. Traffic entering the park from Lexington Road may be traveling above the 25 mph speed limit, so caution is advised when making the turn. Ledge Road leads a short distance into the park, where it feeds into the Cherokee Park Scenic Loop. The loop is a one-way road that continues straight ahead past the traffic island.

0.1 Continue onto Cherokee Park Scenic Loop

Almost immediately, the road begins to climb a fairly large hill, known to the locals as Dog Hill because of the many dog owners who allow their pets to run loose up and down the hill's east side. The dog owners mostly congregate near the picnic shelter at the top of the hill along the portion of the pedestrian/bicycle lane that is separated from the lane of traffic and not directly on this route, but cyclists should still pay attention to their surroundings when cresting the hill due to the large number of pedestrians in the area.

0.5 Right onto Alexander Road

At the top of the hill, Cherokee Park Scenic Loop curves sharply to the left. Alexander Road branches off straight ahead and continues past Cherokee Golf Course as it winds its way to the park's western entrance at the intersection of Alexander Road and Willow Avenue. Across the street from the end of Alexander Road is Willow Park, one of Louisville Metro's numerous pocket green spaces. There are restroom facilities in Willow Park if they are needed. At the end of Alexander Road, the route continues to the right onto Willow Avenue.

0.9 Right onto Willow Avenue

A few feet from the end of Alexander Road, Willow Avenue intersects Cherokee Parkway. The route turns left onto Cherokee Parkway at the intersection.

0.9 Left onto Cherokee Parkway

Cherokee Parkway is a shaded two-lane road that leads through a residential neighborhood nestled between Cherokee Park and the eastern edge of the Highlands. Along both sides of the road there are several large Victorian homes that are characteristic of this section of the Highlands neighborhood. Most of these homes were built in the early 1890s when Cherokee Park was under development.

Cherokee Parkway soon intersects Cherokee Road at a roundabout. In the center of the traffic circle is a statue of General John Breckinridge Castleman, a Confederate soldier from Lexington who recruited 41 men and formed the Second Kentucky Calvary in Knoxville, Tennessee under General John Hunt Morgan. In 1864, Castleman organized guerilla attacks on Union supply ships in St. Louis, Missouri. He was soon captured in Indiana, convicted of espionage, and imprisoned in Indianapolis. Fearing that Castleman would be executed, his brother-in-law S. M. Breckenridge intervened on his behalf and obtained a stay of execution from President Abraham Lincoln. Castleman was released in 1865 and exiled to France.

Castleman wasted little time in redeeming himself. After being pardoned by President Andrew Johnson in 1866, he returned to Kentucky and settled on a farm that would later become part of the Tyler Park neighborhood. In 1878, Castleman organized a militia unit, and was later appointed as Adjutant General of Kentucky in 1883. His militia became involved in the

John Breckenridge Castleman monument

Spanish-American War in 1898. Castleman was promoted to Colonel, then to Brigadier General, and later served as a military governor in Puerto Rico following ratification of the Treaty of Paris in 1899.

Following his military service, Castleman was again appointed as Adjutant General after the assassination of Governor William Goebel in 1900. By this time, Castleman was well-regarded for his military service and success in business, and his influence was instrumental in calming tensions following the assassination. Castleman was also well known as an advocate for parks and outdoor recreation as a 25-year member of the Board of Park Commissioners.

The monument situated in the roundabout is not a military style statue. Instead, he is dressed in civilian attire atop his prized mare Carolina and appears relaxed. The monument here pays homage to his role in the formation of the American Saddlebred Horse Association, his election as its first president in 1891, and his grand championship at the 1893 Chicago

World's Fair. In August 2017, there were demonstrations calling for the monument's removal due to Castleman's service in the Confederate Army, and the statue was vandalized with spray paint. Currently, the stature remains in place, but its future seems uncertain.

Traffic in the roundabout flows in a counter-clockwise direction, so the route proceeds to the right through the traffic circle. The next turn on the route comes almost immediately, to the right onto Cherokee Road.

1.1 Right onto Cherokee Road at roundabout

Cherokee Road continues through the residential portion of the Highlands, leading through shaded, tree-lined neighborhoods. There are many cars parked along the side of the road through this area, so cyclists should be vigilant and look for cars suddenly entering or exiting the roadway, or for car doors that may open suddenly.

1.8 Left onto Highland Avenue

The route turns to the west on Highland Avenue and leads toward the commercial district of the Highlands along Bardstown Road. The road crosses Bardstown Road at a traffic light. The traffic on Bardstown road may be heavy, and despite the many bicycles and pedestrians that traverse the road, caution is highly advised due to the many vehicles that travel this major thoroughfare.

To the left and the right there is a long expanse of restaurants, bars, coffee shops, art galleries, and small stores that line both sides of Bardstown Road. There are also several bike shops in this area if repairs or supplies are needed. If you have time, Bardstown Road makes an excellent side trip, and many of the shops in this area provide bike racks for cyclists.

Bardstown Road

West of Bardstown Road, Highland Avenue continues through another residential area. The street appears to end at Barret Avenue, although it continues west a little farther north along Barret Avenue. The route, however, continues to the left on Barret Avenue.

2.2 Left onto Barret Avenue

There are many art galleries and shops along Barret Avenue, although the crowds along this street are nowhere as large as the crowds on Bardstown Road. On the right side of the street is the recently closed Lynn's Paradise Café. The café and its delightfully tacky décor have served as a Louisville landmark for many years. The restaurant first opened in the Crescent Hill neighborhood in 1991, but it moved to this location in the Highlands in 1994.

Lynn's Paradise Café was highly successful for many years, and its whimsical, kitschy atmosphere attracted crowds of hungry Aatourists to the Highlands. It was well known for its New Year's Pajama Party and for sponsoring an Ugly Lamp Contest at the Kentucky State Fair. The eatery was even featured on *The Oprah Winfrey Show*, *Man v. Food Nation*, and *Throwdown! With*

Lynn's Paradise Cafe

Bobby Flay. In 2013, Lynn's Paradise Café closed amid allegations of labor law violations and blowback over a controversial tip-sharing policy. The property was purchased in 2016 by a buyer from Nashville, with plans to eventually reopen the restaurant.

A little farther down Barret Avenue, the rows of shops and restaurants give way to homes and eventually to St. Louis Cemetery, which straddles the border between the Highlands and Germantown. Across from the cemetery, the route continues to the right onto Ellison Avenue as it passes through the eastern edge of Germantown.

2.6 Right onto Ellison Avenue

Ellison Avenue leads west, heading out of the Highlands and entering the Germantown neighborhood. As the street continues east, it passes over the South Fork of Beargrass Creek and then by St. Michael's Cemetery, which dates back to 1851. The road then comes to a somewhat confusing intersection with St. Michael's and Spratt Streets. Ellison Avenue continues to the right, with Reutlinger Avenue splitting off directly north of the intersection. The route continues seemingly straight ahead onto Spratt Street, although it is listed as a left turn because Ellison Avenue continues on to the right. Extreme caution is advised in this location, as it is a busy intersection where motorists are often confused by the odd layout of the streets and sometimes run the stop sign. There is a blinking red light overhead that was likely placed here because of the high number of accidents at this intersection.

3.0 Left onto Spratt Street

There is a shared-use bicycle lane on this street. The many well-maintained shotgun houses along Spratt and neighboring streets are typical of Louisville's Germantown neighborhood and blend in with some of the small shotgun houses on the edge of the Highlands. After many decades of neglect and decay, Germantown has made a major comeback, with many of the area's residents taking pride in renovating and maintaining their historic homes.

Spratt Street ends a little over a quarter of a mile later at its intersection with Goss Avenue. Traffic on Goss Avenue may be heavy during the morning and evening commute times, so patience may be required when making the next turn on the route.

3.3 Left onto Goss Avenue

As Goss Avenue continues south back toward Eastern Parkway the traffic volume picks up slightly. Near the end of the road, it widens to four lanes just ahead of a traffic light. Although Goss Avenue and Eastern Parkway are both major cycling routes through the area, caution is still advised.

3.6 Continue onto Poplar Level Road

South of Eastern Parkway, Goss Avenue becomes Poplar Level Road. A bicycle lane appears, easing the coexistence of bicycles and cars. The traffic and speed limit both increase in this area. The terrain becomes much hillier as the road continues toward the southern end of the Highlands.

The next turn on the route, onto Audubon Plaza Drive, comes less than a mile later. Norton Audubon Hospital is on the left side of the road at the intersection, providing a useful landmark. Since Poplar Level Road is a four-lane road, it will be necessary to leave the bicycle lane and move into the left turn lane at the traffic light.

4.4 Left onto Audubon Plaza Drive

Audubon Plaza Drive continues past the hospital. There may be many vehicles entering and exiting the hospital's parking garages, so caution is advised, and it will be necessary to stay as far to the right as possible in this area. At the far end of the hospital there is a back entrance to a shopping center situated between Audubon Plaza Drive and Poplar Level Road. Fortunately, there is little traffic entering and exiting the street in this location. Beyond the shopping center, the route climbs a small hill as the street ends at its intersection with Illinois Avenue.

4.7 Left onto Illinois Avenue

The neighborhoods situated between Poplar Level Road and Newburg Road comprise what locals regarded as the Poplar Level neighborhood. Most of the homes here are working class or middle class, and traffic through the area is minimal. Illinois Avenue is hilly and winding, making it a fun ride on a bicycle.

A little less than a mile later Illinois Avenue seems to end at its intersection with Quarry Hill Road, although the road continues to the left through the stop sign. The route continues to the left, following Illinois Avenue.

5.4 Left to continue onto Illinois Avenue

The Beargrass Creek State Nature Preserve is situated along the left side of the road through this area. The preserve is spread across a 41-acre tract of wetlands and low hilltops along the South Fork of Beargrass Creek and is one of the largest urban nature preserves in the country. The land for the preserve was purchased by the Kentucky State Nature Preserves Commission in 1982 and managed through an agreement the Louisville Nature Center. The Louisville Nature Center is located a little further down Illinois Avenue in a building constructed here in 1997. There are trails through the preserve that are well worth exploring on an afternoon hike.

Joe Creason Park is adjacent to the preserve's southern edge and is part of the same original tract of land from which the nature preserve was formed. There are numerous walking and running trails throughout the park, which stretches along Trevilian Way between Illinois Avenue and KY-1703/Newburg Road. At the edge of Joe Creason Park, the route turns right, onto Trevilian Way. There is often a considerable amount of traffic passing through this intersection, but the traffic circle in front of the Louisville Zoo forces motorists to slow down considerably. Caution is still advised, however, due to the volume of traffic.

5.8 Left onto Trevilian Way

Across Trevilian Way from Joe Creason Park is the Louisville Zoo. There is an entrance into the zoo about one hundred feet to the east, so it will be necessary to take the lane in this location to avoid colliding with right-turning vehicles who may not necessarily be paying attention to the road. On nice spring days when the zoo is extremely busy and the traffic is backed up down Trevilian Way, it is actually quite easy to get around the long column of cars waiting to enter the parking lot.

The Louisville Zoo, founded in 1969 with funding from philanthropist James Graham Brown, is situated on a 169-acre tract of land south of Trevilian Way that was carved from the same tract of land as the Beargrass Creek State Nature Preserve and Joe Creason Park. Accredited by the Association of Zoos and Aquariums, the Louisville Zoo boasts more than 1,700 species of animals and plants, many of which are listed as threatened or endangered.

Louisville Zoo

The Louisville Zoo's signature exhibit is The Islands, the first zoological exhibit in the world that rotates a series of threatened or endangered animal species from the Indonesian wilderness through different habitats in the same exhibit through the day, much as they would do in their natural habitats. Rotating both predator and prey species through the same enclosures at different times of the day provides valuable stimulation for the animals, and also for the zoo's visitors who never quite know what they will see in the exhibit from one day to the next.

There are many other interesting areas of the zoo to visit and explore. Special talks and presentations are given almost every day of the year, even during the dead of winter. As Kentucky's only accredited zoo, the Louisville Zoo is a must-visit attraction for tourists and locals alike.

At the end of the elongated traffic circle a few hundred feet to the east there will be vehicles exiting the zoo. Although the traffic here is not usually as congested, caution is still advised. Past the traffic circle, there is a sharp descent with a sharp curve to the right at the bottom as the road approaches its intersections with KY-1703/Newburg Road. There are two lanes at the intersection; traffic continuing straight onto Trevilian Way shares the right-hand lane with traffic turning right. Bicyclists should take the entire lane here to discourage right-turning vehicles from turning in front of them. The sensors underneath the road controlling the signal should respond to the weight of a bicyclist, although there are normally enough vehicles at the light to ensure that it changes.

East of Newburg Road, Trevilian Way enters the Belknap neighborhood. Although it is now part of Louisville's Highlands, the neighborhood saw scant development until well into the 20th century. Much of the land on which the neighborhood sits was originally owned by the Doup family, who came into the area around 1790. Jonathon Clark, the older brother of William and

Belknap neighborhood

George Rogers Clark, purchased a 1,000-acre tract of land in 1801 and established a farm here, which became known as Trough Springs. Part of his original home still stands on Trough Spring Lane and Dundee Road, although the home has been renovated multiple times over the past two centuries.

As the city of Louisville continued to grow over the next century, portions of the land were eventually subdivided, sold, and developed. In 1901, the Zimlich brothers, who operated a stagecoach stop along Bardstown Road, sold a 24-acre tract of land that was developed into one of the first commercial districts to appear along the Bardstown Road corridor. In 1909, the Eiler family sold a 22-acre easement to the city for the establishment of a street car loop, and the street cars began to run through the area soon afterward. In 1923, the Kaelin family sold a portion of their land for development, and the area's population began to increase.

7.3 Left onto Dundee Road

Dundee Road begins to rise in elevation as it continues northeast toward Bardstown Road. Near the top of the hill it curves to the left as Woodbourne Avenue seems to continue straight ahead. There are numerous yellow signs directing traffic to the left onto Dundee Road. It is not unusual to get lost among the labyrinthine streets of the Highlands, so it will be necessary to pay strict attention to the roads in this area.

Just ahead of the intersection of Dundee Road and Bardstown Road is the next turn of the route, onto Harvard Drive. Dundee Road straight ahead becomes one-way, carrying only inbound traffic from Bardstown Road and Douglass Boulevard. Vehicles wishing to access Bardstown Road must turn right onto Harvard Drive. It is not unusual to see confused motorists here, so caution should be observed when making the turn.

There are many bars, restaurants, and shops along Dundee Road and Harvard Drive ahead of the turn, and it is not unusual to see pedestrians in the area as well. The area ahead is known as the Douglass Loop for the streetcar loop that the Louisville City Railway once operated at this location. Loops such as this were used to turn the trains around. The Douglass Loop was the last of the loops remaining until the tracks were finally paved over in 1948 for further development of the neighborhood.

7.6 Left onto Harvard Drive

Harvard Drive was originally named Diebel; however, the name was changed amid anti-German sentiment following World War I. There are usually many cars parked along the side of the road in this location, so cyclists should be cautious of cars suddenly entering or exiting the lane of traffic in this location. It is recommended that cyclists occupy the full lane of traffic here to avoid car doors opening suddenly.

7.8 Right onto Boulevard Napoleon

The homes along Boulevard Napoleon and its side roads were developed beginning in 1913 when the area was known as Cherokee Plaza.

7.9 Left onto Douglass Boulevard

As Douglass Boulevard curves sharply to the right about a half mile later, it becomes Norris Place.

8.3 Continue onto Norris Place

On the left side of the road just past the curve is the entrance to Bellarmine University, one of Louisville's many colleges and universities. The Catholic university was founded in 1950 by Archbishop John Floersh of the Archdioceses of Louisville and named for Cardinal Saint Robert Bellarmine, an Italian Jesuit who was instrumental in the Counter-Reformation. The college grew rapidly between 1950 and 1970, growing from an initial freshman class of 115 students in 1950 to more than 2,000 by 1970. Today, there are more than 3,500 students enrolled across its seven colleges, which offer Bachelor's and Master's degrees in over 50 academic disciplines.

As Norris Place winds its way northward past Speed Avenue, there is a point of interest about 3 blocks to the west at the corner of Newburg Road and Speed Avenue. The building at the corner, which now houses an Irish pub, was once the home of Kaelin's Restaurant. Kaelin's was a family-run restaurant founded in 1934 that lays claim as the birthplace of that great

Campus of Bellarmine University

American staple, the cheeseburger. The restaurant closed in 2004, and the property was sold to new owners who opened other businesses in the building. A plaque still graces the wall of the building, proclaiming it as the birthplace of the cheeseburger.

Norris Place continues north through the Highlands and Deer Park neighborhoods as it continues back toward Cherokee Park. The road crosses Eastern Parkway at a stoplight before ending two blocks later at Edenside Drive.

9.1 Right onto Edenside Drive

Edenside Drive ends at Bardstown Road and continues straight ahead as Baringer Avenue. There is no stoplight here, so crossing Bardstown Road here can be an exercise in patience, especially on weekends.

At the corner of Edenside Drive and Bardstown Road is St. James Catholic Church. The church

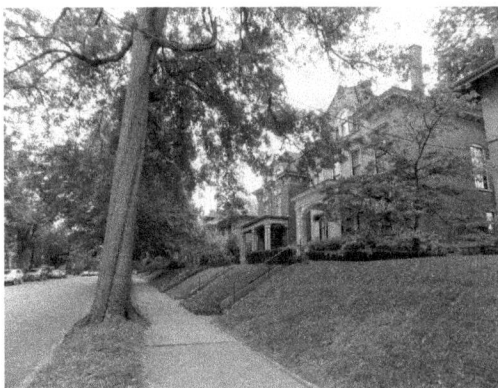

The Highlands neighborhood

is an example of Baroque Byzantine architecture, sporting a tall bell tower and large dome, a red clay roof, and an orange glazed brick exterior. A Highlands landmark for over 100 years, the church first opened in 1913.

9.3 Continue onto Baringer Avenue

The densely-packed homes along Baringer Avenue exhibit the wide variety of architectural styles in the Highlands neighborhood. There are many cars parked along the road through this area, so caution is advised. Baringer Avenue ends at Cherokee Road near the edge of Cherokee Park.

9.8 Right onto Cherokee Road

As Cherokee Road approaches the entrance to Cherokee Park, it intersects with Eastern Parkway at a roundabout. Traffic flows through the roundabout in a counter-clockwise direction.

9.9 Right onto Cherokee Park Road at roundabout

Daniel Boone statue

In the center of the roundabout is a statue of Kentucky pioneer Daniel Boone. In 1775, Boone blazed a trail known as Wilderness Road through the Cumberland Gap from North Carolina and Tennessee into Kentucky. After arriving in Kentucky, Boone founded the town of Boonesborough, the first town west of the Appalachian Mountains. Over the next two decades, hundreds of thousands of settlers followed Wilderness Road into Kentucky.

Boone served as an officer in the militia during the U.S. Revolutionary War. He was captured by Shawnee Warriors in 1778, but escaped and was able to warn the settlers in Boonesborough of an impending raid on the settlement, allowing them to repulse the attackers. Boone also fought in the Battle of Blue Licks in 1782, which occurred well after the surrender of Cornwallis at Yorktown in October 1781. The battle, which occurred in modern-day Robertson County along the Licking River, was the last major victory for the British Loyalists and their Canadian and Native American allies.

Following the war, Boone fell on hard times due to speculative losses and land deals gone bad. Facing mounting legal problems, he moved to Missouri in 1799, outside of the border of the United States. Over the next 20 years, he was able to repay most of his creditors in Kentucky, although it is unclear as to whether or not he actually came back to the state. Boone died in 1820 and was buried in Marthasville, Missouri beside his wife, who had passed away several years earlier. His remains and those of his wife were reinterred in Frankfort, Kentucky in 1845, but it is rumored that the remains that were moved to Frankfort were not the Boones because their original graves were unmarked. Even today, Missouri and Kentucky both lay claim as Boone's final resting place. The statue seen here was sculpted in 1906 by famed sculptor and Louisville native Enid Yandell.

10.0 Continue onto Cherokee Park Scenic Loop

Immediately upon entering the park, you will need to bear to the right to follow Cherokee Park Scenic Loop through the park back toward the ride start on Ledge Road. The road is one-way, traveling around the park in a roughly counter-clockwise direction. The road begins to climb a fairly large hill, ending at a picnic pavilion and Hogan's Fountain, a popular landmark within the park. Past the fountain, the road makes a swift descent toward its intersection with Barret Hill Road. Here, the road curves sharply to the left as Barret Hill Road continues almost straight ahead. The next turn on the route, onto Ledge Road, occurs just before the Scenic Loop climbs Dog Hill. There is a triangular traffic island at the intersection that is a convenient landmark for the turn.

11.0 Left to continue onto Cherokee Park Scenic Loop

11.5 Right onto Ledge Road

11.6 Left into parking lot

5 AUDUBON PARK, SCHNITZELBURG, AND GERMANTOWN

Distance: 9.4 miles

Difficulty: Easy. Moderate traffic in a few areas.

Points of Interest: George Rogers Clark Park, Audubon neighborhood, City of Audubon Park, Germantown neighborhood, Schnitzelburg neighborhood, Hauck's Handy Store

Germantown, as the name suggests, is a neighborhood of Louisville that was first populated by German immigrants. The area was first settled in the 1850s when the new arrivals moved southward down Shelby Street into the newly developed suburbs from the overcrowded Phoenix Hill neighborhood where most of the established German immigrants had settled. The influx accelerated after the Bloody Monday riots in 1855 as many recent immigrants moved into newly opened suburban neighborhoods to escape the discrimination they were subjected to in the city. By the 1870s, many small family farms, shops, and businesses dotted the landscape, interspersed with pockets of suburban homes.

The South Fork of Beargrass Creek runs through Germantown. Although the water source attracted many farmers to the area, it soon became a nuisance due to the constant flooding that plagued the area. The frequent floods earned the neighborhood the nickname "Frogtown" and touched off countless malaria and cholera epidemics. By the 1890s, the creek was rerouted into a deep channel that was encased in concrete sometime during the 1920s. The original course of the creek was converted into a sewer.

With these changes, the flooding problems lessened and touched off a population boom in the area. To cope with the need for housing, many of the area's farms were soon partitioned into subdivisions that were soon covered with large numbers of shotgun houses and modest cottages.

Like Phoenix Hill, many of the original shotgun houses built in Germantown are still standing today. There are many small stores, bars, and taverns sprinkled throughout the neighborhood, many of which are still in business or have recently reestablished themselves. Many of the homes have been renovated as the neighborhood has experienced a wave of revitalization. With its hip, urban vibe, a large number of young urban professionals and families has swept through the neighborhood, making it one of the city's up and coming neighborhoods. However, the area still retains much of its sense of community, and its heavily German-American heritage still dominates.

Schnitzelburg is a portion of the Germantown neighborhood that seems to have acquired its own identity, with a hip, urban vibe similar to the Frankfort Avenue corridor. It makes up the core of the Germantown neighborhood, situated roughly between Shelby Street and Goss Avenue, extending southward to Eastern Parkway. Its many coffee shops and pubs are a Louisville tradition, attracting an eclectic mix of young professionals, college students, and blue collar workers.

The nearby city of Audubon Park was established 1,000 acres of land that were part of a land grant awarded to Colonel William Preston in 1773 for his service in the French and Indian War. The Preston family, which includes former Congressman and Confederate General William Preston, maintained the tract as pasture land for well over a century. In 1906, most of the land was sold to G. R. Hunt, who developed the land as a suburb and established a golf course and country club on a nearby parcel of land that was leased. The land was next to the Interurban, a commuter rail line that led from many of Louisville's far-lying suburbs into downtown. Development, however, was slow at first, with 65 houses in the development by 1916.

War soon displaced the area's population when Camp Zachary Taylor was established here in 1917. After the conclusion of World War I, the planned installation of gas and electric lines in the early 1920s attracted residents back to the area and finally fueled the neighborhood's growth. As new homes were built, they were laid out along straight, tree-lined streets that emphasized green spaces, a more natural environment, and ample recreational opportunities for its residents. Keeping with this theme, the neighborhood was named Audubon Park after naturalist John James Audubon, with all but two streets named for birds.

Audubon Park was incorporated as a sixth-class city in 1941. By 1947, all of the lots in the city had finally been sold, and by 1977, the city was elevated to fifth-class status. Today, Audubon Park has a population of about 1,500 residents and still boasts the shaded, tree-lined streets and green spaces that were envisioned by its developers. It remains an island of greenery amidst the expanse of the Kentucky Fair and Exposition Center directly to the west, Standiford Field to the southwest, and the heavily developed KY-61/Preston Highway, which replaced the Interurban Railway as cars and trucks replaced trains and buses.

The tour begins at George Rogers Clark Park, situated in the Audubon neighborhood that is located directly between Germantown and Audubon Park. The Audubon neighborhood was developed in the early 1940s, with the developer banking on the area's proximity to Audubon Park and the nearby George Rogers Clark Park. It envisioned the construction of simple, affordable homes on small lots. Audubon Park residents opposed the plan but were unable to stop the neighborhood's development.

George Rogers Clark Park

Route Directions – Audubon Park, Schnitzelburg, and Germantown

0.0 Left onto Thruston Avenue
0.3 Left onto Pindell Avenue
0.8 Continue onto Oriole Drive
1.2 Left onto Cardinal Drive
1.6 Continue onto Nightingale Road
2.0 Left onto Audubon Parkway
2.3 Right onto Bobolink Road
2.5 Right onto Hess Lane
2.5 Left onto Bobolink Road
2.7 Left onto McKinley Avenue
3.2 Right onto Pindell Avenue
3.5 Right onto Parkway Drive
3.6 Left onto E Burnett Avenue
4.1 Right onto Texas Avenue
4.5 Left onto Samuel Street
4.6 Right onto Spratt Street
4.8 Right onto Ellison Avenue
5.2 Left onto Barret Avenue
5.8 Left onto E Breckinridge Street
6.4 Left onto S Shelby Street
6.8 Left onto E Oak Street
7.1 Right onto Swan Street
7.1 Continue onto Ellison Avenue
7.4 Right onto Spratt Street
7.6 Right onto Goss Avenue
7.7 Left onto Hoertz Avenue
8.1 Left onto E Burnett Avenue
8.3 Right onto Texas Avenue
8.5 Left onto Delor Avenue
8.5 Right to continue onto Delor Avenue
9.0 Left onto Thruston Avenue
9.4 Left into parking lot at Thruston Avenue and Dixie Street

Route Description – Audubon Park, Schnitzelburg, and Germantown

0.0 Left onto Thruston Avenue

At the exit from the park, there is a historical marker on the side of Thurston Avenue that describes the history of Mulberry Hill, the former Clark family estate that once stood at the site now occupied by George Rogers Clark Park. Mulberry Hill was built from 1784-1785 on land that John Clark purchased from the family of George Meriwether. John moved his family here, including his wife, Ann, and his four youngest sons, which includes famed explorer William Clark (1770-1838). The Clark family and their descendants lived at Mulberry Hill until 1863, when the home passed out of the family. The home fell into disrepair by the early 1900s and was finally razed in 1917 when the land became part of Camp Zachary Taylor during World War I.

In 1921, some of the Clark family heirs purchased the land on which Mulberry Hill once stood and established George Rogers Clark Park. While most of the Clark family had been interred elsewhere, the graves of Ann and John Clark are still located within the park.

0.3 Left onto Pindell Avenue

Pindell Avenue continues south through what is referred to as the Audubon neighborhood (as opposed to Audubon Park just south of here), passing St. Steven Martyr Church and Audubon Traditional Elementary School before coming to a stop sign at Hess Lane. Across Hess Lane, the road becomes Oriole Drive as it enters Audubon Park.

0.8 Continue onto Oriole Drive

Audubon Park is shaded with many mature trees along the roadside and usually remains a few degrees cooler than the surrounding areas during the summertime. Most of the roads through the neighborhood are named for birds and retain their original

Audubon Park Neighborhood

names. The homes within Audubon Park include a mixture of modest Craftsman-style bungalows,

Tudor Revival and Colonial Revival architectural styles.

At the intersection of Oriole Drive with Audubon Parkway there is a small traffic circle that must be navigated in order to continue on Oriole Drive. The road ends at Cardinal Drive.

1.2 Left onto Cardinal Drive

Cardinal Drive rolls past the northern edge of Audubon Country Club. It becomes Nightingale Road as it passes the entrance to a large condominium building on the right.

1.6 Continue onto Nightingale Road

Nightingale Road soon curves to the left and passes a cluster of apartment buildings. The road ends at Audubon Parkway near its intersection with Poplar Level Road. Speeding cars may enter Audubon Parkway suddenly from Poplar Level Road, so caution is advised when making the next turn.

2.0 Left onto Audubon Parkway

Audubon Parkway begins rising in elevation, climbing about 50 feet as it heads back into the Audubon Park neighborhood. A bike route sign pointing to the right marks the next turn on the route onto Bobolink Drive.

2.3 Right onto Bobolink Road

2.5 Right onto Hess Lane

After a short distance on Hess Lane, Bobolink Road continues again on the left. Hess Lane is a major thoroughfare that runs between KY-61/Preston Highway and KY-864/Poplar Level Road, and traffic may be heavy at certain times of the day.

2.5 Left onto Bobolink Road

2.7 Left onto McKinley Avenue

McKinley Avenue passes along the southern edge of George Rogers Clark Park.

3.2 Right onto Pindell Avenue

3.5 Right onto Parkway Drive

3.6 Left onto E Burnett Avenue

North of Clarks Lane, E Burnett Avenue enters the Schnitzelburg neighborhood. Soon, the road crosses the very busy Eastern Parkway at a traffic light. Caution is advised here due to a large number of cars that attempt to run the traffic light after it turns red. There is a pedestrian crossing button at the corner that may help if the light does not turn in response to your bicycle.

As the road continues north of Eastern Parkway it passes DuPont Manual Memorial Stadium, which has served as the football stadium from DuPont Manual High School since 1924. The school itself is located in the Old Louisville neighborhood just north of the University of Louisville. DuPont Manual High School has a long, proud football tradition, having claimed the Kentucky state football championship in 1925, 1938, 1948, 1959, and 1966. The team was named as the national champion in 1925 and 1938, although the 1925 title is in dispute because there was no tournament or championship game held that year.

Manual's football tradition dates back to the school's founding in 1892, and its famed rivalry with Male High School began in 1893. It is the longest running high school sports rivalry in the state.

Schnitzelburg neighborhood

4.1 Right onto Texas Avenue

The homes along Burnett and Texas Avenues are very representative of the architectural style of the neighborhood. Most of them are shotgun houses like those in Phoenix Hill and Shelby Park. Texas Avenue continues eastward through Schnitzelburg before crossing Goss Avenue at a traffic light. Texas Avenue ends shortly ahead at St. Michael's Cemetery, and the route continues to the left onto Samuel Street. There is a bike route sign marking the way.

4.5 Left onto Samuel Street

4.6 Right onto Spratt Street

There is a shared use lane marked on the road in this location. The road soon comes to an end at an awkward five-way intersection. Straight ahead and slightly to the right, the road becomes Ellison Avenue as it continues eastward.

4.8 Continue onto Ellison Avenue

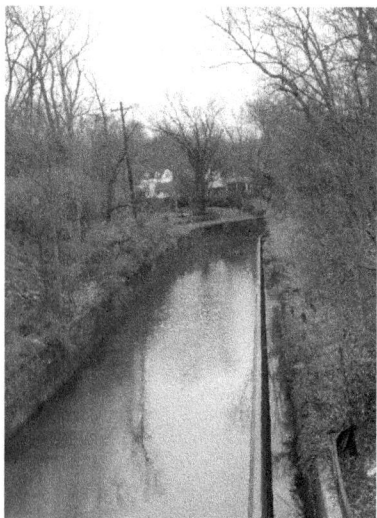

South Fork of Beargrass Creek

The shared use lane markings continue on Ellison Avenue as the road passes the northern edge of St. Michael's Cemetery on the right side of the road. The cemetery, opened in 1851, was one of the first German Catholic cemeteries in the area. There are over 40,000 burials in the 48-acre cemetery.

Continuing east, the road passes over the South Fork of Beargrass Creek. On both sides of the bridge, the creek flows northward through the neighborhood within a concrete-encased channel. The concrete walls were added in the 1920s to alleviate flooding problems and sewage overflows that were a consequence of the increase in population. A true urban stream, the South Fork is still plagued by sewage overflows and point source pollution, and is heavily monitored by the Metropolitan Sewer District (MSD). Contact with the stream's water is highly discouraged, especially after heavy rains.

The bridge, built in 1914, bears a plaque with an inscription that bears the name of Mayor John Henry Buschemeyer. He was the last of Louisville's mayors elected under John Henry Whallen's Democratic political machine. The term "political machine" originates from the large top-down political party organizations that controlled the local governments of many large U.S. cities during the late 19th and early 20th centuries. The most notable of these was New York's Tammany Hall. The party boss held most of the power and commanded the allegiance of most of the city's elected officials, public servants, and business leaders. During this time, most cities under this system experienced widespread government corruption and inefficiency while struggling with large population increases.

Buschemeyer was elected mayor in 1913 behind Whallen's powerful political machine. He is best known for signing a 1914 ordinance mandating racial segregation among the city's neighborhoods. The NAACP quickly challenged the ordinance, which effectively barred black residents from residing in majority white neighborhoods. Soon

Inscription on Bridge over Beargrass Creek

afterward, a property transfer dispute between a black property buyer and a white seller precipitated a Supreme Court case. The court's 1917 decision in the case of Buchanan v. Warley essentially overturned the city's ordinance on the grounds that it violated the fourteenth amendment to the U.S. Constitution. Native son Louis Brandeis was one of the justices involved in the Buchanan decision.

Buschemeyer was defeated in the 1917 election by Republican John Weissinger Smith, who ran on an anti-corruption campaign. Although Whallen's death in 1913 had significantly weakened the political machine in Louisville, Smith's victory effectively ended this infamous era of Louisville politics.

5.2 Left onto Barret Avenue

The traffic volume picks up slightly on Barret Avenue, so it may require patience and caution to make the turn. The speed limit is only 35 mph, but many cars travel faster than this because Barret Avenue is a major thoroughfare between Germantown and the Highlands.

Barret Avenue traces the easternmost edge of Germantown along its border with the Highlands as the road passes north of Oak Street. Although traffic increases slightly here, most of the drivers are used to sharing the road with bicycles here and are generally courteous. The next turn on the route is roughly a half-mile north, onto E Breckenridge Street. The turn is marked by an old church on the corner.

5.8 Left onto E Breckinridge Street

Breckenridge Street is one-way, heading west. A protected bike lane appears here, so it is best to use this lane whenever possible. There is a buffer zone on both sides of the lane that helps to protect cyclists from traffic and from car doors opening suddenly in the parking lane along the left side of the road.

6.4 Left onto S Shelby Street

Shelby Street leads back through the eastern edge of the Smoketown and Shelby Park neighborhoods. The next turn on the route, onto Oak Street, is marked by the enormous Sojourn Community Church, which now occupies the former St. Vincent de Paul Church. Built in 1884, the church is a Shelby Park neighborhood landmark.

6.8 Left onto E Oak Street

Past the intersection of Oak and Logan Streets, the route re-enters Germantown. There are several small shops and bars that mark the next turn on the route, onto Swan Street.

7.1 Right onto Swan Street

Jim King Memorial Rain Garden

One block beyond the turn, Swan Street ends as the road curves sharply to the left and becomes Ellison Avenue. Directly ahead is the Jim King Memorial Rain Garden, a small patch of wetland plants wedged between Swan Street, Ellison Avenue, and Dandridge Avenue. Created by MSD in response to the frequent combined sewage overflows that occur during heavy rains in Germantown, the rain garden helps filter pollutants from surface water runoff after rain events. In turn, this eases the demand on the city's water treatment plants and helps reduce the amount of pollution that enters waterways. There are several such rain gardens throughout the city, including one at the corner of 7th and Cedar Streets near MSD's downtown headquarters.

7.1 Continue onto Ellison Avenue

A shared use lane appears on Ellison Avenue as it crests a small hill and leads back into the heart of Germantown. The road is lined with well-kept shotgun houses, typical of the Germantown neighborhood. Ellison Avenue then leads downhill to a stop sign at the same awkward five-way intersection that was encountered earlier in the route. In this case, the route continues onto Spratt Street, to the right.

On the left side of the road near the stop sign is Gnadinger Park. At a mere 0.1 acres, it is by far the smallest of Louisville's many pocket parks and green spaces. The land for the park was donated to the city by the Gnadinger family in 1976.

7.4 Right onto Spratt Street

7.6 Right onto Goss Avenue

Goss Avenue is busy, particularly around the morning and evening commutes. Fortunately, most drivers in Germantown are courteous to cyclists and pedestrians, as many of them are avid cyclists as well.

7.7 Left onto Hoertz Avenue

At the corner of Hoertz and Goss Avenues is Hauck's Handy Store, a Germantown tradition since 1912. It's not only a good spot to refill a water bottle or buy snacks on a hot afternoon, it's also a must visit landmark. The store is still family-owned by George Hauck, who lives upstairs.

Hauck's is best known for its annual Dainty Contest, held on the last Monday in July. The contest has been ongoing since 1971, but the game of Dainty actually traces its roots back to the mid-19th century when German immigrants first settled the area. Among the traditions that the immigrants brought was Dainty, a children's game in which a batter hits a small pointed stick off the

Hauck's Handy Store

ground with a broomstick and then attempts to whack the little stick mid-air to propel it down the street like a baseball. There are markings on the street to measure how far the batter has hit the dainty, which are still visible most of the year.

These days, the World Famous Dainty Contest is limited to kids 45 years of age or older, but the contest includes many events for youngsters in the under-45 category as well. A large street festival surrounds the event every year and raises funds for the Little Sisters of the Poor.

8.1 Left onto E Burnett Avenue

At the corner of E Burnett Avenue and Hickory Street is Check's Café, another Schnitzelburg tradition. Check's offers a large variety of inexpensive beers and pub grub, and is a popular neighborhood destination.

8.3 Right onto Texas Avenue

The route retraces its tracks through Schnitzelburg along Texas Avenue and past DuPont Manual Memorial Stadium. The next turn on the route may be a little difficult to understand. The intersection of Texas Avenue and Delor Avenue appears to be a five-way intersection. Here, Delor Avenue forks as it continues to the left; the left fork becomes Keswick Boulevard, and the right fork continues as Delor Avenue. The route turns left at the intersection and then follows Delor Avenue down the right-hand fork.

8.5 Left onto Delor Avenue

Again, Delor Avenue forks almost immediately, becoming Keswick Boulevard on the left, and continuing as Delor Avenue to the right. The route continues to the right and follows Delor Avenue.

8.5 Right to continue onto Delor Avenue

As Delor Avenue crosses Eastern Parkway, there is no traffic light to assist. Extreme caution should be used when crossing Eastern Parkway because traffic is usually well in excess of the 35 mph speed limit.

9.0 Left onto Thruston Avenue

9.4 Left into parking lot at Thruston Avenue and Dixie Street

Dainty game markings on Hoertz Avenue

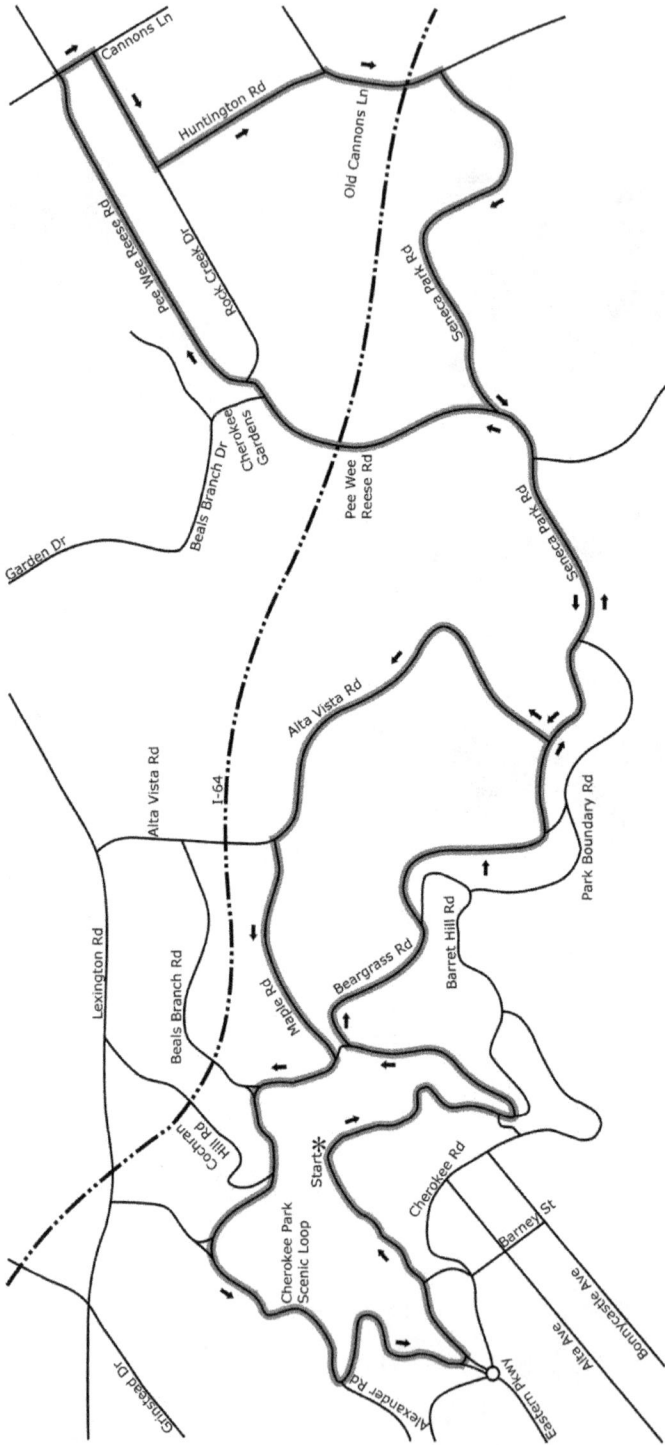

6 CHEROKEE AND SENECA PARKS

Distance: 8.2 miles

Difficulty: Moderate. A few hills; some traffic along Seneca Park and Pee Wee Reese Roads

Points of Interest: Cherokee Park; Hogan's Fountain; Seneca Park; Louisville Seminary

Cherokee and Seneca Parks, located between the Highlands and many of Louisville's east end neighborhoods, are considered by many to be the crown jewels of the city's Olmstead Park system. The two parks sprawl across more than 900 acres on Louisville's east side and are connected by the Middle Fork of Beargrass Creek. Cherokee Park opened in 1891, touching off a population boom nearby that is largely credited for spurring the development of the city's east end. The park is extremely popular, listed as the 69th most visited public park in the United States.

Louisville's Olmstead Parks System was first proposed in 1887 to create much needed recreational space for the city's residents. The plan called for the development of three parks at the city's western, eastern, and southern ends connected by a system of parkways. Cherokee Park was the first of the three to be developed, opening in 1891. The land chosen for the park was located in a hilly area along the Middle Fork of Beargrass Creek that was visually beautiful but generally unsuitable for farming.

Despite its popularity, Cherokee Park has been involved in several controversies over the years. The first of these controversies arose during the late 1960s when the construction of Interstate 64 called for the roadway to run through the park's northern portion. An outcry by a large number of conservation groups eventually forced a compromise in which two tunnels were constructed to pass the highway underneath Cochran Hill.

Crime in Cherokee Park has also been a source of controversy, as the area has been plagued by crime at various times throughout its history. Most of the early problems were just minor cases of vandalism, but by the 1970s the park experienced major problems with gangs of teenagers and youths gathering around Hogan's Fountain to buy and sell drugs or engage in sexual activity. A major police crackdown on crime in the park, along with a redesign of portions of the park, was necessary to finally rid the park of its crime problems. And even though crime in the park has plummeted since the 1970s, an occasional major crime still occurs here, such as the 2014 murder of a 12-year-old child by a homeless man. Despite the occasional headline-grabbing crime, however, the park is very safe.

Cherokee Park

Cherokee Park was severely damaged by a large tornado on April 3, 1974. The tornado damaged the popular Hogan's Fountain Pavilion and destroyed thousands of mature trees. After the disaster, the Olmstead Parks Conservancy initiated a major replanting program in an effort to restore the park to its original appearance, aided by disaster funds granted by the federal government. Signs of this and of other efforts to restore natural habitats within the park are evident around many of the dozens of trails that lead through the park.

Seneca Park is located adjacent to Cherokee Park and was the last of the five Olmstead Parks to be developed, opening to the public in 1928. The park occupies a 330-acre tract of land that was originally part of an estate inherited by a German army officer and later sold to the Louisville Parks Commission. It boasts an 18-hole golf course, hiking trails, recreational and sports fields, and other amenities. The park's great lawn, located between Interstate 64 and Cannons Lane, is a very popular recreational space and often serves as a rendezvous point for cycling groups in the area.

This tour begins in Cherokee Park at a small parking lot adjacent to the Hogan's Fountain Pavilion where parking is usually available. On days when the park is extremely busy the parking lot may be full, but there is usually parking available along Cherokee Park Scenic Loop, the road circling the main portion of the park. The route's mileage begins at the far end of the Hogan's Fountain parking lot.

Route Directions – Cherokee and Seneca Parks

0.0 Right onto Cherokee Park Scenic Loop
0.6 Right onto Beargrass Road
1.3 Left to continue onto Beargrass Road
1.6 Left onto Seneca Park Road
2.0 Continue onto Pee Wee Reese Road
3.1 Right onto Cannons Lane
3.2 Right onto Rock Creek Drive
3.4 Left onto Huntington Road
3.8 Right onto Old Cannons Lane
4.0 Right onto Seneca Park Road
4.7 Left onto Pee Wee Reese Road
4.8 Continue onto Seneca Park Road
5.1 Right onto Beargrass Road
5.3 Right onto Alta Vista Road
6.1 Left onto Maple Road
6.5 Right onto Cherokee Park Scenic Loop
7.0 Left to continue onto Cherokee Park Scenic Loop
8.2 Right into parking lot

Route Description – Cherokee and Seneca Parks

0.0 Right onto Cherokee Park Scenic Loop

From the parking lot at the top of the hill beyond Hogan's Fountain, Cherokee Park Scenic Loop continues to the right. The road is one-way with a recreational lane on the left side of the road that is separated from the lane

of traffic by a solid yellow line. Signs throughout the park indicate that the recreational lane is for pedestrians and cyclists and that the lane of traffic is for cars and bicycles. It is up to you to decide which lane is appropriate. Generally, traffic through Cherokee Park is well behaved, so at most times of the day it is best to use the traffic lane to avoid the many pedestrians walking or running through

Scenic Loop in Cherokee Park

the park. This is especially true on weekends when the park is extremely busy. At times when the park is not so busy, it is also fine to ride in the recreational lane. However, it will be necessary to move back into the traffic lane in a few locations when making turns out of the park.

The road very soon begins to descend a rather large hill. During the descent, the road curves sharply to the left, and then to the right, making it necessary to gently feather the brakes down the hill. At the bottom of the hill, there is an exit that leads out of the park onto Cherokee Road. Beyond the exit, Cherokee Park Scenic Loop curves very sharply to the left as the exit onto Barrett Hill Road appears on the right, making it necessary to brake sharply in some cases. The route continues to follow the Scenic Loop around the sharp curve.

Cherokee Park Scenic Loop may seem confusing to some, but the secret to navigating the park is to always turn left when confronted with a fork in the road in order to continue circling the park. Turning to the right always leads to an exit.

Past the sharp curve, the road continues slightly downhill through the park for 0.5 miles before coming to a stop sign at an intersection with Beargrass Road. The route continues to the right onto Beargrass Road.

0.6 Right onto Beargrass Road

Beargrass Road does not have a wide recreational lane like Cherokee Park Scenic Loop, but there is a widened shoulder most of the way that is often used by pedestrians and cyclists that wish to stay out of the lane of traffic. Cyclists are not required to use the shoulder, and it is usually best to remain within the lane of travel to prevent motorists from passing in an unsafe

Historic bridge over Beargrass Creek

manner. The road is mostly flat at first and follows the Middle Fork of Beargrass Creek most of the way. Barrett Hill Road appears again on the right, and then the road continues next to the creek until it forms a fork. Beargrass Road continues on the left side of the fork, away from the historic bridge straight ahead.

1.3 Left to continue onto Beargrass Road

After the left turn, the road continues alongside Beargrass Creek. East of Alta Vista Road, Beargrass Road begins to climb a small hill that rises about 40 feet in elevation. Fortunately, the road here is not steep, but the wide shoulder momentarily disappears. There are some good views of Beargrass Creek from the top of the hill, but it is advised to pay close

Beargrass Creek

attention to traffic. After cresting the hill, the road descends the hill before ending at its intersection with Park Boundary and Seneca Park Roads.

1.6 Left onto Seneca Park Road

Seneca Park Road leads between Cherokee and Seneca Parks. The widened shoulder reappears here, and the road passes a few well-maintained homes before coming to a three-way stop next to the Seneca Park Golf Course. Due to occasional heavy traffic, it is best to fully occupy the lane of travel before reaching the intersection to increase visibility and to prevent vehicles from turning right in front of you. Beyond the stop sign, Seneca Park Road becomes Pee Wee Reese Road.

2.0 Continue onto Pee Wee Reese Road

Great Lawn in Seneca Park

The volume and speed of traffic increase on Pee Wee Reese Road. Many drivers use it as a shortcut between Cannons Lane and Taylorsville Road and are frequently speeding and/or not paying attention to traffic. There are also many pedestrians in this area, so cyclists should ride fully within the lane of traffic, as far to the right as possible while allowing plenty of room to pass pedestrians safely.

The road begins to rise in elevation beyond the golf course, rising about 75 feet in elevation as the road crosses over Interstate 64. The road curves to the right, then to the left, and then parallels a pedestrian loop around a lawn with tennis courts and soccer fields. Seneca Park's great lawn is a very popular recreational space, and there will be many cars parked along the road on both sides here. It will probably be necessary to move fully into the lane of traffic in order to avoid car doors opening suddenly. This portion of the park is a popular meeting place for many cycling groups who use it as a rendezvous point, so it is not unusual to see other cyclists in this area.

Pee Wee Reese Road ends at Cannons Lane at a four-way stop. It may be tempting to hop onto the pedestrian trail around the loop to avoid Cannons Lane, but the traffic is not usually heavy here, and there are usually far too many pedestrians on the narrow trail for bicycles to easily cut through it.

3.1 Right onto Cannons Lane

The route continues to circle the lawn at Seneca Park, turning right onto Rock Creek Drive about 150 feet to the east.

3.2 Right onto Rock Creek Drive

Rock Creek Drive continues alongside the great lawn of Seneca Park. The road ends at Pee Wee Reese Road, but the route leaves the park before the end of the road to head southeast on Huntington Road.

3.4 Left onto Huntington Road

Huntington Road leaves Seneca Park and enters the neighborhood to the southeast. The road is a little rough through this area, but there is little traffic to contend with. The road begins to head downhill and soon ends at an awkward intersection with Old Cannons Lane.

3.8 Right onto Old Cannons Lane

It may not seem immediately evident which of the roads at the intersection is Old Cannons Lane, as there are two roads that seemingly branch off to the right. The road on the immediate right simply makes a triangle with Old Cannons Lane and provides access to a few additional residential streets. Proceeding what seems like straight through the intersection will lead onto Old Cannons Lane, which soon veers off to the right toward Interstate 64. If you're confused, simply follow the shared use lane markings on Old Cannons Lane.

The road heads down a hill and passes underneath Interstate 64 and then over Beargrass Creek. The next turn on the route follows shortly after crossing the creek and can be easy to miss.

4.0 Right onto Seneca Park Road

Seneca Park Road leads through a residential area and then re-enters Seneca Park near the golf course.

4.7 Left onto Pee Wee Reese Road

4.8 Continue onto Seneca Park Road

Seneca Park Road ends at its intersection with Beargrass and Park Boundary Roads. The route follows the bike route sign pointing to the right that leads back onto Beargrass Road.

5.1 Right onto Beargrass Road

5.3 Right onto Alta Vista Road

Alta Vista Road branches off to the right from Beargrass Road and ascends the hill on the park's northern edge. It continues through a residential area and then passes the Louisville Seminary on the left near the 5.7-mile mark of the route. The facility, previously known as the Louisville Presbyterian Theological Seminary, was built in 1963. The seminary moved to this location when the construction of Interstate 65 threatened the seminary's previous location at the corner of 1st Street and Broadway. The beautiful Gothic-style building that once housed the seminary is currently owned by Jefferson Community and Technical College.

Louisville Seminary on Alta Vista Road

The upcoming turn onto Maple Road is easy to miss if you're not paying close attention. The sign marking the street is on the right side of the road, across the street from the intersection.

6.1 Left onto Maple Road

Maple Road is a narrow, tree-lined road that is barely wide enough for two normal-sized vehicles to pass each other. Fortunately, there is plenty of room for both a car and a bicycle, and there is seldom much traffic on this street. The rough pavement on this street makes it unwise to build up too much speed for the descent back into Cherokee Park. Maple Road ends at the bottom of the hill on Cherokee Park Scenic Loop.

6.5 Right onto Cherokee Park Scenic Loop

From the end of Maple Road, the scenic loop continues through a flat area of Cherokee Park where there are several recreational fields for the next half mile. The recreational lane on the left is available for cyclists, but using the main traffic lane is preferable when there are many pedestrians using the recreational lane.

The road appears to fork as it approaches a large hill. Keeping with the rules of the park, Cherokee Park Scenic Loop continues to the left, toward the hill. The road branching off to the right exits to Lexington Road.

7.0 Left to continue onto Cherokee Park Scenic Loop

The road begins to rise in elevation again for the next half mile. Fortunately, the hill is not extremely steep. If there is a significant amount of vehicle traffic through the park, it is a good idea to move over into the recreational lane if there are not too many pedestrians using it. Near the top of the hill, the road curves very sharply to the left as Alexander Road branches off to the right seemingly straight ahead.

After the road curves back around to the right, the recreational lane diverges from the roadway to circle around a picnic shelter at the top of Baringer Hill. Although Baringer Hill is its official name, it is usually referred to as "Dog Hill" due to the many dog owners who let their pets run off-leash up and down the hill in violation of park policy and the city's leash law. It is strongly

Baringer Hill

recommended that bicyclists remain in the main traffic lane and bypass Dog Hill, especially when the park is busy, to avoid dogs running in and out of the recreational lane.

South of Baringer Hill the road descends and makes a hairpin turn at the park's entrance from Eastern Parkway. If you're in the main travel lane, be on the lookout for vehicles entering the park.

After the road swings all the way around, it begins to climb again as it heads back toward the ride start at the parking lot near Hogan's Fountain. This hill is fairly steep in a couple of places, particularly near the top of the hill. The road flattens as it crests the hill, with Hogan's Fountain on the left side. The fountain, commissioned by W. J. Hogan and sculpted by famed Louisville sculptor Enid Yandell, was installed here in 1905 and is a popular landmark within the park. It originally served as a drinking fountain for dogs and horses.

On the right and across from the fountain is the Hogan's Fountain Pavilion, commonly known as the "teepee" or "witch's hat" by locals. The pavilion was built in 1965 but sustained considerable damage in a 1974 tornado. By 2010, the structure had seriously deteriorated, and the Parks Department and the Olmstead Conservancy drafted plans to eventually remove the structure. After a massive outcry, the plans were scrapped, and money was raised to rehabilitate it.

8.2 Right into parking lot

The "witch's hat" at Hogan's Fountain Pavilion

Hogan's Fountain in Cherokee Park

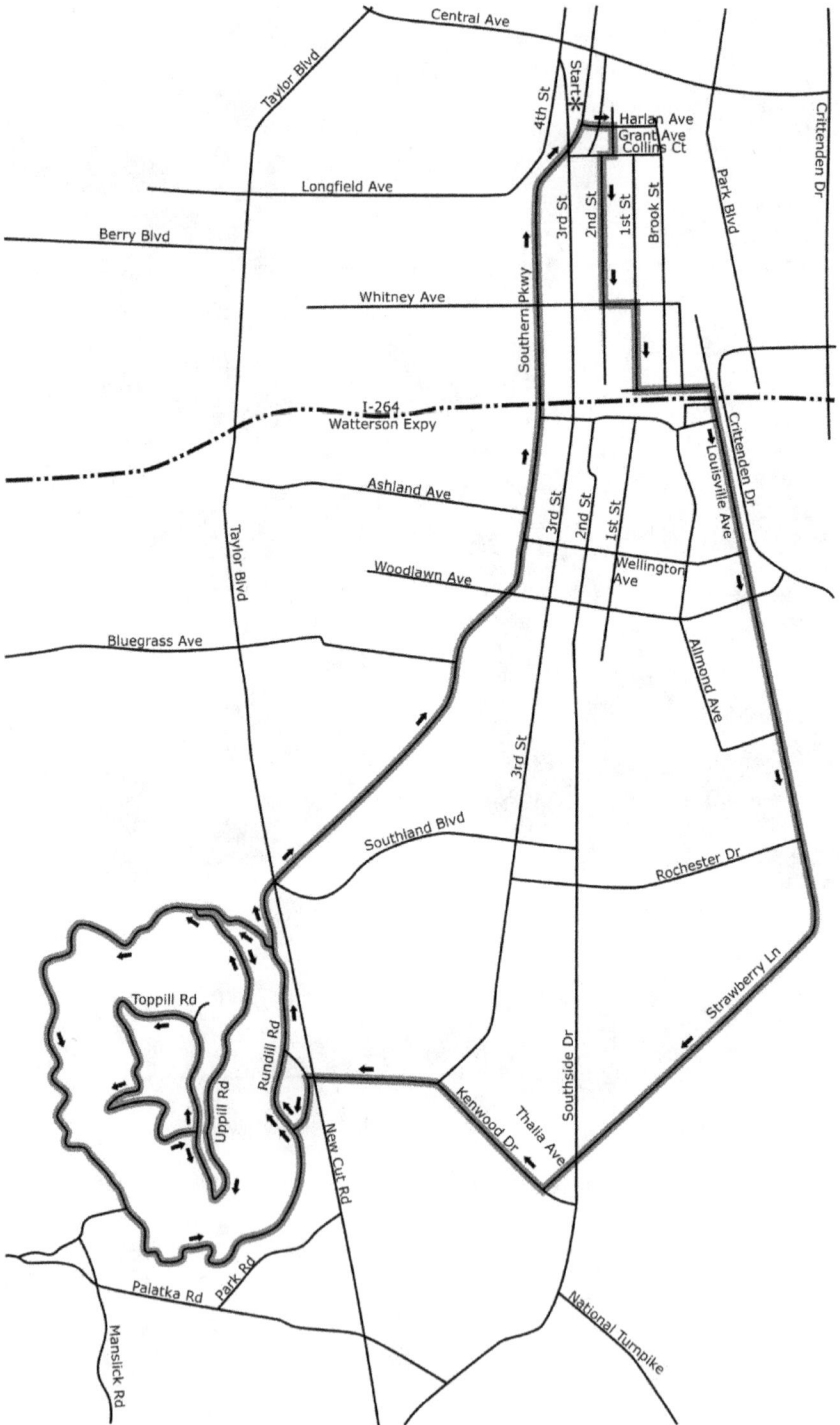

Central Ave

Taylor Blvd

4th St

Start

Harlan Ave
Grant Ave
Collins Ct

Crittenden Dr

Park Blvd

Longfield Ave

3rd St

2nd St

1st St

Brook St

Berry Blvd

Southern Pkwy

Whitney Ave

I-264
Watterson Expy

Ashland Ave

3rd St

2nd St

1st St

Crittenden Dr

Louisville Ave

Taylor Blvd

Woodlawn Ave

Wellington Ave

Bluegrass Ave

Allmond Ave

3rd St

Southland Blvd

Rochester Dr

Toppill Rd

Rundill Rd

Strawberry Ln

Uppill Rd

New Cut Rd

Kenwood Dr

Thalia Ave

Southside Dr

Palatka Rd

Park Rd

National Turnpike

Manslick Rd

7 SOUTHERN LOUISVILLE

Distance: 15.0 miles

Difficulty: Moderate. Light traffic in most areas, with moderate traffic at times on Southern Parkway. Mostly flat with a few large hills within Iroquois Park.

Points of Interest: A. D. Ruff Memorial Wheelmen's Bench, World War II veterans' memorial, Wilder Park neighborhood, former site of Highland Park neighborhood, Beechmont neighborhood, Kenwood Hill neighborhood, Little Loom House, Iroquois Gardens, Iroquois Park

The neighborhoods south of Eastern Parkway are generally regarded as Louisville's south end. These neighborhoods are mostly centered around Southern Parkway, which runs from 3rd Street near Churchill Downs to the entrance of Iroquois Park, which is located at the intersection of Southern Parkway with New Cut Road and Taylor Boulevard. Although Louisville's southern neighborhoods have traditionally been off the beaten path, the new South Points Scenic Area project has been very successful in drawing visitors to the area and highlighting the many points of interest that it has to offer.

Iroquois Park, located in Louisville's south end, was one of the three original Olmstead Parks built along the outskirts of Louisville in the early 1890s. The park can be seen from quite a distance away, highlighted by a large knob rising from the landscape, and is considered by many to be the true jewel of Louisville's Olmstead Park system. The land for the park was acquired in 1889 when Mayor Charles Jacob purchased a large parcel of land at the southern edge of the city with the vision of creating a public park at the location. Jacob also purchased the right-of-way for what would eventually become Southern Parkway, leading from the city's southern edge to the new park. In 1891, Frederick Law Olmstead signed a contract with the city to develop its park system. Jacob's new park, renamed as Iroquois Park, was included in this contract. Construction on the park was completed in 1897.

During the Great Depression, the Works Progress Administration made many improvements to the park. One such improvement was the construction of a large amphitheater near the park's northern entrance. Ground was broken in April 1938, and the open-air facility opened later that year with a production of *Naughty Marietta*. Over the years, many patchwork repairs were done to preserve the facility, but by the early 2000s the facility was showing its age. In 2003, Iroquois Amphitheater received an $8.9 million upgrade that both preserved much of the facility's original structures and gave it some much-needed modern upgrades. Today, the facility attracts many prominent musicians and hosts many movies, plays, and other events.

Iroquois Park has many modern amenities, including a disk golf course, hiking and running trails, an archery range, a spray park, a riding stable, and a golf course. However, the major attraction of Iroquois Park is the panoramic view of the city of Louisville from the large knob in the center of the park. When the land for the park was purchased in 1889, the large hill in the center of the parcel was known as Burnt Knob due to the natives' practice of burning the forest and savannah at the top of the knob to create an open area for hunting. Parts of the knob's summit have been maintained in that state, and there are trails through the park that traverse the open field there as well as many other diverse habitats that exist along the slopes of the knob.

This tour also explores portions of Wilder Park and Beechmont, two of Louisville's south end neighborhoods. Wilder Park, where the tour begins, was first developed as the Greenland Racetrack in 1866. Greenland closed in 1888 and became a park, but was soon targeted for development. Between 1891 and 1901, many homes were built in the new neighborhood named for Mrs. Wilder Collins. Streetcar lines soon connected the neighborhood to Iroquois Park and to the many factories that had set up shop in south Louisville. Most of Wilder Park's residents were attracted here due to its proximity to the Nashville and Louisville Railroad Company's rail yard, which was once located just east of the neighborhood. Although the rail yard is long gone, remnants of it can still be seen over a fence to the east of Brook Street, and trains still ply these tracks constantly. In 1904, Wilder Park was incorporated into the city of Oakdale, located on the west side of Southern Parkway. Oakdale was annexed by the city of Louisville in 1922, and Wilder Park became one of Louisville's many neighborhoods.

Beechmont was originally developed as a neighborhood of the city of Highland Park in the 1890s. The neighborhood's name originated from the many beech trees that stood on the swampy patch of land that the neighborhood was developed from. The large stately homes intermixed with well-kept cottages were originally intended to serve as summer homes for the city's wealthier residents. By 1900, a streetcar line was extended to Beechmont from 4th Street, and the neighborhood soon became a very desirable area to live in due to its proximity to Iroquois Park. It quickly attracted an eclectic mix of writers, artists, and aristocrats, and was soon annexed by the city of Louisville.

Beginning in the late 1940s, smaller, less expensive homes were added to the neighborhood to accommodate the many soldiers returning home and the residents who were affected by the 1937 flood. Adjacent south end neighborhoods were also added to Beechmont between the 1940s and 1960s, changing the feel of the area dramatically. Long-time residents were upset at the changes and voted with their feet, fleeing to the rapidly developing eastern suburbs. Following the exodus, some of the area's large stately homes were demolished and redeveloped into smaller homes, and others were subdivided into apartments. By 1960, a population decline was particularly evident, with many vacant homes and rapidly falling property values. But after more than a half century of decline, Beechmont and Wilder Park are experiencing an urban renewal. In recent years, the two neighborhoods have become highly desirable places to live due to their proximity to the University of Louisville, Interstates 264 and 65, and downtown Louisville. Although Beechmont today is still primarily a working class neighborhood, many pockets of the neighborhood's former grandeur still remain intact today,

Churchill Downs

particularly along Southern Parkway. With the explosive growth occurring in the Highlands area just east of downtown, Beechmont has begun to reacquire some of its earlier character, attracting many artists, writers, and performers fleeing soaring rents and congestion.

Less than one-half mile north of the ride's start and within view of Wayside Park during the winter months is world-famous Churchill Downs, one of Louisville's most iconic landmarks. Churchill Downs is located at the junction of Louisville's south end and the Algonquin neighborhood located west of Taylor Boulevard. The track's enormous video display and famed twin spires are easily visible from a long distance away. Churchill Downs was founded in 1875 by Colonel Meriwether Lewis Clark Jr., the grandson of explorer William Clark, who leased an 80-acre tract of land south of Louisville from his uncles John and Henry Churchill. The new track was located close to the Louisville and Nashville Railroad, facilitating easy transport of horses to and from the track. The Kentucky Derby and the Kentucky Oaks races were run for the first time during the track's opening season and were fashioned after the racing events Clark had watched in England. Opening day at Churchill Downs on May 17, 1875 attracted a crowd of more than 10,000 spectators who watched Aristides win the inaugural Kentucky Derby. The tradition continues today on the first Saturday in May as crowds of more than 170,000 spectators crowd the Downs each year to watch horse racing's premier event. The city of Louisville celebrates the Derby every year with its Kentucky Derby Festival, which runs for two weeks prior to the race.

In 1893, the track was sold to William Applegate, who shortened the Kentucky Derby to its current 1 1/4 mile distance and built the facility's grandstand and trademark twin spires. Since this time, the facility has undergone numerous additions and renovations, and the Kentucky Derby itself has become a world-class event. In 1985, the Kentucky Derby Museum was opened on the grounds of Churchill Downs; the museum is easily visible from the track's north side along Central Avenue and is open to visitors year-round. Between 2001 and 2005 the clubhouse was replaced and many luxury suites were added as part of a major renovation. In 2014, a 90-foot high-definition display board, known as the "Big Board," was added along the track's back stretch. It is currently believed to be the world's largest ultra high-definition display.

Churchill Downs hosts three racing meets per year: a spring meet, beginning one week prior to the Kentucky Derby and lasting through early July; a fall meet, beginning in late October and running until Thanksgiving weekend; and a September meet, which was added in 2013. Going to the races at Churchill Downs is a must-do for any Louisville resident or visitor, particularly during the spring racing season when the weather is almost always pleasant and inviting.

The tour begins and ends at Wayside Park, which is located at the intersection of South 3rd Street, Southern Parkway, and Oakdale Avenue. Wayside Park is home to the Ruff Memorial Wheelmen's Bench, a local landmark that was erected in 1898 in memory of cycling legend Alexander D. "Pap" Ruff, a well-known Kentucky cyclist who rode all the way from his home in Owingsville to Yellowstone Park in 1893. Ruff died in 1896, leaving a large amount of money to the Kentucky Division of the League of American Wheelmen. The club commissioned famed Louisville sculptor Enid Yandell to erect this stone bench and fountain in Ruff's honor. Known to local cyclists as "Wheelmen's Bench," it is a frequent meeting place for cyclists organizing rides in the area. From here the tour winds through Wilder Park, passes under Interstate 264/Watterson Expressway, and then continues along the edge of an industrial area on the eastern border of the Beechmont neighborhood. Parking is available on S 3rd Street or on one of the many side streets of the adjacent Wilder Park neighborhood. The mileage for the ride begins at the intersection of S 3rd Street and Harlan Avenue.

Wilder Park neighborhood

Route Directions – Southern Louisville

0.0 Left onto Harlan Avenue
0.1 Right onto Grant Avenue
0.2 Right onto W Collins Court
0.2 Left onto S 2nd Street
0.7 Left onto W Whitney Avenue
0.8 Right onto S 1st Street
1.0 Left onto E Adair Street
1.2 Right onto Louisville Avenue
1.8 Continue onto Strawberry Lane
3.8 Continue onto Thalia Avenue
4.0 Right onto E Kenwood Drive
4.7 Continue onto Knoll Gate Road
4.8 Right to stay on Knoll Gate Road
5.0 Right onto Rundill Road
5.3 Left onto Rundill Road
5.6 Left onto Uppill Road
6.8 Continue onto Toppill Road
7.1 Left to continue onto Toppill Road
8.1 Right onto Uppill Road
9.3 Left onto Rundill Road
12.3 Continue onto Iroquois Park Road
12.5 Continue onto Southern Parkway
14.9 Continue onto S 3rd Street
15.0 End at Wayside Park

Route Description – Southern Louisville

0.0 Left onto Harlan Avenue

The tour begins in the southbound lanes of 3rd Street at Wayside Park, one of Louisville's many pocket green spaces located at the intersection of Southern Parkway, South 3rd Street, and Oakdale Avenue. The A. D. Ruff Memorial Wheelmen's Bench at the park's center is frequently used as a launching point for many group rides, and it is not unusual to see other cyclists here. Viewed from above, the bench actually resembles the wheel of a bicycle.

A.D. Ruff Memorial Wheelmen's Bench in Wayside Park

Third Street heads south from this location and branches off slightly to the left at the intersection at the park's southernmost point. Straight ahead, the road continues as Southern Parkway. A few dozen feet north of this intersection and directly across from Wheelmen's Bench, Harlan Avenue branches off to the left. The route continues down Harlan Avenue for two blocks before turning right onto Grant Avenue.

0.1 Right onto Grant Avenue

Grant Avenue ends at W Collins Court. To the right, W Collins Court intersects S 3rd Street at a very busy intersection near the intersection of S 3rd Street with Southern Parkway. Many of this neighborhood's residents use Collins Court to access the main artery, so there are occasionally cars that may come down Collins Court at high speeds. There are also many residents' cars parked along the road, obstructing motorists' lines of sight. It is highly advised for cyclists to use caution in this area.

0.2 Right onto W Collins Court

After a very short distance on W Collins Court, 2nd Street again branches off to the left.

0.2 Left onto S 2nd Street

World War II Veterans Memorial on 2nd St.

The street soon becomes a divided boulevard with a shaded grassy median. At the northernmost (nearest) end of the median there is a small memorial dedicated to the veterans of World War II. About half a mile later, the street appears to end at Interstate 264/Watterson Expressway. It actually continues on the other side of the expressway, but because of this obstacle, it will be necessary to travel down side streets to get under the expressway.

0.7 Left onto W Whitney Avenue

0.8 Right onto S 1st Street

1.0 Left onto E Adair Street

E Adair Street runs parallel to the expressway but ends before intersecting with 2nd Street, so there is no through traffic on Adair Street to contend with. However, cyclists should be on the lookout for cars running the stop signs at the end of Brook Street and Allmond Avenue, as motorists in this area are not accustomed to dealing with bicycles or other traffic on Adair Street.

Adair Street parallels the westbound lanes of the Watterson Expressway, and in a few places it seems that all there is to separate Adair Street from the busy freeway is a curb and a chain link fence. To the east, the elevated roadway of the Watterson Expressway provides a natural barrier from the fast, noisy traffic it carries and also provides some much-appreciated shade during the hot summer months. During the winter, however, the elevated roadway creates a near permanent shadow that causes any standing water in the roadway to freeze solid.

Adair Street ends at its intersection with Louisville Avenue. Cyclists should be wary of northbound traffic on Louisville Avenue, which has a limited line of sight as it emerges from the underpass.

1.2 Right onto Louisville Avenue

Louisville Avenue begins two blocks north of the intersection, runs under the expressway, and then heads south into a light industrial area at the edge of the Beechmont neighborhood. Immediately after Louisville Avenue emerges from underneath Interstate 264/Watterson Expressway, Allmond Avenue resumes to the right, running parallel to the expressway before curving sharply to the south. Traffic coming from Allmond Avenue has a limited line of sight around the expressway, so cyclists should be on the lookout for vehicles as they emerge from beneath the overpass.

Neglected for many years because of its somewhat inaccessible location and the demolition of most of the Highland Park neighborhood that it once served, Louisville Avenue had become an iconic sign of the area's decaying infrastructure. Pockmarked with potholes, the road was a hazard to bicycles, pedestrians, and automobiles alike. Several potholes were so large and deep that they exposed long-buried railroad and streetcar tracks below the modern roadway. In 2015, Louisville Avenue and Strawberry Lane were finally repaved after many decades of neglect, perhaps due to the actions and persistence of local cyclists.

South of I-265/Watterson Expressway, Louisville Avenue passes through an industrial area that is wedged between the eastern edge of the Beechmont neighborhood just one block to the west and a busy set of railroad tracks to the east. With the recent reconfiguration of Crittenden Drive, the many side streets that once crossed the tracks and led to the east were permanently closed, and a wall was erected on the east side of the railroad tracks.

Although this small, seemingly forgotten area is now considered an enclave of the Beechmont neighborhood, it was once a thriving part of Louisville's now-defunct Highland Park neighborhood that encompassed the area between Adair Street and Woodlawn Avenue and stretched eastward toward Crittenden Drive. The neighborhood was first developed in the 1880s, and like Wilder Park attracted many workers from the Louisville & Nashville Railroad Company's nearby facility. The name Highland Park was chosen because it was on higher ground than many of the surrounding south end neighborhoods. The neighborhood was incorporated as a city in 1890 and annexed by the city of Louisville in 1922 along with Wilder Park and Beechmont.

In contrast to the relatively peaceful Wilder Park neighborhood, Highland Park always had a seedy reputation and was well known for crime and violence. There were many bars and taverns along Louisville Avenue, including one that was fittingly named the Bloody Bucket. Throughout most of the 20th century Highland Park's many bars were well known for violence, particularly on the weekends.

Highland Park eventually fell victim to time and progress. As the

Watterson Expressway was built between 1948 and 1975, most of the traffic that once crossed this troubled neighborhood used the new expressway to avoid it altogether. This sent the neighborhood into a serious tailspin, and many of its businesses closed or moved elsewhere. The decline of the Louisville & Nashville Railroad Company in the 1970s put many people out of work, accelerating the neighborhood's decline. The impending expansion of Standiford Field and the nearby UPS facility in 1989 finally sounded the death knell for Highland Park. The remaining homes were bought out, and nearly all that remained of the neighborhood was demolished. Today, what little remains of the neighborhood can be seen on the side streets that head eastward from Louisville Avenue toward Beechmont.

As Louisville Avenue passes under the Woodland Street overpass and exits the Highland Park area, it becomes Strawberry Lane.

1.8 Continue onto Strawberry Lane

Strawberry Lane continues along the edge of an industrial area of south Louisville. Louisville Water Company has a facility near the corner of Strawberry Lane and Allmond Avenue, and a post office is located one block west on Allmond Avenue. There is a considerable amount of traffic passing through this intersection, so cyclists should remain aware of traffic in this location. During the winter months, there is frequently a strong headwind from the south in this location that may slow all but the most determined of cyclists.

Traffic increases past Allmond Avenue, and soon the road climbs a small hill. A large ramp rises to the right and leads over to another industrial area along Crittenden Drive on the other side of the railroad tracks. Large semis often turn onto Strawberry Lane from this ramp, adding to the traffic. On the other side of the hill, there is an extremely rough railroad crossing sitting at an oblique angle to the road that will make it necessary to slow down or even walk your bicycle over the tracks due to the danger of getting a narrow wheel stuck within the tracks. Beyond the railroad crossing, the road curves sharply to the right and passes through a mixed residential and industrial area before ending at Southside Drive. Across the intersection, the road becomes Thalia Avenue.

3.8 Continue onto Thalia Avenue

4.0 Right onto E Kenwood Drive

Kenwood Drive passes through the Kenwood Hill neighborhood, an upscale area that was developed in the 1960s around a hill northeast of Iroquois Park. There are many large, stately homes and tall, majestic trees here that provide welcome shade during the hot summer months.

A point of interest in the Kenwood Hill neighborhood is the Little Loom House, a historic cabin located on the hill on the south side of Kenwood Drive. At the intersection of Kenwood Drive and Kenwood Hill Drive is a historical marker that details the story of the Little Loom House and the Hill sisters, who penned the song "Happy Birthday to You." The Little Loom House is not just one house, but a collection of three small cabins that were built on Kenwood Hill in the late 19th century. The first cabin built here, Esta Cabin, was constructed by charcoal maker Beoni Figg in 1870. The home was acquired by artist Etta Hest in 1898 and refitted in the board and batten style. Hest hosted annual gatherings for artists and writers who occupied summer homes in the area. In 1939, the cabin was purchased by Lou Tate, who

Esta Cabin

ran her weaving business from the property until her death in 1979. Over the years many prominent people have visited the site, including First Lady Eleanor Roosevelt, who accidentally destroyed a floorboard during her visit.

The Little Loom House is also known as the birthplace of the song, "Happy Birthday to You." Kenwood Hill residents Patty (1868-1946) and Mildred Jane Hill (1859-1916), both prominent educators, penned the song "Good Morning to All" in 1893. On a visit to Elsa Cabin for a birthday party, it was suggested that the lyrics be changed to "Happy Birthday to You." The song's alternate lyrics were published in 1912 and quickly grew in popularity. But it was not until 1935 that the song was finally copyrighted with the new lyrics. After a number of court cases, the sisters were finally credited as the song's authors. It is considered by many to be the most-recognized song in the English language and has been translated into many other languages as well.

Kenwood Drive ends at its intersection with New Cut Road. At the corner is Colonial Gardens, a dilapidated building that is classified by the Louisville Metro Landmarks Commission as an individual local landmark. The building was constructed in 1903 by Frederick Senning and was originally known as Senning's Park. The facility hosted picnics, political rallies, and dances, and benefitted from being located near the 4th Street streetcar line that served Louisville's south end neighborhoods. In 1920, Senning opened a zoo at the facility, which operated until 1939. In 1940, the building was sold and began a new life hosting numerous restaurants, bars, nightclubs, and even a beer garden at one time. It is said that Jerry Lee Lewis and Elvis Presley performed here, but these claims have not been substantiated. The last business in Colonial Gardens closed in 2003, at which time the building was abandoned by its owners. Its fate has remained in the balance ever since, with many area residents wanting the dilapidated structure demolished to eliminate blight. Others, however, have made efforts to conserve the structure, and in 2013, the Louisville Metro Council voted 16-3 to purchase the building.

Kenwood Drive ends at its intersection with New Cut Road at a traffic light. Across the intersection, the road becomes Knoll Gate Road as it enters Iroquois Park. New Cut Road carries a large amount of very fast-moving traffic, so it is imperative for cyclists to sit in the lane with traffic and wait for the light to cross New Cut Road. Less experienced cyclists may opt to cross New Cut Road at the crosswalk and walk their bikes across the road at this intersection.

4.7 Continue onto Knoll Gate Road

4.8 Left to stay on Knoll Gate Road

Knoll Gate Road forks as it enters the park. The left fork leads to Iroquois Amphitheater and a large parking lot that is used by the many runners and walkers who use the park. The right fork passes through a smaller parking area where restrooms and a water fountain are located. The spray park behind the restrooms makes a compelling reason to stop and cool off on hot summer days. The route continues left at the fork, passing the amphitheater, and then turns right onto Rundill Road at the base of the hill.

5.0 Right onto Rundill Road

Rundill Road makes a complete 3.3-mile circuit around Iroquois Park. Traffic on Rundill Road on the eastern side of the park is one-way and usually light. Most visitors park their cars in this area and walk to the park's facilities. On the left side of the road, there is a recreational lane for pedestrians and cyclists that fully circles the park. Due to the large number of runners, walkers, and strollers in this lane, it is usually best for cyclists to stay in the lane of traffic to avoid dodging and weaving around the pedestrians. There are usually cars parked along the side of the road on this side of the park, so cyclists should watch for car doors opening suddenly.

5.3 Left onto Rundill Road

At the stop sign, the loop around the park continues to the left. The road also begins climbing steeply, making it necessary to shift into a lower gear to make it to the top. At the top of the hill, there is a 3-way stop and a small parking lot for some of the hiking trails ascending the hill. Vehicles often fail to stop at the stop sign here, so cyclists should remain alert to traffic in the area. The route turns left at the stop sign to ascend the hill.

5.6 Left onto Uppill Road

Just past the entrance to the parking lot, there is a gate that blocks vehicle access to Uppill Road. Cars are allowed on this road on Wednesdays, Saturdays, and Sundays from May through October, but it is open to pedestrians and bicycles all year. Vehicle traffic has been severely restricted on the roads at the top of the knob because the heavy traffic they invite has been causing considerable damage to the pavement. If the gate is closed, it may be necessary to stop, dismount, and walk your bicycle around the gate.

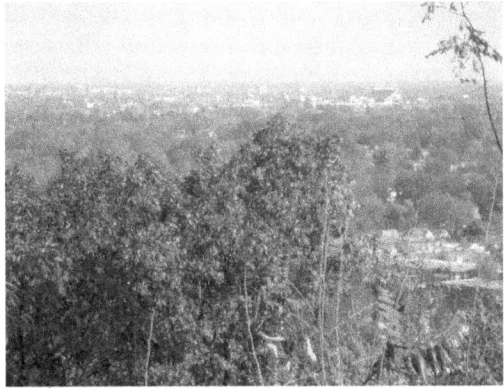

Overlook from Iroquois Park

Uppill Road climbs the knob, rising nearly 200 feet in elevation over the next mile. Although the road is not as steep as the previous hill, it is a constant climb that will be a moderately challenging workout for all but the most physically fit cyclists. If the gate is open, cyclists should be wary of vehicles descending the hill that are almost always far in excess of the 25 MPH speed limit and often veer into the other lane of traffic around the curves on the road. The heavy tree cover may make the roadway on the eastern side of the hill dark in the afternoon or early evening hours, so it is a good idea to turn on your lights or otherwise ensure that your bicycle is highly visible to motorists.

As Uppill Road nears the top of the hill, the grade increases and the road curves sharply. As you come around the curve there is an overlook that gives an excellent view of the knobs extending from southern Jefferson County through northern Bullitt County. The steep portion of the hill ends just beyond the overlook as Uppill Road becomes Toppill Road.

6.8 Continue onto Toppill Road

Iroquois Park Road continues past a small basketball court and a road branching off to the left. The road to the left is Toppill Road, which is a one-way street. Several signs prohibit traffic, including bicycles, from entering the road at this point.

The road continues to climb very slightly as it reaches the top of the knob. At the top, there is a small pavilion and a large open prairie-like area that has been maintained in this state since the park's opening. This opening was created for hunting by the natives who once inhabited the area before settlers arrived, and it is the reason that the hill was once referred to as Burnt Knob. A short gravel nature trail leads through the prairie, and many beautiful wildflowers can be seen here during the summer and fall months.

Just past the prairie-like opening, the road forks and Toppill Road branches off the left. Straight ahead, the road becomes Downill road, which crests a small hill and ends at the northern overlook. The northern overlook gives a beautiful view of the entire city of Louisville. It is an excellent place to take a quick break and enjoy the view. The overlook itself, however, has fallen into disrepair over the last few decades, and a major construction effort is now underway to restore it.

7.1 Left to continue onto Toppill Road

As Toppill Road continues along the knob's summit, it passes through a densely forested area with many majestic oak and hickory trees that provide welcome shade during the hot summer months. The road soon curves sharply to the left as it continues past a small WPA-era wall and passes the far side of the meadow. The road makes many twists and turns along the top of the knob, making it necessary to slow down in a few areas in order to avoid running off the side of the road. Near the end of the road, there is one more overlook bounded by a rock wall. Past the overlook, the roadway turns suddenly and climbs a very steep but short hill. The road ends back at Uppill Road near the basketball court that is located just beyond the hairpin turn near the knob's summit.

8.1 Right onto Uppill Road

Uppill Road descends back down the knob to the 3-way stop sign near Iroquois Golf Course on Rundill Road. It is very easy to gain a large amount of speed coming down the hill, but cyclists should stay aware of the road to avoid a few potholes and the numerous sharp curves on the road. If the road is closed to traffic, it will be necessary to again walk your bicycle around the metal gate at the bottom of the hill. Past the gate, Uppill road ends at a three-way stop sign with Rundill Road. The route continues left at the intersection to finish circling the park.

9.3 Left onto Rundill Road

Rundill Road continues to circle the park at the base of Burnt Knob, beginning with a swift descent past Iroquois Golf Course. The road climbs and descends a few small hills, and there are several sharp curves along the way. The speed limit along most of the road is 25 mph due to the curves in the road, but it is common for speeding vehicles traveling through the park to veer into the oncoming lane, so cyclists should remain alert to any traffic in the area. There is a stable along the right side of the road and an archery range on the left. Just past the archery range, a steel gate blocks traffic from continuing on Rundill Road, forcing cars to turn right onto Sanders Gate Road and exit the park. Cyclists should use caution in this area, as vehicles often run the stop sign at the end of Sanders Gate Road when turning left onto Rundill Road. Most cyclists will opt to walk their bicycles past the gate here, but it is possible to continue riding past the gate on the far left side of the road on a small bit of pavement that goes around the gate post.

Vehicles are usually not allowed beyond the metal gate, so bicyclists, walkers, and runners may use the entire road. The street descends a small hill and curves slightly to the left before ascending a steep, winding hill that climbs about 50 feet in elevation. Thankfully, the hill is short, but it may be challenging for some cyclists. After cresting the top of the hill, the road

Rundill Road in Iroquois Park

makes a steep descent back toward the parking lot on the park's east side. There may be debris in the roadway, such as leaves and tree branches, so caution is advised here. The route continues past the parking lot and amphitheater to the next stop sign. Instead of turning left to continue circling the park as before, the route continues straight ahead onto Iroquois Park Road toward the park's main entrance at the intersection of New Cut Road and Southern Parkway.

12.3 Continue onto Iroquois Park Road

The park's entrance road descends a hill and then ends at the intersection of New Cut Road and Southern Parkway. The intersection is a 5-way intersection with Southland Boulevard beginning straight ahead and to the right, Southern Parkway straight ahead, New Cut Road to the right, and Taylor Boulevard to the left. The light has a very long cycle, and a bicycle is not heavy enough to trigger the weight sensor to change the light. Unless a car pulls up to the intersection, it may be necessary to dismount and press the pedestrian crossing button next to the crosswalk.

12.5 Continue onto Southern Parkway

Southern Parkway is a well-known bicycle route, and it is not uncommon to see other cyclists traveling up and down the road. There are four lanes, giving vehicles plenty of room to pass. However, vehicles on side streets will often dart out in front of bicycles into traffic, so cyclists should use plenty of caution when traveling on this road.

Southern Parkway was formerly known as the Grand Boulevard and first opened to traffic in 1893. It passes through a portion of the Beechmont neighborhood, and many of the neighborhood's original stately homes can be seen lining the street on both sides. Woodlawn Avenue crosses Southern Parkway at the first traffic light. To the left, there are roads leading into the heart of the Beechmont neighborhood. To the right, there are a number of shops lining the street, including Sunergos Coffee shop, a popular local hangout.

The route continues ahead on Southern Parkway. As the road passes Interstate 264/Watterson Expressway, vehicles turning onto Southern Heights Avenue or traveling west on Florence Avenue to access the expressway may suddenly turn in front of bicyclists, so extreme caution is advised in this area. It is important to maintain good visibility in this area, especially in the early morning or evening hours.

14.9 Continue onto S 3rd Street

Southern Parkway ends at its intersection with S 3rd Street. Wayside Park, where the route ends, can be seen on the other side of the street from the intersection. If desired, S 3rd Street can be used as a connector to Eastern Parkway, which connects Iroquois Park with Cherokee Park.

15.0 End at Wayside Park

Toppill Road in Iroquois Park

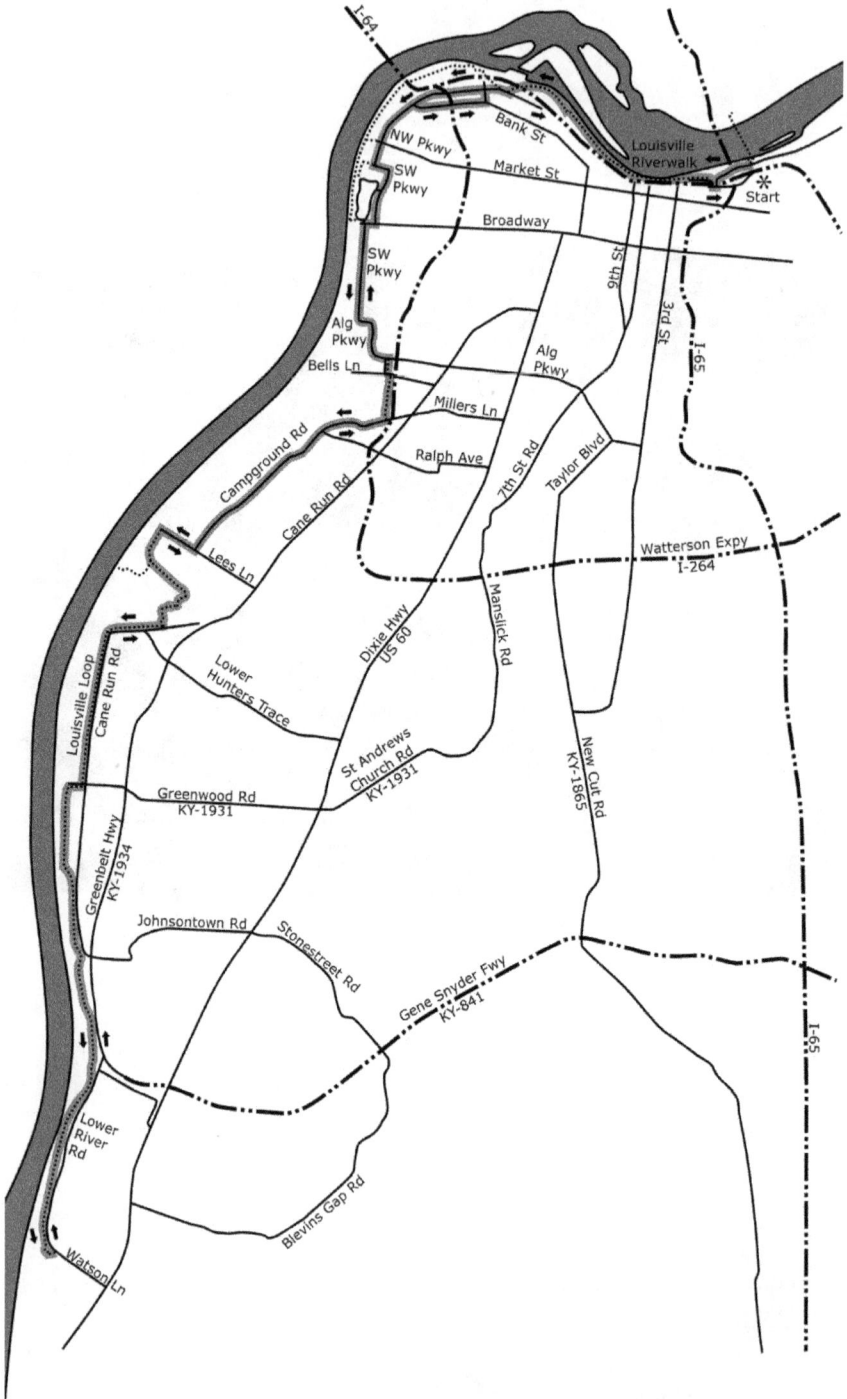

8 LOUISVILLE LOOP

Distance: 50.5 miles

Difficulty: Easy. Shorter routes are possible by utilizing other trailheads.

Highlights: Waterfront Park, Belle of Louisville and Spirit of Jefferson, Lannan Park, Portland, Shawnee Park, Chickasaw Park, Rubbertown, Lake Dreamland neighborhood, Riverside Gardens neighborhood, Cane Run Generating Station, Riverview Park, Riverside, the Farnsley-Moremen Landing

The Louisville Loop is a proposed 100-mile bicycle and pedestrian pathway that will encircle the city of Louisville and provide access from many of Louisville's neighborhoods to area attractions and recreational areas. Utilizing a combination of asphalt and concrete greenways, bicycle lanes, and shared use lanes, the Louisville Loop will provide recreational opportunities and alternative transportation options between many points within the Louisville metropolitan area. The Louisville Loop has been divided into five sections that correspond to the physiographic regions of Jefferson County: the Ohio River Valley, the Knobs, the Shale Lowlands, Floyds Fork, and the Limestone Belt. Currently, around 35% of the project has been completed, with portions of the Ohio River Valley, Floyd's Fork, and the Shale Lowlands sections of the loop currently open to pedestrian and bicycle traffic. The remaining portions of the trail are in the planning stages, with the construction of several new sections slated to begin in the near future.

The Ohio River Valley section of the loop, featured in this route, is a 24.6-mile trail that stretches from the Big Four Bridge at Waterfront Park to Watson Lane near the Mill Creek Generating Station in the Valley Station area of southwestern Jefferson County. This portion of Jefferson County is generally characterized by rich, alluvial soils and was home to many farms throughout Louisville's early history. Between the 18th and early 20th centuries, the Ohio River served as a major transportation hub across the eastern United States, and many factories sprung up along the river to take advantage of easy access to the many riverboats and barges that carried their goods to distant locations. Although its importance to the city's economy has waned, the river shipping industry still maintains a heavy presence throughout this region.

The Knobs section of the Louisville Loop encompasses much of the land south of Interstate 265/Gene Snyder Freeway between Valley Station and Interstate 65. It is a scenic area consisting of a series of large hills that rise approximately 200 to 400 feet above the surrounding river valley. They are classified as monadnocks, which are small isolated hills on a plain that are the result of erosion. The slopes consist primarily of shale and silt dating to the Mississippian and Devonian ages that are covered by a thin layer of poor soil. Despite the poor soil quality, the knobs contain many rich, diverse ecosystems. Portions of these unusual ecosystems have been preserved as Jefferson Memorial Forest, an urban forest located merely 12 miles south of downtown Louisville. The preserve contains numerous trails, streams, lakes and outdoor recreation areas, and it is often considered one of the city's hidden treasures. When the Louisville Loop is completed through the knobs, it will link the loop to some of the main hiking trails into the forest.

The Shale Lowlands section of the Louisville Loop encompasses an area just north of the Knobs that extends northward toward downtown Louisville and eastward toward Newburg and Okolona. Known as the "wet woods" to many of the pioneers who settled the area, this area of Jefferson County is a low elevation wetland with poor soils and carbon-rich mud that is prone to frequent flooding. Much of the area is drained by Pond Creek, a large creek that drains much of south central and southwestern Jefferson County into the Ohio River. As the area was developed and settled, many of the area's streams and ponds were channeled into man-made ditches to drain the swampy areas and mitigate flooding. As a result, most of the area's streams and ponds are now inhospitable to aquatic life. Current conservation efforts in the area seek to restore many of the area's wetlands and portions of Pond Creek. The inclusion of the Louisville Loop through this area constitutes a major effort at restoring and preserving what remains of this unique habitat.

Currently, a short 1.5-mile section of the Louisville Loop in the shale lowlands running from W Manslick Road westward to a point approximately 0.5 miles west of Lamborne Boulevard has been built and is open to pedestrian and bicycle traffic. The trail parallels Pond Creek and is prone to flooding after heavy rains like much of the surrounding area. The trail was not well maintained at first, but since the Metropolitan Sewer District has taken over some of the trail's maintenance, the situation has improved greatly. Once this section is joined to the other portions of the loop, traffic will increase and the trail's maintenance will undoubtedly improve.

The Floyds Fork section of the Louisville Loop traverses the Floyds Fork river valley in the far eastern portion of the county. The Floyds Fork is a 62-mile tributary of the Salt River that arises from springs in Henry County and converges with the Salt River near Shepherdsville, just south of Louisville. Elevations in the Floyds Fork valley drop from over 700 feet in elevation to a little over 400 feet, creating some very dramatic and beautiful landscapes just minutes from the city of Louisville. The sharp drop in elevation also creates many waterfalls, such as Fairmount Falls, along the river and its tributary streams and creeks.

This physiographic region is now home to the Parklands of Floyds Fork, the city's largest public park endeavor since the creation of the Olmstead Parks in the 1890s. There are five parks located along the river in this area: Beckley Creek Park, Pope Lick Park, The Strand, Turkey Run Park, and Broad Run Park. A 19-mile section of the Louisville Loop provides easy access to these parks and is featured in another tour within this guide.

The Limestone Belt region is located in northeastern Jefferson County and encompasses the cities of Middletown, Anchorage, and Prospect as it extends southward toward Fern Creek. The area is characterized by multiple layers of limestone, and the land slowly rises in elevation to the northeast. Historically, the soils in this region made it suitable for farming, and the many farms established in this area caused it to remain largely rural until the latter half of the 20th century when the city's eastern suburbs were developed. The Louisville Loop in this area is currently in the planning stages, with construction slated to begin within a few years. The cities of Middletown, Anchorage, and Prospect, which are rich in history, are featured in later routes in this guide.

This tour begins in Waterfront Park at the foot of the Big Four Bridge and explores the completed 24.6-mile section of the Louisville Loop in the Ohio River Valley section. Parking is available in any of the adjacent parking lots in Waterfront Park along E River Road. The tour follows the trail as it travels along the riverfront in the downtown area before leaving the waterfront to explore the Portland, Shawnee Park, Rubbertown, Lake Dreamland, and Riverside Gardens neighborhoods as the trail winds through the river valley toward Watson Lane in southwestern Jefferson County. The route is out-and-back, and the distance is quite long for most cyclists unless they are part of a larger group that has access to a shuttle vehicle at the end of the trail. For most riders, it is best to divide the trail into shorter sections of 10-25 miles that can be easily explored over a weekend afternoon. If a shorter route is desired, any of the following Louisville Loop trailheads can be used. For each access point, the nearest mile marker of the trail is indicated.

Big Four Bridge, mile 0
Lannan Park, mile 3
Shawnee Park northern entrance, mile 6
Shawnee Park southern entrance, mile 7
Chickasaw Park, mile 8
Riverside Gardens Park, mile 14
Riverview Park, mile 19
Riverside, the Farnsley-Moremen Landing, mile 22
Watson Lane, mile 25

Waterfront Park in downtown Louisville

Route Directions – Louisville Loop

0.0 Right onto E River Road
0.6 Right onto E Witherspoon Street
0.8 Right onto Bingham Way
1.0 Left onto Louisville Loop
4.1 Right onto Northwestern Parkway
5.9 Continue onto Southwestern Parkway
6.2 Left to continue onto Southwestern Parkway
6.5 Right to continue onto Southwestern Parkway
7.2 Right onto W Broadway
7.4 Left onto Southwestern Parkway
8.6 Continue onto Algonquin Parkway
9.4 Right onto Louisville Loop at S 41st Street
10.1 Right onto Campground Road
13.4 Right onto Lees Lane
13.9 Left onto Louisville Loop
14.3 Left to continue onto Louisville Loop
24.6 Turn around at Watson Lane
35.3 Right to continue onto Louisville Loop
35.8 Right onto Lees Lane
36.3 Left onto Campground Road
39.4 Left onto Louisville Loop
40.3 Left onto Algonquin Parkway
41.1 Continue onto Southwestern Parkway
42.3 Right onto W Broadway
42.4 Left onto Southwestern Parkway
43.1 Left to continue onto Southwestern Parkway
43.3 Right to continue onto Southwestern Parkway
43.7 Continue onto Northwestern Parkway
44.3 Right onto Bank Street
45.2 Left onto N 33rd Street
45.4 Right onto Northwestern Parkway
45.7 Left onto Louisville Loop
48.7 Right onto Bingham Way
48.8 Left onto E Witherspoon Street
49.1 Left onto E River Road
49.8 Left into Big Four Bridge parking lot

Michael W. Thompson

Route Description – Louisville Loop

0.0 Right onto E River Road

The Louisville Loop begins at the foot of the Big Four Bridge and runs east along the sidewalk on E River Road and E Witherspoon Street. Waterfront Park is extremely popular, and on virtually any day of the year there will be throngs of walkers and runners, families, and other park visitors. At most times of the day, it is far safer and easier for cyclists to ride directly on the road in this area to avoid weaving in and out of the pedestrian traffic on the Louisville Loop. There are often cars parked along the side of the road on Witherspoon Street, so cyclists should ensure that they remain far enough into the lane of traffic to avoid car doors opening suddenly.

The intersection of E River Road and E Witherspoon Street is controlled by a traffic light and is very busy on most days. Cars often run through red lights here and are not always looking for bicycles, so caution is advised in this area. Additional caution should be used when there are events going on at the stadium on the corner.

0.6 Right onto E Witherspoon Street

0.8 Right onto Bingham Way

Bingham Way leads from E Witherspoon Street to W River Road. The Louisville Loop follows the sidewalk along Bingham Way, and there is a large curb that prevents bicycles from easily hopping on and off of the Louisville Loop here. Again, it is usually best for cyclists to remain in the lane with traffic to avoid the large number of pedestrians that are usually present here.

As Bingham Way ends, it passes under Interstate 64 and becomes W River Road. The end of Bingham Way branches off to the right at the curve and terminates in a small cul-de-sac that doubles as a drop-off point for people patronizing the many restaurants and tourist attractions along the riverfront. There is a small valet station at the entrance to the cul-de-sac. Cyclists should turn right into the cul-de-sac at the end of Bingham Way and pull up directly onto the sidewalk at the end of it to follow the Louisville Loop. The trail intersects with this sidewalk as it continues along the riverfront, and there are Louisville Loop mileage markers along the sidewalk here that mark the route. Although it is generally illegal for cyclists to operate on the sidewalk in the city, it is permitted here because the sidewalk doubles as a bike route.

1.0 Left onto Louisville Loop

The Louisville Loop continues past the restaurants and through a few

162

parking lots as it continues under Interstate 64 before emerging into the light again near the site where the Belle of Louisville is docked on the Ohio River. Cyclists following the trail should look closely for signs and markings on the pavement that mark the bike route because they are not always easy to see. Cyclists should slow down here due to the heavy pedestrian traffic and the many cars backing out of parking spaces through this area.

The Belle of Louisville and the Spirit of Jefferson, which offer sightseeing excursions up and down the Ohio River, are docked next to the loop. The riverboats are popular riverfront attractions that offer lunch and dinner cruises, a cash bar, and a gift shop for those so inclined.

Belle of Louisville and Spirit of Jefferson

The Belle of Louisville was built in 1914 in Pittsburgh, PA, and was originally named the *Idlewild*. The *Idlewild* was first used as a ferry between Memphis, Tennessee and West Memphis, Arkansas, but later was used to travel the inland river system of the United States between Mexico and Canada. In 1948, the ship was renamed Avalon and sold to a group of investors in Cincinnati where the boat become the most widely traveled steamboat in history.

In 1962, the Avalon was sold and brought to Louisville and renamed as the Belle of Louisville. After a number of repairs, the Belle was raced against the Delta Queen in the first ever Great Steamboat Race on April 30, 1963. That tradition continues even today as a part of the city's Kentucky Derby Festival.

The Spirit of Jefferson was built in 1962 in Dubuque, Iowa and immediately put into service in New Orleans as the Mark Twain. From 1970 to 1995, she served as an excursion ship in St. Louis, Missouri under the name Huck Finn. In 1995, the Huck Finn was brought to Louisville and renamed the Spirit of Jefferson in honor of Thomas Jefferson and Jefferson County, Kentucky.

Past the riverboats, the Louisville Loop continues underneath Interstate 64 where the trail narrows due to the many large support pillars for the elevated roadway. Signs direct bicycle traffic to stay to the right. It will be necessary for bicyclists to slow down due to the uneven pavement and heavy pedestrian traffic in the area. The trail soon emerges from underneath the expressway and then continues along the riverfront past panoramic views of

Louisville's skyline, museum row, and other downtown attractions.

There is a fork in the trail just beyond the 2-mile mark. The right-hand fork is a spur trail that descends a small knoll and heads down toward the river bank. The spur trail is very rough and often carries heavy pedestrian traffic. The left-hand fork leads through a barren field away from the river. The pavement here is smoother and carries far less pedestrian traffic, so it is the preferred route through the area. Less than 0.3 miles to the west the two forks again converge as the trail continues west. The trail passes underneath a tall railroad bridge over the Ohio River and then continues parallel to the railroad tracks running along the river.

Trail at N 26th Street near Lannan Park

At the 3.0-mile mark the trail makes several sharp turns and crosses the railroad tracks as it climbs to the top of the levee. Atop the levee, the trail enters Lannan Park, a small pocket green space that serves the Portland neighborhood. On the other side of the park, the trail crosses N 26th Street. Traffic on N 26th Street has a limited line of sight, so caution should be observed when crossing the road.

At the 4.0-mile mark, the Louisville Loop curves southward and runs parallel to N 30th Street. The trail turns to the right and merges with the sidewalk along Montgomery Street, passes underneath a railroad trestle, and then seemingly ends as Montgomery Street curves sharply to the left and becomes Northwestern Parkway. Although the Louisville Loop originally turned to the right and entered Portland Wharf Park at this point, extensive flooding destroyed portions of the trail in 2012. The Louisville Loop currently follows a detour along a shared use lane on Northwestern Parkway to bypass the damaged trail.

4.1 Right onto Northwestern Parkway

Northwestern Parkway travels through the historic district of Portland. It is a one-lane road west of its intersection with Portland Avenue, heading west as it runs parallel to the river toward Shawnee Park. The first few blocks are not very scenic, but the road soon widens and passes through an area full of tall, majestic trees and lovingly maintained Victorian homes with immaculately-manicured lawns.

As the road passes southwest of Bank Street it again becomes a two-way road. On the right is Shawnee Golf Course, one of the city's municipally-owned golf courses and a part of Shawnee Park. Built in 1927, the facility is a full 18-hole course complete with a driving range, pro shop, and 3-hole youth golf course. The Olmstead firm in charge of the city's park

Northwestern Parkway

system originally did not want to develop a golf course near Shawnee Park, contending that it would be a danger to children and visitors to the park. The parks commission finally bowed to public demand 30 years later and built the course.

Near the 6.0-mile mark of the route, Northwestern Parkway becomes Southwestern Parkway.

5.9 Continue onto Southwestern Parkway

As Southwestern Parkway crosses W Market Street, the Louisville Loop becomes a protected bike lane, and portions of Shawnee Park come into view on the right side of the road.

6.2 Left to continue onto Southwestern Parkway

Southwestern Parkway continues through a neighborhood flanking Shawnee Park. There are many stately houses throughout this neighborhood that were once home to the city's elite, but the decline of Louisville's western neighborhoods after the 1950s is evident in some areas.

6.5 Right to continue onto Southwestern Parkway

Southwestern Parkway continues along the edge of Shawnee Park, which is one of the three original flagship parks of Louisville's Olmstead Park System. It was originally proposed in 1890, but did not open until 1895 due to difficulties in obtaining land for the park. Access points to the park were developed between 1896 and 1899. Dozens of subdivisions appeared soon after the park opened, comprising what is regarded today as Louisville's Shawnee neighborhood.

Southwestern Parkway

7.2 Right onto W Broadway

Southwestern Parkway seems to come to an end at its intersection with Broadway. The road, however, continues just a short way to the west from this intersection, while W Broadway ends at a parking lot just to the west of Shawnee Park's southern entrance. The parking lot is often used as an access point for Shawnee Park and for the Louisville Riverwalk, which ends near the southern end of the park. The parking lot may also be used as a launching point for shorter routes along the Louisville Loop.

7.4 Left onto Southwestern Parkway

The Louisville Loop continues along Southwestern Parkway south of Shawnee Park as a bike lane. Chickasaw Park is located along Southwestern Parkway near the 7.8-mile mark. A short road leads through the park and makes an excellent side trip if desired. There is a spray park that makes a compelling reason to stop here on hot summer days, and there are excellent views of the Ohio River from the park as well.

Chickasaw Park was developed between 1923 and the early 1930s under the Olmstead firm. In 1924, the Louisville Parks Commission segregated the Olmstead parks, and Chickasaw Park was designated as a park for the Louisville's African-American community, as was Sheppard Park at 17th and Magazine Streets. In the wake of the U.S. Supreme Court's *Brown v. Board of Education of Topeka* decision, Mayor Andrew Broaddus signed an order desegregating the city's parks and pools in 1955, amid pressure from the NAACP.

Southwestern Parkway curves sharply to the east and becomes Algonquin Parkway as it continues toward I-265/Watterson Expressway.

Chickasaw Park

8.6 Continue onto Algonquin Parkway

Algonquin Parkway soon curves back to the south, and then east again, as it continues away from the Ohio River. On the right side of the road just south of Gibson Road is the Metropolitan Sewer District's Morris Forman Wastewater Treatment Plant. It is Louisville's largest wastewater treatment facility, producing over 70 tons of biosolids daily. The biosolids are sold as fertilizer, marketed as "Louisville Green." Occasionally, the smell from the facility may be bothersome, but it is not dangerous. Every city's greenway must pass by the water treatment plant, and Louisville is no exception.

There is a historical marker nearby that marks the former site of Fort Southworth, the westernmost fortification that protected the city of Louisville during the U.S. Civil War.

9.4 Right onto Louisville Loop at S 41st Street

As Algonquin Parkway approaches Interstate 265/Watterson Expressway, the Louisville Loop trail suddenly branches off to the right on the far (eastern) side of S 41st Street. The trail continues next to 41st Street for a few hundred feet before crossing Bells Lane. Traffic on Bells Lane, which consists of mostly semis and tanker trucks, often blocks the road when trying to turn to or

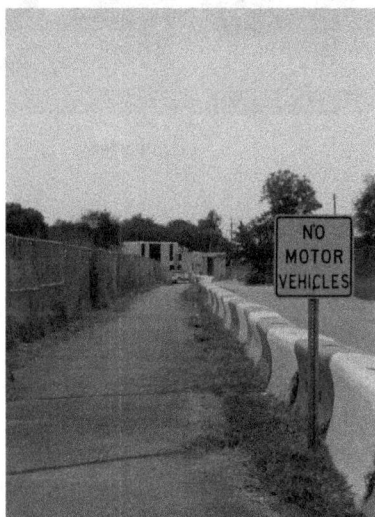

Loop Trail near Bells Lane

from S 41st Street. Since these trucks often obstruct cyclists' line of sight, considerable caution should always be used when crossing Bells Lane. Often, it is preferable to simply ride in the lane with traffic on S 41st Street to ensure that you are visible to traffic.

On the other side of Bells Lane, the trail makes a sharp left turn and passes a small brick building. It then crosses a driveway and makes a sharp right turn before ascending a slight hill, well away from the busy road. The trail then travels next to a recycling facility as it heads toward Campground Road. There are sometimes swarms of mosquitoes and other insects in this area, especially after rain events, so trail users should be prepared.

10.1 Right onto Campground Road

The Louisville Loop again becomes a bicycle lane as it continues southwest along Campground Road. Campground Road leads into the Rubbertown neighborhood, which is named for the rubber facility that

 operated here during World War II. The land was originally developed as an industrial area in 1918 when Standard Oil opened a refinery here. Other companies soon followed suit, refining oil into gasoline, kerosene, and other petroleum products. In 1941, the U.S. Office of War Production convinced DuPont, National Carbide, and B.F. Goodrich to open facilities nearby. In 1945,

Rubbertown

several companies under the banner of National Synthetic Rubber built a facility nearby to manufacture styrene-butadiene rubber for use in tires to support the war effort. Today, the American Synthetic Rubber continues this tradition, producing synthetic rubber for automobile tires. Eleven chemical companies, including DowDuPont and Zeon Chemical, currently call Rubbertown home. Rubbertown is well known as a major point source of air pollution, responsible for nearly half of the industrial emissions in Jefferson County.

Most of the area's chemical facilities are located along Campground Road just beyond its intersection with Ralph Avenue. Although the companies doing business in Rubbertown are fairly vigilant about maintaining the road and keeping the bike lane clear of debris and obstructions, there may still be significant amounts of gravel and other debris in the bike lane due to the many large semis and other trucks that pass through this area.

Louisville's infamous Lake Dreamland neighborhood comes into view on the right side of the road just beyond Kramers Lane. The neighborhood was originally developed in 1931 as a summer resort for the wealthy. The homes were cottages that encircled a small lake created by damming a stream feeding into the Ohio River. The name for Lake Dreamland came from an unknown critic who said that the development was a "dream that would never amount to anything."

Unfortunately for the developer, Lake Dreamland became a nightmare. Frequent flooding, including the Ohio River flood of 1937, plagued the area and damaged or destroyed many of the homes. The floodwall that followed the 1937 flood ran directly through the middle of the neighborhood, effectively cutting it in half. Furthermore, the lack of

Lake Dreamland neighborhood

infrastructure, including running water, sewers, and paved roads, prevented investors from sinking any more money into the project and drove many potential buyers and tenants away. But with the industrial boom in nearby Rubbertown in the 1940s, many of the workers at the various chemical plants rented the homes, albeit for much less than hoped, and some of them built new homes nearby. However, because the developer retained ownership of the land, the homes here were not eligible for federal funds to rehabilitate them, and the neighborhood languished.

After decades of neglect and decline, Lake Dreamland homeowners organized and formed a neighborhood association in 1983. By 1988, the group had arranged government buyouts of individual homes, but this arrangement was abandoned in the early 1990s. The new agreement encouraged individual home ownership, created grants and loans for repair of the homes, and provided funds for rehabilitation of the environment surrounding the neighborhood. In return, the property deeds stipulated that once the current landowners and their families leave, the land reverts to the county and becomes part of a land trust that will eventually return the area to its original state as a wetland.

Campground Road ends a half mile later at Lees Lane. Although the route and the Louisville Loop turn right at the intersection, turning left and riding 0.2 miles leads to Riverside Gardens Park. This park also serves as a trailhead for the Louisville Loop. Restrooms, picnic facilities, and parking are available here.

13.4 Right onto Lees Lane

Lees Lane passes through the Riverside Gardens neighborhood as it leads back toward the Ohio River. Riverside Gardens was developed in 1926 as a resort neighborhood, complete with amenities such as a clubhouse, bath house, and beautiful views of the Ohio River. But like Lake Dreamland, the neighborhood was plagued with frequent flooding. After the Great Flood of 1937, the neighborhood lost its luster and fell into serious decline.

The 1937 flood, however, was not the end of Riverside Gardens residents' woes. By the 1940s, the area was plagued with toxic emissions from Rubbertown, which lies only a mile to the north. The Cane Run Generating Station was built nearby in 1954, and coal ash from the facility added to the toxic emissions floating over the neighborhood. The neighborhood's miseries were compounded by toxic emissions from the nearby Lees Lane Landfill, which operated from 1940-1975.

Riverside Gardens neighborhood

Riverside Gardens made national headlines in 1975 when methane emissions from the landfill caused flash fires in seven homes in the neighborhood. Other toxic gases have since been detected in the neighborhood, and the wells that provided drinking water were found to contain numerous dangerous chemicals. Stories abound of children in the neighborhood developing cancer, epilepsy, and other maladies early in life.

Numerous court battles over the toxic mess in Riverside Gardens have been waged since the late 1970s. Among the lawsuits filed, one was settled in the early 1990s with 23 companies agreeing to contribute a total of $2.4 million to clean up the pollution. A class-action lawsuit against LG&E for coal ash emissions from the Cane Run Generating Station was settled recently, with terms of the settlement remaining sealed. Other lawsuits are still pending, and will not likely be resolved for many years, if not decades.

The Louisville Loop continues past the end of Lees Lane as an asphalt greenway. There are several poles that prevent motor vehicles from entering, and it is even a narrow squeeze for many bicycles. Just beyond this entrance, the Louisville Loop continues to the left along a levee.

13.9 Left onto Louisville Loop

The Louisville Loop continues to the south on the far side of Riverview Gardens. The trail then turns left, heading eastward toward the Cane Run Generating Station. A spur trail leads off to the right, descends the levee, and ends at a small overlook at the bank of the Ohio River. If you decide to follow this trail, it is important to heed the signs and stay on the trail to avoid the toxic chemicals that occasionally seep from the ground.

This area sits next to the site of the former Lees Lane Landfill, which operated from 1940 until 1975, and is the main source of toxic pollution that has plagued Riverside Gardens. The site was originally a sand and gravel quarry, but it was soon put into service as a municipal landfill. Much of the waste that was buried at the facility was toxic chemical wastes from Rubbertown. Many of these chemicals, including benzene, phenols, and heavy metals, were dumped directly into the ground without any containment, as oversight was lax and many such practices were not against the law at the time.

In 1980, a methane collection system was installed at the former landfill, and the site was capped with a clay liner and large boulders to prevent chemicals from seeping into the river. By 1983, the Lees Lane Landfill site was added to the federal Superfund list, providing much-needed federal funds to assist in its cleanup. Gas and groundwater wells were installed, and the site was finally removed from the federal Superfund list in 1988.

Currently, authorities assure that the site is no longer a health hazard to Riverview Gardens residents. Despite official reassurances, many area residents contend that the Lees Lane Landfill continues to pose a health hazard. In 1998, the methane collection system was found to have failed. Metropolitan Sewer District is currently under an agreement to maintain the site until 2020, and the EPA is currently monitoring the site for other problems. In 2011, the EPA agreed to reevaluate the containment efforts at the site, and these studies are still ongoing. Public access to the site is prohibited by law, but many area residents illegally use it as an informal off-road site for ATVs and other motorized vehicles.

14.3 Left to continue onto Louisville Loop

The Louisville Loop continues along the levee past the sharp left curve. At the 14.8-mile mark, the trail descends the levee and enters a wooded area. The descent is short and steep, and it may be necessary to reduce your speed here in order to successfully negotiate the curves in the trail ahead. There is often gravel on the trail where it descends the levee toward the woods.

For the next half mile, the trail twists and turns through the woods before crossing a bridge over Mill Creek. The trail soon emerges from the woods, turns to the south, and runs along the eastern side of the Cane Run Generating Station. Cyclists should be wary of gravel and other debris on the trail through this area, as well as a rough railroad crossing near Cane Run Road.

Bridge over Mill Creek

As the trail approaches Cane Run Road it curves sharply to the right and continues between Cane Run Road and the Cane Run Generating Station. Near the curve, new transmission lines have been erected to deliver electricity from the facility's new natural gas facility. This new facility will take over much of the job of electricity generation as some of the older coal-burning generators are mustered out of service. With time, this change should greatly reduce the toxic emissions that have plagued nearby neighborhoods, including Riverside Gardens, for many decades.

River Valley Cemetery

Near the 16.5-mile mark there is a small restaurant that sits opposite the intersection of Cane Run Road and Lower Hunters Trace. The trail passes in front of the restaurant, and although Louisville Loop traffic has the right-of-way over traffic entering and exiting the restaurant, caution should be observed.

A little further down the trail from the power plant, the Louisville Loop crosses a small access road that leads to the River Valley Cemetery. Since 1988 the city of Louisville has used the site as a potter's field, where the homeless and the indigent are given a respectful burial. The city parks department maintains the site, and many volunteers help to maintain grave sites and to keep the grounds mowed and clear of debris. The plots in this cemetery have nearly all been used, so the city has turned to another site located in the Valley Station area.

The trail continues along Cane Run Road with minimal disruptions for the next two miles, passing through the Jefferson Riverport Industrial Park. Around the 18.8-mile mark, the trail passes the Pleasure Ridge Park Fire Training Facility before reaching a stop sign at its intersection with Greenwood Road. This intersection lies immediately west of the intersection of Greenwood Road and Cane Run Road. Traffic crossing Cane Run Road is supposed to yield to trail users who have previously stopped before proceeding across the intersection, but they are seldom inclined to do so, and thus caution is urged.

The trail curves sharply west and crosses a rough set of railroad tracks before ascending a short but steep hill to climb back onto the levee next to the Ohio River. At the top of the levee, a side trail leads down the levee on the other side and into Riverview Park. In addition to serving as a Louisville Loop trailhead, the park contains a playground, splash park, and boat launch ramp.

Louisville Loop Trail

The trail turns sharply south and continues atop the levee for the next 3.5 miles as it passes a few scattered industrial sites and a few homes. At the 20.5-mile mark is Mike Linnig's, a well-known restaurant that has been serving up seafood since 1925. Many restaurant patrons can be seen walking up and down the Louisville Loop near the restaurant on summer evenings. The restaurant is a Louisville tradition and makes a nice destination for dinner after a long day of pedaling on the Louisville Loop.

Immediately past Mike Linnig's, the trail descends from the levee to cross Johnsontown Road before immediately climbing back onto the levee. Although there is little traffic to contend with on this short stretch of Johnsontown Road, extreme caution is advised in this area because motorists have a very limited line of sight and cannot see cyclists or pedestrians descending the trail.

At the 21-mile mark the trail passes the historic Moremen chapel, which is located on the grounds of Riverside. Originally built in 1888, the small church hosted the Bethany United Methodist congregation. The chapel was relocated here from its original location at Bethany Lane and Dixie Highway in 2006 and was subsequently restored at a cost of just over $900,000. Today, the chapel is available for weddings and other special events. It is connected to the Farnsley-Moremen landing by a short access road.

At the 22.5-mile mark, the Louisville Loop crosses Moorman Road. A trailhead branches off to the right and leads to Riverside, the Farnsley-Moremen Landing. Riverside is a historic site along the Ohio River that served as a riverboat landing from the 1820s until the 1880s. The Farnsley-Moremen house, built in 1837 by Gabriel Farnsley, sits nearby. It was first home to the Farnsley family and was later purchased by the Moremen family in 1862. Both families made a living farming the fertile river valley and trading with the riverboats that once plied the Ohio River. The Moremen family continued to purchase land adjacent to the farm, increasing its size to nearly 1,500 acres. At its time, it was the largest farm in Jefferson County.

Ohio River from Farnsley-Moremen landing

In the late 19th century, the farm was divided among the Moremen heirs, many of whom remained in the area over the next century. In 1988, the property was sold to Jefferson County. Today, the house has been repurposed as a museum. The museum contains many artifacts from the home and farm, an auditorium, and information about farm life along the Ohio River in the 19th century. The home's original detached kitchen has been lovingly restored, and there is an operational garden nearby. There is a large parking lot here, making it an excellent launching point for rides along the Louisville Loop, and a visit to the museum is an excellent idea for a weekend afternoon.

The Louisville Loop continues beyond Farnsley-Moremen for a little over two miles along the levee next to the river. As the trail ends, it descends the levee with a sharp S-curve and then ends at the Watson Lane trailhead around the 24.6-mile mark. On the south side of the trailhead is the Mill Creek Generating Station, LG&E's largest coal-fired electrical generating plant. Construction on the facility began in 1968, with the plant going into service in 1972 and becoming fully operational in 1982. The three large cooling towers that are visible from many miles away were built to help cool the plant's discharges into the Ohio River and protect aquatic life in the river.

24.6 Turn around at Watson Lane

From the Watson Lane trailhead, the route retraces itself for the next 20 miles until reaching the one-way section of Northwestern Parkway that will force loop traffic to utilize Bank Street to return to the main trail.

35.3 Right to continue on Louisville Loop

35.8 Right onto Lees Lane

36.3 Left onto Campground Road

39.4 Left onto Louisville Loop

40.3 Left onto Algonquin Parkway

41.1 Continue onto Southwestern Parkway

42.3 Right onto W Broadway

42.4 Left onto Southwestern Parkway

43.1 Left to continue onto Southwestern Parkway

43.3 Right to continue onto Southwestern Parkway

43.7 Continue onto Northwestern Parkway

44.3 Right onto Bank Street

Northwestern Parkway north of Bank Street is one-way, so traffic must turn right onto Bank Street at the 44.3-mile mark of the route. There are orange bicycle route detour signs that direct trail traffic onto Bank Street just before the turn.

Bank Street is one-way heading east, and the right lane contains signage indicating that it is a shared-use lane. The next turn, onto N 33rd Street, is also indicated by an orange detour sign that is easy to miss. At this point, loop traffic should signal and move into the left lane before making the turn to avoid turning in front of traffic coming up from behind in the left lane.

45.2 Left onto N 33rd Street

North 33rd Street leads north toward Northwestern Parkway, where it comes to a five-way intersection with Northwestern Parkway and Portland Avenue. The intersection may seem confusing to some, and the bike route detour signs may be difficult to see. To continue along the Louisville Loop, it is necessary to turn right and take the left-hand fork to make the turn onto Northwestern Parkway, which carries two-way traffic in this area. Although it is tempting to turn right on the red light after stopping, it is highly discouraged because this intersection often confuses motorists as well.

45.4 Right onto Northwestern Parkway

45.7 Left onto Louisville Loop

48.7 Right onto Bingham Way

As the Louisville Loop again passes the row of restaurants along the Ohio River just east of the Belle of Louisville, the trail continues along the sidewalk parallel to Bingham Way. Due to the heavy pedestrian traffic on the trail in this area, many cyclists may choose to head straight out of the cul-de-sac onto Bingham Way. Since Bingham Way turns into W River Road and becomes a divided highway near this point, it will be necessary for cyclists following the road to turn right into the cul-de-sac, and then cautiously head straight out from the cul-de-sac and turn left onto Bingham Way at the traffic light.

48.8 Left onto E Witherspoon Street

49.1 Left onto E River Road

49.8 Left into Big Four Bridge parking lot

Louisville Loop trailhead at Watson Lane

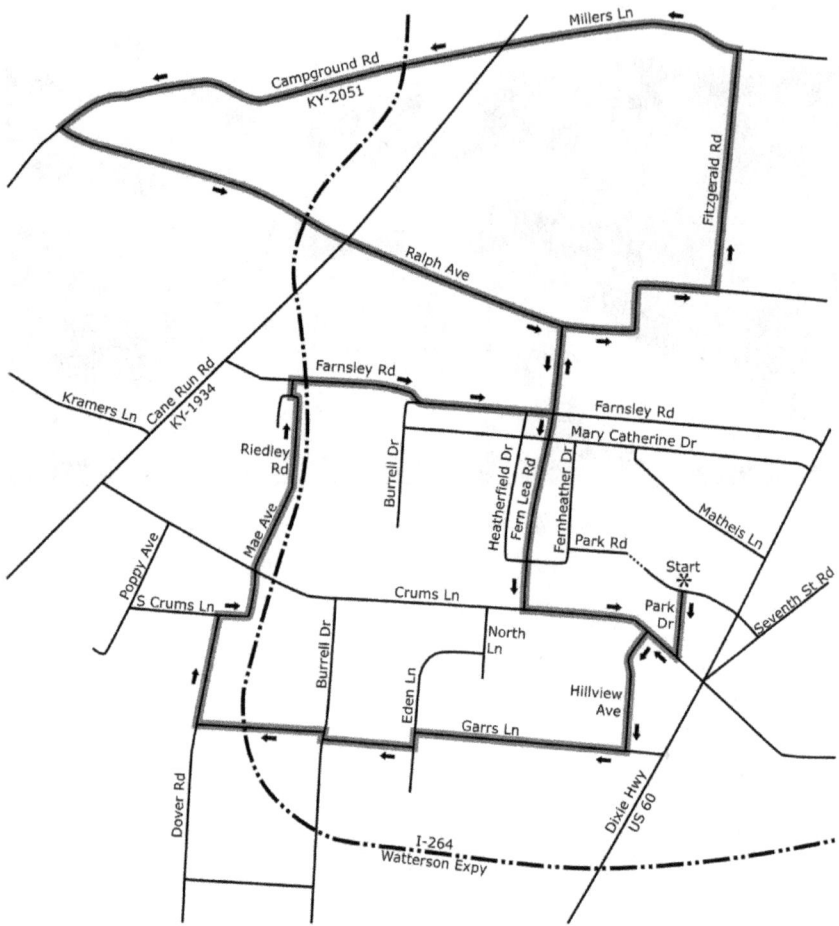

(about)(about)(about)(about)(about)(about)(about)(about)(about)(about)(about)(about)(about)(about)(about)(about)(about)

9 SHIVELY

Distance: 9.5 miles

Difficulty: Easy. Heavy traffic and rough pavement in a few areas.

Points of Interest: Shively Park; City of Shively; Garrs Lane United Methodist Church; Stitzel-Weller Distillery

The city of Shively is located within the southeastern portion of Jefferson County, encompassing a 20 square mile area roughly bounded by Millers Lane to the north, Interstate 264/Watterson Expressway to the west, 7th Street to the east, and Rockford Lane to the south. It is directly south of the Algonquin neighborhood, with the Rubbertown industrial area situated due west of the city. Shively is a third-class city within Metro Louisville with a population of just under 15,000 and has its own local government with a mayor, city council, and police force.

Shively was founded around 1810 when Christian Shively settled on a 1,000-acre tract of land in the area where Dixie Highway and 7th Street Road cross. Shively built and operated a mill along what is now known as Mill Creek. Other settlers soon followed and established large farms in the area. The area was soon known as the Shively Precinct and began to develop during the late 19th century with the arrival of a large number of German immigrants.

Shively remained relatively quiet and rural until the end of Prohibition in the 1930s when a number of whiskey distilleries opened up near town. With the Great Depression in full swing, the city of Louisville attempted to annex the land and tax the distilleries to fill the city's empty coffers. The distillers, however, fought back. In 1938, they managed to convince Shively to incorporate and include the land on which the distilleries were built. The tax revenue from the distilleries greatly enriched the new city, and it began to grow rapidly.

Shively's rapid growth accelerated during the 1950s as Louisville's residents began a mass movement toward the suburbs. The city's settlement pattern, however, had a very dark side. In the early 1950s, Shively was well known as a whites-only neighborhood. The mass migration of city residents toward the suburbs accelerated this pattern. But as integration swept the nation in the 1950s, segregation in Shively was soon challenged.

In 1954, activists Carl and Anne Braden helped Andrew Wade, a black Korean War veteran, secure a home in suburban Shively. The Bradens purchased a home that Wade and his wife had chosen and then deeded the home over to the Wades. Violence soon followed. Bricks were thrown, guns were fired at the family's home, a cross was burned in an adjacent lot, and a bomb was even detonated under the house. Fearing for their safety, the Wades left in 1958, and few African-American families dared to move into the area until well into the 1970s. The incidents made national news, drawing attention to the plight of black families in the south under Jim Crow.

The hate crimes that occurred in the Wade case were never prosecuted, but the Bradens were. Carl Braden was tried and found guilty of sedition in the case and was sentenced to 15 years in prison. Braden was freed after serving 7 months when his conviction was overturned in the wake of the U.S. Supreme Court's *Pennsylvania v. Nelson* decision, which pre-empted Kentucky's sedition laws.

Racial injustice wasn't the only woe afflicting Shively during the 1950s and 1960s. Changing consumer preferences and a tax increase caused most of the area's distilleries to close during the 1960s, leading to economic depression and blight. The losses in tax revenue from the distillery closures caused massive budget shortfalls by the early 1970s, and the shrinking budgets unleashed a major decline in government services and police protection. The decreased police presence led to a spike in crime, which was especially acute along the 7th Street corridor where a large number of bars and lounges were located. Shively's residents voted with their feet and moved out, further intensifying the city's budget crisis. By 1980, Shively had depopulated by nearly 15% and its budget situation became dire.

In a desperate attempt to address the city's shrinking budget, Shively attempted to annex the Pleasure Ridge Park neighborhood to the west in 1984. This attempt failed, and later that year Police Chief Michael Donio admitted to taking bribes for ignoring prostitution along the city's 7th Street corridor. After the scandal, and in light of the serious crime problems along the north side of town, locals began to refer to the city as "Lively Shively."

Like much of Jefferson County, Shively's fortunes began to improve in the 1990s. The city modernized much of its infrastructure and increased police protection, persuading many chain restaurants and hotels to move into the area and provide badly-needed jobs. With the recent renewal of Kentucky's bourbon industry, several of Shively's distilleries have reopened. With time and patience, the future looks much brighter for Shively.

The tour begins at Shively Park, located west of U.S. Highway 31W/Dixie Highway and north of Crums Lane. The entrance to the park is on Park Road. Past the new police station, a short road on the right leads into a parking lot where plenty of parking is usually available.

Rickhouses at the Stitzel-Weller distillery on Fitzgerald Road in Shively

Route Directions – Shively

0.0 Continue onto Park Drive
0.2 Right onto Crums Lane
0.3 Left onto Hillview Avenue
0.6 Right onto Garrs Lane
1.1 Left onto Eden Lane
1.2 Right onto Garrs Lane
1.4 Right onto Burrell Drive
1.4 Left onto Garrs Lane
1.7 Right onto Dover Road
2.0 Right onto S Crums Lane
2.2 Continue onto Mae Avenue
2.5 Continue onto Riedley Road
2.8 Right onto Farnsley Road
3.1 Left to continue onto Farnsley Road
3.5 Left onto Fern Lea Road
3.7 Right onto Ralph Avenue
4.2 Left onto Fitzgerald Road
4.8 Left onto Millers Lane
5.5 Continue onto KY-2051/Campground Road
6.7 Left onto Ralph Avenue
8.1 Right onto Fern Lea Road
8.9 Left onto Crums Lane
9.3 Left onto Park Drive
9.5 Continue into parking lot

Route Description – Shively

0.0 Continue onto Park Drive

The route continues straight ahead onto Park Drive from the parking lot instead of onto Park Road, which leads back to U.S. Highway 31W/Dixie Highway. Park Drive ends a short distance ahead at Crums Lane.

0.2 Right onto Crums Lane

Crums Lane is a busy road, particularly during the morning and evening commute times. In addition, the road frequently backs up when Butler Traditional High School is dismissing in the mid-afternoon. Caution should be used in pulling out onto the road, as drivers are frequently not paying attention to traffic in this area.

0.3 Left onto Hillview Avenue

0.6 Right onto Garrs Lane

A few blocks after making the turn, the far side of Butler Traditional High School can be seen on the right. Another block away, on the left side of the road, is Garrs Lane United Methodist Church. Although the church building here is not historic, the church itself was formed in 1816 from land that was donated by the Shively family. The church has moved many times over the past two centuries, and the current church was formed when the congregation merged with the nearby Hazelwood Methodist Church and moved to this location in 2007.

1.1 Left onto Eden Lane

Garrs Lane continues heading west after a short distance on Eden Lane.

1.2 Right onto Garrs Lane

1.4 Right onto Burrell Drive

Garrs Lane continues heading west after a short distance on Burrell Drive.

1.4 Left onto Garrs Lane

Garrs Lane soon ends at Dover Road, where it will be necessary to turn right to continue following the route.

1.7 Right onto Dover Road

Dover Road ends a short distance to the north at its intersection with S Crums Lane.

2.0 Right onto S Crums Lane

S Crums Lane approaches Interstate 264/Watterson Expressway, then makes a sharp turn to the left and becomes Mae Avenue.

2.2 Continue onto Mae Avenue

Mae Avenue continues across Crums Lane, which is a major thoroughfare through Shively. North of Crums Lane, the road continues parallel to the Watterson Expressway. A short distance later, the road curves slightly to the left and becomes Riedley Road.

2.5 Continue onto Riedley Road

Reidley Road continues parallel to the expressway. With the exception of the traffic noise, it is hard to realize that the road is right next to the expressway due to the heavy foliage that blocks the view (and most of the noise) to the east. Near its end, the road curves sharply to the left, then sharply to the right, and ends at its intersection with Farnsley Road.

2.8 Right onto Farnsley Road

Farnsley Road continues back into northern Shively. Soon, the road comes to a stop sign at a slightly confusing intersection. The route follows Farnsley road, which continues to the left past the stop sign. Bicyclists should exercise caution when making the turn to check for vehicles that commonly exceed the speed limit in this location. Vehicles coming from the right are coming around a tight curve and may have a limited line of sight.

3.1 Left to continue onto Farnsley Road

3.5 Left onto Fern Lea Road

3.7 Right onto Ralph Avenue

Ralph Avenue continues through an area of well-kept middle-class homes with meticulously manicured lawns. A few blocks further east, the road curves sharply left, then sharply right, and enters an industrial area.

4.2 Left onto Fitzgerald Road

Whiskey rickhouses on the grounds of the Stitzel-Weller Distillery line the left side of the road. With the bourbon industry's recent revival and overseas demand for the liquor at an all-time high, distilling is serious business in Kentucky. The Stitzel-Weller Distillery, located here on Fitzgerald Road, played a major role in the history of bourbon and has enjoyed a revival in recent years as the home of Bulleit bourbon. Founded in 1935 and recently reopened in 2014, the distillery is one of Louisville's must-see attractions.

Bourbon pioneers Julian P. "Pappy" Van Winkle and Alex Farnsley, both of whom were former employees, bought the W. L. Weller and Sons company in 1908. During Prohibition, the Weller Company continued selling whiskey to pharmacies for medicinal purposes. They bought their whiskey from Alfred Stitzel's distillery on Story Avenue, one of only six distilleries that were allowed to continue distilling whiskey during Prohibition.

After Prohibition's repeal in 1933, Van Winkle, Farnsley, and Stitzel joined forces and began construction on the Stitzel-Weller distillery, which opened on Derby Day in 1935 with Van Winkle as its president. The facility produced several brands, including the venerable Old Fitzgerald, and began development of a unique wheated bourbon recipe that has regained popularity in recent years.

Van Winkle died in 1965, and the business passed to his son Julian P. Van Winkle. At the time, the bourbon industry was in serious decline, and many of the surrounding distilleries had closed. Under pressure from shareholders, Van Winkle sold the distillery to Norton-Simon in 1972. The name was changed to Old Fitzgerald Distillery, and the quality of the whiskey being made went into a long slow decline that ignominiously ended with the facility's closing in 1992. Later that decade, the Old Fitzgerald and Cabin Still brands were sold to the Heaven Hill company, and the wheated bourbon recipe once produced here was sold to Buffalo Trace in Frankfort. The company still produces the recipe as W. L. Weller.

Julian Van Winkle continued making bourbon after the sale of Stitzel-Weller. He created the Old Rip Van Winkle brand, bought bourbon from Stitzel-Weller, and bottled it himself. Julian's son, Julian Van Winkle III, expanded the business and created Van Winkle Family Reserve 15, 20, and 23-year bourbons, which have become the gold standard of high-end bourbon. In 2002, the Van Winkles partnered with Buffalo Trace, moving their aging barrels of whiskey to Buffalo Trace's Frankfort facility where the brand is still produced today. The Van Winkle Family Reserve bourbon that was produced from whiskey distilled here at Stitzel-Weller is much sought after and commands a very high price on the secondary market.

The road ends at Millers Lane, on the northern edge of the city of Shively.

4.8 Left onto Millers Lane

Millers Lane continues west, exiting the city of Shively as it heads toward the Ohio River and the Rubbertown neighborhood. A shared use lane appears west of the road's intersection with Old Millers Lane, although cyclists should beware of several patches of rough pavement in the area. As the road crosses Cane Run Road, it becomes KY-2051/Campground Road.

5.5 Continue onto KY-2051/Campground Road

Campground Road passes underneath Interstate 264/Watterson Expressway, crosses a set of railroad tracks, and then merges with the Louisville Loop where a bike lane appears. The route continues to follow the Louisville loop for about one mile, before turning left onto Ralph Avenue as it enters Rubbertown.

6.7 Left onto Ralph Avenue

8.1 Right onto Fern Lea Road

8.9 Left onto Crums Lane

City of Shively

Again, Crums Lane may be busy during the morning and evening commutes and during the mid-afternoon on weekdays when school is in session. Butler Traditional High School, one of the city's larger high schools with nearly 1,700 students, is located on the right side of the road on Crums Lane near the entrance into Shively Park.

If the road is significantly backed up, it is possible to avoid Crums Lane by turning left onto Shadow Fern Lane from Fern Lea Road two blocks north of Crums Lane, and then right onto Park Drive, which ends with a pass-through into one of the parking lots within Shively Park.

9.3 Left onto Park Drive

9.5 Continue into parking lot

Stitzel-Weller Distillery

187

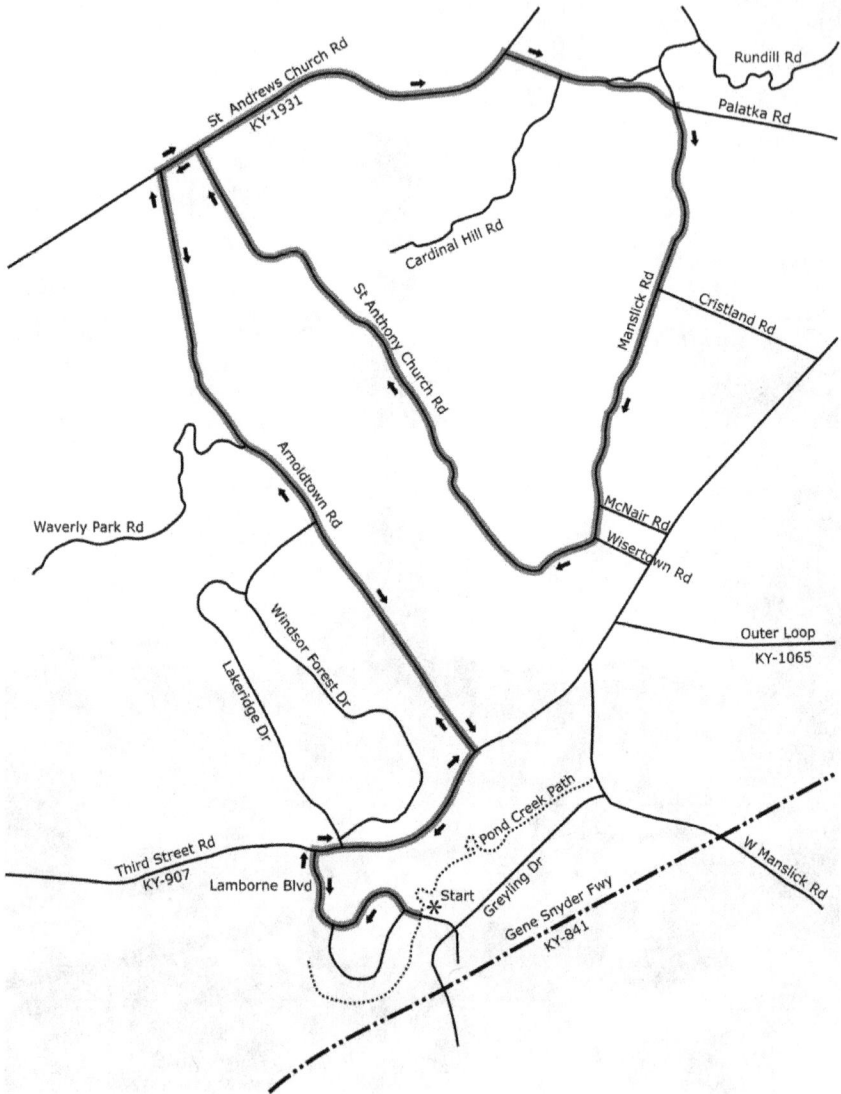

10 WAVERLY HILLS

Distance: 13.2 miles

Difficulty: Difficult. A few hills, including one difficult climb. Moderate to heavy traffic in a few areas at certain times of day.

Points of Interest: Pond Creek Path Greenway; Waverly Hills Park; Cardinal Hill; Cardinal Hill Reservoir; Iroquois Park; St. Andrews Church Cemetery

The Waverly Hills neighborhood encompasses the area bounded by U.S. Highway 60/Dixie Highway to the west, Third Street Road to the south, St. Andrews Church Road to the north, and KY-1865/New Cut Road to the east. The neighborhood lies just south of Iroquois Park and includes Cardinal Hill, the large hill situated due south of the park. Waverly Hills, as the name implies, is quite hilly, and was largely rural and wooded until the 1990s. Development has now caught up to Waverly Hills, and there are numerous small neighborhoods that have been built on the area's rugged hillsides.

This portion of the city is best known for the Waverly Hills Sanatorium, the large tuberculosis hospital that opened in the area's densely wooded hills in the early 20th century. A task force was formed in 1906 in response to the alarming rise in tuberculosis infections in the Louisville area. The voters of Jefferson County approved a levy to fund the effort, and ground was broken on the hospital soon afterward. The facility admitted its first patients in 1911. Over the next decade, the hospital's patient load grew rapidly, with nearly 400 patients of all age groups residing at the hospital by the 1920s. The hospital was expanded in 1924 to accommodate the growing number of patients, and at the time boasted a playground, library, farm, and school. Waverly Hills Sanatorium was almost fully self-sufficient, and most of the nurses, doctors, and other employees who worked at the facility lived on site with their families. At the height of its operation, Waverly Hills Sanatorium offered state-of-the-art therapies for the treatment of tuberculosis.

The 1943 discovery of streptomycin, an aminoglycoside drug that interferes with bacterial ribosomes, revolutionized the treatment of tuberculosis. Tuberculosis treatment soon became an outpatient procedure that could be performed in doctor's offices, and there was no longer any need for facilities like Waverly Hills. The hospital closed in 1961, and the building was converted into a nursing home and a facility for the mentally handicapped. Waverly Hills closed for good in 1980 and was abandoned, left to deteriorate.

In recent years Waverly Hills Sanatorium has gained notoriety as one of the most haunted hospitals in the United States and was even featured on several television shows. There are obviously many urban legends that surround the old hospital, including many that claim that over 10,000 people died at the hospital over its history. The real number, however, is probably far fewer. There is also an urban myth that room 502 is haunted by a nurse who was either murdered or committed suicide after discovering that she had contracted tuberculosis and become pregnant by the sanatorium's owner.

Pond Creek Path Greenway

Since the facility's closing, there have been multiple plans to redevelop the property. However, none of them have ever materialized to this date. For the last few years, Waverly Hills has hosted a haunted house during the Halloween season.

The tour begins in the parking lot at the Lamborne Boulevard trailhead of the Pond Creek Path greenway. Although the greenway will eventually be linked up to the Louisville Loop as more segments of the project are finished, the greenway is, for now, an isolated 1.6-mile segment that runs between West Manslick Road and an isolated spot behind Scarborough Avenue where it comes to a dead end. For a slightly longer ride, it is possible to park at the West Manslick Road trailhead 0.8 miles to the east and travel to this location on the greenway to follow the route described here. However, this section of the greenway may contain mud or standing water after heavy rains, particularly in the spring.

Route Directions – Waverly Hills

0.0 Right onto Lamborne Boulevard
0.6 Right onto KY-907/Third Street Road
1.3 Left onto Arnoldtown Road
3.7 Right onto KY-1931/St. Andrews Church Road
5.0 Right onto Palatka Road
5.7 Right onto Manslick Road
7.2 Continue onto St. Anthony Church Road
9.3 Left onto St. Andrews Church Road
9.5 Left onto Arnoldtown Road
11.9 Right onto Third Street Road
12.6 Left onto Lamborne Boulevard
13.2 Left into parking lot

Route Description – Waverly Hills

0.0 Right onto Lamborne Boulevard

Lamborne Boulevard passes through a small neighborhood south of Third Street Road. It soon widens and becomes a divided road with a grassy median in the center, then crosses a set of railroad tracks. The road then climbs slightly and ends at Third Street Road.

0.6 Right onto KY-907/Third Street Road

Traffic on Third Street Road may be traveling above the speed limit. Eastbound vehicles are coming over a small hill next to the church on the left and have a limited line of sight, so caution is advised. The road continues east past a gas station, and then to an intersection with Arnoldtown Road at a traffic light. The weight sensors under the road will respond to bicycles, so stopping and standing at the stop bar in the turn lane is normally enough to trigger the left turn signal.

1.3 Left onto Arnoldtown Road

The speed limit on this road is 35 mph, but it is a busy thoroughfare, and traffic often exceeds this limit. The first major climb of the route comes after another half mile, ascending the ridge as it continues northward. There are a few twists and turns along the ascent, so it is advisable to stay to the right as much as possible. The climb is long, but not particularly steep. After cresting the hill, the road descends gently, curving back and forth, as it passes the entrance to Waverly Park on the left.

If you're up for a challenge, Waverly Park Road makes a nice scenic detour. The hill is somewhat steep, but the views along the way are well worth the extra effort. The road comes to a dead end at the park's end, so it will be necessary to turn around there if you do make the side trip. The Waverly Hills Sanatorium is located just west of the end of the road on the other side of the golf course, but it is not accessible from Waverly Park. The facility's entrance is on Paralee Lane, which is accessible from East Pages Lane several miles away.

Beyond the entrance to Waverly Park, the road continues to descend gently toward its end at St. Andrews Church Road.

3.7 Right onto KY-1931/St. Andrews Church Road

St. Andrews Church Road can be busy at times, especially around the morning and evening commutes, and especially around school dismissal time.

The road is a major thoroughfare that carries traffic between some of the neighborhoods of Louisville's south end, centered around Iroquois Park and the Pleasure Ridge Park neighborhood along Greenwood Road west of Dixie Highway. Fortunately, the road is wide enough to accommodate bicycles and cars at most points, and school traffic tends to slow the cars down. Doss High School is located along the right side of the road, nestled among numerous apartment complexes and a few small residential neighborhoods. The long hill in the distance is Cardinal Hill, and many of the apartment complexes and businesses along St. Andrews Church Road are named for it.

The road soon passes through a small commercial district. A right turn lane appears near the end of it, at the road's intersection with Manslick Road and Palatka Road. Beyond the intersection, St. Andrews Church Road becomes Manslick Road. The route continues to the right, onto Palatka Road.

5.0 Right onto Palatka Road

Palatka Road heads east toward Iroquois Park and New Cut Road. The first road on the right is Cardinal Hill Road, which climbs Cardinal Hill and ends at Cardinal Hill Reservoir. The reservoir was built by the Louisville Water Company in 1932 to serve the burgeoning population of the south end neighborhoods. The structure is on the National Register of Historic Places and is an example of Classical Revival architecture. The reservoir is not open to the public.

Palatka Road climbs a small hill and then descends past the southern edge of Iroquois Park. There are two entrances to the park on the left along Palatka Road, at Dogwood Road and Sanders Gate Road. Dogwood Road merges with Sanders Gate Road and intersects with Rundill Road, the loop around Iroquois Park, near the gate that blocks vehicles from the far side of the park. If desired, a trip through Iroquois Park will add about 3.5 miles to the tour.

The next turn on the route, onto Manslick Road, is at a traffic light. Manslick Road is across the road from Sanders Gate Road and the entrance to Iroquois Park.

5.7 Right onto Manslick Road

If it seems like half of the roads in southern Jefferson County are named Manslick, it's only because Manslick Road is fragmented into multiple segments. Despite the snickers that the road's name often elicit, its name is derived from the town of Mann's Lick, which disappeared in the 1890s. Manslick Road continues to circle the base of Cardinal Hill, running roughly parallel to Third Street Road. The road is slightly hilly, but none of the hills are particularly troublesome.

As the road reaches the southern edge of Cardinal Hill, it curves sharply to the right and becomes St. Anthony Church Road.

7.2 Continue onto St. Anthony Church Road

St. Andrews Catholic Cemetery

St. Anthony Church Road continues to circle Cardinal Hill, tracing its west side. The road twists and turns, passes a small church on the right, and then begins to climb Cardinal Hill for the second major climb of the ride. The hill is a fairly challenging climb, rising over 200 feet in elevation, but flattens out in several spots to allow cyclists to catch a breather before resuming the climb. People living near the top of the hill allow their dogs to run loose in the road, so caution is advised in this area.

As the road crests the hill, St. Andrew Cemetery appears on the left side. The cemetery was established in 1851 and surrounded a church that once stood at this site atop Cardinal Hill. The land for the church was donated by John Jacob Wiser, an early settler in the area who owned a farm here.

The road makes a steep descent past the cemetery and curves sharply to the right. It will likely be necessary to feather the brakes on the descent, or in some cases to walk part of it, in order to avoid running off the side of the road. The road ends not far beyond the bottom of the hill at St. Andrews Church Road.

9.3 Left onto St. Andrews Church Road

The route turns left, back onto St. Andrews Church Road, and then very quickly turns left onto Arnoldtown Road to head back to the ride start. There is a left turn lane for traffic to turn onto Arnoldtown Road.

9.5 Left onto Arnoldtown Road

From here, the route heads back toward the ride start at the Pond Creek Path Greenway. The road begins to climb again as it heads past the entrance to Waverly Park, but the climb is not particularly difficult.

11.9 Right onto Third Street Road

As the next turn on the route approaches, oncoming vehicles have a limited line of sight due to a small hill at the intersection with Lamborne Boulevard. Caution is advised when making the turn.

12.6 Left onto Lamborne Boulevard

13.2 Left into parking lot

Waverly Hills Sanatorium

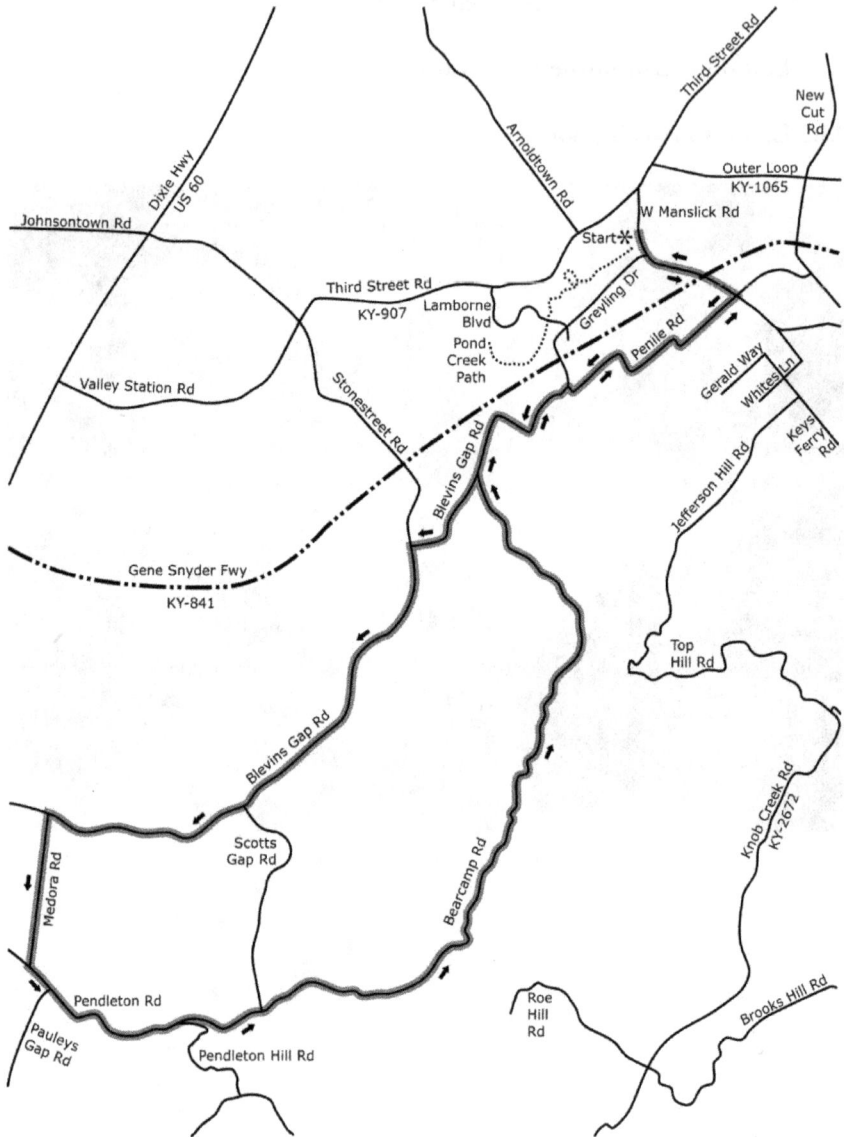

Michael W. Thompson

196

11 FAIRDALE AND JEFFERSON MEMORIAL FOREST

Distance: 18.7 miles

Difficulty: Moderate. A few hills, but little traffic.

Highlights: Pond Creek Path greenway, Penile, Fairdale, Jefferson Memorial Forest

Fairdale is a former census-designated town in southern Jefferson County that is roughly defined as the area south of KY-1065/Outer Loop to the north, South Park Road to the east, West Manslick and Keys Ferry Roads to the west, and Bullitt County to the south. Settlers arrived at the end of the 18th century, attracted by the many salt licks located nearby. Mann's Lick, which was located just north of Fairdale, was named for pioneer John Mann and operated by Joseph Brooks. The town of Mann's Lick was soon chartered. Newtown, where many of the mine's workers settled, was chartered a few years later.

Mann's Lick soon found itself unable to compete with the larger salt licks in Bullitt County. Cheaper salt was soon being imported via steamboat down the Ohio River, and Mann's Lick closed. The population of Mann's Lick and nearby Newtown dwindled by the mid-1800s, and the two towns fully disappeared in the 1890s due to a change in the state constitution. Today, the only trace of Mann's Lick that remains is the name of what seems like half of the roads in southern Jefferson County.

The area around the former towns developed a bad reputation not long after their founding, preventing the area from developing quickly. There were many disputes over land ownership between 1830 and 1860, and violent confrontations often ensued. Between the violence and the closing of Mann's Lick, most of the area's residents moved elsewhere, never to return. The few residents who remained eked out a living selling charcoal from the richly wooded hillsides nearby, which became known as Woods Precinct. But the area's bad reputation lingered as it was largely regarded as a hideout and gathering place for criminals.

The turn of the 20th century saw positive changes in the area, despite the disappearance of Newtown and Mann's Lick. The area's population began to increase between 1880 and 1910 after the opening of a general store near the intersection of modern day Mount Holly and Mitchell Hill Roads. In 1910, residents of the Woods Precinct community voted to rename the town as Fairdale to distance itself from its prior reputation. In 2003, Fairdale officially became a neighborhood of Metro Louisville with the merger of the county and city governments. Fairdale today attracts many residents looking for a home in an area with a more remote feel, but that is still convenient to the city of Louisville.

This tour also passes through Jefferson Memorial Forest, a 6,500-acre urban forest located in southernmost Jefferson County. The preserve was created in 1946 by the county government as an effort to preserve the natural history of the southern portion of Jefferson County. Between 1946 and 1985, approximately 5,000 acres were obtained, with a few smaller acquisitions occurring after 1985. The forest is located within the Knobs region of Kentucky, also known as the Muldraugh Escarpment, which separates the Bluegrass and Pennyrile regions of Kentucky. It is composed of hundreds of primarily round, conical hills, or monadnocks, that were created by the erosion of the northern portion of the Mississippian Plateau in southern and central Kentucky. The slopes of the knobs contain mostly shale and siltstone dating to the Mississippian and Devonian ages.

Jefferson Memorial Forest offers many recreational facilities, including camping areas, Tom Wallace Lake, and well over 50 miles of hiking trails. In the 1990s, the forest's ranger station, located in an old schoolhouse, was renovated to create a visitor's center. Despite the rugged terrain and poor soils of the area, Jefferson Memorial Forest hosts a diverse variety of plants and wildlife that includes bobcats, coyotes, red foxes, and ten species of oak. It is well worth time spent exploring the many trails that pass through the area, especially on hot summer afternoons when the cool, shaded forests make a welcome diversion. There is a trailhead for the Siltstone Trail on Bearcamp Road.

The route described here departs from the W Manslick Road trailhead of the Louisville Loop, where parking is available. A short 1.6-mile section of the Louisville Loop's Shale Lowlands section begins here and runs next to Pond Creek. The trail then crosses Lamborne Boulevard before ending less than 0.5 miles to the east. Additional parking is available at the Lamborne

Boulevard trailhead if desired. From here, the route crosses KY-841/Gene Snyder Freeway and travels through the Penile community before heading into Jefferson Memorial Forest via Blevins Gap Road.

Scenery along Bearcamp Road

Michael W. Thompson

Route Directions - Fairdale and Jefferson Memorial Forest

0.0 Right onto West Manslick Road
0.7 Right onto Penile Road
2.2 Left onto Blevins Gap Road
4.0 Left to continue onto Blevins Gap Road
7.5 Left onto Medora Road
8.5 Left onto Pendleton Road
9.1 Continue onto Bearcamp Road
15.4 Right onto Blevins Gap Road
16.5 Right onto Penile Road
18.0 Left onto West Manslick Road
18.7 Left into Louisville Loop parking lot

Route Description – Fairdale and Jefferson Memorial Forest

0.0 Right onto West Manslick Road

West Manslick Road begins at Third Street Road near its intersection with Outer Loop and continues south, passing the Louisville Loop parking lot and crossing KY-841/Gene Snyder Freeway as it continues toward the Fairdale community. The name of the road is derived from the town of Mann's Lick, which once stood near this site.

0.7 Right onto Penile Road

The turn onto Penile Road is at a four-way stop, but caution should be employed when turning, as impatient motorists often run the stop sign. Soon, there is a large trailer park that arises on the right side of the road, and the Gene Snyder Freeway can be seen off to the north. Penile Road is flat and fairly straight with smooth pavement, but there are several sharp curves in the road that may force cyclists to slow down.

Penile Road

The Penile community (pronounced pa-nilē by local residents) was founded around 1840 and has been a source of snickers from locals and visitors alike ever since. According to most accounts, Penile's name was derived from the Biblical story of Jacob wrestling with an angel at Peniel as detailed in the book of Genesis. Despite its proximity to the Gene Snyder Freeway, it still maintains a rural look and feel.

Penile Road ends suddenly as it becomes Greyling Drive and passes back over Interstate 265. On the left side of the road is Penile Baptist Church, which sits at the intersection of Penile Road, Greyling Drive, and Blevins Gap Road. The church was at one time Penile Elementary School, which was founded around the same time as Penile. The original school building was a small one-room log cabin. The current building located here was constructed in 1933 and subsequently sold to a Baptist mission in 1955.

2.2 Left onto Blevins Gap Road

Traffic on Penile Road is not required to stop before turning onto Blevins Gap Road, but southbound drivers on Greyling Drive may not necessarily be looking for left turning vehicles or bicycles as they cross over the freeway. Cyclists should check for oncoming traffic here before making the turn.

Soon after the turn, the road begins climbing a few minor hills, but they should not be challenging to most cyclists.

4.0 Left to continue onto Blevins Gap Road

Just short of the 4-mile mark of the route, Blevins Gap Road descends a large hill and comes to a stop at its intersection with Stonestreet Road. Although Blevins Gap Road continues on to the left here, this intersection can be dangerous because traffic descending the steep hill here is required to stop and yield to southbound traffic from Stonestreet Road and northbound traffic from Blevins Gap Road. Cyclists should be prepared to brake fairly hard to avoid darting out into the intersection.

Immediately after the turn, the road begins to climb a fairly large hill. Because of the stop sign, there is no momentum to carry riders up the hill, so cyclists should be prepared to shift down quickly in order to make it up the hill. There are a few more hills to climb and descend over the next 3 miles as the route passes through the northernmost reach of the Jefferson Memorial Forest and heads west toward Valley Station. Just before the route's next turn, there is a railroad crossing, but the tracks here are easily passable.

7.5 Left onto Medora Road

Medora Road runs parallel to the railroad before making a short descent that is followed immediately by a quick climb. Medora Road ends one mile ahead at its intersection with Pendleton Road.

8.5 Left onto Pendleton Road

Cyclists must cross the railroad tracks again immediately after turning onto Pendleton Road and should be on the lookout for trains at the intersection. There is a signal here, but there are no barriers. Passing trains pose a danger to impatient motorists, pedestrians, and bicyclists who ignore the signal and do not check for trains before crossing the tracks.

9.1 Continue onto Bearcamp Road

Bearcamp Road crosses briefly into Bullitt County as it travels through a densely wooded area. After a brief descent, the road begins climbing slowly for the next few miles. Near the top of the hill, Pendleton Hill Road branches off to the right and ascends a very large hill, heading toward KY-1526/Knob Hill Road in Bullitt County. The road is passable for a quick side trip,

Bearcamp Road

but it is extremely steep and can only be conquered by the fittest and most experienced cyclists.

Another mile farther down Bearcamp Road, the road re-enters Jefferson County and enters the Tom Wallace area of Jefferson Memorial Forest. At this point, the forest canopy increases, and the road makes a long, steady descent as it turns slightly and heads back toward Blevins Gap Road. A trailhead for the Siltstone Trail of Jefferson Memorial Forest is located on the right side of the road about one mile after crossing the county line.

15.4 Right onto Blevins Gap Road

From this point, the route retraces Blevins Gap Road and Penile Road as it heads back toward the parking area at Pond Creek Path.

16.5 Right onto Penile Road

18.0 Left onto West Manslick Road

18.7 Left into Louisville Loop parking lot

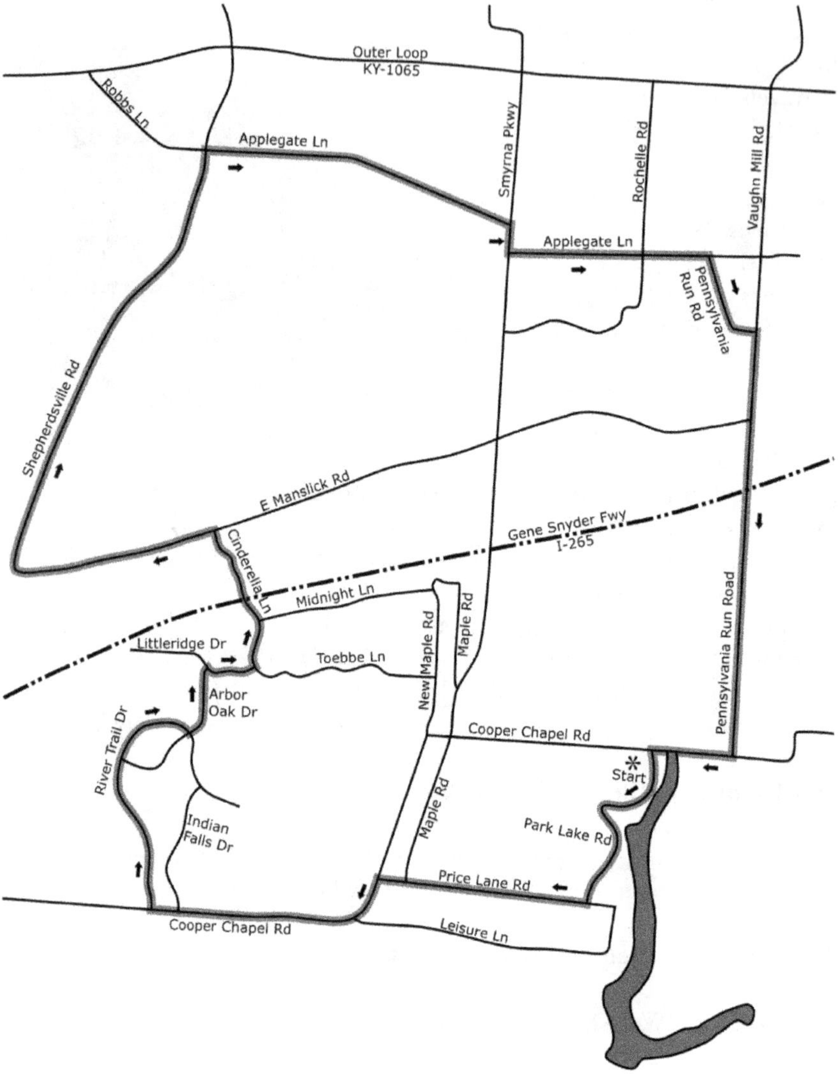

Outer Loop
KY-1065

Robbs Ln

Applegate Ln

Smyrna Pkwy

Rochelle Rd

Vaughn Mill Rd

Applegate Ln

Pennsylvania
Run Rd

Shepherdsville Rd

E Manslick Rd

Gene Snyder Fwy
I-265

Cinderella Ln

Midnight Ln

Littleridge Dr

Maple Rd

New Maple Rd

Pennsylvania Run Road

Arbor
Oak Dr

Toebbe Ln

River Trail Dr

Cooper Chapel Rd

*
Start

Indian
Falls Dr

Maple Rd

Park Lake Rd

Price Lane Rd

Cooper Chapel Rd

Leisure Ln

12 OKOLONA

Distance: 8.7 miles

Difficulty: Easy, with only a few minor hills. Very heavy traffic on E Manslick and Shepherdsville Roads.

Points of Interest: Okolona, McNeely Lake Park, Korean War Memorial, Pennsylvania Run Presbyterian Church Cemetery

Okolona is one of Louisville's southernmost suburbs and is centered mostly around the extremely busy intersection at KY-61/Preston Highway and KY-1065/Outer Loop. There are numerous restaurants, retail shops, and other assorted businesses in the area, as well as many apartments, condominiums, and residential neighborhoods. Jefferson Mall, one of Kentucky's first indoor shopping malls, opened in Okolona in 1978. Although most of the roads in this area of town are choked with rude, heavy, fast-moving traffic, there are a few decent roads accessible to cyclists and several sites of interest that make the area worth exploring.

Farmers migrating from Virginia and Pennsylvania founded Okolona in the late 18th century. The new arrivals quickly founded two churches in the area: Cooper Memorial United Methodist Church and Pennsylvania Run Presbyterian Church. The area remained largely rural for the next century, but around the turn of the 20th century the town had grown and a post office was established. The name Lone Oak was chosen for the small town for the large oak tree that sat near the center of town. However, since a community in McCracken County had already taken the name Lone Oak, the name was rearranged to make "Okolona."

Okolona remained primarily rural from the late 19th century through the middle of the 20th century. The town developed a bad reputation stemming from the many unsavory characters who resided here and in nearby Fairdale, which kept many people from settling in the area. But that changed in 1953 with the construction of General Electric Appliance Park on Shepherdsville Road just northeast of town. Suddenly, the undeveloped land around Okolona became prime real estate for the many workers taking jobs at the plant. Combined with the massive suburban shift that began around the same time, Okolona boomed. By 1980, Okolona's explosive population growth had greatly exceeded the ability of city planners to accommodate the increase in traffic and changing land use patterns.

The city of Louisville attempted to annex Okolona and much of the surrounding land in the early 1980s, and outraged residents attempted to incorporate as a fourth-class city to prevent it. The struggles culminated in a 1986 Kentucky State Supreme Court case that was decided against the city of Louisville, and annexation efforts were halted. But with the merger of Louisville and Jefferson County that resulted in the creation of Metro Louisville in 2003, the city finally won out and Okolona officially became a suburb of Louisville.

McNeely Lake

The tour begins and ends at McNeely Lake Park, which is located along Cooper Chapel Road in southern Okolona. The park opened in 1961 on 750 acres surrounding an impound-ment of Pennsylvania Run Creek, which is a tributary of the Floyds Fork River. In addition to the lake, the park includes caves, a large woodland area, and two state endangered species: Kentucky Glade Cress (*Leavenworthia exigua*) and Eggleston's Violet (*Viola egglestonii*). Both of these rare wildflowers occur in the limestone glades that are common throughout southern Jefferson County and northern Bullitt County. In the near future, McNeely Lake Park will become part of the Louisville Loop in an ongoing effort to create a 100-mile network of greenways and shared use roadways around the city of Louisville. It is expected to be a key access point linking the Floyds Fork region with Jefferson Memorial Forest to the west.

The ride begins at the park entrance on Cooper Chapel Road. There are several parking lots available along the lake's edge and behind the Korean War memorial. The mileage listed for the route is measured from the parking lot nearest the park entrance by the boat ramp.

Route Directions – Okolona

0.0 Left onto Park Lake Road
0.5 Right onto Price Lane Road
1.2 Left onto Cooper Chapel Road
1.9 Right onto River Trail Drive
2.6 Left onto Arbor Oak Drive
2.8 Right onto Littleridge Drive
3.0 Left onto Cinderella Lane
3.4 Left onto E Manslick Road
4.0 Continue onto Shepherdsville Road
5.4 Right onto Applegate Lane
6.3 Right onto Smyrna Parkway
6.4 Left onto Applegate Lane
7.0 Right onto Pennsylvania Run Road
7.3 Right to continue onto Pennsylvania Run Road
8.5 Right onto Cooper Chapel Road
8.6 Left onto Park Lake Road
8.7 Left into parking lot

Route Description – Okolona

0.0 Left onto Park Lake Road

Korean War memorial in McNeely Lake Park

Park Lake Road is the unmarked road that passes through McNeely Lake Park. Several parking lots and picnic areas are located on the side of the road, and there are many beautiful views of the lake from this road. The pavement, however, is in poor condition, with numerous potholes, cracks, and rough areas, so cyclists should pay close attention to the road.

Near the 0.3-mile mark there is a memorial to the Korean War and to the area's veterans who served their country in that war. The road ends at Price Lane Road across the street from Wilt Elementary School. Traffic in the area will be very heavy early in the morning and around dismissal time in the mid-afternoon between August and May.

0.5 Right onto Price Lane Road

1.2 Left onto Cooper Chapel Road

Traffic on Cooper Chapel Road may be busy at times, especially around the morning and evening commute times due to its proximity to KY-61/Preston Highway, the major highway serving Okolona and other nearby suburbs. Fortunately, the speed limit is 35 mph, which does significantly calm the traffic here. The road was recently widened to add a center turn lane and a bicycle lane. These changes have helped to alleviate the heavy traffic on this busy corridor.

The next turn on the route, onto River Trail Drive, may be difficult to see. The sign marking the road is black and white instead of the standard green road sign. The sign also sits a significant distance away from the roadway. However, there is a small median dividing the road at the entrance to the neighborhood that will make it a little easier to find. River Trail Drive is the second such entrance.

1.9 Right onto River Trail Drive

River Trail Drive is one of the main streets leading through the Indian Falls neighborhood. The modest middle-class homes here are typical of many of the small developments that have recently sprung up throughout Okolona and other surrounding suburbs as the area's population began to swell again during the 1980s.

There are a few gently rolling hills through the neighborhood, as well as a few parked cars along the road, that may occasionally make it necessary to veer toward the center line of the road. Overall, traffic flows smoothly through the neighborhood, and the pavement is in good condition.

Prior to the next turn on the route, Arbor Oak Drive appears on the right. If you accidentally turn onto the road at this point instead of at the four-way stop ahead, it is possible to continue along Arbor Oak Drive to pick up the route again.

2.6 Left onto Arbor Oak Drive

It may seem confusing to have to turn right at the end of Arbor Oak Drive because the Gene Snyder Freeway is within earshot; however, Littleridge Drive leads to a dead end on the left. The route continues to the right.

2.8 Right onto Littleridge Drive

3.0 Left onto Cinderella Lane

Cinderella Lane leads down a slight hill and then passes under Interstate 265/Gene Snyder Freeway as it leaves the neighborhood and continues northward toward Manslick Road. At the end of Cinderella Lane there are two drainage gratings that lie perpendicular to the roadway and extend across the road. These gratings are dangerous, and can easily catch and snag bicycle tires. It will be necessary to fully dismount, carry your bicycle over the gratings, and remount to resume riding on Manslick Road.

3.4 Left onto E Manslick Road

Traffic picks up slightly on Manslick Road. The speed limit is 35 mph, but if it seems as if most vehicles are greatly exceeding that speed it is because they are. Speeding and unsafe passes by cars are a major problem along this roadway, so cyclists should use caution here and pay close attention to their surroundings.

East Manslick Road soon curves sharply to the right, descends a small hill, and then becomes Shepherdsville Road as it heads northward. The road here runs roughly parallel to KY-61/Preston Highway, the major thoroughfare through Okolona.

4.0 Continue onto Shepherdsville Road

Before long, E Manslick Road continues off to the left at a four-way stop. North of the four-way, the road becomes Shepherdsville Road. Traffic in this area picks up considerably, especially during the afternoon and early evening hours. As with E Manslick Road, speeding traffic and distracted or impatient motorists may be a problem along this stretch of the road. Extreme caution, patience, and defensive cycling will likely be necessary.

5.4 Right onto Applegate Lane

Applegate Lane leads away from the hubbub of Shepherdsville Road and enters a residential area. Although it's not as busy as Shepherdsville Road, there is still considerable traffic here since many residents use it as a shortcut between KY-1065/Outer Loop and Smyrna Parkway. There are also many vehicles making turns and entering or exiting the roadway to access the homes that are directly along the road, which does calm traffic somewhat.

The road begins climbing almost immediately after the turn, rising about 100 feet in elevation over the next mile or so. Fortunately, it is not steep.

6.3 Right onto Smyrna Parkway

Smyrna Parkway is a busy road, but thankfully this segment of the route is very short. A little patience will be needed in turning onto the road here. Applegate Lane soon continues off to the left, and there is a turn lane that makes it easier to get out of the way of traffic when making the turn. The Smyrna Bait and Tackle Shop, which serves the many fishermen who frequent McNeely Lake and Fisherman's Park nearby, is at the corner.

6.4 Left onto Applegate Lane

Applegate Lane east of Smyrna Parkway is more suburban, and thankfully it carries significantly less traffic.

7.0 Right onto Pennsylvania Run Road

Pennsylvania Run Road begins to head south, back toward the Gene Snyder Freeway and McNeely Lake. The road also begins a moderate descent to a narrow bridge and a sharp left turn before climbing again and seemingly ending at Vaughn's Mill Road. Vaughn's Mill Road, however, actually ends here and becomes Pennsylvania Run Road as it continues southward toward McNeely Lake.

Just before reaching the stop sign at the next turn on the route is the historic Pennsylvania Run Presbyterian Church and Cemetery, located at the corner of Vaughn's Mill and Pennsylvania Run Roads. Although the church building is now occupied by the Emmanuel Freewill Baptist Church, the cemetery, which dates back to at least 1795, is still in use. William Cummings, one of the church's founders, is buried here, and there are many other graves and monuments in the cemetery that are nearly as old.

Pennsylvania Run Cemetery

Vaughn's Mill Road is fairly busy, and a little patience may be needed to make the turn onto Pennsylvania Run Road from the stop sign.

7.3 Right to continue onto Pennsylvania Run Road

Pennsylvania Run Road continues southward, climbing a small hill to cross over the freeway. There are several small hills on the south side of the freeway before the road ends at the bottom of a swift descent to a stop sign at Cooper Chapel Road.

8.5 Right onto Cooper Chapel Road

Cooper Chapel Road heads back toward the ride's start at McNeely Lake Park, passing the Quail Chase Golf Course and crossing the northern end of McNeely Lake. The entrance back into the park lies just beyond the bridge over the lake.

8.6 Left onto Park Lake Road

8.7 Left into parking lot

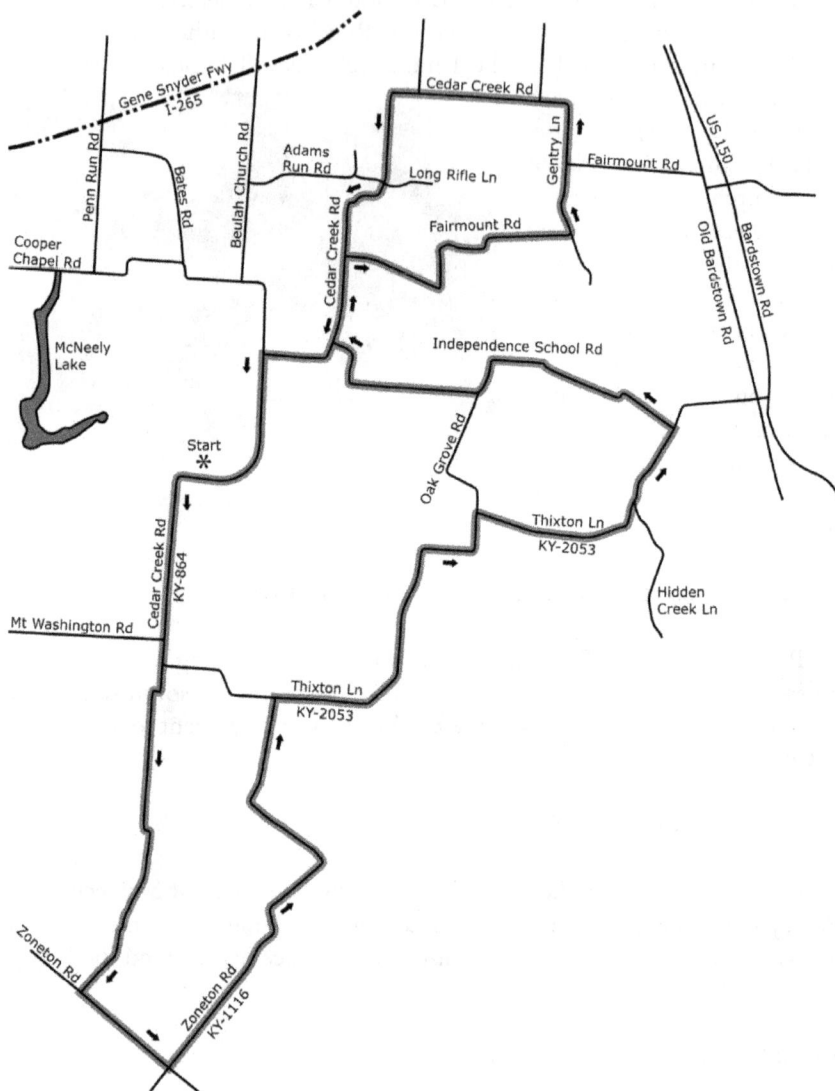

13 FERN CREEK

Distance: 17.4 miles

Difficulty: Moderate. A few rolling hills, but no significant climbs. Light traffic on most roads, although there may be moderate traffic on portions of Cedar Creek Road during the morning and evening commute hours.

Points of Interest: McNeely Lake Park, Fairmount Falls

The Fern Creek area of Louisville features the lush rolling hills and creek bottoms that line either side of KY-150/Bardstown Road through south central Jefferson County. The name Fern Creek probably refers to the creek that arises near the northernmost border of the area at Watterson Trail and meanders toward KY-2052/Shepherdsville Road. The center of activity in Fern Creek is Bardstown Road, formerly Bardstown Pike, which was originally constructed as a toll road between Louisville and Bardstown. But like the many businesses that have come and gone along Bardstown Road, the only constant in the history of Fern Creek has been change.

The area was first settled in the 1770s by a pioneer named James Guthrie, who accepted a 400-acre tract near Cedar Creek as payment for his service during the U. S. Revolutionary War. Within a few decades, many farms and mills were operating throughout the area, attracted by fertile land and abundant clean water. Bardstown Pike was built in 1838 and opened travel between Louisville and Bardstown. Many hotels, restaurants, businesses, and homes soon sprung up along the road, and Fern Creek became a popular stagecoach stop. But a little more than two decades later, Bardstown Pike and the many fruit orchards that had sprung up in the area became far too attractive for the many Union and Confederate soldiers traveling the turnpike, who often raided the area.

After the end of the U. S. Civil War, the farmers who owned the many orchards in the area organized a fair to showcase their wares and attract customers. The first fair was held in 1877 at the Beulah Church, which was located at the current site of Beulah Presbyterian Church. The event was formally organized as the Fern Creek Fair in 1880 and moved to the new fairgrounds located along Fairground Road between Fern Creek and Jeffersontown. The annual fair in Fern Creek was a popular annual event until 1900 when the fair board allowed its incorporation to lapse. That year, the event became the Jefferson County Fair and continued running until 1928 when competition from Jeffersontown's Community Fair and the Kentucky State Fair drew away most of the event's attendees.

The construction of General Electric Appliance Park on Shepherdsville Road just to the east in 1953 soon breathed new life into the community. Attracted by the new subdivisions being built on patches of farmland through the area, Fern Creek's population boomed, topping 10,000 residents by 1965. The boom continued as Louisville residents fled to the area's suburbs, and Fern Creek's population topped 16,800 by 1980. Fern Creek's population boom continues even today as improved infrastructure and more dependable cars have enabled residents of far-flung suburbs to commute into the city cheaply and reliably. Today, U.S. Highway 150/Bardstown Road and Fern Creek are choked with heavy, fast-moving commuter traffic, but there are still plenty of lightly-traveled rural roads south of Interstate 265/Gene Snyder Freeway that are well worth exploring by bicycle.

The tour begins from the large parking lot at the entrance to McNeely Park South. This portion of the park serves the numerous soccer fields at the park's southern edge in Fern Creek. Although the lake and walking trails are not accessible from this lot, it is a good starting location for rides through the area. The route passes through the rural areas of Fern Creek in the Cedar Creek area, which contains much of the area's still undeveloped farms and forested areas. The route stays within the rural portion of Fern Creek, passing through areas still filled with lush, rolling hills, wooded creek bottoms, and scenic farms.

Route Directions – Fern Creek

0.0 Right onto Cedar Creek Road
1.0 Right to continue onto Cedar Creek Road
2.8 Left onto KY-1116/Zoneton Road
3.4 Left to continue on KY-1116/Zoneton Road
5.8 Right onto KY-2053/Thixton Lane
8.9 Left onto Independence School Road
11.1 Right onto Cedar Creek Road
11.6 Right onto Fairmount Road
13.4 Left onto Gentry Lane
13.8 Continue onto Cedar Creek Road
16.4 Left to continue onto Cedar Creek Road
17.4 Right into parking lot

Route Description – Fern Creek

0.0 Right onto Cedar Creek Road

Cedar Creek Road curves sharply left immediately past the exit from the McNeely Lake South parking lot. There is a scenic farm, complete with barn and silo, in the distance at the curve in the road. Past the farm, there is a series of gently rolling hills as the road heads southward through a mixture of small farms and suburban homes.

The next turn on the route occurs immediately past Mt. Washington Road. The road curves sharply left and becomes Thixton Lane, as indicated by the large yellow and black arrow sign on the side of the road. Cedar Creek Road continues slightly to the right (almost straight ahead) as it continues into Bullitt County.

1.0 Right to continue onto Cedar Creek Road

After making the slight right turn onto Cedar Creek Road, Thixton Lane Church will be on the left side of the road. Cedar Creek Road curves sharply to the right, and then to the left, and then continues to wind back and forth through the hills of southern Jefferson and northern Bullitt Counties as it heads toward the Zoneton area of Bullitt County.

After two miles, the road makes a swift descent toward a creek bottom and then ends with a fairly steep climb up to KY-1116/Zoneton Road. The hill is a bit steeper than it first appears, so be ready to shift into a climbing gear if necessary. Traffic on Zoneton Road is not heavy, but cars may be traveling well above the speed limit.

2.8 Left onto KY-1116/Zoneton Road

After dealing with the near constant hills of the past 2 miles, the relatively flat terrain of this portion of northern Bullitt county comes as a relief. After a half mile or so, the road comes to a 3-way stop with Bates Lane. The route continues to the left as it continues to follow KY-1116/Zoneton Road.

3.4 Left to continue on KY-1116/Zoneton Road

Zoneton Road zigzags back to the north as it leaves the flat terrain and passes numerous quiet subdivisions interspersed with large, sprawling farms. Though the road has many twists and turns, this section of KY-1116 is nowhere near as twisty as Cedar Creek Road, and there are only two curves in the road that might slow down cyclists. The road re-enters Jefferson County and then ends at Thixton Lane at the crest of a small hill.

5.8 Right onto KY-2053/Thixton Lane

Thixton Lane passes near the Jefferson-Bullitt County line before turning back to the north and following the low ridge west of the Floyds Fork River. There are many gently rolling hills, farm fields, horses, and black wooden fences that are reminiscent of Kentucky's Bluegrass region along this portion of the road.

Around the 7.5-mile mark, Thixton Lane passes

KY-2053/Thixton Lane

through the unincorporated town of Oakgrove, which consists of little more than a church and a few homes. A little over one mile past Oakgrove is Fairmount Falls, a small pocket park that is a hidden gem of Louisville's Metro Parks system. A creek flowing along Thixton Lane near Hidden Creek Lane suddenly plunges 40 feet into the river bottom before joining the Floyds Fork River nearby. Often, the sound of the falls is so loud that the water crashing down into the river valley can be heard from Thixton Lane, particularly after heavy rains. Sometimes the falls run dry, especially during the dry season between August and October. During the winter months, the falls can be seen from Hidden Creek Lane after the leaves have fallen. Currently, Fairmount Falls is only open by permit from the Natural Areas Management division of Louisville Metro Parks.

8.9 Left onto Independence School Road

The road becomes much rougher for the first hundred feet following the turn onto Independence School Road. There are also many sharp curves in the road, and vehicles traveling too quickly often emerge around the curve on the wrong side of the road. Cyclists should be very cautious and keep to the very right side of the road when rounding the curves in this area.

Just beyond the 10-mile mark, the road curves sharply to the left and crests a small hill beside a scenic red barn before descending gently and turning sharply to the right. Cyclists should note the sharp curve in the road at the bottom of the hill where the other end of Oakgrove Road intersects with Independence School Road, and avoid building up too much speed. The route continues to follow Independence School Road here as it curves sharply to the right.

Barns along Independence School Road

Before long, the road crosses Cedar Creek and begins rising again in elevation as it curves sharply right, then left, before ending at Cedar Creek Road at the top of the hill. The hill is somewhat steep, and may necessitate shifting into a climbing gear. Riders should also be aware of cars traveling down the hill in the opposite direction, as they usually fail to negotiate the curves properly and may suddenly pop out from around the curve on the wrong side of the road.

11.1 Right onto Cedar Creek Road

11.6 Right onto Fairmount Road

One-lane bridge on Fairmount Road

Fairmount Road returns to more rural surroundings. It is well shaded, providing some much-needed relief during the hot summer months. The road soon begins descending a hill as it heads down toward Cedar Creek. At the bottom of the hill there is a sharp curve to the left. There are often sticks, limbs, and leaves along the road here, as well as a rough patch in the road. Cyclists should watch the road very closely in this location and avoid riding too fast. The view of beautiful Cedar Creek, however, is a tempting diversion.

Multiple signs along the road warn of a one-lane bridge on Fairmount Road. The bridge is at the 8.2-mile mark of the route as the road crosses Cedar Creek. It will be necessary to check for oncoming traffic before crossing because the bridge lies just beyond a sharp curve in the road. The concrete bridge was built in 1940 and is currently listed as structurally deficient, although it is definitely strong enough to support bicyclists.

One mile past the bridge, Fairmount Road curves sharply to the right as Gentry Lane branches off very slightly to the left. The road appears to continue almost straight ahead, and many GPS-based maps mark this intersection incorrectly. Traffic making the slight left turn onto Gentry Lane must yield to oncoming traffic on Fairmount Road before making the turn, so cyclists must be extremely cautious and ensure that there are no oncoming cars to their right before leaving Fairmount Road for Gentry Lane, which lies directly ahead and slightly to the left.

13.4 Left onto Gentry Lane

Gentry Lane connects Fairmount Road back to Cedar Creek Road. The road ends about one-half mile later and becomes Cedar Creek Road as it continues straight ahead. The other portion of Cedar Creek Road ends at the bottom of a hill where Gentry Lane becomes Cedar Creek Road. Although traffic from Gentry Lane has the right of way, cyclists should be wary of cars running the stop sign or turning left in front of them.

13.8 Continue onto Cedar Creek Road

Cedar Creek Road soon begins climbing a long gentle hill. The hill is not particularly steep, but it will thoroughly test the legs after vigorously pedaling for the past 13 miles. The road continues climbing past a sewage treatment plant, rolls up and down a series of moderate hills that pass through a few areas of bland suburban sprawl, and then comes to a stop sign at its intersection with Cooper Chapel Road. Although the area here is topographically interesting, the bland cookie-cutter suburban sprawl is generally unappealing and nowhere near as scenic as the past 9 miles.

Cooper Chapel Road ends at the intersection, becoming Cedar Creek Road. From this intersection, the route continues left onto Cedar Creek Road. There is a limited line of sight here, so cyclists should exercise extreme caution when turning left to continue along the route. Traffic on Cooper Chapel Road is descending a fairly large hill and may be well in excess of the 35 MPH speed limit.

The main entrance to McNeely Lake Park, highlighted in an earlier route, is accessible via Cooper Chapel Road by turning right at this intersection instead of left. The lake is located near the park's main entrance, and there are picnic facilities and walking paths adjacent to the lake.

16.4 Left to continue onto Cedar Creek Road

From this point, it is approximately one mile back to the parking area at

McNeely Lake Park South. The road passes through the city of Heritage Creek, which was incorporated in the 1960s during a period when many of the city's expanding suburbs were incorporating to resist annexation into the city of Louisville. This mentality among many suburbanites has persisted, and a few minor cities like Heritage Creek escaped the 2003 city-county merger that created Louisville Metro.

The police in Heritage Creek often run radar along Cedar Creek Road, and there is often an automated radar unit positioned along the right side of the road measuring the speed of passing vehicles. Fortunately for cyclists, this tends to calm traffic and reduce the number of cars traveling in gross excess of the 35 MPH speed limit. On the other hand, it is extremely fun for cyclists to watch their speed on the sign while descending the hill to see how fast they can ride.

17.4 Right into parking lot

Fairmount Falls

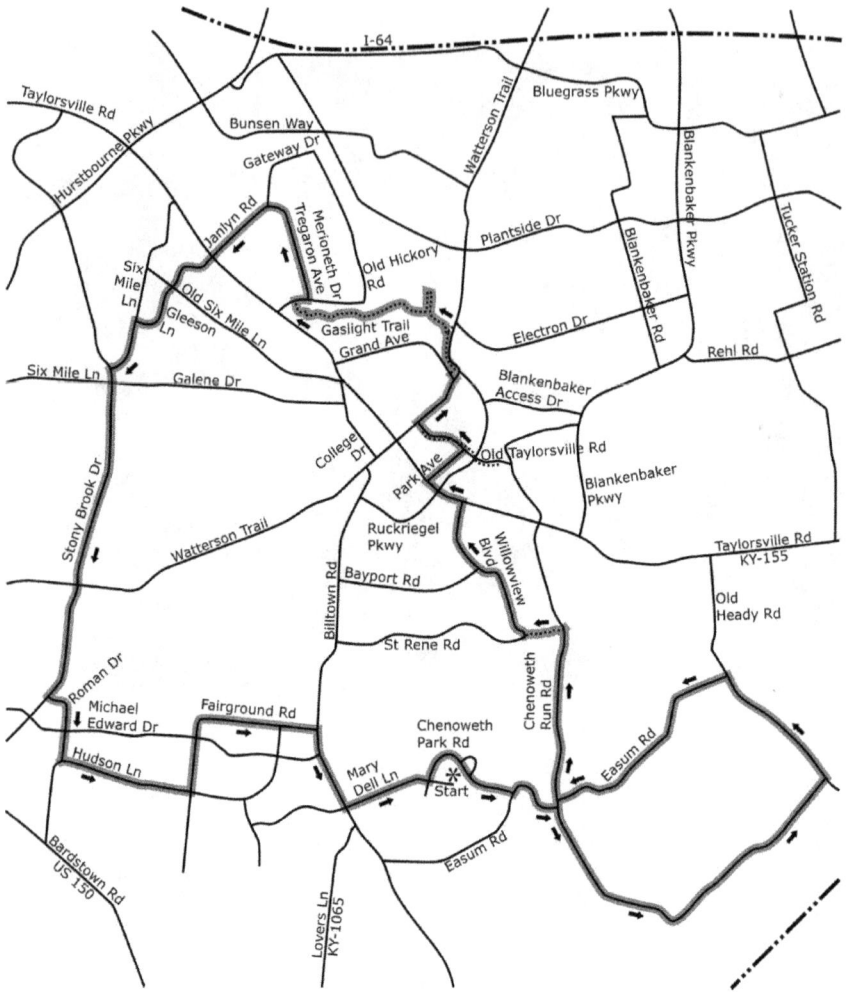

14 JEFFERSONTOWN

Distance: 15.9 miles

Difficulty: Moderate. Moderately heavy traffic on Six Mile Lane and Stony Brook Drive; light traffic elsewhere.

Points of Interest: Vettiner Park, Veterans' Memorial Park, City of Jeffersontown, German Reformed Presbyterian Church Cemetery, Skyview Park, Gaslight Recreational and Workforce Trail

Jeffersontown, referred to as "J-town" by most Louisville residents, is an independent city within Jefferson County that escaped consolidation when the city of Louisville and Jefferson County merged to form Metro Louisville in 2003. While many of Jeffersontown's residents commute to and from jobs in downtown Louisville, the city is well known for its affordable housing, sprawling industrial parks, and historic downtown district. The city is roughly bounded by U.S. Highway 150/Bardstown Road to the west, Blankenbaker Parkway to the east, Interstate 64 to the north, and Fairground Road to the south. A section of the city also extends north of the interstate, encompassing the shopping centers and neighborhoods centered around Linn Station Road near KY-1747/Hurstbourne Parkway.

The area was first settled in the late 18th century as Revolutionary War veterans migrated westward in search of farmland. A number of these settlers found fertile land atop a ridge near Chenoweth Run Creek. The early settlers' wagons had created a natural crossroad as they moved through the area. In 1794, Abraham Bruner bought 120 acres near this crossroad with the intent of founding a town. Soon, merchants purchased land from Bruner to set up their shops, and the area became known as Brunerstown. Eventually, hotels, blacksmiths, and brewers came to Brunerstown, and the town flourished.

The city was incorporated in 1797 as the city of Jefferson, named for President Thomas Jefferson. Eventually, it became known as Jeffersontown, although the locals continued to refer to it as Brunerstown for the next 100 years. Throughout the 19th century, the city continued to develop into a major commerce center as tailors, stonecutters, wheelwrights, bakers, and tobacconists set up their businesses here.

City of Jeffersontown, Kentucky

In the late 1800s, the Louisville and Taylorsville Pike came through town. The new crushed stone road replaced the old dirt road and greatly improved transportation through Jeffersontown. In 1903, a railroad depot was added, offering a direct commuter line into downtown Louisville. With these and other infrastructure improvements, Jeffersontown experienced a new era of prosperity. Later in the 20th century, the mass migration toward the suburbs continued to add to the city's growth, especially as the Hurstbourne Lane interchange at Interstate 64 opened and made the commute into the city of Louisville even easier than before.

The 1960s also saw the development and opening of Blue Grass Research and Industrial Park, one of the first developments of its kind. The development attracted many businesses in the manufacturing and service sectors, continuing Jeffersontown's storied history as a major commerce center. The development, now known as Bluegrass Commerce Park, is currently home to more than 800 businesses. More than 30,000 people work in and around Jeffersontown, making it one of the state's largest economic engines.

The tour begins just south of Jeffersontown in Charlie Vettiner Park. From here, the route explores some of the back roads around Chenoweth Run Creek before heading into the heart of Jeffersontown and passing by Veterans Memorial Park. Plenty of parking is available along Chenoweth Park Road, or along a small loop near the park's center.

Route Directions – Jeffersontown

0.0 Left onto Chenoweth Park Road
0.3 Left onto Easum Road
0.6 Right onto Chenoweth Run Road
2.6 Left onto Old Heady Road
3.3 Left onto Easum Road
4.5 Right onto Chenoweth Run Road
5.3 Left onto St. Rene Greenway
5.4 Continue onto St. Rene Drive
5.6 Right onto Willowview Boulevard
6.4 Left onto KY-155/Taylorsville Road
6.6 Right onto Park Avenue
6.9 Left onto Old Taylorsville Road
7.2 Right onto Watterson Trail
7.4 Left onto Grand Avenue
7.5 Right onto Jeffersontown Greenway Trail
7.8 Left onto Electron Drive
7.9 Right onto Gaslight Recreational and Workforce Trail
8.1 Left to continue onto Gaslight Recreational and Workforce Trail
8.2 Left to continue onto Gaslight Recreational and Workforce Trail
8.9 Left onto Grassland Drive at end of trail
9.0 Right onto Merioneth Drive
9.1 Left onto Tregaron Avenue
9.7 Continue onto Janlyn Road
10.0 Continue onto Gleeson Lane
10.6 Left onto Six Mile Lane
10.9 Left onto Stony Brook Drive
12.6 Left onto Roman Drive
13.0 Left onto Hudson Lane
13.7 Left onto Fairground Road
14.6 Right onto Billtown Road
15.0 Left onto Mary Dell Lane
15.6 Left onto Chenoweth Park Road
15.9 Left into parking lot

Route Description – Jeffersontown

0.0 Left onto Chenoweth Park Road

The climb out of the parking lot is fairly steep and may pose some difficulty for less experienced cyclists or to riders on heavier bikes. However, it is easy to simply walk out onto the road and mount your bicycle on the side of the road. Chenoweth Park Road is the main road that leads through Charlie Vettiner Park, which has soccer fields, a disc golf course, a playground, and a dog run in addition to the 18-hole golf course located at the park's western border.

Chenoweth Park Road descends a large hill as it leads down to the park's eastern entrance on Easum Road. There are a few speed bumps along the road, but they are not so large that they're likely to cause an accident. However, it is advisable for cyclists to feather the brakes when descending the hill to avoid running the stop sign at the bottom of the hill because traffic on Easum Road has a limited line of sight.

0.3 Left onto Easum Road

Easum Road continues downhill before ending at Chenoweth Run Road.

0.6 Right onto Chenoweth Run Road

Chenoweth Run Road remains flat for a short distance, but it soon curves sharply to the left and begins a long sustained climb near the 1.4-mile mark, rising about 150 feet in elevation. Fortunately, the hill is not extremely steep. The road ends at the top of the hill at its intersection with Old Heady Road.

2.6 Left onto Old Heady Road

3.3 Left onto Easum Road

Easum Road heads back toward Vettiner Park. There are numerous new subdivisions that have sprung up along the road that contrast with the more rural feel of Chenoweth Run and Old Heady. Soon, the road begins descending the hill back toward Chenoweth Run Road, but the sharp curves, numerous potholes, and rough patches in the road will make it necessary to watch your speed during the descent.

4.5 Right onto Chenoweth Run Road

The next turn on the route heads back onto Chenoweth Run Road, this time heading away from Vettiner Park and toward the center of Jeffersontown. The scenery is somewhat rural, but there are signs of development due to the road's proximity to the center of Jeffersontown and convenient access to Interstate 265/Gene Snyder Freeway. A creek, Chenoweth Run, flows alongside the road in many locations and provides a buffer from the many subdivisions to the west. At around the 5.3-mile mark, there is a small greenway that leads from Chenoweth Run Road to the subdivision immediately to the west of the creek, providing a convenient transportation corridor toward Billtown Road.

5.3 Left onto St. Rene Greenway

The greenway leads from the left side of Chenoweth Run Road and crosses the creek. The turn is easy to miss, and cyclists much watch for southbound traffic before turning. There may be flooding or mud on the greenway after heavy rains, particularly in the spring.

The bridge over the creek is a bit rough, and the wood surface may be slippery in the early morning or after it has rained. On the far side of the bridge, there is a rough patch of pavement where the greenway has collapsed into the creek. Repairs will be necessary, but until then, it will likely be necessary to walk your bicycle across this short area.

A very steep hill immediately follows; fortunately, it is short, rising only 50 feet in elevation. However, the steep pitch of the hill will most likely require a significant downshift in order to keep moving. The greenway soon ends at a cul-de-sac located at the end of St. Rene Drive.

5.4 Continue onto St. Rene Drive

5.6 Right onto Willowview Boulevard

Willowview Boulevard leads out of the residential neighborhood, ascending a significant hill as it heads northward toward Taylorsville Road. The road is somewhat steep in a few places but is easily manageable by most cyclists. There are several speed bumps on the road that may be jarring, but they have the benefit of greatly calming what little traffic there is in the neighborhood. The road makes a slight descent and then ends at Taylorsville Road.

6.4 Left onto KY-155/Taylorsville Road

Taylorsville Road is busy in places, especially near its intersections with Hurstbourne Lane and Interstate 265/Gene Snyder Freeway. However, this section of the road is not as wide, and the 35 mph speed limit helps to calm traffic. The road is somewhat busy up to its intersection with Ruckriegel Parkway, but traffic lightens greatly past the intersection heading into downtown Jeffersontown.

6.6 Right onto Park Avenue

6.9 Left onto Old Taylorsville Road

7.2 Right onto Watterson Trail

Along with Taylorsville Road, Watterson Trail is one of the original roads along which the city of Jeffersontown was founded. To the left, the road leads toward downtown Jeffersontown. The route continues to the right, toward the industrial parks located along Jeffersontown's north side.

Historic Presbyterian Church Cemetery

At the intersection of Watterson Trail and Shelby Street is the German Reformed Presbyterian Church Cemetery, a historic cemetery that is the fourth oldest in the state of Kentucky. The church and cemetery were established at this site in 1799. The cemetery was in use until 1909 and later fell into disrepair. The graveyard was restored in the 1960s, but it has once again fallen into disrepair.

Beyond the cemetery, the road begins a gentle descent as it heads northward toward Ruckriegel Parkway. It will likely be necessary to slow down in order to make the turn onto Grand Avenue.

7.4 Left onto Grand Avenue

Less than one block after making the turn, a bike trail begins on the right side of the road. The route continues along the bike trail.

7.5 Right onto Jeffersontown Greenway Trail

The greenway trail crosses a creek and then runs alongside Ruckriegel Parkway, separated from the roadway by a large concrete retainer wall. The trail ends near the intersection of Ruckriegel Parkway and Electron Drive at the entrance to Skyview Park.

7.8 Left onto Electron Drive

Electron Drive continues into the park, curving back to the left and heading downhill toward the railroad tracks where it then passes underneath Ruckriegel Parkway. The greenway trail resumes near the bottom of the hill and heads into Skyview Park.

7.9 Right onto Gaslight Recreational and Workforce Trail

The Gaslight Recreational and Workforce Trail begins at Skyview Park. The trail soon enters the edge of the park's parking lot, then continues off to the left back into the park. The trail continues past a baseball field, enters the woods, and then ascends a slight hill. It will then be necessary to make a sharp left turn to continue along the trail. In the other direction, the trail leads back to the parking lot.

Gaslight Recreational and Workforce Trail

8.1 Left to continue onto Gaslight Recreational and Workforce Trail

The trail continues over a small bridge. Immediately past the bridge, the trail continues to the left as another paved pathway continues straight ahead toward the park's sports facility.

8.2 Left to continue onto Gaslight Recreational and Workforce Trail

The trail heads down a small hill and back into a wooded area. Tree limbs, twigs, mud, and other debris may cover the pavement at times, and there are numerous sharp turns along the pathway that will make it necessary to watch your speed as the trail continues through the forest. The trail then runs parallel to Grassland Drive for a short distance before re-entering the woods.

The trail ends a little less than a mile later at Grassland Drive near an apartment complex. The tour continues to the left, onto Grassland Drive.

8.9 Left onto Grassland Drive at end of trail

Grassland Drive ascends a small hill before ending abruptly at Merioneth Drive.

9.0 Right onto Merioneth Drive

A bike lane begins along the right side of the road and continues to the top of the hill. The road then begins a modest descent, and the bike lane suddenly disappears as Tregaron Drive appears on the left.

9.1 Left onto Tregaron Avenue

The road climbs as it passes through a residential neighborhood and passes Cochrane Elementary School. It curves to the left and becomes Janlyn Road as it crosses Ballard Boulevard.

9.7 Continue onto Janlyn Road

Janlyn Road ends at KY-155/Taylorsville Road and continues on the west side of the road as Gleeson Lane. There is no traffic light at this location, so caution should be employed when crossing Taylorsville Road.

10.0 Continue onto Gleeson Lane

10.6 Left onto Six Mile Lane

Six Mile Lane ends at Stonybrook Drive. Traffic on Stonybrook Drive occasionally backs up in this location due to a set of railroad tracks and a traffic light off to the left.

10.9 Left onto Stony Brook Drive

The best strategy here is to integrate into the lane of traffic, which will be slow through this area, and cross the intersection with the light in the traffic through lane on the right. Cyclists should take the entire lane here to avoid getting clipped by traffic turning right onto Six Mile Lane, which branches off to the right at this intersection.

Stonybrook Drive is somewhat hilly, and it will be necessary to ride as far to the right as possible to accommodate traffic that may pass irresponsibly in areas where drivers cannot see oncoming traffic over the hill. The speed limit is 35 mph here, but many cars travel above the speed limit due to the lack of stop signs and large numbers of traffic lights through this stretch. Stonybrook

Drive crosses Watterson Trail at a light as it rises in elevation, potentially making it difficult to cross. For this reason, it is advised to take the entire lane of traffic when crossing the intersection to avoid crossing paths with cars turning right onto Watterson Trail.

12.6 Left onto Roman Drive

Roman Drive curves to the left and then makes a swift descent as it ends at Hudson Lane.

13.0 Left onto Hudson Lane

13.7 Left onto Fairground Road

This road passes along the northern edge of the Fern Creek neighborhood near the area where the Jefferson County Fairgrounds were located between 1900 and 1928. The area was largely rural until the mass migration toward the suburbs in the 1960s converted it into a residential neighborhood.

14.6 Right onto Billtown Road

Traffic picks up slightly along Billtown Road, but it is easily accessible to bicycles. The next turn on the route is easy to spot due to the blinking yellow caution light and a very prominent pedestrian crosswalk.

15.0 Left onto Mary Dell Lane

Mary Dell Lane heads downhill, but it is difficult to build up too much speed due to the presence of speed bumps. The road reaches the bottom of the hill at the entrance to Vettiner Park, then begins to climb a small hill before coming to a stop sign. The route continues to the left, onto Chenoweth Park Road, which is the main road leading through the park.

15.6 Left onto Chenoweth Park Road

15.9 Left into parking lot

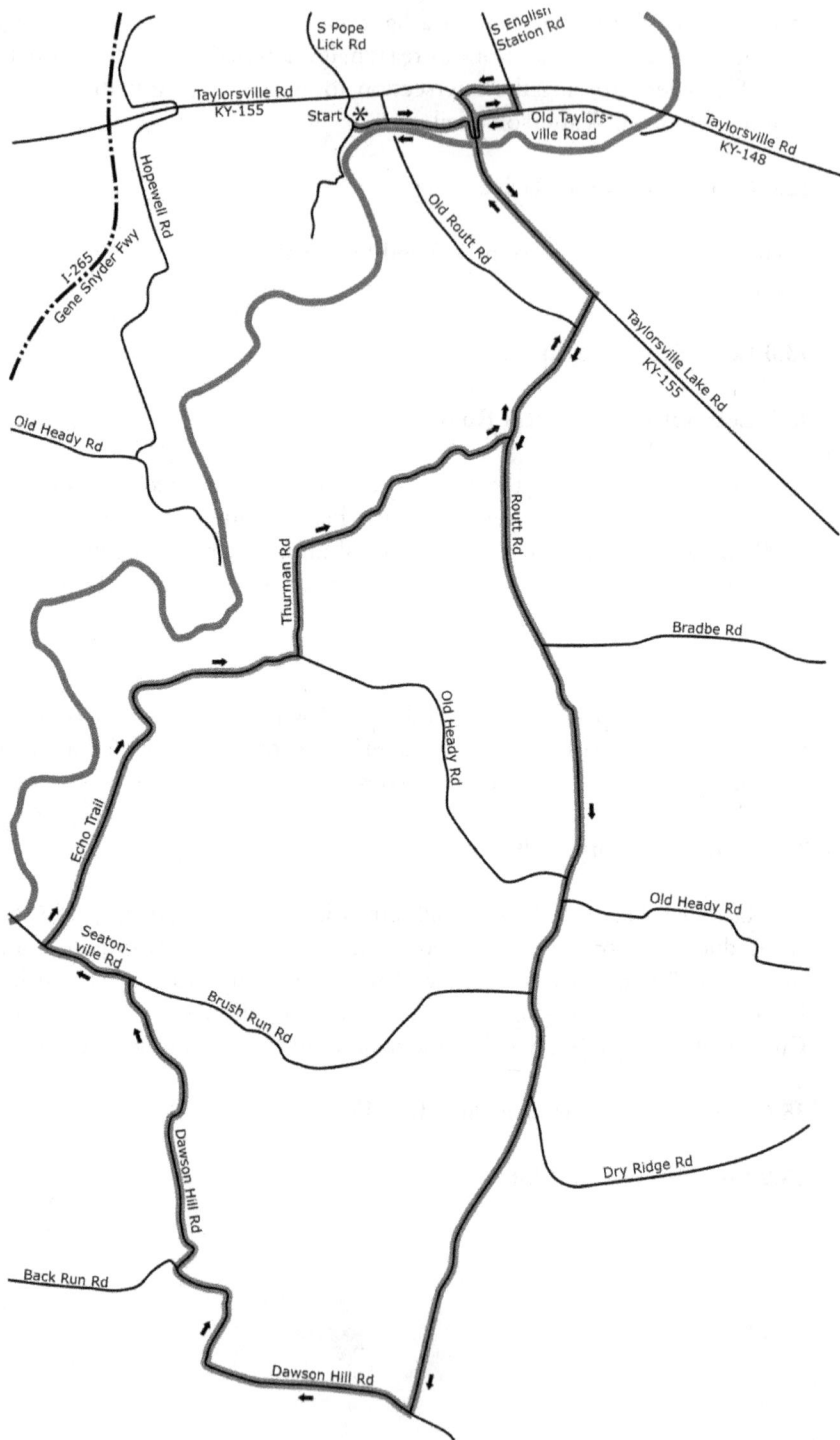

Michael W. Thompson

15 SEATONVILLE

Distance: 20.0 miles

Difficulty: Difficult. Several large hills, with one significant climb. Light traffic in most places, except for Taylorsville Lake Road.

Points of Interest: Pope Lick Park, Fisherville Paddling Access, Turkey Run Park, Cane Run Canoe Access Area

Seatonville refers to a defunct settlement that once thrived near the confluence of Chenoweth Run and the Floyds Fork River. Today, the site of the former town is located near the end of Seatonville Road where it becomes Brush Run Road. The town was named for George Seaton (1781-1835), who was one of the area's first magistrates and a son of one of the area's first settlers.

Due to government policies at the time, the first arrivals in this area could obtain land claims for a mere ten dollars with few limits on the amount of land that could be claimed. Obviously, this policy led to many overlapping claims, causing many disputes over land ownership. Often, these disputes led to violence. It was only after a larger number of settlers arrived in the early 19th century that order was established and the violence subsided.

A road leading from Jeffersontown to Taylorsville passed through the area, and several mills were built in the area. The main mill in the area was Funk's Mill, and the facility drew enough traffic into the area that a town was established along the floodplain of the Floyds Fork River. The Funk family continued operating the mill until the late 1800s, and the town continued to grow. By the end of the century, Seatonville boasted 75 residents, several mills and lumber operations, and a school. A post office opened around 1900, and the town was incorporated as Malott. The post office closed in 1908, and in 1919 the citizens of the area petitioned to return the town's name to Seatonville.

Seatonville Cemetery

Seatonville slowly disappeared over the 20th century as automobiles improved transportation, and the small family farms in the area were unable to compete with larger farms. Today, locals use the name Seatonville in reference to the southeastern portion of Jefferson County near its border with Bullitt and Spencer Counties. Geographically, the Seatonville area is characterized by a series of hills and ravines cut by the many creeks that run eastward through the area toward the Floyds Fork River. The earliest roads cut through the area followed the creeks and ravines, a fact that is still evident today when traveling the roads through this portion of the county. Generally, the land in this area of Jefferson County is rugged with poor soils, and erosion proved problematic for many early settlers attempting to establish farms in the area.

This tour begins at a parking lot at the entrance to Pope Lick Park and explores the many scenic roads that lie to the south and east of the Parklands of Floyds Fork. This route is rated as difficult due to the rugged terrain, and will challenge most cyclists. Since much of the route passes through a remote area with very little traffic, a spare tube, a first aid kit, and a cell phone are recommended, especially when traveling alone.

Route Directions – Seatonville

0.0 Left onto Old Taylorsville Road
1.0 Left onto English Station Road
1.1 Left onto KY-148/Taylorsville Road
1.3 Left onto KY-155/Taylorsville Lake Road
2.6 Right onto KY-1531/Routt Road
8.5 Right onto Dawson Hill Road
10.3 Right to continue onto Dawson Hill Road
11.9 Left onto Brush Run Road
12.3 Right onto Echo Trail
14.6 Left onto Thurman Road
16.4 Left onto KY-1531/Routt Road
17.4 Left onto KY-155/Taylorsville Lake Road
18.6 Right onto KY-148/Taylorsville Road
18.8 Right onto Old Taylorsville Road
20.0 Right into parking lot

Route Description – Seatonville

0.0 Left onto Old Taylorsville Road

Old Taylorsville Road leads away from Pope Lick Park and heads toward the eastern Jefferson County community of Fisherville. For this first half mile, the road is pockmarked with numerous cracks and potholes. Sections of the road may flood after heavy rains, particularly in the early spring, so cyclists should be alert for water covering the road during these times. Because the pavement is so rough, it is also recommended that cyclists check the air pressure in their tires prior to riding to avoid pinch flats, which are a common problem in this area.

Soon, the road becomes much smoother. On the right side of the road is the Fisherville Paddling Access, a staging area for canoes and kayaks that is a part of Pope Lick Park. Immediately to the east of the paddling access area, the road takes a large U-shaped turn as it passes underneath Taylorsville Lake Road. Soon after the road emerges from underneath the overpass, the next turn, onto English Station Road, appears on the right.

1.0 Left onto English Station Road

1.1 Left onto KY-148/Taylorsville Road

To access points south of Pope Lick Park, it is necessary to travel a short distance on Taylorsville Road. Fortunately, this portion of Taylorsville Road is not as busy and congested as the portion west of Taylorsville Lake Road, since most traffic through the area has been re-routed down the newly-widened KY-155. KY-148 ends soon with a traffic light at its intersection with KY-155. To the right, the road becomes KY-155/Taylorsville Road and continues back toward Pope Lick Park and the city of Louisville. To the left, the road becomes KY-155/Taylorsville Lake Road. The route continues south along Taylorsville Lake Road as it heads toward the remote and scenic Seatonville area of southeastern Jefferson County.

1.3 Left onto KY-155/Taylorsville Lake Road

Taylorsville Lake Road is an extremely busy four-lane road with heavy, fast-moving traffic. Fortunately, there is an extremely wide shoulder that is suitable for cycling. A wide rumble strip separates the general traffic lanes from the shoulder, discouraging inattentive motorists from accidentally drifting out of the lane of traffic. However, cyclists should remain aware of traffic and keep a watch for roadside debris on the shoulder that can occasionally force cyclists into the roadway.

The road begins a slow, steady climb that begins at the overpass over Old Taylorsville Road and the Floyds Fork River and ends near the intersection of KY-155 and KY-1531/Routt Road at the next turn on the route. Approaching this turn, cyclists should watch for motorists turning right onto Routt Road from Taylorsville Lake Road who may not be looking for cyclists entering the road with them at the intersection. If this is a concern, it would be wise to move into the full lane with traffic before proceeding with the turn.

2.6 Right onto KY-1531/Routt Road

Routt Road continues climbing for another quarter mile after the turn. The road soon flattens out, and traffic becomes more sparse as the route traverses a series of gently rolling hills over the next six miles. Before the widening of KY-155/Taylorsville Lake Road drew most of the traffic away, Routt Road was one of the major thoroughfares through the southeastern portion of Jefferson County toward Bullitt and Spencer Counties. Near its end, Routt Road enters Bullitt County.

8.5 Right onto Dawson Hill Road

Dawson Hill Road heads over a small hill and around a curve before re-entering Jefferson County. The rolling suburban landscape soon gives way to the more scenic, tree-covered rural roads typical of the Seatonville area. The road soon heads into a long descent that is followed quickly by a sharp S-curve that turns first to the right, then to the left about a half

Dawson Hill Road

mile later. Cyclists should pay close attention to the road and avoid building up too much speed through this area.

North of the S-curve the road continues straight ahead along the bottom of the wide ravine and around a gentle left-hand curve as it becomes Back Run Road. The route continues along Dawson Hill Road, which branches off to the right just before the road becomes Back Run Road. The turn is easy to miss, so pay close attention. At the turn, the road sign indicating Dawson Hill Road may be misaligned, as it seems to indicate that Dawson Hill Road continues straight ahead.

10.3 Right to continue onto Dawson Hill Road

Dawson Hill Road leaves the creek bottom and heads across the ridge at this point. After a short flat stretch, the road again begins climbing, rising nearly 150 feet in elevation over the next mile. Fortunately, the climb is not extremely steep, and should not be difficult for most cyclists.

After cresting the ridge, the road makes a short, swift descent toward Brush Run Road and ends at a 3-way stop. The road curves back and forth at this point, so it will likely be necessary to feather the brakes to avoid building up too much speed. It is especially important to avoid running through the stop sign at the bottom of the road because traffic on Brush Run Road can appear very suddenly.

11.9 Left onto Brush Run Road

Brush Run Road heads toward the former town of Seatonville. Just beyond the next turn of the route, the road passes the Seaton Family Cemetery, a small concrete walled cemetery located on the left side of the road. Many of the area's pioneers are buried here. Immediately west of the cemetery is the entrance to Turkey Run Park, which is one of the parks that makes up the Parklands of Floyds Fork. On the right is the entrance to The Strand, a portion of the Parklands of Floyds Fork and Louisville Loop that links Turkey Run Park to Pope Lick Park. If desired, the Louisville Loop may be used to return to the ride's start point at the northern end of Pope Lick Park.

Brush Run Road

12.3 Right onto Echo Trail

Echo Trail runs along the eastern side of the Floyds Fork River, remaining mostly within the river valley. The river valley is quite wide in this area, and there are many stately homes with beautiful fences, large pastures, and well-manicured lawns. The Cane Run Paddling Access area, another staging area for canoes and kayaks along the Floyd's Fork River, is located about halfway up Echo Trail toward its intersection with Thurman Road. The left turn is located at the bottom of a short descent and may be easy to miss if you are traveling too fast.

14.6 Left onto Thurman Road

Thurman Road continues through a flat area containing many palatial homes and estates. Very soon after the turn, however, is the largest climb of the route. The road begins a steady ascent toward its end at KY-1531/Routt Road here, rising nearly 200 feet in elevation over the course of a mile and a half. The hill is not extremely steep, so most cyclists should be able to easily climb the hill by shifting onto the climbing ring of the front derailleur.

16.4 Left onto KY-1531/Routt Road

With the turn onto Routt Road, the route heads back toward its beginning at Pope Lick Park. The left turn onto Taylorsville Lake Road at the end of Routt Road, however, can be an exercise in patience. Cyclists should wait for a sufficiently large opening in traffic to ensure that there is ample time to fully cross the busy four-lane road onto the shoulder of Taylorsville Lake Road, keeping in mind that traffic may be traveling well in excess of the posted 55 MPH speed limit.

17.4 Left onto KY-155/Taylorsville Lake Road

The return trip along Taylorsville Lake Road is mostly downhill, and many cyclists may build up considerable speed descending the hill. Cyclists should, however, stay acutely aware of the considerable amount of debris that often accumulates along the side of the road. This is especially true near the bottom of the hill where the road passes over the Floyds Fork River and Old Taylorsville Road, where a large amount of mud and gravel often accumulates. The debris may force bicyclists to move into the right-hand lane with traffic. If this is necessary, proper hand signals should be given to motorists to alert them to the sudden maneuver.

18.6 Right onto KY-148/Taylorsville Road

18.8 Right onto Old Taylorsville Road

20.0 Right into parking lot

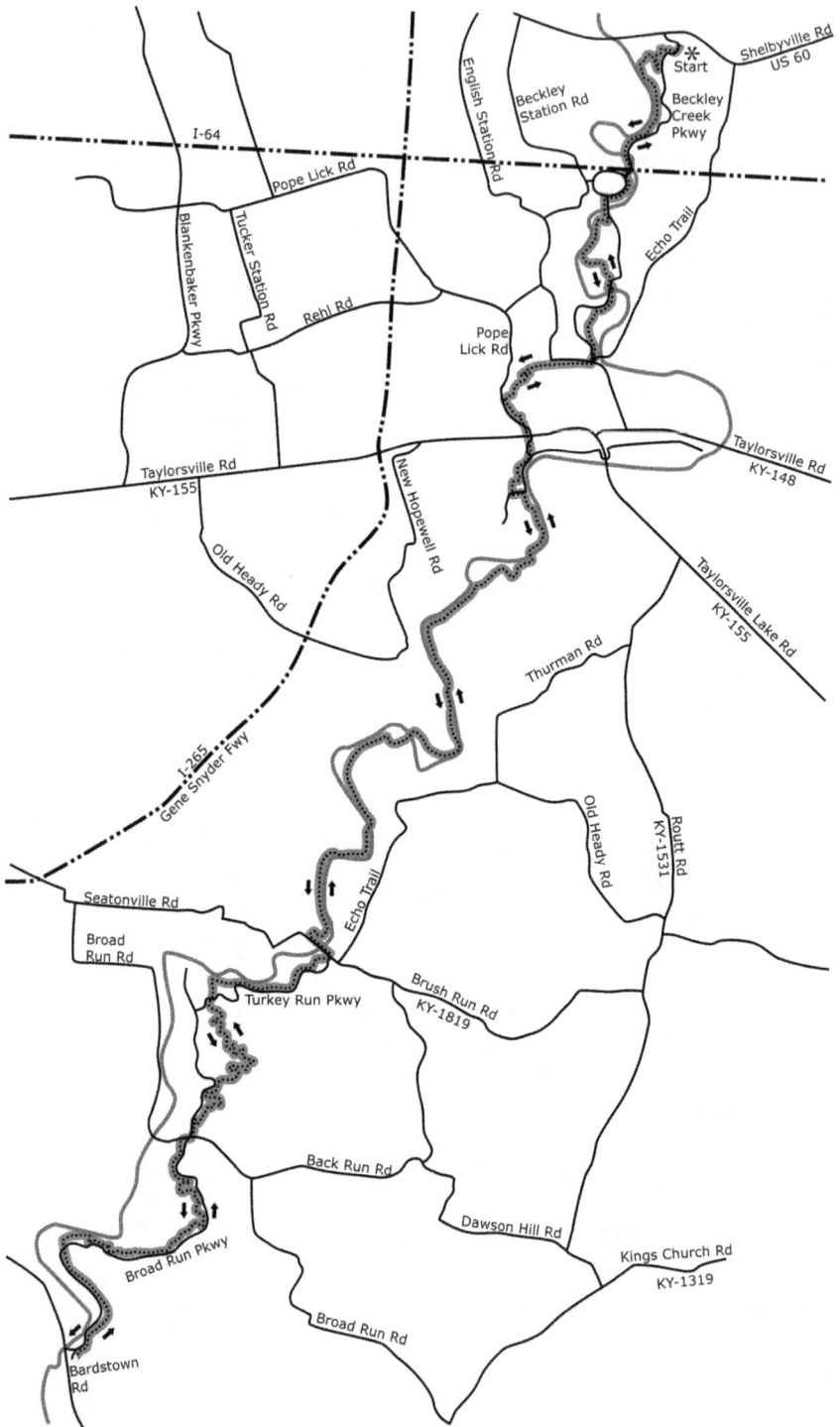

16 PARKLANDS OF FLOYDS FORK

Distance: 38.8 miles (19.4 miles one-way)

Difficulty: Moderate. Numerous hills, several of which may be strenuous for some cyclists. No vehicular traffic, but heavy pedestrian traffic may cause congestion in some areas, particularly in Beckley Creek and Broad Run Parks.

Points of Interest: Beckley Creek Park, Pope Lick Park, The Strand, Turkey Run Park, Broad Run Park, Seaton family cemetery, Brown-Forman Silo Center, Humana Grand Allee, Ben Stout House

The Parklands of Floyds Fork is an ambitious new expansion of Metro Louisville's park system, the first major project in well over a century. While Louisville's Olmstead Parks project created recreational opportunities for residents along the city's periphery at the time, Louisville's rapid eastward and southward growth since the 1890s has fully surrounded the parks. The additional population growth has likewise created demand for more parks and green spaces and exerted pressure on the area's natural resources. With the population's expansion, the few remaining undeveloped areas within the Louisville Metropolitan Area have come under pressure from increasing development and pollution. In response to these needs, 21st Century Parks, a private non-profit corporation, was formed in order to address the need to create new green spaces and preserve Louisville's rapidly disappearing natural areas.

The newly-created Parklands of Floyds Fork encompasses more than 4,000 acres and stretches from US 60/Shelbyville Road near the Jefferson/Shelby County line southward to US 150/Bardstown Road near the Jefferson/Bullitt County line. The Parklands protects a roughly 27-mile stretch of the Floyds Fork River and boasts four major parks: Beckley Creek

Park, Pope Lick Park, Turkey Run Park, and Broad Run Park, which are named for major tributaries of the Floyds Fork River. Pope Lick and Turkey Run Parks are connected by The Strand, a narrow strip of land that passes between existing farms and homes and protects some of the land surrounding the stretch of the Floyds Fork River between the two major parks. The Parklands of Floyds Fork is also home to a 19-mile stretch of the Louisville Loop, the ongoing project that envisions a 100-mile series of greenways encircling the city.

The Floyds Fork River is a tributary of the Salt River that runs through the easternmost and southernmost portions of Jefferson County, the last sparsely developed areas within Metro Louisville. With an increasing focus on water quality in the area and the need to preserve and protect the area's increasingly polluted watersheds, the Parklands of Floyds Fork addresses many of these problems. The project protects the threatened waterway by preserving much of the undeveloped land surrounding it and also provides recreational opportunities for citizens of Metro Louisville that, in turn, fosters an understanding of why the conservation of natural areas is important for the health of the ecosystem.

Floyds Fork River

Beckley Creek Park is the northernmost of the four parks, stretching from U.S. 60/Shelbyville Road to Echo Trail. Completed in 2012, it was the first of the new parks to open. Beckley Creek Park encompasses the already existing Miles Park along Shelbyville Road and boasts four small lakes, an easily accessible canoe and kayak launch area, and the Egg Lawn, a 22-acre recreational area surrounded by a circular road and numerous walking trails. The main visitor's center and the Gheens Foundation Lodge, a facility for meetings and special events, are both located in Beckley Creek Park immediately south of the Egg Lawn. The many parking lots in this area also serve as a convenient staging area for bike rides throughout southern and eastern Jefferson County, and it is not unusual to see lots of other cyclists here.

Pope Lick Park lies just to the south of Echo Trail and encompasses some of the already existing soccer fields located to the south of KY-155/Taylorsville Road and east of I-265/Gene Snyder Freeway. Much of the park is still forested, including a large hillside situated just north

242

of Taylorsville Road, and the Big Beech Woods, which lies south of the recreational fields at the heart of the park near Taylorsville Road.

The Strand is located between Pope Lick and Turkey Run Parks, extending more than 5 miles from the southern end of Pope Lick Park to Seatonville Road. The last of the parks to open, The Strand is not so much a park as it is a green space that protects some of the valuable bottomland along the river and connects Pope Lick Park to Turkey Run. A large portion of the Louisville Loop runs through The Strand, providing continuity to the parks and also providing an easy, vehicle-free shortcut for cyclists and pedestrians through the area. With the park's opening in 2017, it is now possible for cyclists to make their way from Shelbyville Road on the city's east end all the way to Bardstown Road near the southern end of Jefferson County without having to deal with traffic, except for a few road crossings.

Turkey Run Park lies between KY-1819/Seatonville Road and Broad Run Road. Of the four major parks in the system, it is the largest and most heavily forested, and it has the most rugged terrain. These features make it a major draw for trail runners and mountain bikers. It also contains the Brown-Forman Silo Center, which hosts occasional gatherings and events, and the Ben Stout house, a historic home in the area.

Broad Run Park, the last of the four parks to open and the system's southernmost park, stretches from Broad Run Road back toward U.S. 150/Bardstown Road. Although not as rugged as Turkey Run, Broad Run Park features several scenic overlooks, waterfalls, densely wooded hillsides, and large playgrounds and recreational areas.

The ride begins at the northernmost Louisville Loop trailhead in Beckley Creek Park near Shelbyville Road, where parking is available. It is easily recognizable from the tall yellow silo next to the parking lot, and there are water fountains and restroom facilities available here. On busy days, the parking lot here may be full, but there are parking lots located about one mile south on Beckley Creek Parkway, at the canoe/kayak launch site, or surrounding the Egg Lawn, if needed. There are many trailheads for the Louisville Loop throughout the parks, so a shorter ride is easy to plan if desired. For each access point, the nearest mile marker of the Louisville Loop (not the mileage of this route) is indicated.

William F. Miles trailhead, mile 0
North Beckley Paddling Access, mile 0.8
Egg Lawn, mile 1.7
Distillery Bend trailhead, mile 3.5
Pope Lick Park trailhead, mile 5.2
John Floyd Fields trailhead, mile 6
Seaton Valley trailhead, mile 12
Sky Meadow, mile 13.3

Brown-Forman Silo Center, mile 15
Broad Run Valley trailhead, mile 15.7
Limestone Gorge trailhead, mile 16.8
Big Vista Overlook, mile 17.7
Cliffside trailhead, mile 18.7
Cliffside Paddling Access, mile 19.4

Floyds Fork River in Pope Lick Park

Route Directions – Parklands of Floyds Fork

0.0 Right onto Louisville Loop at William F. Miles trailhead
0.8 Continue past North Beckley Paddling Access
1.7 Continue through Egg Lawn
3.5 Continue past Distillery Bend trailhead
5.2 Continue past Pope Lick Park trailhead
6.0 Continue past John Floyd Fields trailhead
12.0 Continue past Seaton Valley trailhead
13.3 Continue past Sky Meadow trailhead
15.0 Continue past Brown-Forman Silo Center
15.7 Continue past Broad Run Valley trailhead
16.8 Continue past Limestone Gorge trailhead
17.7 Continue past Big Vista Overlook
18.7 Continue past Cliffside Trailhead
19.4 Turn around at Cliffside Paddling Access
20.1 Continue past Cliffside Trailhead
21.1 Continue past Big Vista Overlook
22.0 Continue past Limestone Gorge trailhead
23.1 Continue past Broad Run Valley trailhead
23.8 Continue past Brown-Forman Silo Center
25.5 Continue past Sky Meadow trailhead
26.8 Continue past Seaton Valley trailhead
32.8 Continue past John Floyd Fields trailhead
33.6 Continue past Pope Lick Park trailhead
35.3 Continue past Distillery Bend trailhead
37.1 Continue through Egg Lawn
38.0 Continue past North Beckley Paddling Access
38.8 Left into parking lot at William F. Miles trailhead

Route Description – Parklands of Floyds Fork

0.0 Right onto Louisville Loop at William F. Miles trailhead

William F. Miles Louisville Loop trailhead

The Louisville Loop trail begins at the parking lot and immediately crosses Beckley Creek Parkway to descend a large hill as it makes its way toward the river. The hill is not excessively steep, but it will be necessary to watch your speed through this area due to the switchbacks that the trail cuts down the hillside and the large number of pedestrians that are usually present on the trail.

0.8 Continue past North Beckley Paddling Access

The loop turns to the south as it reaches the river, follows it through a heavily wooded area, and then begins to climb a slight hill on the river's eastern side. There is a major canoe and kayak launch area at the entrance to the wooded area where the trail turns to the south, and there are often many paddlers present in the area during the summer.

1.7 Continue through Egg Lawn

As the trail leaves the woods and crests the hill, it continues alongside Beckley Creek Parkway for a short distance and then passes underneath Interstate 64. On the other side of the interstate, the trail turns sharply to the left before crossing Beckley Creek Parkway at the entrance to the Egg Lawn. The parkway makes a 0.75-mile loop here that encircles the Egg Lawn, a large open area that contains numerous walking paths, open recreational spaces, and parking lots. On the west side of the parking lots encircling the Egg Lawn, there are playgrounds, a dog park, and the Parklands visitor's center. The facility is a good source of information for anyone who is interested in the flora and fauna of the park or the area's history. There is bike parking available near the building, water fountains, restrooms, and a large rental facility that hosts many events throughout the year.

The Louisville Loop traces the eastern edge of the Egg Lawn next to the river. As it reaches the southern edge of the Egg Lawn, the trail again crosses the parkway, crosses the river over a large bridge, and then passes to the west of the Humana Grand Allee, one of the more popular areas of Beckley Creek Park. It features a large picnic area, crushed gravel walking trails, and a wetland area crossed by a wooden walkway that gives visitors a glimpse of wetland wildlife. The Louisville Loop continues to the west of the Humana Grand

Humana Grand Allee

Allee. There are many pedestrians on the trail here, as well as many children who may not be paying attention to passing bicyclists. It will be necessary to watch for children who may suddenly dart out in front of traffic, especially on weekends and during the summer months when the park is busy.

3.5 Continue past Distillery Bend trailhead

The trail soon crosses underneath the parkway and makes a loop to cross the bridge over the river and enter an area known as Distillery Bend. The area's name is derived from the Waterfill and Frazier Distillery, which was built here beside the river in 1933 following the repeal of Prohibition. The distillery's main product was Kentucky Supreme bourbon. Charles and Theresa Grosscurth purchased the distillery in 1948 and continued its tradition of making bourbon.

In 1968, the Grosscurth Distillery was consumed in a massive fire. Thousands of barrels of bourbon aging in two warehouses were set ablaze by an explosion that sent burning liquid directly into the Floyds Fork River. The massive conflagration destroyed forests and agricultural fields nearby and caused massive losses for the many farmers who supplied grain to the facility and the scores of people who worked at the distillery. Following the massive fire, the Grosscurths sold the distillery to the Makler Brothers, who then moved production to Bardstown. The distillery has long since been demolished, and there are few to no remains of the facility to this day. The Kentucky Supreme brand is now owned by Heaven Hill, who no longer produces it.

At the southern end of Distillery Bend, the trail begins to climb a large hill. The trail makes several sharp switchbacks, passes underneath the parkway, and then emerges near the top of the hill before crossing English Station Road near its intersection with Echo Trail. The trail continues a gradual ascent to the top of the hill from here, rising slightly in elevation for the next half mile. After cresting the hill, the trail begins to descend as it enters a heavily wooded area. The trail continues to descend the hill for another mile through the woods, but there are many sharp turns on the trail that will make it necessary to watch your speed through this area.

After emerging from the woods, the trail flattens out and again turns to the south, heading toward Taylorsville Road. Just north of Taylorsville Road, there is a large train trestle that runs over Pope Lick creek and a small overhang that makes a convenient place to stop and rest if needed. Although the train trestle looks abandoned, it is still in use, with several trains per day passing over the bridge. This trestle is also the reputed lair of the Pope Lick Monster, site of one of Louisville's many urban legends. The Pope Lick Monster is said to be part man and part goat or sheep and haunts the area around the trestle, luring people onto the tracks in the path of oncoming trains. It is said that the monster uses either hypnosis or mimics a human voice to lure its victims onto the tracks. Some variations of the legend contend that the monster is so hideous that its victims are frightened into jumping off of the trestle.

Pope Lick Trestle

The origin of the legend is unknown, but most accounts contend that the monster was either an outcast member of a circus sideshow who sought revenge after being disrespected, or that it is the hideous reincarnation of an area farmer who sacrificed goats in Satanic rituals. Whatever the case, the trestle has become a destination for thrill-seekers despite many measures being taken to prevent trespassing, such as the large fence surrounding the base of the trestle. In spite of the many warnings from police and from Norfolk Southern Railway, who owns the trestle, there have been a number of deadly accidents on the bridge. The most recent death was in April 2016 when a 26-year-old Ohio woman fell to her death from the trestle after wandering onto the tracks in search of the Pope Lick Monster legend. Trespassing on the structure is prohibited by law, and people ignoring the warnings are subject to arrest and prosecution.

Not far from the trestle, the trail crosses Pope Lick Road and then passes underneath KY-155/Taylorsville Road. The trail under the road is a narrow steel deck walkway, and it will be necessary to dismount and walk your bike across it. Not only is it unsafe to ride on the steel deck, especially when it is wet, but there are likely to be pedestrians coming around the corner who may not expect to see an oncoming bicycle in their path. If you would rather not dismount, it is possible to turn left onto Pope Lick Road and cross Taylorsville Road at the intersection. Taylorsville Road, however, carries such a large volume of fast-moving traffic that it is unsafe (and frustrating) to cross.

5.2 Continue past Pope Lick Park trailhead

On the other side of Taylorsville Road, the trail crosses Pope Lick Road and leads to a trailhead at the corner of Pope Lick and Old Taylorsville Roads. The trailhead makes a convenient stopping point and is also a convenient parking area for shorter rides along the trail. Old Taylorsville Road also leads out toward many of the roads through the southeastern portion of Jefferson County, making it a convenient staging area for many rides through this area.

Bridge over Floyds Fork River

Beyond the trailhead, the trail again crosses Pope Lick Road, narrows greatly, and then crosses a bridge over Pope Lick Creek near its confluence with the Floyds Fork River. There are poles blocking motorized vehicles from accessing the trail that will make it necessary to slow down, especially if pedestrians are present.

6.0 Continue past John Floyd Fields trailhead

After traveling a short distance through the woods, the trail again crosses Pope Lick Road beside a large parking lot near several athletic fields. There is a large building on the right side of the trail here with water fountains and restrooms, making it a convenient stop on longer rides. There are usually many pedestrians in this area, so caution is advised.

The trail continues south from the parking lot and athletic fields, crosses the Floyds Fork River, and then continues through the Prairie Preserve portion of the park. There are many native grass species here, and it is a popular area for bird watching. Immediately to the east is Big Beech Woods, a large tract of bottomland forest that has been preserved as a part of the parklands.

As the trail continues south beyond the Prairie Preserve, it leaves Pope Lick Park and enters the Strand, which connects Pope Lick to Turkey Run Park. The Strand is a 5.5-mile stretch of the trail that follows the Floyds Fork River between the two parks and serves as a buffer to protect water quality from the pollution that has accompanied development in southeastern Jefferson County. The Strand continues southward toward Seatonville Road. As the trail reaches Seatonville Road, it travels parallel to the road, crosses a bridge, and then crosses Seatonville Road at the entrance to Turkey Run Park.

12.0 Continue past Seaton Valley trailhead

The northernmost end of Turkey Run Park near the Seatonville Road entrance is a broad, flat river valley known as the Seaton Valley. The land here was once the home of Irongate Country Club, which was forced into bankruptcy by frequent flooding and its remote location. The land was sold in 1978 to a group of investors who converted the area into a horse stable. Several of the facility's barns are still standing. The view from the valley is remarkable, with the ridges that surround the valley looming tall in the distance.

Turkey Run Park

On the left side of Turkey Run Parkway just south of the Seatonville Road entrance to the park is the Seaton Family Cemetery, which is enclosed by stone walls and an iron gate. The small family plot is one of the oldest cemeteries in Jefferson County and dates back to the early 1800s. The cemetery holds the remains of many members of the Seaton family, who settled in this area around 1781.

From the park's entrance, the Louisville Loop continues through the valley for almost one mile before climbing a fairly large hill. Although it is not excessively steep, the hill is fairly long and may be strenuous for less experienced riders.

13.3 Continue past Sky Meadow trailhead

At the top of the ridge is Sky Meadow, a flat meadow-like area from which several trails emerge. A paved trail leads from the Louisville Loop to Sky Dome, a rocky area that has spectacular views of the surrounding countryside. The loop continues past Sky Dome and Bullfrog Crossing and then descends the hill to cross Turkey Run Creek. The trail begins climbing again on the other side of the creek, but with a much steeper grade than before. It will be necessary to shift down to an appropriate climbing gear to make the ascent, although the climb is not extremely long.

15.0 Continue past Brown-Forman Silo Center

As the trail nears the top of the ridge again, there is a large yellow silo surrounded by several buildings. This area, known as the Brown-Forman Silo Center, is sometimes used to host private gatherings and events. There is bicycle parking available here, and visitors are free to climb the stairs up to the top of the silo for spectacular views of Turkey Run Park and much of the surrounding countryside. On clear days, it is possible to see all the way west to Muldraugh Hill, which lies near the border of Hardin and Meade Counties just north of Fort Knox.

From the Brown-Forman Silo Center, a side trip to the north on Turkey Run Parkway leads to the Ben Stout House. The house was built sometime

View from silo overlook in Turkey Run Park

in the early 1800s by Daniel Omer using limestone quarried nearby and was sold to Ben Stout in 1867. The home's interior is currently being restored by 21st Century Parks in order to preserve it and to teach visitors about life in the area during the pioneer era.

15.7 Continue past Broad Run Valley trailhead

As the Louisville Loop departs the Brown-Forman Silo Center, it descends a fairly steep hill next to Turkey Run Parkway, which ends at its intersection with Broad Run Road and the entrance to Broad Run Park.

Across Broad Run Road, the parkway becomes Broad Run Parkway. Near the bottom of the hill, the Louisville Loop crosses Turkey Run Parkway before crossing Broad Run Road and heading south into Broad Run Park next to the Parkway.

16.8 Continue past Limestone Gorge trailhead

A short distance later, the Louisville Loop departs from Broad Run Parkway and heads back into the woods. The trail ascends a fairly large hill and then flattens out as it reaches the Limestone Gorge area of the park. This geologically unique area features a large limestone gorge with a small stream running through it, and the water has eroded away the soft layers of shale at the surface to create a series of

Broad Run Park

small waterfalls. During the winter and spring, or after heavy rains, the water cascading down the stream bed is a beautiful sight.

17.7 Continue past Big Vista Overlook

The trail passes over the creek next to the waterfall and then continues uphill toward Highland Crossing, a 70-foot tall ridge overlooking the Floyds Fork River. While not as tall as the hills in Turkey Run Park, there is an overlook here that has a nice view of the river valley. At an elevation of 650 feet, the hill towers tall over the surrounding countryside.

18.7 Continue past Cliffside Trailhead

On the far end of Highland Crossing, the trail begins its descent back into the river valley toward the Greensward, a flat recreational area similar to the Egg Lawn in Beckley Creek Park. There are many picnic shelters, playgrounds, and even a spray park that makes an excellent excuse to stop and cool off during the hot summer months. There are usually many pedestrians here, including children, who may not be paying close attention to their surroundings, so it is wise to slow down through this area.

The trail continues past the playgrounds and parking lots of the

Greensward before crossing Broad Run Parkway. It continues next to a wooded hillside and then crosses a bridge over the Floyds Fork River that connects Broad Run Parkway to US 150/Bardstown Road. During the spring, there are many wildflower species along this hillside and throughout the flat river valley.

19.4 Turn around at Cliffside Paddling Access

The trail ends at the bridge just beyond a small parking lot next to the river. From here, the route retraces the Louisville Loop trail back to the ride state at the William F. Miles trailhead.

20.1 Continue past Cliffside Trailhead

21.1 Continue past Big Vista Overlook

22.0 Continue past Limestone Gorge trailhead

23.1 Continue past Broad Run Valley trailhead

23.8 Continue past Brown-Forman Silo Center

25.5 Continue past Sky Meadow trailhead

26.8 Continue past Seaton Valley trailhead

32.8 Continue past John Floyd Fields trailhead

33.6 Continue past Pope Lick Park trailhead

35.3 Continue past Distillery Bend trailhead

37.1 Continue through Egg Lawn

38.0 Continue past North Beckley Paddling Access

38.8 Left into parking lot at William F. Miles trailhead

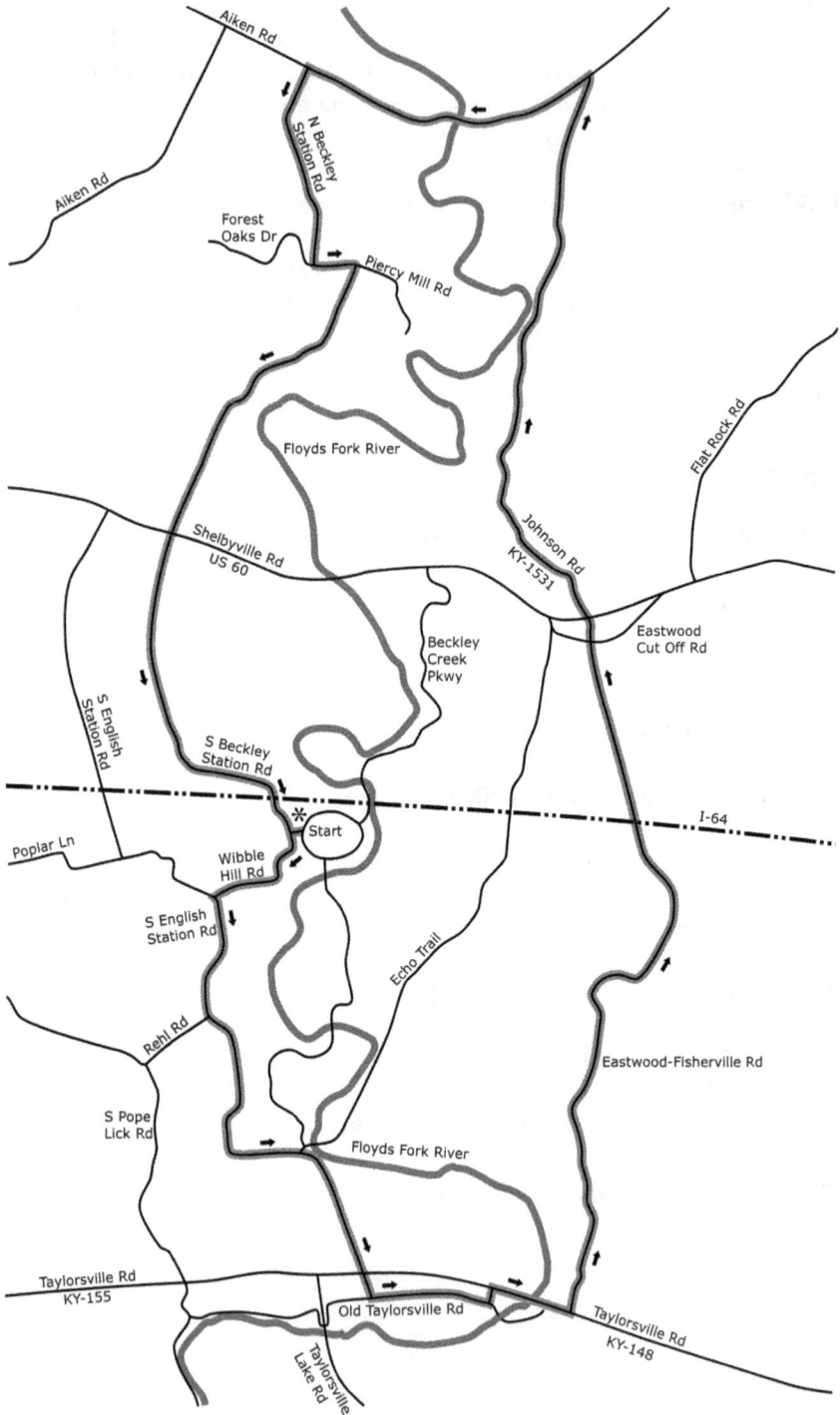

Aiken Rd

N Beckley Station Rd

Aiken Rd

Forest Oaks Dr

Piercy Mill Rd

Floyds Fork River

Flat Rock Rd

Shelbyville Rd US 60

Johnson Rd KY-1531

Beckley Creek Pkwy

Eastwood Cut Off Rd

S English Station Rd

S Beckley Station Rd

I-64

Start

Poplar Ln

Wibble Hill Rd

S English Station Rd

Echo Trail

Rehl Rd

Eastwood-Fisherville Rd

S Pope Lick Rd

Floyds Fork River

Taylorsville Rd KY-155

Old Taylorsville Rd

Taylorsville Rd KY-148

Taylorsville Lake Rd

17 FISHERVILLE AND EASTWOOD

Distance: 15.5 miles

Difficulty: Difficult. Hilly, with two significant climbs. Light to moderate traffic in most areas.

Points of Interest: Beckley Creek Park, Pope Lick Park, Fisherville, Fisherville, Eastwood, Chenoweth Massacre Site

Fisherville is a sparsely populated neighborhood in the southeastern corner of Jefferson County that is centered around the Floyds Fork River and Old Taylorsville Road near its intersection with English Station Road. It lies just to the east of Pope Lick Park, part of the newly developed Parklands of Floyds Fork.

The Fisherville area was first settled in the 1830s. In 1833, a post office was established in the area, which was originally named Curreys after its first postmaster, Edward Currey. Curreys was renamed Fisherville in 1847 for Robert Fisher, who operated a mill on the Floyds Fork River from 1835 until his death in 1845. By the 1850s, the Louisville and Taylorsville Turnpike, which passed through Fisherville, was widened, attracting more travelers and enriching the area's businesses. In 1888, the Southern Railroad passed through town, bringing even more visitors to town.

Fisherville soon became known as a resort town after the discovery of mineral water in a well around the turn of the 20th century. The Blue Rock Hotel was built around the well and opened as a health spa in 1903. The resort prospered as throngs of visitors traveled to the area via the turnpike and the railroad. Some of the mineral water was bottled and shipped for consumption, with the rest diverted into a bathing pool for spa guests.

The good times, however, didn't last long. The well dried up in 1914, and even though the hotel managed to stay open for a few more summers, it eventually closed for good. With the resort's demise, Fisherville was no longer seen as a resort area, and the flood of visitors diminished to a trickle. The hotel was demolished in 1939, and the town returned to being merely another small Kentucky town. In the early 1980s, the newly-widened KY-148/Taylorsville Road bypassed Fisherville, making the area even more isolated. Today, Fisherville is best known for being the home of Hall of Fame Coach Denny Crum, the former basketball coach at the University of Louisville who led the Cardinals to their first two NCAA national championships in 1980 and 1986.

Fisherville

Louisville's Eastwood neighborhood, located along U.S. Highway 60/Shelbyville Road at the easternmost edge of Jefferson County, has a much darker history. Adjacent to Long Run Creek, Eastwood lies along a ridge that was once the site of Boone's Wagon Road. Pioneers fleeing the Painted Stone settlement in Shelby County were killed in the Long Run Massacre that occurred just east of Eastwood on September 13, 1781. Many of the settlers who weren't killed in the massacre fled along the road here, heading toward Linn's Station on Beargrass Creek. Despite its violent history, Eastwood today is a quiet rural suburb of Louisville.

The tour begins in the Parklands of Floyds Fork at the Egg Lawn in Beckley Creek Park. There are many parking lots around the circular lawn, and the park visitor's center is located at the south end of the circle. The parking lots here make an excellent staging area for rides in eastern Jefferson County, and there are usually many other cyclists and runners passing through the area.

Route Directions – Fisherville and Eastwood

0.0 Left onto Beckley Station Road
0.1 Continue onto Wibble Hill Road
0.6 Left onto English Station Road
2.9 Left onto Old Taylorsville Road
3.4 Left to continue onto Old Taylorsville Road
3.5 Right onto KY-148/Taylorsville Road
3.9 Left onto KY-1531/Eastwood Fisherville Road
7.4 Continue onto KY-1531/Johnson Road
9.9 Left onto Aiken Road
11.4 Left onto Beckley Station Road
12.4 Left to continue onto Beckley Station Road
15.5 Left into Beckley Creek Park

Route Description – Fisherville and Eastwood

0.0 Left onto Beckley Station Road

From the park's entrance on the west side of the Egg Lawn, the route turns left (south) onto Beckley Station Road. Beckley Station Road continues a short distance south from the park's entrance, curves sharply to the left, and becomes Wibble Hill Road.

0.1 Continue onto Wibble Hill Road

The first significant climb of the ride comes very quickly after coming around the sharp curve as Beckley Station Road becomes Wibble Hill Road. The road makes a sharp curve to the right as it ascends the hill, so cyclists should watch for vehicles descending the hill that may not be on the correct side of the road. The climb is tough, rising about 140 feet in elevation over a half mile at an average 2.2% grade, but it is not impossible. The hill is a good fitness test, however, because there is not much time to coast prior to beginning the climb. If you find yourself walking up part or most of this hill, you will definitely not be alone. Thankfully, most of the road is well shaded during the summer.

After cresting the hill, Wibble Hill Road soon ends at its intersection with English Station Road. The route continues to the left from the intersection.

English Station Road

0.6 Left onto English Station Road

English Station Road leads southward toward Pope Lick Park and the unincorporated town of Fisherville. The road leads through horse country, with seemingly endless black wooden fences, barns, and large homes. The road, however, is quite rough, and cyclists should be wary of the many potholes, cracks, and uneven patches in the pavement. About one mile from the last turn, English Station Road crosses the Louisville Loop at the southern entrance to Beckley Creek Park. The stop sign at the crossing is on a slight descent, so cyclists should be wary of building up too much speed here due to a large number of pedestrians and cyclists on the Louisville Loop that may be crossing the road here.

South of Beckley Creek Park, English Station Road continues its descent into Fisherville, crossing Taylorsville Road before coming to an end at Old Taylorsville Road.

2.9 Left onto Old Taylorsville Road

Old Taylorsville Road leads away from Pope Lick Park's northern entrance and into the unincorporated town of Fisherville along one of the few relatively flat areas of the route. Although there is not much left of the town, there are a few historic homes along the road and a small post office that is still in operation. Fisherville First Baptist Church, on the left side of Old Taylorsville Road, sits at the site that once housed the old Fisherville School. Just past the church, the road descends slightly and then turns left at the post office. A sign just beyond the post office indicates that the road straight ahead ends at the Floyds Fork River and is no longer in use.

3.4 Left to continue onto Old Taylorsville Road

The short spur of Old Taylorsville Road beside the post office ends a few hundred feet later at KY-148/Taylorsville Road.

3.5 Right onto KY-148/Taylorsville Road

Taylorsville Road may carry a significant amount of traffic at times, particularly during the evening commute hours, but normally this portion of the road is nowhere as busy as the portion of Taylorsville Road between Pope Lick Park and Interstate 265/Gene Snyder Freeway. The route soon turns onto Eastwood Fisherville Road after crossing the Floyds Fork River.

3.9 Left onto KY-1531/Eastwood Fisherville Road

Just after making the turn, there is a one lane railroad underpass. Cyclists should peer around the bend of the road to ensure that there is no traffic coming before entering the underpass. Thankfully, it is short.

Leaving Fisherville, the road again begins to climb, rising nearly 120 feet over the next half mile. There is a series of gently rolling hills for the next 2 miles or so. The road passes under Interstate 64, after which the second significant climb of the ride begins. For the next mile, the road rises about 140 feet in elevation. It is not as steep a climb as Wibble Hill Road, but it is a definite test of the legs. At the top of the hill, Eastwood Fisherville Road

Underpass on Eastwood Fisherville Road

comes to a stop at Eastwood Cutoff Road and the town of Eastwood. There are a few shops here and a post office, so there are a few places to pull off for a quick break if desired. Eastwood Cutoff Road is fairly busy, so caution should be used in this area.

Across Eastwood Cutoff Road, the road makes a sharp descent as it heads toward the extremely busy U.S. 60/Shelbyville Road. It will be necessary to feather the brakes while descending this hill to avoid darting out into fast-moving traffic on the highway.

7.4 Continue onto KY-1531/Johnson Road

On the other side of Shelbyville Road, KY-1531 becomes Johnson Road. The road continues through the rolling farmland of eastern Jefferson County, but there are many signs of development occurring as new subdivisions can be seen here and there along the road. There is one fairly large hill at the 8.4-mile mark of the route, but it is only half as large as the two major climbs already encountered by this point of the route.

9.9 Left onto Aiken Road

Although the speed limit on Aiken Road is 35 MPH, there may be fast-moving traffic in this area, so caution should be used when making the left turn onto Aiken Road. The landscape through this area is mostly rural, with a mixture of forested areas and sprawling farms among rolling hills. Aiken Road begins a long, steep descent as it heads west toward Beckley Station. Occasionally, there is gravel from a few driveways at the bottom of the descent, so caution is advised to avoid skidding. Soon before the next turn, the road begins climbing slightly, so visibility will be limited when turning onto Beckley Station Road.

11.4 Left onto Beckley Station Road

Beckley Station Road begins climbing immediately, rising nearly 100 feet in elevation for the next half mile. After this hill, the route flattens out slightly.

Although there are still constant rolling hills in this area, most of them are much smaller than the hills encountered on the first half of the route. One mile to the south, Beckley Station Road ends at a stop sign and a subdivision on the right. Beckley Station Road continues to the left from this intersection.

12.4 Left to continue onto Beckley Station Road

After the turn, the road continues ahead for a half mile, and then curves sharply to the right and begins a sharp descent. There is a rough railroad crossing at the bottom of this hill that will make it necessary to slow down before reaching the bottom of the descent. The tracks are very uneven and may cause bicycles to lose balance.

This section of the road is more heavily wooded and retains much of its rural character despite the encroachment of suburbs into the area. The road rises and descends a number of small hills, then crests a small hill before coming to a traffic light at its crossing with U.S. 60/Shelbyville Road. The route continues straight ahead on Beckley Station Road, which is mostly downhill from here to the end of the route.

Although Shelbyville Road is extremely busy and definitely not bicycle friendly, a short side trip west along Shelbyville Road leads to a point of interest, the site of the Chenoweth Massacre. From Beckley Station Road, cyclists should turn right onto Lake Forest Drive before reaching Shelbyville Road. At the end of Lake Forest Drive, cyclists should turn left onto Lake Forest Parkway, and immediately right onto Beckley Woods Drive. As Beckley Woods Drive exits the subdivision onto Shelbyville Road there is a small greenway that arises at the corner. The greenway runs alongside Shelbyville Road, under the overpass for Interstate 265/Gene Snyder Freeway, and then becomes a sidewalk as it continues up a significant hill along a busy stretch of Shelbyville Road in the Middletown area. The sidewalk ends at a historical marker that commemorates the Chenoweth Massacre, the last Native American attack on settlers in Jefferson County during the pioneer era.

Captain Richard Chenoweth, who built Fort Nelson at a site near this marker, was attacked along with his family by a large group of Native Americans on July 17, 1789. Three of Chenoweth's children and two guards were killed. Chenoweth's wife was wounded by an arrow and faked death to avoid being killed outright by the raiders. One of the raiders cut off a portion of her scalp as a trophy as she remained motionless. The raiders impaled several of the dead guards on spikes near a springhouse, setting the bodies on fire as a warning.

15.5 Left into Beckley Creek Park

At the bottom of the descent, Beckley Creek Parkway arises to the left and leads back into Beckley Creek Park and the parking lots of the Egg Lawn.

Eastwood, from the intersection of Eastwood Cutoff and Eastwood Fisherville Roads

Farmland on Aiken Road

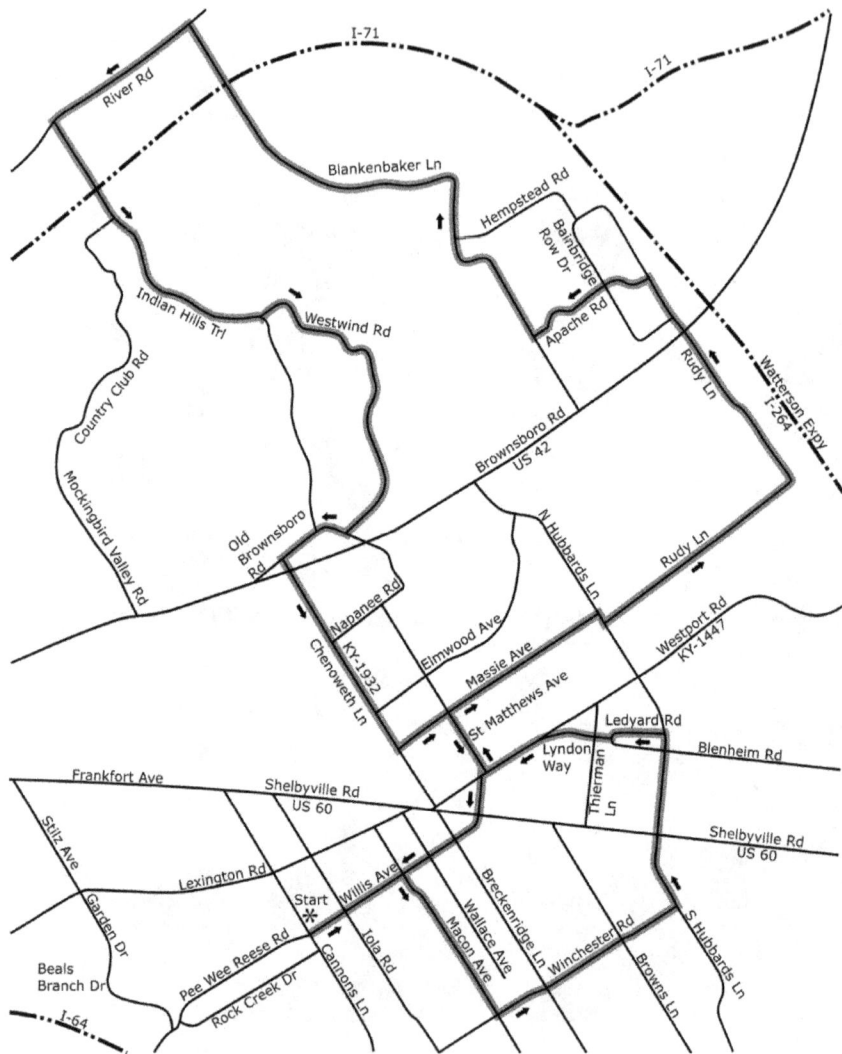

18 ST. MATTHEWS AND INDIAN HILLS

Distance: 14.2 miles

Difficulty: Moderate. Two moderate climbs and some traffic congestion in the St. Matthews area.

Points of Interest: Seneca Park, City of St. Matthews, City of Windy Hills, Zachary Taylor National Cemetery, Zachary Taylor Home, Locust Grove, City of Indian Hills

The city of St. Matthews, situated immediately east of the Crescent Hill neighborhood, is one of the many small cities within Jefferson County that escaped the 2003 consolidation that created Louisville Metro. Like Shively, however, the city is still represented in Louisville's Metro Council. St. Matthews is bounded roughly by Cannons Lane to the west, Interstate 264/Watterson Expressway to the southeast, and Brownsboro Road to the north. St. Matthews is a relatively affluent portion of Louisville and is probably better known to most residents as one of the area's major shopping destinations. Two of the city's major shopping malls, Mall St. Matthews and Oxmoor Center, are located in or near St. Matthews near the junction of Interstate 264/Watterson Expressway and U.S. Highway 60/Shelbyville Road.

The city traces its founding to 1779 when Colonel James John Floyd settled a 2,000-acre tract of land along Beargrass Creek in eastern Jefferson County. He brought his family and erected several cabins and a stockade to form a small settlement originally known as Floyd's Station. The original stockade was located near the Middle Fork of Beargrass Creek at a site near the intersection of Breckenridge Lane and Hillsboro Road. Settlers arriving in the area in the early 18th century built plantations and grew primarily hemp and tobacco.

By the mid-19th century, the settlement had grown, and was centered to the north of its original site near the present-day intersection of U.S. Highway 60/Shelbyville Road, KY-1447/Westport Road, and KY-1932/Breckenridge Lane. In 1851, a post office was opened and the city was renamed St. Matthews after the Episcopal Church that was built nearby. St. Matthews remained largely rural and agricultural, however, until the 1920s when the city's first shopping district was built. In 1938, the Vogue Theater was built along Lexington Road. The theater closed in 1998 and was converted into retail space in the mid-2000s, but the landmark still stands as a monument to St. Matthews' long history as a major shopping and entertainment destination.

After exploring the city of St. Matthews, the route turns north and travels through the city of Windy Hills, a small enclave of historic homes that lies along U.S. Highway 42/Brownsboro Road, before entering the city of Indian Hills. The city of Indian Hills lies along the Muddy Fork of Beargrass Creek on densely forested land atop a low ridge overlooking the Ohio River. Along with Windy Hills and other surrounding neighborhoods, Indian Hills is one of the more prosperous and affluent areas within Metro Louisville and the state of Kentucky. The present city was formed in 1999 by public referendum ahead of the 2003 Metro Louisville consolidation. It stretches from U.S. Highway 42/Brownsboro Road north toward the Ohio River and is bounded by Indian Hills Trail to the west and Interstate 264/Watterson Expressway to the east. Caperton Swamp Park, a preserve located along River Road, lies at the city's northwestern edge.

Indian Hills is named for Indian Hill Stock Farm, the large horse farm that was founded by John Veech, an early settler in the area. Although the Louisville Country Club now occupies about two-thirds of the original farm, the Veech home still stands along Indian Hills Trail near Old Brownsboro Road. Like Anchorage, the heavy tree cover helps to moderate the area's climate during the hot summer months and greatly enhances home values.

Indian Hills, however, is best known for its many battles with the city of Louisville over annexation issues. In the mid-1950s, the city of Louisville proposed the Mallon Plan, which would have annexed most of the city's developing eastern suburbs in order to extend city services such as sewers, fire protection, and garbage collection to residents living in those areas. Suburban voters were incensed, contending that annexation would lead to higher taxes, unnecessary services, and traffic congestion from city buses extending service through the city's eastern suburbs. Voters from Indian Hills and surrounding neighborhoods turned out in large numbers to defeat the proposal.

Buoyed by their success in beating back the annexation proposal, Indian Hills residents began to flex their muscles by drafting restrictive zoning laws.

They used the legal system to force the closure of a used car lot and stop its redevelopment, and then mobilized again in 1988 in an attempt to defeat a proposal to extend sewer service to the neighborhood. Indian Hills residents turned out again in large numbers to vote against the proposal, even though voters in suburbs farther east voted overwhelmingly in favor of the plan. Sewers were eventually extended through the area, but many homeowners in Indian Hills refused connections. In 1999, however, continued problems with septic tank overflows forced many in the area to finally connect to the city's sewer system at great expense.

The tour begins in Seneca Park, a few blocks to the west of the city of St. Matthews, at the intersection of Pee Wee Reese Road and Cannons Lane. Ample parking is available along Pee Wee Reese Road, or along Rock Creek Drive on the southern side of the park's great lawn.

Palmer Products Factory in St. Matthews

Route Directions – St. Matthews and Indian Hills

0.0 Continue onto Willis Avenue
0.4 Right onto Macon Avenue
1.0 Left onto Winchester Road
1.8 Left onto S Hubbards Lane
2.2 Continue onto N Hubbards Lane
2.5 Left onto Ledyard Road
2.6 Right onto Lyndon Way
2.9 Continue onto KY-1447/Westport Road
3.2 Right onto St. Matthews Avenue
3.4 Right onto Massie Avenue
4.1 Right onto N Hubbards Lane
4.2 Left onto Rudy Lane
6.0 Left onto Apache Road
6.5 Left to continue onto Apache Road
6.6 Right onto Blankenbaker Lane
8.6 Left onto River Road
9.3 Left onto Indian Hills Trail
10.4 Left onto Westwind Road
11.7 Right onto Old Brownsboro Road
12.0 Left onto KY-1932/Chenoweth Lane
12.8 Left onto Massie Avenue
13.0 Right onto St. Matthews Avenue
13.3 Right onto KY-1447/Westport Road
13.4 Left onto St. Matthews Avenue
13.5 Continue onto Willis Avenue
14.2 Continue onto Pee Wee Reese Road at Seneca Park

Route Description – St. Matthews and Indian Hills

0.0 Continue onto Willis Avenue

From the stoplight at the end of Pee Wee Reese Road, Willis Avenue lies directly across Cannons Lane. Willis Avenue is one of the main thoroughfares through the western side of St. Matthews.

0.4 Right onto Macon Avenue

1.0 Left onto Winchester Road

Winchester Road, while not a major thoroughfare, carries enough vehicles to warrant a traffic light at its intersection with Breckenridge Lane. Due to the very heavy traffic flow on Breckenridge Lane, it will be necessary to use the traffic light to cross the road safely. Unless there is a car at the intersection to trigger the light, it will likely be necessary to use the pedestrian crossing signal button to cause the light to change.

A few blocks south of this location on the right-hand sidewalk on Breckenridge Lane near its intersection with Hillsboro Road is a series of historical markers that indicates the former site of Floyd's Station and describes the history of the area's earliest residents.

1.8 Left onto S Hubbards Lane

Hubbards Lane is a major north-south thoroughfare through the city of St. Matthews and may be busy during morning and evening commute times. However, this section of the road is not as busy as other sections, and the amount of traffic that the road carries pales in comparison to the volume of traffic that travels U.S. Highway 60/Shelbyville Road at nearly all times of the day.

2.2 Continue onto N Hubbards Lane

Across Shelbyville Road, S Hubbards Lane becomes N Hubbards Lane. Traffic picks up slightly in this area. Ahead of the next turn, southbound traffic has a limited line of sight as it crests a raised railroad crossing, making it necessary to use caution when making the left turn onto Ledyard Road.

2.5 Left onto Ledyard Road

The narrow roadway curves to the left and then ends shortly ahead at its intersection with Lyndon Way. It then continues ahead as Blenheim Road as it curves sharply back to the left, heading back toward N Hubbards Lane. The route continues to the right onto Lyndon Way, which heads west toward the center of St. Matthews.

2.6 Right onto Lyndon Way

Lyndon Way ends abruptly at Westport Road. Westport Road continues straight ahead, heading west toward the center of St. Matthews. Cyclists should use extreme caution in this area to avoid vehicles coming from the right. Westbound traffic on Westport Road travels through an S-curve and across a railroad crossing, and may not be looking for traffic entering the roadway from Lyndon Way.

2.9 Continue onto KY-1447/Westport Road

Immediately past the next turn on the route, there is a bicycle shop, VO2, located along St. Matthews Avenue between Westport Road and Shelbyville Road. It is an excellent place to stop for supplies, a drink of water, or for repair if needed.

3.2 Right onto St. Matthews Avenue

The road crosses a set of railroad tracks and then heads through a small industrial area before entering another residential area.

3.4 Right onto Massie Avenue

Massie Avenue continues through the residential area of St. Matthews and then ends at N Hubbards Lane. The route continues nearly straight ahead onto Rudy Lane, which lies a short distance south across N Hubbards Lane.

4.1 Right onto N Hubbards Lane

To access Rudy Lane, it will be necessary to turn left across traffic on N Hubbards Lane. The road can be busy at times, especially around the morning and evening commutes, and patience will likely be needed. Cyclists should be assertive and take the full lane in this area to prevent cars from trying to squeeze by when making the left turn onto Rudy Lane.

4.2 Left onto Rudy Lane

The traffic calms along Rudy Lane as the houses become larger and spaced farther apart. Soon, the road passes through the city of Windy Hills, a small enclave tucked away between St. Matthews and the Watterson Expressway. The topography changes slightly as the route enters the small hamlet. While most of St. Matthews was flat with a few small rolling hills in places, the hills here a little larger, although they are still not large enough to cause problems for most riders.

As Rudy Lane approaches and crosses U.S. Highway 42/Brownsboro Road, there are several small shopping centers along the right side of the road. On the left side of the road, there is a small park that marks the northeast corner of the city of Windy Hills, and there is a historical marker here. On the north side of the marker, the history of George Rudy is given. George Rudy was one of the earliest settlers in eastern Jefferson County and is the man for whom Rudy Lane is named. The other side of the marker is dedicated to Lieutenant Colonel Robert Taylor, the father of President Zachary Taylor. Taylor, a veteran of the U.S. Revolutionary War, bought a tract of land in the area in 1792. He built a home on the land and later sold the house to George Rudy. Taylor moved onto his farm, which was located nearby just north of U.S. Highway 42/Brownsboro Road. The home is still standing and is located on Apache Drive in Windy Hills a little west of this location.

A bit to the west down Brownsboro Road is the Zachary Taylor National Cemetery, where President Zachary Taylor is buried. It also serves as a veterans' cemetery, although burials are no longer held here. Although the cemetery is a national shrine that does not allow bicyclists or runners, a large monument to the former president and a mausoleum housing his

Tomb of President Zachary Taylor

remains can be seen from the intersection of Rudy Lane and Brownsboro Road. Taylor's father, Robert Taylor, is also buried in the cemetery. A closer view of the cemetery requires a short trip down Brownsboro Road, a very busy four-lane road with no shoulder that is not friendly to cycling.

At the intersection of Rudy Lane with Brownsboro Road, there are two lanes. The left lane carries traffic turning left or continuing straight ahead, while the right lane is meant only for vehicles turning right onto Brownsboro Road. To avoid blocking vehicles turning right, cyclists should move into the left-hand lane at this point. If traffic is sparse and there are no vehicles available to set off the sensors under the roadway, there is a pedestrian crossing button on the corner. It is preferable to use the button on the left-hand corner of the intersection to avoid dealing with traffic entering and exiting the shopping center on the right side of the road, although cars turning right onto Rudy Lane from westbound Brownsboro Road may be a problem.

Once across Brownsboro Road, there is another shopping center on the corner, and then the road flattens out and enters the edge of the city of Indian Hills. The next turn on the route, onto Apache Road, is the second turn on the left just to the north of this location.

6.0 Left onto Apache Road

Indian Hills, like Anchorage, is one of Louisville's more wealthy suburbs. Signs along the side of the road welcome you to Springfield, the name of the farm on which the family of Zachary Taylor lived in the early 19th century. The road passes behind the Zachary Taylor National Cemetery and then comes to a stop sign. Beyond the stop sign the road curves slightly, and the Zachary Taylor house stands on the left-hand side of the road. There is a historical marker in the home's yard that gives a bit of the home's history as well as that of Zachary Taylor himself.

Zachary Taylor house

Zachary Taylor was born in Virginia in 1784. His father, Lieutenant General Robert Taylor, had served in the Continental Army during the U.S. Revolutionary War. With the return of peace to the land, Taylor moved his family to his farm, Springfield, located on a 400-acre tract of land along the Muddy Fork of Beargrass Creek in what is now Jefferson County, Kentucky. The house seen here was built in 1790, and Zachary Taylor lived in the home along with his family until 1808 when he enlisted in the U.S. Army. He returned to the home in 1810, where he was married to Margaret Smith.

Zachary Taylor served in the War of 1812 and was known for his successful defense of Fort Harrison, Indiana against an attack by the Shawnee Chief Tecumseh. He then served in the Black Hawk War between 1828 and 1832, and then in the Second Seminole War, where he earned the nickname "Old Rough and Ready." A Brigadier General by this time, Taylor was again called to service in 1844 during the Mexican-American War. During this war,

General Taylor commanded forces at the Battle of Palo Alto and the nearby Battle of Resaca de la Palma, and also at the Battle of Monterrey. Taylor is best known, however, for the very decisive victory against the Mexican forces under General Santa Anna at Buena Vista. At Buena Vista, Taylor's forces were vastly outnumbered, but his armies forced a humiliating retreat by the Mexican army.

Banking on his successful military service, Zachary Taylor entered the 1848 U.S. Presidential Election as a candidate for the Whig Party along with his running mate Millard Fillmore. Before his entry into politics, Taylor had not announced his ideological leanings, but he found himself more aligned with the Whig Party. Although Taylor was a slave owner, he supported maintaining the federal union above all else. Pragmatic by nature, Taylor found it unwise to roil the existing political order by taking a stand on issues such as the extension of slavery into the newly acquired territories.

Taylor's reticence to address the slavery issue led to the Crisis of 1850, which roiled the nation. Taylor's presidency, however, was cut short before this and other issues were resolved. Zachary Taylor contracted cholera suddenly after a meal in the White House and passed away on July 9, 1850. In the wake of Taylor's death, the U.S. Senate passed the Compromise of 1850 as a set of 5 related bills, and President Millard Fillmore signed them. Overall, the bills granted statehood to California as a free state, organized the Utah and New Mexico Territories, enacted a harsher Fugitive Slave Act, and left the question of slavery in the newly-acquired territories to the legislatures of those territories.

The sudden death of Zachary Taylor, a man who was generally known for his robust health, left many unanswered questions. Over the years, many historians have suggested that a political opponent may have poisoned Taylor with arsenic or heavy metals, especially in light of Taylor's symptoms and their sudden onset. In 1991, Taylor's remains were exhumed by the Jefferson County Coroner's Office and sent to several independent laboratories for analysis. A few weeks later, the coroner's report indicated that there was no evidence of arsenic poisoning that could be found, and Taylor's death was officially ruled as due to natural causes.

West of the Zachary Taylor house, the road again straightens and then continues ahead through a four-way intersection. One block beyond this intersection is the next turn of the route, onto Blankenbaker Lane.

6.5 Left to continue onto Apache Road

6.6 Right onto Blankenbaker Lane

Blankenbaker Lane twists and turns through Indian Hills, and then begins to climb as it passes Hempstead Road. About one mile farther north, amid

Locust Grove

wooden fences and rolling hills, Locust Grove comes into view along the right side of the road. The Georgian mansion, built in 1790 by William and Lucy Clark Croghan, was also the final home of George Rogers Clark, who lived here from 1809 until his death in 1818. William Clark and Meriwether Lewis also stopped here in 1806 following their 1803-1804 expedition through the Louisiana Territory. The farm originally encompassed 700 acres and was adjacent to Springfield, the family farm of Zachary Taylor's family.

The Croghan family sold Locust Grove in 1878 to James Paul, who then sold the property to Richard Waters in 1883. The farm was purchased by Jefferson County and the State of Kentucky in 1961. The mansion and grounds were restored and opened to the public soon afterward. There is a museum here, and tours are conducted daily. For history buffs and visitors to the area who are interested in local lore, Locust Grove is a must-see attraction.

North of Locust Grove, the road gently descends toward the Ohio River, passes underneath Interstate 71, and then ends at its intersection with River Road.

8.6 Left onto River Road

River Road is a popular cycling route, and it is not uncommon to see other cyclists here during the warmer months. There are many beautiful views of the Ohio River on this section of the route. Around the 9-mile mark, River Road passes the Louisville Boat Club. Established in 1879, it was Louisville's first boat club and only the third in the United States. Further up the road, on the left side, is the Louisville Islamic Center, the area's first mosque, which was founded in 1980.

Immediately prior to the next turn, at the corner of River Road and Indian Hills Trail, is Caperton Swamp Park. The park is a 30-acre nature preserve that protects a large variety of waterfowl and other wildlife. The land was donated to the city as a park by the organization River Fields, which is dedicated to preserving and maintaining land along the Ohio River corridor.

9.3 Left onto Indian Hills Trail

Indian Hills Trail leads away from the river and back into the city of Indian Hills. The road is flat for the first half mile, but then begins to slowly climb as it heads toward the tall hills looming to the south. The next turn on the route, onto Westwind Road, may be difficult to see if you are not paying close attention to the road.

10.4 Left onto Westwind Road

Turning left onto Westwind Road seems to avoid the large hill that was looming directly ahead on Indian Hills Trail. The respite, however, merely postpones the inevitable climb back up from the river valley. The pitch of the hill becomes somewhat steep for a few hundred yards, but then moderates as it crests the hill.

Westwind Road ends at Old Brownsboro Road, a spur of U.S. Highway 42/Brownsboro Road. Traffic entering Old Brownsboro Road from the main highway may be moving at high speed, so caution should be observed when turning from the intersection.

11.7 Right onto Old Brownsboro Road

Although this road helps to alleviate interruptions in traffic from vehicles entering and leaving the Indian Hills area, there is still a considerable amount of traffic in the area. Near the next turn on the route, there is a shopping center that sits on a small triangular plot of land that is surrounded by U.S. Highway 42, Old Brownsboro Road, and Chenoweth Lane. In 1957, Indian Hills residents, buoyed by their victory in defeating the Mallon Plan and the annexation of the eastern suburbs by the city of Louisville, used zoning laws to force the closure and annexation of a used car lot that was once located here.

The next turn on the route is easy to miss, especially when dealing with the heavy traffic that may be present here during the morning and evening rush hours. Old Brownsboro Road ends shortly ahead at U.S. Highway 42, but the turn onto KY-1932/Chenoweth Lane is merely a quarter-mile from the previous turn. The pharmacy on the corner of the triangular lot serves as a useful landmark when making the turn.

12.0 Left onto KY-1932/Chenoweth Lane

Chenoweth Lane crosses U.S. Highway 42 at a stoplight and then heads south back toward St. Matthews. Unless there are vehicles at the light to trigger the sensor under the road (and there usually are), it may be necessary to activate the pedestrian crossing signal to force the light to change. U.S. Highway 42 carries a large volume of fast-moving traffic, and caution must be used when crossing here because vehicles nearly always run the red light just after the signal changes.

Chenoweth Lane may be busy at times, especially during the morning and evening commutes. The speed limit is 35 miles per hour because it is a residential area, but most drivers through this stretch are unusually courteous toward cyclists. It is not unusual to see other cyclists passing through this area.

12.8 Left onto Massie Avenue

13.0 Right onto St. Matthews Avenue

13.3 Right onto KY-1447/Westport Road

After a short distance on Westport Road, St. Matthews Avenue continues on the left. Oncoming traffic has a stop sign and must yield to traffic turning onto St. Matthews Avenue, but cyclists should exercise extreme caution here to avoid motorists who often ignore the stop sign or are not paying attention to their surroundings.

13.4 Left onto St. Matthews Avenue

St. Matthews Avenue is a designated bike route, and there is a shared usage lane painted on the road here. The road ends at U.S. Highway 60/Shelbyville Road and continues straight ahead as Willis Avenue.

13.5 Continue onto Willis Avenue

Willis Avenue passes through the heart of St. Matthews. This is a thriving urban business district with many shops, restaurants, and businesses, so there may be vehicles pulling in and out of traffic without notice. The road crosses the busy KY-1932/Breckenridge Lane at a traffic light; there is a pedestrian crossing button that will change the light if there are no cars around to trigger it. Past Breckenridge Lane, Willis Avenue retraces the early portion of the route as it heads back toward Seneca Park.

14.2 Continue onto Pee Wee Reese Road at Seneca Park

St. Matthews Avenue in the heart of St. Matthews

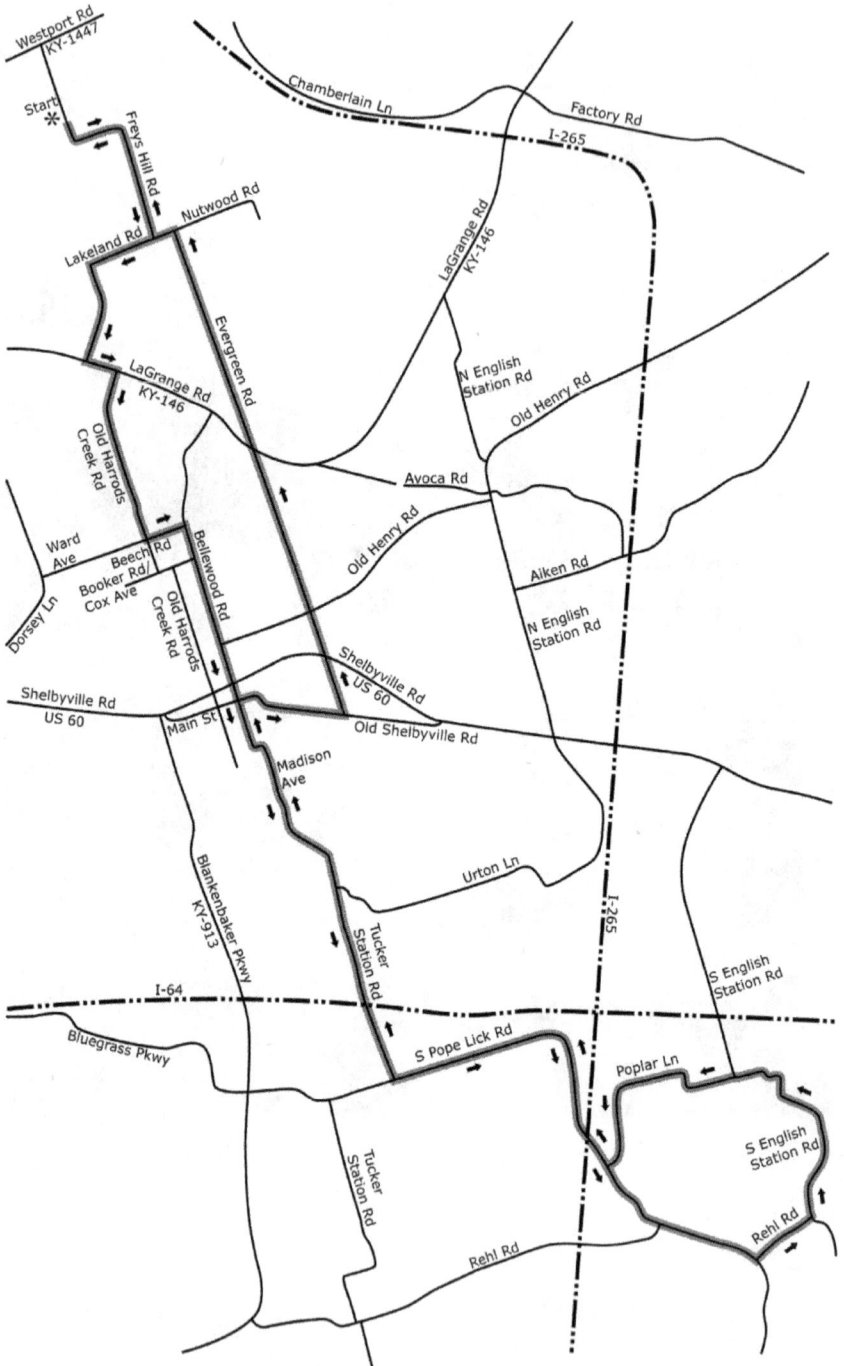

19 ANCHORAGE AND MIDDLETOWN

Distance: 19.0 miles

Difficulty: Moderate. A few rolling hills, with one significant climb. Light to moderate traffic on most roads, although there may be considerable traffic on Freys Hill Road near E.P. Sawyer Park.

Points of Interest: E. P. "Tom" Sawyer Park, Sawyer Hayes Center, Central State Hospital, City of Middletown, City of Anchorage

The cities of Anchorage and Middletown, located in the far eastern portion of Jefferson County just beyond Louisville's city limits, are two fourth class cities that escaped the 2003 Louisville-Jefferson County merger that formed Metro Louisville. Both cities have a very long history that dates back to the late 18th century when the area was first settled.

The city of Anchorage, where the tour begins, is roughly bounded by the southern boundary of E.P. "Tom" Sawyer State Park to the north, Central State Hospital and Old Harrods Creek Road to the west, KY-146/LaGrange Road to the east, and Old Henry Road to the south. The land on which the city lies was originally granted to Isaac Hite in 1773 for his service in the French and Indian War and was referred to as Hite's Mill. In 1849, the Louisville and Frankfort Railroad built a line through the area. The area where the railroad entered town became known as Hobbs Station, and the introduction of reliable rail service through the area fueled its growth.

The city incorporated in 1878 and derived its nautical-sounding name from the name of the home of former riverboat captain James Goslee, one of the area's earliest residents who was ironically killed at a railroad crossing in 1875. When the town incorporated a few years later, it took its name from the name of Goslee's estate, the Anchorage, in his honor. At the center of town, there is a locomotive wheel with an anchor in the center that was taken from Captain Goslee's ship, the *Matamora*, which had previously been used as a decoration on his lawn. Anchorage's heavily wooded land attracted many of Louisville's wealthiest residents, who began migrating to the area in the early 1900s in search of summer homes away from the heat of the city.

Today, the city of Anchorage retains much of its earlier character with tall, majestic trees that provide much appreciated shade during the heat of the summer. Although many of Anchorage's larger estates have since been carved up into smaller properties, most of the area's homes are still large and upscale. Anchorage is well known throughout Metro Louisville as the home of many of Louisville's wealthiest and most prominent citizens. The city's center is has been listed on the National Register of Historic Places since 1982.

Middletown

The nearby city of Middletown was chartered in 1797. It was established from a plot of 500 acres owned by Jacob Meyers and Culbert Harrison, and was incorporated in 1866. The origin of the city's name is still uncertain, but it is commonly thought that it was because the town was nearly equidistant between the cities of Louisville and Shelbyville. Another common theory about the town's name is that before the Louisville and Portland Canal was built, goods being shipped down the Ohio River were unloaded from ships at Westport and moved on ox carts to Shippingport, where they were reloaded. Since Middletown was located about halfway between these points, it was commonly used as an overnight stopping point.

Regardless of the origin of the city's name, Middletown become an important trading post for the many farms in eastern Jefferson and western Shelby counties due to its location on the turnpike connecting Louisville and Lexington. Later, as the railroads came through and an interurban commuter line through the area was added in the early 1900s, Middletown began to evolve into a suburb of Louisville. This trend continued during the remainder of the 20th century as improvements in automobiles and Kentucky's road system allowed easy travel between Middletown and Louisville. With the suburban migration that began in the 1960s, Middletown's population began to grow.

Middletown's city government went seemingly dormant after 1919.

Elections were not held, city taxes went uncollected, and by 1960 the state of Kentucky revoked the city's charter. In 1976, Middletown was revived with the restoration of its government and city commission as a sixth class city. With population increases driven by the suburban migration in the late 20th century, Middletown became a fourth class city in 1982. As of the 2010 census, its population stood at 7,200, and continues to grow. Middletown today is still thought of much as a suburb of Louisville, although it still retains much of its historical small town charm for those intrepid individuals who care to venture off the main highway

This tour begins at E.P. "Tom" Sawyer Park. The park was created from 550 acres of land formerly occupied by Central State Hospital in 1974 and was named in honor of Erbon Powers "Tom" Sawyer, the father of noted journalist Diane Sawyer. E. P. Sawyer served as Jefferson County Judge/Executive for many years, but he was killed in an auto accident in 1969 while still in office. The park has many amenities, including soccer fields, lighted tennis courts, a BMX bike trail, many cross country running trails, and an indoor activity center that boasts an Olympic-sized swimming pool. The Louisville Astronomical Society also has its Urban Astronomy Center within the park. There are many 5K and 10K races held in the park on weekends, but there are lots of visitors present here any day of the week.

Plenty of parking is available in the main parking lot located near the park's eastern entrance on Freys Hill Road. This park is extremely busy, particularly during evenings and on weekends, and there are often many cars driving in and around the parking lot. Hand signals should always be used in this area, and caution should always be observed when riding through the parking lot or near the park's entrance because most drivers here are usually extremely distracted. The tour begins at the park's entrance on Freys Hill Road, heading south toward the city of Anchorage.

Route Directions – Anchorage and Middletown

0.0 Right onto Freys Hill Road
0.9 Right onto Lakeland Road
1.8 Left onto KY-146/LaGrange Road
2.0 Right onto Old Harrods Creek Road
2.9 Left onto Beech Road
3.1 Right onto Bellewood Road
3.5 Continue onto Madison Avenue
4.3 Continue onto Tucker Station Road
6.1 Left onto S Pope Lick Road
8.6 Left onto Rehl Road
8.9 Left onto English Station Road
10.0 Left onto Poplar Lane
11.2 Right onto S Pope Lick Road
12.8 Right onto Tucker Station Road
14.7 Continue onto Madison Avenue
14.9 Right onto Main Street
15.0 Continue onto Old Shelbyville Road
15.5 Left onto Evergreen Road
17.9 Left to continue onto Evergreen Road
18.2 Right onto Freys Hill Road
19.0 Left into parking lot

Route Description – Anchorage and Middletown

0.0 Right onto Freys Hill Road

Traffic in the parking lot of Sawyer Park is usually very heavy. There are many access roads through the parking lot that intersect the rows of parking spaces at odd angles, so cyclists should be very wary of the many cars moving around within the parking lot because drivers may not be paying proper attention to pedestrians or bicycles. There are often many other cyclists and runners in the area, and there is safety in numbers. Besides, it's simply much more fun.

The turn onto Freys Hill Road may require some patience. As busy as Sawyer Park is, there is a considerable amount of traffic on Freys Hill Road. Most of the traffic is traveling southbound from Westport Road towards the park's entrance. Most of the cars turning into the park do not use their turn signals as required, so it is highly advised to wait for traffic to clear up before turning. Fortunately, the pavement on this road is in very good condition and there is beautiful scenery here that is reminiscent of the Bluegrass region of central Kentucky. Freys Hill Road ends at its intersection with Lakeland Road at the bottom of a short but steep hill that will necessitate braking during the descent to avoid running out into oncoming traffic.

0.9 Right onto Lakeland Road

Lakeland Road skirts the southern edge of Sawyer Park and the northwestern edge of the city of Anchorage. The heavily wooded roadside in this area is typical of far eastern Jefferson County. During the summer, Anchorage and the immediately surrounding areas may be as much as 5 to 10 degrees cooler than downtown Louisville because of Louisville's urban heat island effect. For this reason, many Louisville cyclists prefer to ride in eastern Jefferson County or across the river in southern Indiana to avoid the heat and humidity during the height of the summer.

At around the 1.25-mile mark, the road curves sharply to the left. Due to the limited visibility here and the entrance to the Sawyer Hays Center on the right at the curve, there is a 3-way stop at the intersection. This also provides an opportunity to explore the Sawyer Hayes Center, a small pocket of Sawyer Park that was the former site of the Lakeland Asylum. A narrow road makes a short loop to a parking lot, and a side road leads to a community center that now sits at the site. At the far end of the loop next to a levee are a historical marker and informational kiosk that describe the asylum that once stood here.

Lakeland Asylum was built on a parcel of land that was purchased by the state from the Hite family, which owned much of the land in this area and the land that would later become the city of Anchorage. The facility was built in 1869 along Lakeland Drive and was originally named the Home for Juvenile Delinquents at Lakeland. In 1873, the facility was repurposed for the treatment of mental illness and renamed as the Central Kentucky Lunatic Asylum. The facility was one of only four within the state of Kentucky that was dedicated to the treatment of mental illness. Its name was later changed to the Central Kentucky Asylum for the Insane, and later to Central State Hospital.

Former site of Lakeland Asylum

There were allegations of abuse, neglect, and unethical practices at the hospital almost from the beginning, but by 1920, many of these allegations became public. Many of these allegations were quite disturbing, including the institutionalization of individuals who were merely developmentally disabled, homeless, or elderly, but not mentally ill. Later, there were also charges that shock therapy and lobotomies were performed at the institution until nearly the 1950s.

Overcrowding of the hospital was also a major issue. The original facility was built to house around 200 patients. It was expanded to house up to 1,600 patients by 1900. In 1941, however, a grand jury noted that there were often more than 2,400 patients at the institution at any one time. The grand jury also stated that the living conditions in the wards were deplorable, and in gross violation of the state's fire codes. Pressure was put onto the institution for major reform, but little was done until the 1950s when nationwide efforts were made to reform the treatment of the mentally ill. Nobody knows just how many patients died at the facility and were buried unceremoniously on the hospital's grounds, but there are estimates that this number is between 4,000 and 5,000.

In 1986, the old hospital buildings were abandoned, and a new facility was built at the corner of KY-146/LaGrange Road and Lakeland Road. The old facility was demolished in 1996, and the land on which it stood was subsequently incorporated into Sawyer Park.

1.8 Left onto KY-146/LaGrange Road

Although many portions of LaGrange Road carry a large volume of traffic, it is not excessively busy through this area. Thus, it should not be extremely difficult to turn across the road in this area except during morning or evening commute times. The next turn on the route occurs very soon, at the very next right.

2.0 Right onto Old Harrods Creek Road

Immediately after making the turn, the road crosses the railroad tracks. Although the crossing is fairly well maintained, the city of Anchorage has laws prohibiting the use of train horns in the area. Thus, cyclists should look both ways before crossing the tracks.

Old Harrods Creek Road soon crosses into the city limits of Anchorage. There are several sections of rough pavement in this area, and within the city limits of Anchorage, there are also numerous speed bumps that may necessitate slowing down to avoid being thrown or roughly jarred. Although the speed bumps are not especially troublesome and do not appreciably slow the fast traffic in this area, the rough pavement and the many potholes certainly do a better job of it.

2.9 Left onto Beech Road

3.1 Right onto Bellewood Road

Bellewood Road heads out of the city of Anchorage, leading toward Shelbyville Road and the city of Middletown. Situated between Anchorage and Middletown about two blocks to the west, between the cross-streets of Cox Avenue and Robert Road, is the Griffytown neighborhood. During Reconstruction following the U.S. Civil War, the city's settlement patterns changed rapidly. Dan Griffy, an African-American settler who had been living in the area, purchased a small parcel of land from Silas O. Witherbee of Middletown in 1879 and moved a small log cabin onto it. Later, Witherbee sold other nearby lots to additional African-American settlers. Many of the lots were subsequently subdivided further and resold to newer arrivals. Throughout the late 19th and early 20th centuries, Griffytown remained a primarily African-American settlement. In the 1960s, the Griffytown area was redeveloped through an urban renewal program.

The road ends at a traffic light at its intersection with Shelbyville Road. This light will require patience, as even with sensors the light still takes several minutes to turn green for traffic to cross the extremely busy U.S. Highway 60/Shelbyville Road. If the light doesn't turn, there is a pedestrian crossing button at the corner of the sidewalk that may help.

3.5 Continue onto Madison Avenue

Bellewood Road becomes Madison Avenue on the other side of Shelbyville Road and begins climbing a small hill toward Middletown's city center. There is a four-way stop at its intersection with Main Street. At the corner on the right is the Little Bit of Bybee shop, which sells pottery produced by the Bybee Pottery company. Bybee Pottery was founded in 1809 in the Madison County town of Bybee and is still run by the Cornelison family. Although there have been many rumors of the company's demise due to the suspension of operations in 2011, the company's products are still being sold in Middletown, Frankfort, and Bybee.

On the left side of the road is the historic Middletown Inn. The inn was built first as a log building around 1800, and soon afterward bricked in and expanded. The inn also hosted a tavern that was the center of much of the town's business at one point in time. The tavern was closed around 1890 by members of the temperance movement, and the inn finally closed its doors sometime around 1920. The building has since been used as a private residence, and today also houses a law office and a small business.

As Madison Avenue continues south, it curves sharply to the left and then to the right. Cyclists should beware of speeding cars that may be on the wrong side of the road as they emerge from around the curves in this area. Beyond the hairpin turns, the road becomes Tucker Station Road.

4.3 Continue onto Tucker Station Road

Tucker Station Road is a fun series of rolling hills through the southern portion of Middletown. The road soon descends a hill and passes under Interstate 64, then passes just to the east of Jeffersontown and comes to a stop sign at its intersection with S Pope Lick Road. The route turns right onto S Pope Lick Road, heading away from Jeffersontown and toward the Parklands of Floyds Fork.

6.1 Left onto S Pope Lick Road

Pope Lick Road begins to head into the more rural portion of eastern Jefferson County. The speed limit in this area is 35 MPH, although cars in this area are usually traveling well in excess of it. The road begins climbing for the next half mile as it passes over Interstate 265/Gene Snyder Freeway. The bridge joints of the overpass are quite rough, and caution must be used when crossing this bridge to avoid the sharp metal edges where the bridge joins the road and to avoid getting a tire stuck in the gap between the road and the bridge. The smoothest area is near the middle of the lane, between the wheel ruts in the road.

After cresting the hill and crossing the interstate, the road begins to descend into the Floyds Fork River valley as it continues south past Poplar Lane. There are a few rough patches in the road and one sharp curve that may force cyclists to slow down; otherwise, it is a smooth ride through this area.

Rehl Road, the next turn on the route, is not marked, and the turn is easy to miss. Cyclists should look for the first road branching off to the left past Poplar Lane; it is located a little less than half a mile past the other section of Rehl Road that branches off to the right. There is what appears to be a small electrical substation on the right side of the road immediately before the turn that serves as a useful landmark.

8.6 Left onto Rehl Road

Rehl Road immediately begins climbing away from S Pope Lick Road. The climb may be a little steep for some cyclists, particularly if it was necessary to stop and yield to oncoming traffic before turning onto Rehl Road. The road continues climbing as it ends a quarter mile later at English Station Road.

8.9 Left onto English Station Road

English Station Road continues climbing for another half mile, rising nearly 130 feet in elevation, before flattening out near Wibble Hill Road. Thankfully, the hill is not extremely steep, and shouldn't be a problem for most cyclists. After cresting the hill, the road continues a short distance through the scenic rural countryside of the Floyds Fork region.

The next turn on the route occurs at a sharp turn in the road with a limited line of sight. Poplar Lane is a slight left turn off the road, but oncoming traffic negotiation the sharp curve on English Station Road cannot see northbound traffic. Cyclists traveling

Farmland along Poplar Lane

through this area should be EXTREMELY cautious when making this turn.

10.0 Left onto Poplar Lane

After making the turn, the road descends a small hill. There are a few potholes in the road on the descent, so it may be necessary to pay close attention to the road. At the bottom of the hill, there is a small church, Poplar Level Baptist Church, on the left side of the road as it curves sharply to the right. Past the church, Poplar Lane curves sharply to the left, then again to the left, before ascending a hill and ending back at Pope Lick Road.

11.2 Right onto S Pope Lick Road

After the turn back onto Pope Lick Road, the route retraces itself back to Madison Avenue in Middletown.

12.8 Right onto Tucker Station Road

As the route continues back toward Middletown, cyclists should be mindful of the stop sign and flashing red light at the intersection of Tucker Station Road and Ellingsworth Lane that is located near the bottom of a long descent.

14.7 Continue onto Madison Avenue

The route continues back into Middletown on Madison Avenue, past the two hairpin curves. At the intersection of Madison Avenue and Main Street, the route turns right onto Main Street instead of continuing ahead on Madison Avenue.

14.9 Right onto Main Street

Main Street leads through Middletown's historic district, past the Middletown Inn and toward a small triangular point of land with a large clock sitting at the corner. There is a parking lot just beyond the clock with a large Catalpa tree planted at the edge. A small plaque underneath the tree indicates the tree was planted in 1997 in honor of Blaine A. Guthrie, Jr., a longtime Middletown resident who served as a local historian. Upon his death in 1997, the city planted the Catalpa tree here in his memory.

As the road continues around a shallow S-curve, it becomes Old Shelbyville Road.

15.0 Continue onto Old Shelbyville Road

As Main Street becomes Old Shelbyville Road, there is a historic building on the left side of the road that once housed the Davis Tavern and currently serves as Middletown's city hall. There is a historical marker at the corner that commemorates the life and career of Lawrence W. Wetherby (1908-1994), Kentucky's 48th Governor and a native of Middletown. Despite the

Middletown City Hall

fact that Jefferson County is Kentucky's most populous county, Wetherby remains just one of only two governors ever elected from the county throughout its long history. Elected Lieutenant Governor in 1947 under the Earle C. Clements administration, Wetherby was elevated to Governor after Clements resigned in 1950 to take a U.S. Senate seat. In 1951, he was re-elected to serve a full four-year term. During his administration, the state saw many improvements in its road system, including the construction of the Kentucky Turnpike connecting Louisville and Elizabethtown. Wetherby was also instrumental in reforming mental health treatment. During his term in office, he oversaw the creation of a state Department of Mental Health.

15.5 Left onto Evergreen Road

Evergreen Road connects Old Shelbyville Road to the very busy U.S. Highway 60/Shelbyville Road. Past this intersection, the road continues north and crosses back into Anchorage. Many of Louisville's wealthiest citizens live along or near this road, as evidenced by the many large, stately homes with their beautiful, shaded lawns. It is one of the area's most scenic roads, and there

Anchorage

are often other cyclists traveling this road.

After crossing KY-146/LaGrange Road, the road leads past the city center of Anchorage, including city hall, a fire station, and a few restaurants. Just past this area is a confusing three-way intersection with Station Road. The stop sign occurs much earlier than would be expected for traffic heading north. After stopping, traffic may turn left onto Station Road or continue north on Evergreen Road. Traffic from Station Road turning left (north) onto Evergreen Road must stop at the intersection about 25 yards to the north and yield to oncoming traffic that has already stopped and is now continuing through the intersection. More often than not, cars turning left onto Evergreen Road from this intersection fail to yield to traffic as required by law.

A little over a mile later, Evergreen Road comes to a stop sign at its intersection with Nutwood Road. At this intersection, cyclists must turn left to continue on Evergreen Road.

17.9 Left to continue onto Evergreen Road

Shortly after the turn, Evergreen Road ends and becomes Lakeland Drive as it passes Freys Hill Road, the next turn on the route.

18.2 Right onto Freys Hill Road

The route returns to E. P. "Tom" Sawyer Park on Freys Hill Road. There is a short but steep hill immediately after making the turn that may necessitate shifting into a climbing gear for a short distance.

19.0 Left into parking lot

The Middletown Inn

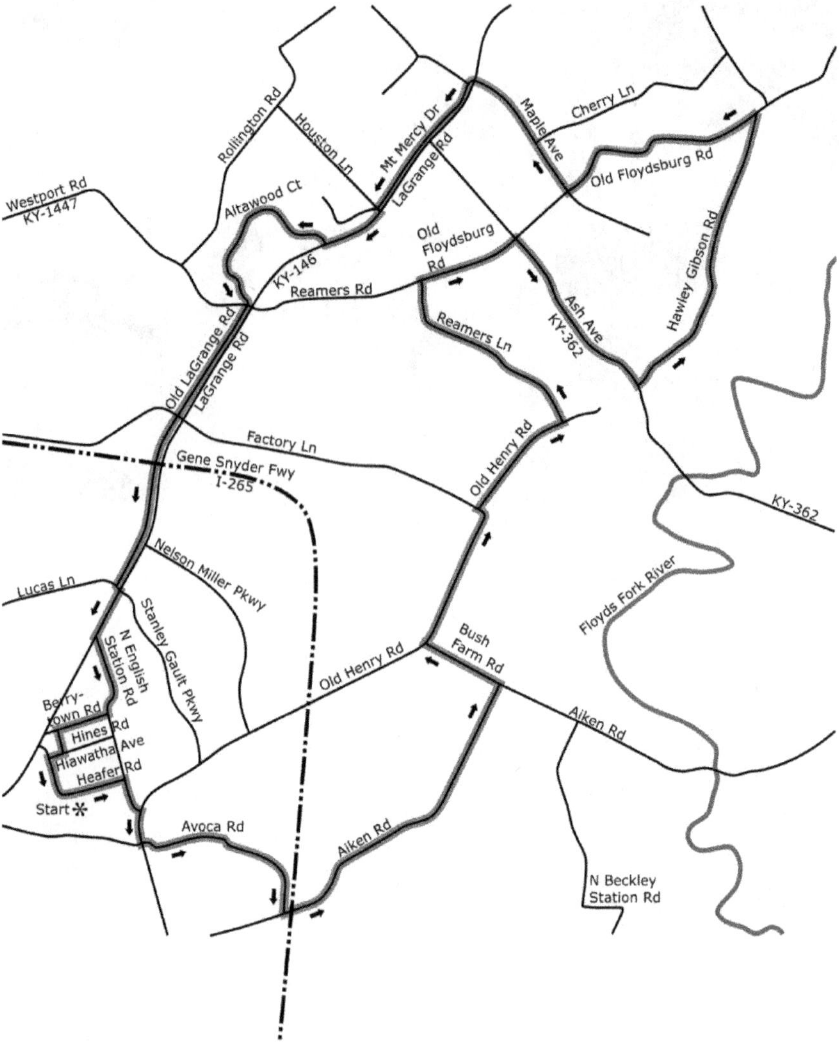
Rollington Rd
Houston Ln
Mt Mercy Dr
LaGrange Rd
Maple Ave
Cherry Ln
Old Floydsburg Rd
Westport Rd
KY-1447
Altawood Ct
Old Floydsburg Rd
KY-146
Reamers Rd
Hawley Gibson Rd
Reamers Ln
Ash Ave
KY-362
Old LaGrange Rd
LaGrange Rd
Factory Ln
Gene Snyder Fwy
I-265
Old Henry Rd
KY-362
Nelson Miller Pkwy
Lucas Ln
Stanley Gault Pkwy
N English Station Rd
Floyds Fork River
Bush Farm Rd
Old Henry Rd
Berry-town Rd
Hines Rd
Hiawatha Ave
Heafer Rd
Aiken Rd
Start
Avoca Rd
Aiken Rd
N Beckley Station Rd

20 BERRYTOWN AND PEWEE VALLEY

Distance: 15.5 miles

Difficulty: Moderate, due to heavy traffic and very rough pavement in a few areas. A few hills, but no significant climbs.

Points of Interest: Berrytown neighborhood, Berrytown Cemetery, Pewee Valley, Kentucky Confederate Cemetery

With the population boom that began at the end of World War II, Louisville experienced a population boom that soon found many of the city's residents searching for more affordable housing in a more suburban setting. This set the stage for the opening of new suburban developments in eastern Jefferson County beginning in the 1950s, with the pace of migration increasing between 1960 and the mid-1980s. The trend has continued throughout the remainder of the 20th century and the first two decades of the 21st century. As a result, many roads, especially Shelbyville Road, have become choked with heavy traffic with the surge in commuters. However, Louisville's east end still has plenty of less-traveled roads to be explored by bicycle, and there are many important historical sites to see in this area of Metro Louisville. This route begins in an area north of Middletown between Shelbyville and Westport Roads and travels eastward toward western Oldham County.

The tour begins and ends in the Berrytown neighborhood that lies east of KY-146/LaGrange Road and west of English Station Road. Berrytown was established in 1874 when Alfred Berry bought a 10-acre plot on the outskirts of Anchorage that became the nucleus for a predominantly African-American neighborhood. Similar to Griffytown, Berrytown's development was spurred by the many African-American residents migrating here after the end of the U. S. Civil War looking for work on many of the farms and homes in affluent Anchorage. While Berrytown also experienced urban decay like many other areas of the city in the latter half the 20th century, the neighborhood's homeowners generally refused urban renewal efforts in the 1960s, in contrast to Griffytown.

From Berrytown, the route heads toward Oldham County and the town of Pewee Valley, which was established in 1852 as a stop along the Louisville and Frankfort Railroad. Originally named Smith's Station, the town was renamed Pewee Valley in 1856 when its post office was established. Residents voted to name the city after the eastern wood pewee (*Contopus virens*), a bird of the tyrant flycatcher family that is locally abundant in the woods around town.

For most of its history, Pewee Valley has remained a small, quiet town on the outskirts of Louisville within easy commuting distance. Despite the town's peacefulness, however, a few controversies have arisen over the past 150 years. In 1902, the Sons of Confederate Veterans purchased the abandoned Villa Ridge Inn and sought to repurpose it as a retirement home for Confederate veterans. Most local residents opposed the project and actively fought against it, appealing to both the Governor and Attorney General. In the end, however, the city lost the battle, and the home was established in 1904. The facility served over 700 veterans over the course of its operation, many of whom had served under General John Hunt Morgan. The home operated until 1934, at which time the five remaining residents were moved to the Pewee Valley Sanitorium to live out their remaining days.

After the closing of the veterans' home, another controversy soon arose when the state proposed opening the Kentucky Correctional Institution for Women on the home's former site. Furious, over 300 Pewee Valley residents stormed the Kentucky State Capitol with a signed petition opposing the plan. The state relented and eventually built the prison on a site just across the Floyds Fork River in Shelby County. The Kentucky Correctional Institution for Women, opened in 1938, is still known unofficially as the Pewee Valley Correctional Institute for Women. Ironically, the prison is one of the area's largest employers.

The tour begins and ends at Berrytown Park, which lies on the southern edge of the Berrytown neighborhood. There is ample parking available in a parking lot on Heafer Road at the park's edge, and traffic through the neighborhood is minimal and generally very courteous.

Route Directions – Berrytown and Pewee Valley

0.0 Right onto Heafer Road
0.3 Right onto N English Station Road
0.4 Right onto Old Henry Road
0.6 Left onto Avoca Road
1.5 Left onto Aiken Road
3.1 Left onto Bush Farm Road
3.5 Right onto Old Henry Road
4.3 Right to continue onto Old Henry Road
4.8 Left onto Reamers Lane
5.9 Right onto Old Floydsburg Road
6.4 Right onto KY-362/Ash Avenue
7.3 Left onto Hawley Gibson Road
8.8 Left onto Old Floydsburg Road
9.9 Right onto Maple Avenue
10.6 Continue onto Mount Mercy Drive
10.9 Left onto Central Avenue
11.0 Right onto KY-146/LaGrange Road
11.7 Right onto Altawood Court
12.7 Continue onto Old LaGrange Road
14.2 Left onto Lucas Lane
14.2 Right onto KY-146/LaGrange Road
14.4 Left onto N English Station Road
14.8 Right onto Berrytown Road
15.1 Left onto Hines Road
15.2 Right onto Hiawatha Avenue
15.3 Left onto Heafer Road
15.5 Right into Berrytown Park parking lot

Route Description – Berrytown and Pewee Valley

0.0 Right onto Heafer Road

From Berrytown Park, the route turns right onto Heafer Road and heads downhill toward N English Station Road. The road ends at the bottom of the hill, making it necessary to begin braking early in order to avoid running out onto the busy English Station Road.

0.3 Right onto N English Station Road

This section of N English Station Road ends shortly after the turn, at its intersection with Old Henry Road. Cyclists should check traffic to the left before pulling out onto Old Henry Road since cars traveling on this street are usually traveling very fast and have a limited line of sight over a hill.

0.4 Right onto Old Henry Road

This road can be busy at times, as it carries a large number of vehicles that are exiting from Interstate 265/Gene Snyder Freeway. There is a wide shoulder here, so it is possible to ride on the shoulder to avoid the heavy, fast-moving traffic. If riding on the shoulder, cyclists should note that the next turn, onto Avoca Road, is to the left, making it necessary to move left across two lanes of traffic before crossing a set of railroad tracks and making the turn. The traffic on this section of Old Henry Road is impatient, rude, and relentless, so patience will be necessary here. Fortunately, the traffic dies down after the next turn.

0.6 Left onto Avoca Road

Avoca Road begins with a swift descent on the east side of the railroad tracks. Traffic is not much of a problem here, but the pavement is cracked and quite rough, with many potholes. There is often gravel, dirt, and debris on the road from the many trucks that enter and exit the concrete facility located here, so cyclists should pay very close attention to road conditions and be on the lookout for occasional truck traffic. At the bottom of the hill, there are two sets of railroad tracks that lie at oblique angles to the roadway. Cyclists should slow down or walk their bicycles across these tracks to avoid getting narrow tires wedged between the rails and the roadbed.

1.5 Left onto Aiken Road

Aiken Road leads from the Middletown area eastward toward Beckley

Station and Eastwood. This road may be busy at times, especially around the morning and evening commute times.

3.1 Left onto Bush Farm Road

3.5 Right onto Old Henry Road

Old Henry Road carries a large amount of traffic. Fortunately, most of the traffic is between Interstate 265/Gene Snyder Freeway and English Station Road, but the traffic may still be heavy at times through this area. Fortunately, the speed limit drops to 35 MPH as the road narrows to two lanes from this point eastward. The pavement here is extremely rough and will force cyclists to slow down and take the entire lane. Fortunately, the rough pavement seems to slow the cars down just as much as it slows cyclists down. Sometimes, potholes can be a blessing in disguise.

About 0.7 miles from the last turn, the road turns sharply to the left before coming to a 3-way stop. Straight ahead, the road becomes Factory Lane. The route continues to the right as it continues to follow Old Henry Road.

4.3 Right to continue onto Old Henry Road

This section of the route carries considerably less traffic because most of the vehicles continue straight at the previous intersection. There are a few small subdivisions in this area, and the condition of the pavement improves greatly. The road ascends a gentle hill and then ends a half mile beyond its intersection with Reamers Lane.

4.8 Left onto Reamers Lane

Reamers Lane branches off to the left from Old Henry Road near its easternmost terminus and hugs the very edge of Jefferson County as it heads northwest. A little less than a mile later, the road turns to the north as it enters Oldham County and begins climbing slightly in elevation.

5.9 Right onto Old Floydsburg Road

After making the turn, the road continues to rise in elevation as it heads toward Pewee Valley. The road comes to a stop at KY-362/Ash Avenue. Caution should be used in making the turn since traffic on KY-362 is not required to stop at the intersection and is often traveling well in excess of the speed limit.

6.4 Right onto KY-362/Ash Avenue

Ash Avenue in Oldham County

KY-362/Ash Avenue passes through the scenic farmland of western Oldham County. The road has no shoulder, and there is a ditch just off the edge of the road. Thus, cyclists should take the lane to avoid being squeezed off the edge of the road if a vehicle makes an illegal pass or otherwise fails to share the road courteously. The road is mostly downhill from Old Floydsburg Road to the next turn at Hawley Gibson Road, so it is possible to gather a good amount of speed along this stretch of the route.

7.3 Left onto Hawley Gibson Road

Hawley Gibson Road continues through the scenic farmland of the Pewee Valley area. The road begins to climb almost immediately after the turn.

Although the hill is not steep, it seems to go on forever, climbing about 100 feet in elevation for a little more than one mile. The road ends at its intersection with Old Floydsburg Road about a half mile beyond the crest of the hill.

8.8 Left onto Old Floydsburg Road

The route turns back onto Old Floydsburg Road and resumes climbing in elevation for a short distance before leveling off. After this point, the road ascends and descends a series of small hills through a sparsely populated area, none of which are challenging. The scenery along this portion of the route, however, is well worth the effort. Tall, majestic trees provide valuable shade during the hot portion of the year, and lots of exposed limestone seeps and babbling streams give the area a very

Old Floydsburg Road

remote feel, despite being no more than a few miles away from Metro Louisville.

Prior to the next turn on the route, there are a few homes along the road as it nears a residential area of Pewee Valley. The next turn on the route is to the right onto Maple Avenue, but there is a point of interest to the left. About one block down Maple Avenue is the Pewee Valley Confederate Cemetery, which sits at the former site of the Kentucky Confederate Home. It is the only state burial ground for Confederate veterans and contains 313 graves.

Although the cemetery was originally established in 1871, it was not until 1902, when the Kentucky Confederate Home was established nearby, that the cemetery was used to bury Confederate Civil War veterans. At that time the cemetery was divided into three sections: one for blacks, one for whites, and one for Confederate veterans. Between 1904 and 1934, a total of 313 veterans were buried in the Confederate cemetery, many of whom served under General John Hunt Morgan. The cemetery's entrance was fashioned from the former gate of the veterans' home. Within the cemetery, there is an unusual monument that is fashioned from zinc.

Kentucky Confederate Cemetery

9.9 Right onto Maple Avenue

The city of Pewee Valley has a distinct small town feel despite lying just across the county line from Metro Louisville. Along the way toward the center of town, there is a home with a small plaque commemorating the burial of a time capsule. Near the end of Maple Avenue, as it intersects with KY-146/LaGrange Road, a state historical marker describes the Kentucky Confederate home and the cemetery that lie at the other end of Maple Avenue just south of its intersection with Old Floydsburg Road.

10.6 Continue onto Mount Mercy Drive

Mount Mercy Drive lies across the highway from the end of Maple Avenue, leading into the heart of Pewee Valley as it runs parallel to KY-146 on the opposite side of the railroad tracks. There is a stop sign at the road's intersection with Central Avenue near a cluster of historic shops. On the left just before the stop sign is an old restored railcar and a small pocket park

Pewee Valley

dedicated to Annie Fellows Johnston, author of the Little Colonels series of children's books upon which the 1935 Shirley Temple movie *The Little Colonel* was based.

Mount Mercy Drive continues straight ahead, passes St. Aloysius church and school, and then crosses over the railroad tracks and ends at KY-146/LaGrange Road.

10.9 Left onto Central Avenue

11.0 Right onto KY-146/LaGrange Road

The highway can be busy at times, especially during the morning and evening commutes. Thankfully, this section of the route is very short. KY-146 soon crosses back into Jefferson County, and the next turn, onto Altawood Court, comes very quickly after crossing the county line. The road is not marked and very easy to miss. It ascends a short, steep hill to cross the railroad tracks.

Entrance to Altawood Court

11.7 Right onto Altawood Court

Altawood Court enters a small hidden neighborhood that is tucked away on the eastern edge of Jefferson County. This neighborhood is a hidden gem, with a beautiful, mature tree canopy that provides much welcome shade during the hot summer months, and little traffic to contend with in contrast to the busy highway nearby.

Altawood Court ends a mile later at its intersection with KY-1447/Westport Road. Across the intersection, the road becomes Old

LaGrange Road. Just to the left, Westport Road intersects with KY-146/LaGrange Road, and although signs warn motorist against blocking this intersection, there are usually vehicles blocking the intersection here when the light is red. Before proceeding across the intersection, cyclists should cautiously check for oncoming traffic. This can be a dangerous intersection.

12.7 Continue onto Old LaGrange Road

Old LaGrange Road runs parallel to KY-146/LaGrange Road, which was widened to accommodate the large volume of commuter traffic that now passes through this area. With nearly all of the traffic redirected onto the new road, the old road makes a good bicycle-friendly route through this portion of eastern Jefferson County. The only traffic to deal with is the cross traffic on Chamberlain Lane, and there is a traffic light at this location that mostly takes care of that problem. The road then passes under Interstate 265/Gene Snyder Freeway and ends at Lucas Lane in Anchorage.

14.2 Left onto Lucas Lane

Lucas Lane continues directly ahead as Stanley Gault Parkway, which leads into an industrial park. The route turns right here, onto KY-146/LaGrange Road. Thankfully, most of the traffic that was on LaGrange Road lies east of the interstate, so traffic in this area is not especially problematic.

14.2 Right onto KY-146/LaGrange Road

14.4 Left onto N English Station Road

14.8 Right onto Berrytown Road

Although it is easy to get back to Berrytown Park by continuing down English Station Road and turning right onto Heafer Road, the final portion of the tour explores the historic Berrytown neighborhood. On the left, about 1/4

Berrytown Cemetery

mile from the turn, is Berrytown Cemetery. There are over 300 people buried here, including many members of the Berry family for which the neighborhood is named. The cemetery is meticulously cared for by many of the neighborhood's residents.

15.1 Left onto Hines Road

If the roads in Berrytown seem to have been laid out in a haphazard fashion, it is not by accident. Berrytown, like Griffytown, was targeted for urban renewal in the 1960s, but resistance by residents of the neighborhood prevented a redesign of the streets to link English Station Road with KY-146/LaGrange Road. As a result, most of the streets here are laid out in the same fashion as they have been for over a century. Just as many of the exclusive enclaves of Louisville's east end contain many cul-de-sacs and dead end streets to discourage traffic from passing through the neighborhood, Berrytown's residents also enjoy their peace and quiet away from speeding motorists looking for a shortcut.

15.2 Right onto Hiawatha Avenue

15.3 Left onto Heafer Road

15.5 Right into Berrytown Park parking lot

Historic district in Pewee Valley, Kentucky

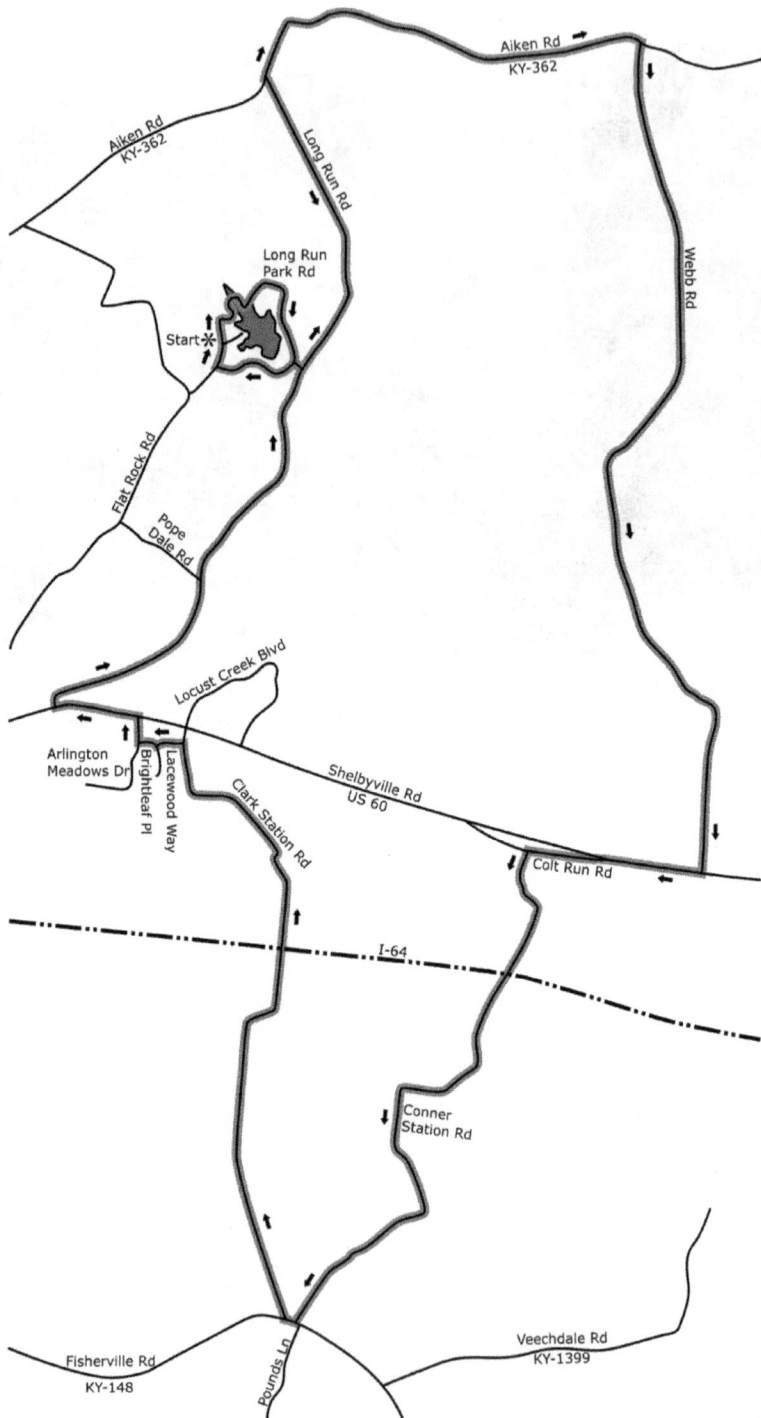

21 LONG RUN AND SIMPSONVILLE

Distance: 22.6 miles

Difficulty: Moderate. Nearly constant hills, but no significant climbs. Light traffic along most of the route, but very heavy traffic along U.S. Highway 60/Shelbyville Road.

Points of Interest: Long Run Park, Simpsonville, Whitney M. Young birthplace, Lincoln Institute, Long Run Massacre and Floyd's Defeat sites

Simpsonville, Kentucky is a sixth-class city in Shelby County that lies a few miles east of Jefferson County along U.S. Highway 60/Shelbyville Road. It is best known to most residents of Louisville as the home of the Outlet Shops of the Bluegrass and a convenient place to stop for cheap gasoline on their way out of the city. The city was founded in 1816 and incorporated in 1832. It was named for Captain John Simpson, a prominent lawyer in Shelby County who represented the county in the Kentucky General Assembly and was later elected to the United States House of Representatives. Captain Simpson was killed in action at the Battle of River Raisin in the War of 1812, and thus did serve his full term in office.

Today, Simpsonville is known as the "Saddlebred Capital of the World" due to the large number of horse farms and trainers in the area. Although it technically lies outside of Kentucky's Bluegrass region, the countryside surrounding Simpsonville looks a lot like the Bluegrass with its numerous horse farms and gently rolling hills. Due to its proximity to the city of Louisville, the city's population has increased greatly in recent years. In 1960, the city was home to a little over 200 residents, but in 2010 there were nearly 2,500 people who called Simpsonville home.

About two miles west of the Jefferson-Shelby County line along U.S.

60/Shelbyville Road is Long Run Creek. The creek was dammed to form a small lake around which modern-day Long Run Park lies. It is a tributary of the Floyds Fork River, and its confluence with the river is located a few miles south of this location. Today, the area around Long Run Creek is filled with sleepy suburban neighborhoods, but the area was once the site of several major skirmishes between some of the earliest settlers in the Louisville area and native tribes under the command of British forces.

The pioneers of the Painted Stone settlement, which was located near present-day Shelbyville, realized that their isolated location and exposed position left them vulnerable to attack by Indian forces under the command of British Captains Joseph Brant and Alexander McKee. After several groups of marauders raided Painted Stone in 1781, the settlers decided to abandon the site for the more heavily fortified settlements to the east along Beargrass Creek. On September 13, 1781, the residents of Painted Rock packed their belongings and made their way down Boone's Wagon Road, which ran atop a ridge where modern-day Eastwood is located, heading toward Linn's Station, the easternmost settlement along Beargrass Creek.

As the settlers crossed Long Run Creek, the anticipated attack occurred. Some of the settlers simply dropped their packs and fled. Many of the men stood their ground but quickly realized that they were outnumbered and outmaneuvered along the narrow road, with their militia far behind the line of wagons on the narrow road. Faced with almost certain death, the men decided to flee and run the remaining 9 miles to Linn's Station. Their retreat left the remaining settlers in the wagons vulnerable to attack, and the attack soon became a massacre. Many of the pioneers were shot as they fled, with heavy casualties among the women and children.

Few survivors made it to Linn's Station. Here they rejoined the militia, which arrived in Linn's Station later that evening after having taken a detour once they realized the settlers were under attack. News of the attack, later known as the Long Run Massacre, alarmed people living up and down Beargrass Creek. In response, Colonel James John Floyd quickly gathered up a small militia and headed to Linn's Station, fearing that it might be under attack. Linn's Station was safe when Floyd's militia arrived, but the presence of the armed militia helped to allay the fears of those who witnessed the massacre earlier that day.

The next morning, Floyd set out for Painted Stone with a force of 27 men that was organized into three columns. Anticipating this move, the Native and British forces prepared an ambush with a force of nearly 200. Although Floyd's forces arrived before the Indians and the British had fully set their trap, they quickly found themselves badly outnumbered. Seventeen of Floyd's men were killed in Floyd's defeat, and the remaining ten (including Floyd himself) barely eluded capture.

Floyd's defeat, however, had a positive side for the settlers. Floyd's forces had managed to kill a few of their attackers, including the Chief of the Hurons. Dejected, the Huron warriors simply headed back north and abandoned their British allies. This saved the remaining pioneers at Painted Stone from further attack, and a force of nearly 300 from Louisville was able to march to Painted Rock to rescue the remaining families there. Today, a marker placed along Shelbyville Road just east of Long Run commemorates the early residents who died in the Long Run Massacre and Floyd's defeat.

The tour, which explores the area around Long Run Park, Simpsonville, and portions of western Shelby County, begins in the parking lots on the west side of the lake in Long Run Park. A road runs through the main parking lot and ends with a boat ramp at the edge of the lake. This is usually the best area for parking due to the abundant shade. From here, the route follows the road circling the lake before exiting the park to explore the surrounding area via Long Run Road.

Long Run Park

Route Directions – Long Run and Simpsonville

0.0 Right onto Long Run Park Road
1.1 Left onto Long Run Park Road
1.2 Left onto Long Run Road
3.0 Right onto KY-362/Aiken Road
5.4 Right onto Webb Road
10.4 Right onto U.S. Highway 60
10.9 Left onto Colt Run Road
11.4 Left onto Connor Station Road
14.8 Right onto KY-148/Fisherville Road
14.9 Right onto Clark Station Road
18.5 Right onto Lacewood Way
18.7 Right onto Brightleaf Place
18.9 Right onto Arlington Meadows Drive
19.0 Left onto U.S. Highway 60/Shelbyville Road
19.4 Right onto Long Run Road
22.0 Left onto Long Run Park Road
22.1 Left onto Long Run Park Road
22.6 Right into parking lot

Route Description – Long Run and Simpsonville

0.0 Right onto Long Run Park Road

The road running through the parking lot ends at the edge of the park's lake. The road ascends a hill and then ends at Long Run Park Road, which circles the lake. Cyclists may circle the road in either direction to reach the park's exit onto Long Run Road, but the more scenic route lies to the right. The road around the lake is a series of twists and turns over small undulating hills, and there are numerous places for cars to park along the side of the road and for people to access the lake. Cyclists should be wary of speeding, inattentive, or distracted drivers circling the park in the opposite direction, but the road is wide enough to easily accommodate both bicycles and cars.

At the park's exit, there is a grass-covered traffic island on the left side of the road. A small brick sewage pumping station is visible in the distance. The route turns left onto the park's entrance road, which is unmarked, to exit the park onto Long Run Road.

1.1 Left onto Long Run Park Road

The entrance road ends a short distance after the turn at Long Run Road. The route turns left onto Long Run Road, toward the small brick building visible to the left side of the road.

1.2 Left onto Long Run Road

A few hundred feet from the park's entrance, Long Run Road leaves Jefferson County and enters Shelby County. From this point, the road rises nearly 100 feet in elevation over the next 2 miles. The climb is not steep, with several flat areas and small downhill stretches that allow tired legs to rest. In several locations, Long Run Creek runs alongside the road. The road ends on an incline about 3 miles into the route at KY-362/Aiken Road.

3.0 Right onto KY-362/Aiken Road

Traffic on Aiken Road can be moderate to heavy at times, especially around the morning and evening commute times, since this road is often used as a shortcut to the Middletown area. Fortunately, Long Run Road is at the edge of the busiest section of the road, so traffic is not usually much of a problem here. Cyclists should use caution, however, as eastbound traffic has a limited line of sight coming around a curve in the road and may be traveling in excess of the speed limit.

Scenery along Aiken Road

The Floyds Fork River flows just to the north of the road, and in this area it forms the border between Shelby and Oldham Counties. Along the way, there are a number of small hills, scenic farms, and historic homes. The next turn on the route, onto Webb Road, occurs a couple of miles to the east. The turn may be difficult to see because it is located at the bottom of a short descent.

5.4 Right onto Webb Road

Webb Road leads through the undulating hills of western Shelby County as it rolls southward toward the city of Simpsonville. This portion of the route begins with a short but somewhat steep climb, rising about 50 feet in elevation. From this point, the road is a fun series of rolling hills that passes through horse pastures, scenic farms, and wooded areas. This road is easily the highlight of the route and is a well-kept secret among many area cyclists. For most of the next 5 miles, there is little or no traffic to contend with, no traffic lights, and no stop signs. It's just beautiful scenery and a fun series of

Webb Road

climbs and descents.

At the 9.5-mile mark, there is a short, steep climb that rises about 100 feet in elevation that will test many cyclists' resolve, but most riders will easily conquer it. Shortly after this hill, traffic picks up a little as the road approaches its end at U.S. Highway 60 just west of Simpsonville. The route continues to the right at this point.

10.4 Right onto U.S. Highway 60

A short ride along the very busy U.S. Highway 60 will be necessary to reach the next portion of the route. Traffic here is fast, rude, and just plain unpleasant. It is possible to ride along the shoulder of the road through this area, but it is barely wide enough for a bicycle. There is usually a considerable amount of road debris along the shoulder, and there are rumble strips that are cut uncomfortably close to the edge of the shoulder in a couple of spots. Riding on the shoulder here also encourages cars to violate cyclists' 3-foot zone and is definitely not recommended. Fortunately, this portion of the route is quite short. There are, however, two points of interest along this short stretch of highway.

Across the street from the end of Webb Road is a historical marker that commemorates the vicious massacre that occurred at this site during the U. S. Civil War. At this site in January 1865, 22 members of the 5th United States Colored Cavalry, based at Camp Nelson in Louisville, were killed by Confederate guerillas while driving a herd of cattle back to Louisville. Local residents buried the soldiers in a mass grave near this site, which was later used as an African-American cemetery. There is a memorial here now that bears the names of the soldiers killed in the massacre. There is currently an effort underway to locate the men's graves and place a proper memorial directly at the burial site.

A little further west there are two historical markers on the south side of the highway that flank a side road. The first marker indicates the former site of the Lincoln Institute, a boarding school for African-American students that operated between 1912 and 1966. The school was located just south of the highway at this location. The school served

Lincoln Institute

as both a high school and a junior college and offered vocational classes as well. After 1933, the institute served primarily as a high school when Kentucky State University in Frankfort took over this role from the Lincoln Institute.

The Lincoln Institute was founded and operated by Berea College in response to the 1904 Day Law that mandated the segregation of schools and forbade black students from attending schools within 25 miles of white-only schools. At the time, Berea College was the only integrated school operating

311

within the state, and the college was fined the sum of $1,000 for violating the new law. The conviction and fine were contested, but they were upheld by the U. S. Supreme Court's *Berea College v. Kentucky* decision in 1908. In its decision, the court cited the 1896 *Plessy v. Ferguson* decision in upholding the law. Ironically, U. S. Supreme Court Justice and Boyle County native John Marshall Harlan issued one of the two dissenting opinions in the ruling and was the court's lone dissenting vote in the 1896 *Plessy v. Ferguson* ruling. Harlan died in 1911 after serving nearly 34 years on the court. The University of Louisville Law School's Harlan Scholars Program was named in his honor.

In response to the court's ruling, Berea College's trustees raised $200,000. Combined with a matching grant from the Carnegie Foundation, the college purchased this tract of land in western Shelby County and built the Lincoln Institute on it. The school closed its doors in 1966, and today is home to the Whitney M. Young Job Corps Center. The organization opened at this location in 1972 to provide job placement and training services.

The second historical monument at this location marks the birthplace of Whitney Moore Young (1921-1971), the Lincoln Institute graduate and prominent civil rights leader for whom the Job Corps Center now located here is named. Young was the son of Whitney M. Young, Sr., president of the Lincoln Institute and a well-known African-American educator. Valedictorian of his class, Young went on to Kentucky State University and earned a Bachelor of Science degree in social work. During World War II, he worked his way through the ranks very quickly and soon found success in mediating racial disputes between groups of soldiers.

After the war, Young went to the University of Minnesota and earned a master's degree in social work. He became president of the National Urban League's Omaha, Nebraska chapter, and eventually became Dean of Social Work at Atlanta University in Atlanta, Georgia. He was instrumental in transforming the National Urban League into a major player in the civil rights movement during the 1960s and is considered one of the "Big Six" leaders of the movement.

Soon, Colt Run Road appears on the left side of the highway, heading to the southwest at a shallow angle. The route turns left onto this road, away from the heavy traffic of Shelbyville Road.

10.9 Left onto Colt Run Road

After descending a small hill, Conner Station Road appears on the left.

11.4 Left onto Connor Station Road

The road becomes hillier as Conner Station Road continues south toward Fisherville in eastern Jefferson County. After the narrow road passes under

Interstate 64, the hills become smaller and less strenuous. At the 14.2-mile mark, the road crosses a set of railroad tracks and then ends at KY-148/Fisherville Road. At this point, the route turns right, onto KY-148/Fisherville Road.

14.8 Right onto KY-148/Fisherville Road

Almost immediately after turning onto KY-148/Fisherville Road, the next turn of the route, onto Clark Station Road, appears on the right side of the road.

14.9 Right onto Clark Station Road

Clark Station Road crosses the railroad tracks again soon after the turn and then crosses back into Jefferson County. This portion of the route is also very scenic, passing through beautiful wooded areas and scenic hillside farms as the road twists and turns its way back toward the Long Run area. The road climbs about 100 feet in elevation for most of the first two miles, crosses over Interstate 64, and then makes a steep, swift descent, dropping nearly 150 feet in elevation as the road continues northward.

Near the end of Clark Station Road at U. S. 60/Shelbyville Road, the route turns left onto Lacewood Way and travels through a small subdivision to bypass much of the very busy U.S. 60/Shelbyville Road.

18.5 Right onto Lacewood Way

18.7 Right onto Brightleaf Place

18.9 Right onto Arlington Meadows Drive

19.0 Left onto U.S. Highway 60/Shelbyville Road

This second trip down Shelbyville Road is much less stressful than the first. Although there is still heavy traffic in this area, the road is mostly downhill, so this segment of the route feels much shorter than the first. The next turn, back onto Long Run Road, is located just beyond the bridge over Long Run Creek. The entrance to the road is partially hidden from view until you reach the end of the bridge, so watch carefully and anticipate the turn.

Halfway through the descent, there are two historical markers on the right side of the road. The first one commemorates the Long Run Massacre, which occurred near the site of the marker at a ford across Long Run Creek. The second marker retells the killing of Captain Abraham Lincoln by Indians in 1786. The elder Lincoln, the grandfather of U.S. President Abraham Lincoln, was born in Pennsylvania in 1738. After the U.S. Revolutionary War, he moved his family to a farm on the Floyds Fork River near the site of this marker. In 1786, he and his sons were working in the fields when a sniper from the forest shot and killed the elder Lincoln in plain sight of his three sons.

Lincoln's eldest son Mordecai ran to the cabin nearby where Abraham kept his gun. After a few moments, the sniper emerged from the woods to examine the body while Abraham Lincoln's youngest son, Thomas Lincoln, kept watch. Mordecai took aim and killed the sniper.

After her husband's slaying, Bathsheba Lincoln moved the family to Washington County near Springfield. Young Thomas Lincoln, who would later become the father of President Abraham Lincoln, was forced to abandon his schooling and go to work at a very early age. His first-hand tale of his father's massacre undoubtedly left an impression on the young president.

The elder Abraham Lincoln was buried near his cabin, which sat at the present-day site of Long Run Cemetery. The cemetery is located just off Long Run Road about a half-mile south of the entrance to Long Run Park around the 21.5-mile mark of the route. A memorial to Lincoln was placed in the cemetery in 1937.

19.4 Right onto Long Run Road

Long Run Road leads north, back toward the ride start at Long Run Park. The road climbs approximately 120 feet in elevation from its intersection with Shelbyville Road to the park's entrance, but fortunately, the climb is barely noticeable since it is spread over a 2-mile stretch. The route turns left into Long Run Park at the same entrance from which the route departed.

22.0 Left onto Long Run Park Road

Immediately after re-entering the park, the route continues to the left past the traffic island and back onto Long Run Park Road.

22.1 Left onto Long Run Park Road

The last half mile climbs a small hill, passes by the southern edge of the lake, and then returns to the parking lot entrance that the route departed from.

22.6 Right into parking lot

Farmland on Webb Road in western Shelby County

22 PROSPECT AND WESTERN OLDHAM COUNTY

Distance: 23.0 miles

Difficulty: Difficult. Many hills, with two significant climbs. Light to moderate traffic on most roads with very heavy traffic along a short stretch of U.S. Highway 42.

Points of Interest: Hays Kennedy Park, Harrod's Creek, City of Prospect, Norton Commons, Wolf Pen Branch Conservation Area

The city of Prospect lies at the far northeastern corner of Jefferson County and borders Oldham County. Along with Anchorage, it is one of the wealthiest cities in the state, with a median household income of over $110,000 per year. The city can be roughly defined as the land lying between Harrod's Creek to the south, Hays Kennedy Park and U.S. Highway 42 to the west, and Oldham County to the east.

The city was founded in the late 1700s when settlers traveling down the Ohio River reached the area on flatboats by traveling up nearby Harrod's Creek. The population remained low for the next century until the Harrod's Creek and Westport Railroad built a line through the area in the 1870s. At the time, the area was known as Sand Hill due to the expansive sandy beaches along the river. The area's first residents were an eclectic mixture of wealthy landowners, poor migrant farmers, and former slaves.

Like many of Louisville's outlying suburbs and towns, Prospect remained sparsely populated until the 1960s when Hunting Creek opened, boasting its own country club and golf course. The development soon attracted many wealthy residents who were fleeing the city for the suburbs in the great suburban migration that began in the 1950s. U.S. Highway 42, which runs through the middle of town, provided an easy route for residents to commute into and out of downtown Louisville and fueled Prospect's population growth. Prospect incorporated as a fourth-class city in 1974 with a population of just under 2,000 residents. By 2000, the population of Prospect had more than doubled as more land was opened to development, but growth has slowed greatly since. Today, Prospect is best known as one of Louisville Metro's prosperous eastern suburbs and is centered around U.S. Highway 42, the main artery leading into western Oldham County.

Oldham County lies immediately to the east of Prospect and northeast of the bulk of Jefferson County. The county was established in 1823 from portions of Jefferson, Shelby, and Henry counties. It was named for Colonel William Oldham, who served as a Captain in the U.S. Revolutionary War and as a Colonel in the Kentucky Militia afterward. Oldham was killed in action at the Battle of the Wabash in 1791 at what later became known as St. Clair's Defeat.

Oldham County remained primarily rural with very few developed towns or cities until the Louisville and Frankfort Railroad Company introduced a rail line through the area. The railroad brought relatively little population growth until the suburban exodus of the 1950s and 1960s led to explosive growth in many of the small towns within commuting distance of Louisville. In the early 1970s, the construction of Interstate 71 between Louisville and Cincinnati opened the area to further development, and the western portion of Oldham County became more suburban. Today, Oldham County is Kentucky's wealthiest and second best educated county, and although it serves as a major bedroom community for the city of Louisville it is well known for its rural beauty, beautiful horse farms, and rugged, hilly terrain.

This tour explores the westernmost portions of western Oldham County, including the communities of Goshen and Brownsboro. The city of Goshen is a small city near the Ohio River with a population of 900. The city was founded in 1849 and originally named Saltillo for the Mexican city near the Battle of Buena Vista during the Mexican-American War. It was renamed Goshen in 1851 when the post office opened, for the Biblical land of Goshen. The Kentucky General Assembly officially incorporated Goshen as a fifth-class city in 1990.

Brownsboro is an unincorporated town lying in the northeastern portion of Oldham County adjacent to the Jefferson County border and south of Goshen. Although the area is primarily rural today, it was a thriving community during the 19th century. Settlers arrived in the area around 1788 and established a town near the site of Fort Kuykendahl that later became known as Brownsville. A post office was established in 1827, and sometime in the following decade the name of the town was changed to Brownsboro. Although the town was well established and populated when Oldham County was officially formed that year, it was passed over for the newer settlement of La Grange when the county seat was formally selected in 1838.

Brownsboro was a prosperous town, boasting a tannery, blacksmith, and carding mill. Its economy was powered by an influx of settlers and by its proximity to the city of Louisville. But prosperity did not last. During the 1850s and 1860s, a series of plagues swept through the area and decimated the population. During the U.S. Civil War a few years later, large numbers of Union and Confederate Army deserters plundered the area's remaining farms, and in spite of railroad lines that had been established nearby, the area fell into decline. Although the town has long disappeared, many of Brownsboro's original families remain in the area, joined by a number of wealthy citizens looking to distance themselves from the traffic and congestion of the city.

The tour begins just west of the city of Prospect in the parking lot of Hays Kennedy Park. The park is located on Bass Road, which is accessible from River Road a little less than one mile from its end at U.S. Highway 42. There are two parking lots available, although occasional events, such as soccer games, may cause a lack of parking here.

Hays Kennedy Park

Michael W. Thompson

Route Directions – Prospect and Western Oldham County

0.0 Right onto Bass Road
0.8 Left onto River Road
1.0 Left onto Sedgwicke Drive
1.2 Right onto Windham Parkway
1.3 Right onto Greenmere Boulevard
1.5 Left onto U.S. Highway 42
2.0 Left onto KY-3222/Rose Island Road
5.3 Right onto Mayo Lane
7.6 Continue onto Locke Lane
9.0 Left onto KY-329/Covered Bridge Road
11.7 Right onto KY-1694/Sleepy Hollow Road
15.1 Right onto Chamberlain Lane
16.5 Right onto Wolf Pen Branch Road at roundabout
18.9 Right to continue onto Wolf Pen Branch Road
19.7 Right to continue onto Wolf Pen Branch Road
20.8 Right onto River Road
22.2 Left onto Bass Road
23.0 Left into parking lot

Route Description – Prospect and Western Oldham County

0.0 Right onto Bass Road

Adjacent to the park is the Garvin Brown Preserve, a 46-acre riverfront nature preserve that is owned by the preservationist group River Fields. Rich in native plants and wildlife, the preserve is open to the public. It can be reached by a small trail located adjacent to the soccer field on the east side of Bass Road and is well worth a sunny afternoon spent exploring and enjoying the day.

Bass Road leads out of Hays Kennedy Park, rises very slightly in elevation as it passes through a small residential area, and then ends at its intersection with River Road.

0.8 Left onto River Road

River Road is a popular cycling route, beginning near Waterfront Park and the Big Four Bridge and ending at U.S. Highway 42 in Prospect. Before reaching the end of River Road, however, the route turns left and travels through the Sutherland Farms neighborhood, which was developed from one of the area's historic farms.

1.0 Left onto Sedgwicke Drive

1.2 Right onto Windham Parkway

1.3 Right onto Greenmere Boulevard

Greenmere Boulevard ends at U.S. Highway 42. The next turn on the route, onto the highway, requires both caution and patience.

1.5 Left onto U.S. Highway 42

U.S. Highway 42 is extremely busy, carrying a large volume of fast-moving traffic that is generally rude and unfriendly to bicycles despite the fact that this stretch of the highway is frequently traveled by cyclists. However, there is no way to continue any further east without traveling at least a short distance on this busy thoroughfare. The shoulder here is narrow and cut with rumble strips, and it will be necessary to ride at the far right side of the right lane or even on the white line at the edge of the road. This, however, may encourage motorists to pass cyclists in an unsafe manner. Fortunately, this section of the route is very short. It is best to travel this portion of the route with other cyclists, maintain visibility, and exercise extreme caution. Some cyclists may choose to walk their bicycles along the side of the road up to the next turn on the route.

The highway passes by Hunting Creek, the early subdivision in Prospect that helped fuel its growth. KY-329/Covered Bridge Road appears on the right just as the next turn on the route looms ahead. There is a gas station on the right side of the road that is situated on the former site of the Prospect General Store that once served as a gathering place for the area's residents. To make the next turn, it will be necessary to move into the left lane and turn across two lanes of traffic. Thus, it will be necessary to check both the traffic ahead and behind you before proceeding.

2.0 Left onto KY-3222/Rose Island Road

Rose Island Road

Rose Island Road leaves the hubbub of U.S. Highway 42 for more lightly traveled areas. The road is popular with area cyclists, and it is not unusual to see other bicycles on the road here.

There is an S-curve in the road soon after the turn, and just beyond the curve is Henry's Ark, an exotic petting zoo that is a popular local attraction. Admission is free to the public, but donations are accepted to help fund food and veterinary care for the animals.

Rose Island Road continues a few miles along the Ohio River, through scenic wooded hillsides and flat river bottomland. The next turn on the route, onto Mayo Lane, leads away from the river and toward the first major climb of the route.

5.3 Right onto Mayo Lane

Soon after making the turn, the road begins climbing a large hill. The hill rises more than 150 feet in elevation over the river valley and is quite steep at several points. Most cyclists will find it necessary to shift into a climbing gear. Many cyclists will end up walking up part or most of this hill, and if you do so, you will have plenty of company.

Mayo Lane ends at U.S. 42, continuing directly ahead as Locke Lane. Traffic on U.S. 42 is usually traveling at speeds well above the speed limit, so caution should be used when crossing the highway at this point.

7.6 Continue onto Locke Lane

Locke Lane continues through scenic Oldham County, amid horse farms, sprawling estates, and wooded hillsides. The road ends at the bottom of a long descent at its intersection with KY-329/Covered

Mayo Lane

Bridge Road. Cyclists should use caution and feather the brakes near the bottom of the hill to avoid running out onto Covered Bridge Road, which carries a moderate amount of traffic.

9.0 Left onto KY-329/Covered Bridge Road

Covered Bridge Road leads atop a small ridge just across the county line on the Oldham County side. The road soon crosses Harrod's Creek as it gently winds back and forth among wooded hillsides. This portion of the route can be spectacular in late October and early November when the trees are ablaze in shades of yellow, orange, and red.

Waterfall near Covered Bridge Road

Just beyond the bridge over the creek, the road begins climbing again, running alongside a small stream that is a tributary of Harrod's Creek that is separated from the road by a guard rail and a steep ravine. There are many small riffles and waterfalls along the creek, which may create quite a show in the spring or after heavy rains.

The road flattens, continues past several small subdivisions, and then continues eastward toward the next turn on the route, onto KY-1694/Sleepy Hollow Road.

Michael W. Thompson

11.7 Right onto KY-1694/Sleepy Hollow Road

Dam on Harrod's Creek near KY-1694

Sleepy Hollow Road soon begins descending a large hill through a heavily wooded area. The descent is steep in a few areas and may necessitate feathering the brakes to avoid gaining too much speed. The plentiful shade is certainly welcome during Kentucky's hot, humid summers, and the road is nice and smooth. The whole area has a rural, remote feel to it, despite being minutes away from Metro Louisville. As the road reaches the bottom of the ravine, it flattens out and passes near a small dam on Harrod's Creek (on the left side of the road) before crossing the creek over a small bridge.

There are two urban legends surrounding this area. The first is the legend of the black hearse, which holds that an ethereal black hearse may suddenly appear from out of nowhere, chasing drivers (and perhaps cyclists as well) down the hill and running them off the road into the steep ravine that lies beside the road. The second legend revolves around the bridge at the bottom of the hill, which is known to many locals as "Cry Baby Bridge." The legend states that the covered bridge that once stood at the site of the modern bridge was used by pioneer families to discard sick, dying, and unwanted babies into the swift waters of the creek below. On clear nights when there is a full moon, the legend states that the sorrowful cries of innocent children can be heard rising up from the waters of the creek.

After crossing Cry Baby Bridge, the road again begins to climb, rising nearly 150 feet from the bottom of the ravine. Fortunately, this hill is not extremely steep. With proper gearing, most cyclists should be able to make the ascent without difficulty. Near the top of the hill, Sleepy Hollow Road becomes Brownsboro Road as it re-enters Jefferson County. The next turn on the route, onto Chamberlain Lane, occurs very soon after passing St. Bernadette Church.

15.1 Right onto Chamberlain Lane

There are portions of Chamberlain Lane throughout eastern Jefferson County, but this portion is the easternmost, and skirts the edges of the newly established Norton Commons housing development. Named for WAVE-TV founder George Norton, the mixed-use development is situated on the former site of Norton's farm. As the suburban exodus of the late 20th century wore on, Norton's heirs developed the site in a model that emphasized the importance of community and convenience, rather than just allowing the land to become yet another sprawling Louisville suburb.

About 1.5 miles later there is a roundabout that leads into Norton Commons. The next turn of the route, onto Wolf Pen Branch Road, occurs at the first exit from the roundabout. Although this intersection is not usually busy, cyclists should be wary of vehicles in the roundabout who may not be looking for cyclists.

16.5 Right onto Wolf Pen Branch Road at roundabout

This road is named for Wolf Pen Branch, a small creek that is a tributary of the larger Harrod's Creek. The road is one of eastern Louisville's hidden treasures and is a must-do for any area cyclist. The road twists and turns through a very scenic area of Metro Louisville, and there are spectacular views of the small creek as it cascades down the hill toward

Wolf Pen Branch Road

Harrod's Creek. Like much of western Oldham County, this area is particularly scenic during the spring and fall months. A modicum of caution should be observed, however, due to the tendency of motorists to greatly exceed the 30 MPH speed limit.

Along the right side of the road lies Wolf Pen Branch Mill Farm, a historic farm that has been preserved by the organization River Fields. Although it is now surrounded on all sides by suburban sprawl, the land is home to a reconstructed grist mill and to the endangered running buffalo clover (*Trifolium stoloniferum*), a small plant that was once very abundant in Kentucky but has mostly disappeared since the area's settlement.

A little over two miles later, the road seems to end at a stop sign. Wolf Pen Branch Road, however, continues to the right at the stop sign.

18.9 Right to continue onto Wolf Pen Branch Road

Wolf Pen Branch Road continues straight ahead through the scenic Prospect area before passing underneath KY-841/Gene Snyder Freeway and coming to a stop at its intersection with Barbour Lane and Green Spring Drive. The route follows Wolf Pen Branch Road, which continues on to the right past the stop sign.

19.7 Right to continue onto Wolf Pen Branch Road

As the road continues to make its way toward the center of the city of Prospect, the traffic volume picks up greatly. Soon, the road crosses the horribly busy U.S. Highway 42, but there is a traffic light that will help immensely. Although there is no pedestrian crossing signal and the sensor is not triggered by the presence of bicycles, there is usually enough vehicular traffic at the intersection to cause the light to change. Despite recent improvements in the area's infrastructure, few efforts have been made to accommodate alternative forms of transportation.

Wolf Pen Branch Road ends at its intersection with River Road, not far from the confluence of Harrod's Creek with the Ohio River. This section of the road is narrow, with rocky outcroppings along the side of the road. Near its end, there are guard rails very close to the edge of the road. It is recommended that cyclists fully take the lane in the area to discourage motorists from passing in an unsafe manner. Since the intersection at the end of the road lies at an angle and sits at the bottom of a small hill, caution is essential when approaching the stop sign. The route continues right, onto River Road, as it heads back toward Hays Kennedy Park.

20.8 Right onto River Road

River Road passes over Harrod's Creek and past a scenic marina as it continues back toward Hays Kennedy Park and the city of Prospect.

22.2 Left onto Bass Road

23.0 Left into parking lot

Wolf Pen Branch Road in eastern Jefferson County

23 BIG FOUR BRIDGE, UTICA, AND JEFFERSONVILLE

Distance: 27.5 miles

Difficulty: Moderate. Heavy traffic through Jeffersonville, with lighter traffic east of Jeffersonville. Lightly rolling hills, with one significant climb.

Points of Interest: Big Four Bridge, Jeffersonville historic district, Howard Steamboat Museum, Jeffboat Shipyards, Utica, Ammo Hill

The city of Jeffersonville, Indiana lies directly across the river from eastern Louisville in Clark County, Indiana. Jeffersonville was one of the original communities that developed along the Ohio River at the Falls of the Ohio. The city was first settled around 1802 at the site of an abandoned fort, and its early growth was fueled by the river shipping industry which needed to offload cargo and transport it over land around the falls. Located near the top of the falls, Jeffersonville was well situated to take advantage of the large volume of river traffic along the Ohio River. But with the construction of the Portland and Louisville Canal on the Kentucky side of the river in the first half of the 19th century, Louisville soon became the dominant city in the region.

Although some of the area's other settlements shrank or disappeared after the canal was built, Jeffersonville persisted, and her fortunes soon turned to shipbuilding. In 1834, James Howard founded a shipbuilding business and built his first steamboat, the *Hyperion*, at his facility in Jeffersonville. After briefly moving the business upriver, Howard returned to Jeffersonville in 1849 and established the Howard Ship Yards just east of town. From the heydays of the 1850s until well into the 1920s, the Howard Ship Yards was the largest builder of steamboats in the country.

The United States Navy took control of the facility in 1925, and many landing vessels were constructed here until the early 1940s. Later, the facility was again privatized and became home to the Jeffersonville Boat and Machine Company, colloquially known as "Jeffboat." Jeffersonville's shipyards have long been a source of jobs and income to the city, and today remains as one of the area's largest employers.

Because of its deep river harbor and quick access to points northward by rail and to most of the south via the Louisville & Nashville Railroad, Jeffersonville became strategically important to the Union Army during the U.S. Civil War. Jeffersonville hosted a large garrison for Union troops during the war, and a large army hospital was built near Port Fulton. The hospital operated from 1864 to 1866 and was later repurposed as a storage facility for the United States Army during the late 1800s. Although the facility has long since disappeared, a historical marker at 301 East Park Place stands testimony to the hospital that once stood here.

During the later stages of the Civil War, Jeffersonville became home to the Ohio Falls Car & Locomotive Company, which manufactured railroad locomotives and boxcars. After a bankruptcy in 1866, a fire in 1872, and another bankruptcy in 1873, the company reorganized as the Ohio Falls Car Manufacturing Company and resumed manufacturing railroad cars for the narrow gauge tracks that were appearing nationwide. By the late 1880s, the company was again profitable, and in 1899, it merged with 13 other builders to form the American Car and Foundry Company. The company operated up through the Great Depression before closing, but was reopened temporarily during World War II. Today, what remains of the facility is occupied by a number of businesses in Water Tower Place, located just to the west of Interstate 65 at the very southern edge of the state of Indiana on Jeffersonville's western border with Clarksville.

The town of Utica, Indiana lies just a few miles upstream of Jeffersonville along the Ohio River. Settled in 1795 by a man named James Noble Woods, the town is one of the oldest settlements in the state of Indiana. Utica was too far from the Falls of the Ohio to attract business from the shipping industry, but it was perfectly situated for a ferry business since the falls were considered too dangerous for river crossings at the time. The town was formally organized in 1816 and had more than 100 log cabins, several of which are still standing today. Within a few years of its founding, Utica was bustling with new settlers arriving from Pennsylvania.

Like Jeffersonville, Clarksville, and New Albany, Utica's influence and fortunes declined somewhat after the opening of the Louisville and Portland Canal. However, Utica later became known for its lime kilns due to the abundance of porous limestone in the many cliffs surrounding the area. The Utica Lime Company was formed, and two large kilns were built on the outskirts of town. The company operated until 1870 when it was purchased by the Louisville Cement Company.

Today, Utica is a sleepy river town of about 900 residents. However, the town is well positioned to take advantage of an increase in vehicle traffic as the nearly 50-year dream of an east end bridge has finally come to fruition, connecting Louisville's eastern suburbs to Utica and the River Ridge development north of town. With the opening of the new bridge, Utica's history of ferrying people across the Ohio River has come full circle.

This tour also features Louisville's Big Four Bridge, which has become a popular local attraction since its opening in 2014. The bridge was originally built between 1888 and 1895 by the Louisville and Jeffersonville Bridge Company. There were many accidents that occurred during the bridge's construction. In one incident, a wind gust dislodged a crane, sending 41 men into the icy water below and killing 20 of them. This tragedy and several other accidents that occurred during the bridge's construction sent the company into bankruptcy. The bridge was soon sold to the Cleveland, Cincinnati, Chicago, and St. Louis Railway, also known as the Big Four Railway.

By the 1920s, the bridge had become obsolete due to the increasing weight of trains. In response, the bridge was upgraded between 1928 and 1929 using a novel building process in which the existing span was used as a scaffold and support for the new one. The upgrade gave the bridge new life, and it continued to operate for the next 40 years. In 1968, the Big Four Railroad merged with the Pennsylvania Railroad to form the Penn-Central Railroad, and the new company began routing traffic into Kentucky over the Fourteenth Street Bridge, leaving the Big Four Bridge unused. The steel from the bridge's approaches on both sides of the river was sold for scrap, and the bridge went dormant.

In the early 2010s, the long-defunct bridge again saw new life as officials on both sides of the Ohio River made plans to convert the structure into a pedestrian bridge over the river, connecting Louisville's Waterfront Park with Jeffersonville's downtown historic district. New approaches on both sides of the river were constructed, with the approach on the Kentucky side of the river finished in 2013. The approach on the Indiana side was finally completed in the spring of 2014, and after it was equipped with new LED light fixtures, the bridge officially opened to pedestrian and bicycle traffic. Since its opening, the bridge has proven to be a popular local attraction, with many residents walking across the river to visit the many restaurants, bars, and other businesses that have since opened along Spring Street. It is also frequently used by cyclists looking to cross the river to take advantage of southern Indiana's rural roads.

The tour begins at Louisville's Waterfront Park. Ample parking is available in any one of the many parking lots located along River Road or along some of the side streets adjacent to River Road. The mileage reported here begins at the Orange Parking Lot along River Road where there are restrooms and a water fountain available. There are also many shops and restaurants on the Indiana side of the Big Four Bridge for a quick snack or meal before or after the ride, if desired.

Big Four Bridge from Waterfront Park

Route Directions – Big Four Bridge, Utica, and Jeffersonville

0.0 Left onto River Road
0.3 Left onto Big Four Bridge
1.2 Left onto Pearl Street
1.2 Right onto W Chestnut Street
1.3 Continue onto E Chestnut Street
1.5 Right onto Walnut Street
1.6 Left onto E Market Street
4.3 Continue onto Utica Pike
7.7 Right onto Church Street
7.9 Continue onto S Front Street
8.3 Left onto E Market Street
8.4 Right onto N 2nd Street
8.6 Continue onto Upper River Road
10.3 Left onto Paul Garrett Avenue
13.7 Turn around at Patrol Road
17.3 Right onto Upper River Road
18.9 Continue onto N 2nd Street
19.0 Left onto Market Street
19.1 Right onto N Front Street
19.6 Continue onto Church Street
19.7 Left onto Utica Pike
25.9 Continue onto E Market Street
26.1 Right onto Spring Street
26.2 Left onto W Chestnut Street
26.2 Continue onto E Chestnut Street
26.3 Left onto Pearl Street
26.3 Right onto Big Four Bridge
27.3 Right onto River Road
27.5 Right into parking lot

Route Description – Big Four Bridge, Utica, and Jeffersonville

0.0 Left onto River Road

The Louisville Loop actually runs on the sidewalk along River Road in the area surrounding the parking lots of Waterfront Park. Due to the large number of walkers and runners on the loop, as well as the large number of children frequently darting in and out of the way, it is usually best to turn out onto River Road where there are fewer obstacles. When turning onto River Road, cyclists must observe traffic on the Louisville Loop as well as on River Road, so extreme caution is advisable in this area. River Road is usually busy, especially in the evening and on weekends.

0.3 Left onto Big Four Bridge

The approach to the bridge may not be evident to people who have not been on the bridge before. From River Road, there is an entrance into a parking lot that is immediately east of the bridge's approach. The lot is almost always full of cars, walkers, runners, and errant children, so caution is advised. Immediately upon turning into the parking lot's entrance, there is a cutout for wheelchairs and bicycles that leads back onto the loop trail and gives access to the bridge. The cutout is easy to miss. There is also vehicular traffic exiting the parking lot that cyclists will need to contend with before entering the Louisville Loop to access the bridge.

Big Four Bridge

Upon reaching the Louisville Loop, the bridge's approach is immediately to the north toward the river. The approach spirals upward, and it will be necessary to shift into an easier gear. The ramp may be a slightly steep climb for some novice cyclists. It is also nearly impossible to ride more than 5-10 MPH up the ramp and across the bridge due to the extremely large number of pedestrians and other bicycles that are usually on the ramp and bridge.

At the top of the approach, the trail turns sharply left, and then the trail straightens out as it crosses the river. Still, it will be nearly impossible to gain speed due to the traffic on the bridge. However, the bridge provides beautiful views of the Ohio River, the Falls of the Ohio, and of Louisville's skyline, so it is highly advisable to slow down and enjoy the view. There are several historical markers along the way, and there is often music playing as well.

The Indiana approach sits at the end of the main span of the bridge. This approach is just as steep as the Kentucky approach, and it will be necessary to apply the brakes sharply to avoid building up too much speed. There is a sharp curve in the approach about halfway down, and it may be necessary to warn pedestrians when passing. At the bottom of the approach, there is a small park with beautiful fountains. On the far side of this small park, there is a sidewalk cutout that leads out onto Pearl Street, where the route continues.

1.2 Left onto Pearl Street

A few feet from the entrance onto Pearl Street, the route continues onto W Chestnut Street on the right.

1.2 Right onto W Chestnut Street

Chestnut Street has a bike lane that brings bicycle traffic from the bridge directly into the business district on Spring Street. There is a parking lot on the left where many people visiting the park on this side of the river park, so there are often vehicles turning in and out of the lot. The bike lane is not well marked, so occasionally there may be vehicles parked along the side of the road.

The first cross street is Spring Street, which leads through a thriving business district that the opening of the Big Four Bridge has energized. There are restaurants, bars, breweries, and shops in nearly every storefront along the road. Spring Street lies near the center of Jeffersonville's historic district, and there are many historic buildings and monuments through this sector of the city. One of the nearby businesses that has benefitted from the traffic from the Big Four Bridge is Schimpff's Confectionery, which has been doing business in this location for over 100 years. Schimpff's is off to the left at the intersection of Spring Street and W Chestnut Street, which is just off the route described here, but it is nonetheless worthy of a side trip.

Schimpff's was founded in 1891 by Gustav Schimpff and is the oldest continuously operating family-owned candy maker in the United States. The store is well known for its Modjeskas, which are caramel-covered marshmallows named for Polish actress Helen Modjeska, who visited Louisville in the 1880s where she produced a production of Henrik Ibsen's *The Doll's House*. Schimpff's is also known for its candy fish but is probably best known for their cinnamon red hots that have been produced by the same method for over a century. Staff members often demonstrate this technique right in front of the store's front window and allow the heavenly aroma of cinnamon candies to waft up and down Spring Street, much to the delight of residents and tourists alike. The store also has a small candy museum in the back, which is free of charge to the store's visitors.

1.3 Continue onto E Chestnut Street

Across Spring Street, W Chestnut Street becomes E Chestnut Street. The route continues for three blocks along E Chestnut to avoid the crowding and congestion of Spring Street, which may be very busy in the evenings or on weekends.

1.5 Right onto Walnut Street

1.6 Left onto E Market Street

Market Street heads away from Jeffersonville's historic district, leading toward the former Port Fulton area and Jeffersonville's industrial district. Just beyond Penn Street, the road passes through the floodwall. There are steel plates on the road that cover a large hole. Caution should be used when passing through the floodwall, as there is often debris in the roadway and the steel plates make a large bump in the roadway that can cause pinch flats.

On the other side of the floodwall, Jeffboat's shipyards appear on the right. On the other side of the road, there are many small bars, restaurants, and convenience stores that cater to the men and women who work in the shipyards. The next two intersections have three-way stop signs that vehicles usually fail to stop at; thus, caution should be used in this area.

Howard Steamboat Museum

On the left side of the road across from the Jeffboat facility there is a large Victorian mansion. The home was built by Howard's son, Edmonds J. Howard, at this site in 1894. Today, the mansion houses the Howard Steamboat museum, which is dedicated to preserving the history of Jeffersonville's shipyards and relaying the history of the shipping industry on the Ohio River. The home still contains many of its original furnishings, including a large amount of ornate woodwork.

Near the end of the Jeffboat shipyards, there is an uneven railroad crossing that intersects the road at a slightly unusual angle, making it necessary to pay attention to the road when crossing. Beyond the crossing, the road climbs a small hill as it heads toward Jeffersonville's city limits. At this point, the road is usually referred to as Utica Pike. Traffic is usually moderate to heavy through this area, and an occasional aggressive driver may make it necessary to practice defensive cycling. Fortunately, police have been stepping up enforcement of Indiana's 3-foot law, especially along this stretch of highway that is a popular local cycling route.

4.3 Continue onto Utica Pike

After cresting the hill, the road makes a short, swift descent toward Duffy's Landing. The road again rises as it ascends toward Allison Lane. Traffic from Allison Lane may suddenly dart out in front of bicyclists and other motorists, so caution should be used approaching the intersection. Fortunately, traffic lightens greatly to the east of Allison Lane.

Just before the 6-mile mark the road crosses Lancassange Creek, climbs a very short hill, and then crosses a set of railroad tracks before coming to a 4-way stop at Port Road. Trains frequently cross the road on the tracks parallel to the road, but seldom block the crossing on Utica Pike. Past the intersection, the railroad tracks again cross the road. The road is rough between Port Road and Loop Road, but fortunately, the railroad crossing is very well maintained. On the right is the Port of Indiana – Jeffersonville, a major commerce center and a major employer in Clark County. Spurred in part by the Ohio River Bridges Project, shipments of steel, salt, and grain through the port have increased dramatically since 2013.

The road soon crosses Loop Road at another 4-way stop that carries a considerable amount of truck traffic bound for the riverport. Immediately past the intersection, Brown-Forman Road branches off

Marina near entrance to town of Utica

to the left. The road leads past a small lake that is home to Lakeside Reflections, a facility that hosts many outdoor weddings. Utica Pike then descends a short hill and enters the town of Utica. Upon entering the town, the speed limit drops to 30 mph and a small marina comes into view on the right. The next turn of the route is located immediately past the marina, onto Church Street.

7.7 Right onto Church Street

The route turns right onto Church Street, following the bike route signs toward the river. Soon the road curves sharply to the left as it becomes S Front Street.

7.9 Continue onto S Front Street

Front Street passes next to a small clearing that was once the site of a home that has excellent views of the river. This area makes a great spot for a quick break and a drink of water if desired. Past the clearing, Front Street becomes a one-way street heading southeast, so it will be necessary to turn left onto Market Street.

8.3 Left onto E Market Street

8.4 Right onto N 2nd Street

At the corner of Market and 2nd Street, there is a small outdoor diner that serves lunch to the many boaters, pedestrians, and cyclists that pass through the town during the warmer months of the year. It is an excellent place to stop for a cold drink or a snack, especially on hot summer days.

8.6 Continue onto Upper River Road

Looking ahead, it appears as if 2nd Street ends at a T-intersection with Upper River Road. Actually, N 2nd Street continues to the left at the intersection, and Upper River Road begins at the intersection and curves sharply to the right. The route continues to the right at this intersection onto Upper River Road. Traffic on 2nd Street can simply continue straight through the intersection onto Upper River Road because there is no stop sign. However, westbound vehicles on Upper River Road entering Utica often take the sharp curves on Upper River Road too quickly and are not usually paying attention to oncoming traffic coming from 2nd Street, so caution should be observed when making the turn.

Upper River Road continues along the Ohio River as it heads upriver from Utica. There are many spectacular views of the river through this area. On the left side of the road there is a massive limestone bluff. The road passes underneath the new east end bridge, then climbs slightly and passes through a shady, wooded area.

Not far past the bridge over the Ohio River, on the left side of the road (facing the bluff), is a point of interest. The remains of an old stone fence that is slowly being reclaimed by the forest conceal an old abandoned house. The abandoned house is known as Mistletoe Falls, but is better known to locals as the "Witch's Castle." The house is surrounded by several urban legends. It was also the site of a horrific crime: 13-year-old Shanda Sharer was tortured and beaten by four teenaged girls at the site before being murdered near Madison, Indiana in January 1992. The horrible crime revived the various urban legends surrounding Utica and brought the area into the national spotlight.

The urban legends surrounding the site and the town of Utica revolve around a rumor that the land for the town of Utica was stolen from three sisters of mixed Native American descent who lived in a house at or near the site of the Witch's Castle. The sisters refused to sell the land, and as punishment were beaten and strapped to a wooden raft that was set adrift on the

Mistletoe Falls

river heading toward the Falls of the Ohio. Just before their lives were claimed by the river near the falls, the sisters cursed the town and its residents. Shortly afterward, the Louisville and Portland Canal directed ships downriver to Louisville, and Utica's fortunes declined.

In the 1950s, a home was built at the site, but the owners of the new home were beset with multiple misfortunes. The home later burned and was never rebuilt; all that remains of the home are the foundation, a fireplace, a wall, and many urban legends surrounding the site. For many years it has attracted local teens looking for a thrill. After the sensationalized Sharer case, the urban legends surrounding it have only multiplied. Access to the site is prohibited.

Past the Witch's Castle, there is a road branching off to the left that heads up a steep hill to the top of the bluff and the exclusive Quarry Bluffs neighborhood. Many cyclists and runners use this hill and others in the area for hill repeats.

At the end of Upper River Road is a slightly confusing intersection. The road seemingly continues past a small guard house that lies ahead as it becomes Huntington Beach Road. To the left, there are two roads that branch off toward the bluff. The nearest road heads back into the Quarry Bluff neighborhood. The road farthest away, situated on the other side of a large concrete curb, is Paul Garrett Avenue, which leads up and over the hill to connect Upper River Road with IN-62 and Charlestown. The route continues past the guard shack and onto Paul Garrett Avenue.

10.3 Left onto Paul Garrett Avenue

Paul Garrett Avenue heads into a shady wooded area and very quickly begins climbing the hills of the Ohio River valley east of the Quarry Bluffs neighborhood. While the hill is not exceptionally steep, it is long, climbing steadily for nearly 2 miles before finally leveling off. There is another abandoned guard shack about 1 mile up the hill on the left side of the road, and then the tree canopy disappears. This hill, known as "Ammo Hill" by many area cyclists, is a popular cycling route. On any given day, there are usually a few other cyclists climbing or descending the hill, and the vehicle traffic is very light.

Water tower on Ammo Hill

Ammo Hill passes through the former site of the Indiana Army Ammunition Plant, a facility that was built on this site in 1941 due to its proximity to shipping routes on the Ohio River and its unsuitability for farming. Production at the plant began in April 1941, with the full facility opening in 1942. The plant was operated by E. I. DuPont de Nemours and Company during World War II, and produced smokeless powder. At its peak, the plant produced more powder than all other plants combined through the entirety of World War I. After the war, the plant was temporarily mothballed but was restarted in 1950 during the Korean War. The plant was finally closed for good in 1960. Traces of the plant can still be seen through this area, including the remains of many of the roads and railroad tracks that ran through the facility. Some of the plant's buildings are still standing and can be seen along IN-62 near Charlestown.

In the 1990s, about 4,500 acres of the site was transferred to the Indiana Department of Natural Resources as part of Charlestown State Park, which also includes the former site of Rose Island Amusement Park. In the 2000s, much of the remaining land was repurposed as the River Ridge Commerce Center, a light industrial development along IN-62 that now provides many jobs to the area. Near the end of Paul Garrett Avenue, portions of the new development can be seen off to the left. With the new bridge over the Ohio River now open to traffic, River Ridge seems well poised to become a major economic engine in the Kentuckiana area.

At the top of the hill, the road crosses a set of railroad tracks, passes a water tower and an old cemetery on the right, and another abandoned guard shack on the left as the road widens and flattens out. There is usually a tailwind coming up the hill from the river in this location, which will become a headwind on the return trip down the hill.

13.7 Turn around at Patrol Road

Paul Garrett Avenue ends at a stoplight with IN-62. About 100 feet before reaching this intersection, Patrol Road crosses Paul Garrett Avenue and leads west into the River Ridge Commerce Center. The route turns around at this point to head back down Paul Garrett Avenue.

17.3 Right onto Upper River Road

18.9 Continue onto N 2nd Street

19.0 Left onto Market Street

19.1 Right onto N Front Street

19.6 Continue onto Church Street

19.7 Left onto Utica Pike

25.9 Continue onto E Market Street

26.1 Right onto Walnut Street

26.2 Left onto W Chestnut Street

26.2 Continue onto E Chestnut Street

26.3 Left onto Pearl Street

26.3 Right onto Big Four Bridge

27.3 Right onto River Road

27.5 Right into parking lot

24 CLARKSVILLE AND NEW ALBANY

Distance: 13.7 miles

Difficulty: Easy. Mostly flat, but there may be moderate traffic on Lewis and Clark Parkway, Main Street, and Spring Street in New Albany, especially around morning and evening commute times.

Points of Interest: Ohio River Greenway, Falls of the Ohio State Park, Lewis and Clark Park, George Rogers Clark homesite, Loop Island Wetlands, Sloan-Bicknell-Paris House, Culbertson Mansion

The town of Clarksville and city of New Albany lie along the Indiana shore of the Ohio River flanking the Falls of the Ohio, across the river from the city of Louisville. While both are seemingly overshadowed by the much larger city of Louisville, they were independent settlements of equivalent influence to Louisville prior to the construction of the Louisville and Portland Canal in the 1820s. After the canal's opening, most of the commercial traffic along the Ohio River was routed to the Kentucky side of the river, bypassing Clarksville and New Albany.

Clarksville was founded in 1783 and named for Revolutionary War hero General George Rogers Clark, who used the land north of the Ohio River near Louisville as a base of operations for his militia. Following the war, Clark was granted 150,000 acres of land in the area north of the river in what was known as the Northwest Territory. From this land, Clark granted a 1,000-acre tract for the establishment of a town near the falls. Because of this, the town often bills itself as the "First American Settlement in the Northwest Territory."

Despite owning most of modern-day Clark and Floyd Counties in Indiana at the time, Clark spent most of his later years in debt, trying to elude creditors. In 1793, he lost a large amount of money in a never-realized plan to drive the Spanish out of the Mississippi Valley through an alliance with the French. In 1805, Clark was appointed to the board of directors of the Indiana Canal Company in a failed attempt at building a canal around the Falls of the Ohio on the Indiana side. The company collapsed before work could begin, and two of its board members, one of whom was Vice President Aaron Burr, were later charged with treason. Creditors eventually forced the sale of most of Clark's land, leaving him with only a few dozen acres near his home where he built and worked a grist mill with two slaves. Clark remained here until 1809 when he fell into ill health and was forced to move in with his brother-in-law, Major William Croghan, at Locust Grove just east of Louisville.

The town of Clarksville, despite its proximity to the Falls of the Ohio, never developed beyond a few dozen homes, and the construction of the canal on the Kentucky side of the river ensured that the town would never be more than a dot on the map for many decades to come. Clarksville remained in relative obscurity until the 1870s when the few residents remaining in the area challenged an annexation attempt by a developer. The Indiana Supreme Court ruled in favor of Clarksville, which spurred the re-establishment of its town council.

Colgate-Palmolive clock

Clarksville finally experienced growth and prosperity during the 20th century. In 1923, Colgate-Palmolive opened a toothpaste plant in Clarksville at the former site of the Indiana Reformatory for Men. The plant boasts the world's second largest clock atop one of its towers. With the jobs the plant provided, growth finally came. By 1950, the town had nearly 6,000 residents. In 1968, the Green Tree Mall was built in Clarksville, touching off a building boom that made the town a major shopping destination on the northern side of the river. With the explosive growth provided by the shopping outlets, Clarksville's population now exceeds 21,000. However, Clarksville never formally became a city, and today still retains the original town government under which it was founded.

New Albany, Indiana, located to the east of Clarksville in Floyd County, has a much more prosperous history than Clarksville. New Albany was founded by the Scribner brothers, who arrived at the Falls of the Ohio in 1813. They purchased a tract of land from Colonel John Paul and platted out a town at the site, naming it for Albany, New York. Joel and Mary Scribner built a home at the site in 1814 that still stands today at 106 East Main Street. New Albany was chartered as a town in 1817 and as a city in 1839.

Despite being passed over as a potential site for the establishment of a canal around the Falls of the Ohio, New Albany soon established itself as a major hub for shipbuilding. Situated downstream of the Falls, New Albany shipbuilders specialized in building ships designed to ply the rivers of the American south. With the jobs and trade that shipbuilding provided, New Albany grew quickly and became quite affluent. By the 1850s, it was the largest and wealthiest city in the entire state of Indiana, and its power and influence rivaled that of the larger city of Louisville across the river.

The onset of the U.S. Civil War ended New Albany's shipbuilding boom, essentially killing the city's primary industry and source of wealth. But as the shipbuilding industry dwindled, other industries quickly replaced it. For example, the American Plate Glass Company was established in 1865 and soon became one of the city's major employers. When the factory closed in 1893, it ended New Albany's century of affluence and sent the city into a long, slow economic decline that lasted until the latter half of the 20th century. But with the opening of the Pillsbury Company in 1959, the 1962 construction of the Sherman Minton Bridge, and the 1973 relocation of Indiana University Southeast to a sprawling campus on the northern edge of town, New Albany experienced a renewed boost in economic activity and population growth. New Albany's future continued to brighten in the 2010s with a major revival in its downtown district. There are now many restaurants, bakeries, bars, and breweries that have opened in downtown New Albany, with the promise of more to come.

The tour begins in Clarksville at the easternmost trailhead of the Ohio River Greenway. The greenway project links the town of Clarksville to the cities of Jeffersonville and New Albany along the Ohio River corridor and provides access to the Falls of the Ohio, the Loop Island Wetlands, and many historical sites in downtown New Albany. To the east of this location, the greenway is linked to downtown Jeffersonville, the Big Four Bridge, and the Louisville Loop by the shared use lanes on Riverside Drive. To the west, a bike path leads to Lewis and Clark Park, passing the Falls of the Ohio and the George Rogers Clark home site along the way. Plenty of parking is available in the many parking lots surrounding the greenway, and an ice cream shop and bicycle rental facility are located across the street from the greenway trailhead. There are also many restaurants nearby along Riverside Drive.

Michael W. Thompson

Route Directions – Clarksville and New Albany

0.0 Right onto Ohio River Greenway
1.9 Continue onto Harrison Avenue
2.0 Left to continue onto Harrison Avenue
2.1 Continue onto Jackson Street
2.2 Continue onto Emery Crossing
2.5 Right to continue onto Emery Crossing
3.2 Right onto McCullough Pike
3.6 Continue onto Lewis and Clark Parkway
3.8 Left onto Providence Way
4.8 Continue onto IN-62/E Spring Street
4.9 Left onto Cost Avenue
5.0 Right onto E Market Street
5.2 Left onto Silver Street
5.4 Right onto E Main Street
5.7 Left onto E 18th Street
5.9 Right onto Floyd Street
6.1 Continue onto E Water Street
7.0 Right onto E 6th Street
7.2 Right onto E Main Street
8.5 Left onto Silver Street
8.6 Right onto E Market Street
8.7 Left onto Cost Avenue
8.8 Right onto IN-62/E Spring Street
9.1 Right onto Providence Way via exit ramp
9.3 Right to continue onto Providence Way
10.0 Right onto Lewis and Clark Parkway
10.3 Continue onto McCullough Pike
10.7 Left onto Emery Crossing
11.4 Left to continue onto Emery Crossing
11.7 Continue onto Jackson Street
11.8 Continue onto Harrison Avenue
11.9 Right to continue onto Harrison Avenue
12.0 Left onto Ohio River Greenway
13.7 Left into parking lot

346

Route Description – Clarksville and New Albany

0.0 Right onto Ohio River Greenway

From the parking lot, the greenway trail can be accessed from any one of the ramps that lead up to it from the parking lot. There are numerous places where the trail crosses parking lot entrances, so caution should be used to avoid vehicles entering and exiting the parking lots. During the warmer months of the year, there are many pedestrians on this section of the greenway, and many faster cyclists may feel more comfortable riding on Riverside Drive.

Around the 0.5-mile mark, the trail crosses Riverside Drive and climbs a small hill to the top of a levee. At the top of the levee, there is a stop sign where the trail crosses Winbourne Avenue. It will be necessary to stop and look closely for traffic because vehicles climbing the levee have a limited line of sight. On the other side of the intersection, the museum and headquarters of Falls of the Ohio State Park are located just inside the levee. The park and museum make a compelling reason to stop and explore the area and can be accessed from the end of Riverside Drive back at the bottom of the levee.

The Falls of the Ohio refers to a shallow area of rapids along the Ohio River created by the slow erosion of the Devonian limestone in this location. Across the length of the falls, the river drops about 26 feet in elevation. Instead of a single discontinuity that creates a spectacular waterfall, such as Niagara Falls, the drop in elevation occurs over a length of two miles. The exposed limestone, which

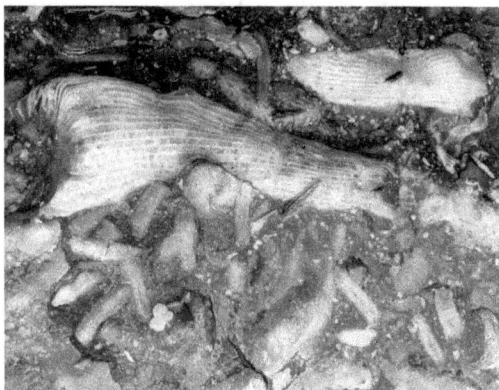

Fossils at the Falls of the Ohio

has been much slower to erode than the surrounding soil and rock, has created a long series of shallow rapids along the river. The exposed limestone was formed approximately 380 to 390 million years ago during the Emsian and Eifelian Ages of the Devonian Period. The formation is referred to as the Jeffersonville Limestone, after the city of Jeffersonville located at the eastern edge of the falls. At the time, this area was part of a shallow inland tropical sea that was inhabited by a number of bizarre sea creatures, including many corals, sponges, bryozoans, brachiopods, and mollusks. Today, the skeletons and shells of many of these creatures remain as fossils embedded

347

in the limestone.

Throughout most of the 18th and early 19th centuries, the Falls of the Ohio posed the only major navigational obstacle to boats traveling up and down the 981-mile long Ohio River. The dangerous rapids at the falls necessitated the movement of passengers and goods over land to waiting ships on the lower side of the falls. This impediment to travel along the river spurred the development of Louisville, Shippingport, Portland, Clarksville, Jeffersonville, and New Albany near the falls. The Falls of the Ohio was also the meeting point for Meriwether Lewis and William Clark for their 1804-1806 journey westward along the Ohio, Mississippi, and Missouri Rivers to explore the territories of the vast Louisiana Purchase.

Today, what remains of the falls has been converted into a state park, with multiple pedestrian trails that lead out to the fossil beds along the river's edge. The best time to explore the fossil beds is between September and November when the river level is at its lowest. During the summer, the oppressive heat can be greatly amplified by the exposed rock, causing the ambient temperature to soar well above 100°F.

Past the Falls of the Ohio, the trail continues along the levee, making several sharp turns as it snakes its way toward Lewis and Clark Park. The trail is very flat and the pavement is in good condition. However, be on the lookout for duck and goose droppings in this area that may make the pavement slippery, especially during and after rain events. The large flocks of geese tend to remain in the area directly behind the museum of the Falls of the Ohio.

Just shy of the 2-mile mark, the bike trail ends at its intersection with Harrison Avenue. This section of Harrison Avenue is a short, dead-end extension of the road that leads to a few homes along the Ohio River. The route continues ahead and slightly to the right onto Harrison Avenue at the end of the bike trail.

1.9 Continue onto Harrison Avenue

This short section of Harrison Avenue ends at a 4-way stop. Directly ahead, the road continues on as Bailey Avenue. Harrison Avenue runs east-west at the intersection and perpendicular to the short dead end extension of the road. The route continues left onto Harrison Avenue at the 4-way stop, toward Lewis and Clark Park. The park can be easily seen from this intersection, so following the route through this area should not be difficult.

If a shorter route is desired, Bailey Avenue continues straight before ending one block later at the entrance to another bike path. This bike path has access points that link the greenway to Miller Avenue and Clark Boulevard, where another bike path extension then links this segment back to Harrison Avenue about one quarter mile east of the earlier trailhead and makes a small loop.

Every town's greenway must pass the sewage treatment plant, and Clarksville is no exception. Beyond the Miller Avenue and Clark Boulevard access points, the greenway continues behind the sewage treatment plant treatment plant before coming to a dead end about one-half mile later.

2.0 Left to continue onto Harrison Avenue

As Harrison Avenue descends a hill and enters Lewis and Clark Park, it becomes Jackson Street.

2.1 Continue onto Jackson Street

Jackson Street continues through Lewis and Clark Park. Near the bottom of the hill, there is a boat ramp facility that is frequented by local residents who fish the river near the Falls of the Ohio. Large signs overhead and along the road warn boaters of the dangerous currents that may exist at the dam adjacent to the boat launch ramp here.

George Rogers Clark homesite

The parking lot for the boat launch ramp also provides access to the George Rogers Clark home site, which lies a short distance southeast of this location. The cabin here is a replica of Clark's original cabin, which burned down in 1854. The land on which it stands, referred to as Clark's Point, has spectacular views of the Falls of the Ohio.

Although Lewis and Clark Park is still not fully developed as of the writing of this book, there are a number of historical markers, informational displays, and a couple of old millstones situated on the right side of the road behind a split rail fence. As the road curves to the right, and then again sharply to the left, it becomes Emery Crossing.

2.2 Continue onto Emery Crossing

Emery Crossing continues along the north shore of the Ohio River, crossing Mill Creek. A few hundred yards to the east, the road curves sharply to the right again as it leads northward through an industrial area. The road is rough and rutted, and there is often debris in the lane of travel. It is crucial to pay very close attention to road conditions here to avoid getting a flat tire, or worse. Thankfully, there is seldom much traffic to contend with in this area.

One block before ending at IN-62/Brown's Station Way, Emery Crossing comes to a four-way stop at its intersection with McCullough Pike. The route continues to the right.

3.2 Right onto McCullough Pike

McCullough Pike climbs a small hill, passes over IN-62/Brown's Station Way, and then widens as it becomes Lewis and Clark Parkway.

3.6 Continue onto Lewis and Clark Parkway

There are two entrance ramps and exit ramps to and from Lewis and Clark Parkway from Brown's Station Way, so extreme caution is highly advised through this area. The next turn, onto Providence Way, occurs at the first traffic light just beyond the point where the road widens to four lanes, so it is best to remain in the left lane and quickly move into the left turn lane as it appears next to the concrete median.

3.8 Left onto Providence Way

Providence Way runs roughly parallel to IN-62/Brown's Station Way, leading past Providence High School and then over Silver Creek as it enters Floyd County, which was carved out of Clark County in 1819. By 1818, the town of New Albany had grown substantially since its founding just five years earlier, so some of the town's residents petitioned the state government to establish a new county with New Albany as its county seat. In early 1819, the Indiana General Assembly established Floyd County from a portion of Clark County. Although there are some historians who maintain otherwise, Floyd County was probably named for Davis Floyd, a local politician and judge who was indicted as a co-conspirator with Aaron Burr in a 1806 incident that later came to be known as the Burr Conspiracy.

Aaron Burr, the third Vice President of the United States, served from 1801-1805 under the administration of President Thomas Jefferson. When it became evident that Jefferson would not include Burr as his running mate in the 1804 election, he ran for governor of New York and suffered a landslide defeat to the relatively unknown Morgan Lewis. After dueling and killing Alexander Hamilton, whom he blamed for his electoral loss, Burr moved westward. He was soon accused of conspiring to provoke a rebellion in Spanish-held territories to the west and southwest in order to form an independent nation there. Kentucky District Attorney Joseph Daveiss brought federal charges against Burr, but failed to convict him.

Davis Floyd, then a member of the territorial legislature, was a fellow member of the Indiana Canal Company along with Burr. Floyd reportedly committed to raising a militia to assist Burr in his goal of destabilizing Spanish territories in the west. With 30 men and a number of ships, Floyd and his troops departed New Albany in 1806, traveling down Silver Creek to the lower side of the falls and then sailed for Louisiana where Burr's forces were waiting.

President Jefferson, aware of the conspiracy, ordered Burr and his co-conspirators arrested and charged with treason. Floyd, Burr, and their associates were tried for treason in 1807, and both men were found not guilty. Ultimately, Floyd was jailed for 3 hours and fined $20. After several years attempting to redeem his name, Floyd eventually returned to public life, serving in various public offices in the following years. In 1819, Floyd lost his home, store, and entire fortune in the Panic of 1819. He later moved to Florida, where he remained until his death in 1834.

Providence Way ends at IN-62/Spring Street in New Albany. Although IN-62 through Clark County is a limited access highway with a high volume of fast-moving traffic, the road is much calmer in New Albany where the speed limit drops to 30 MPH. There is a stop sign at the road's intersection with Beharrel Way. Through the stop sign, the road merges with Spring Street. A yield sign ahead indicates the need to yield to traffic on Spring Street as you continue straight ahead.

4.8 Continue onto IN-62/E Spring Street

After merging onto Spring Street, it will be necessary to move into the left lane as soon as possible in order to make the next turn.

4.9 Left onto Cost Avenue

Cost Avenue provides a shortcut through a residential neighborhood, away from the heavy traffic on Spring Street.

5.0 Right onto E Market Street

5.2 Left onto Silver Street

Silver Street leads back toward the Ohio River, ending at a sharp curve with a stop sign. The abandoned Moser Leather Company factory looms straight ahead at the curve. The company was founded in New Albany in 1878 and operated here until 2002 when the company moved its operations to Ohio.

There is a sign here for the Loop Island Wetlands that are located directly behind the abandoned factory. Loop Island is a small swampy tract of land

surrounded by a loop of Silver Creek. The loop in the creek may have been created as a canal, but that is not known for sure. After the tannery was closed in 2002, the wetland area behind it was preserved, and a portion of the Ohio River Greenway has been built through the area. The wetlands can be accessed from here or from the Ohio River Greenway Trail in New Albany at the 18th Street trailhead. There

Moser Leather Company building

are directions on the window of the abandoned tannery that describe the best ways to access the site.

The Loop Island Wetlands are also thought to be the site of an 1809 duel between Henry Clay, the Speaker of the Kentucky State House of Representatives at the time, and Representative Humphrey Marshall, who harbored animosity toward Clay due to his defense of Aaron Burr in his treason trial. Marshall was elected to the Kentucky House of Representatives in 1807, and tensions soon flared in the capitol. These tensions came to a head in December 1808 when Marshall voted against a bill Clay had introduced that would have required legislators to wear homespun suits to support local manufacturing over British imports. Marshall considered the bill to be grandstanding by Clay and wore a finely tailored British-made broadcloth suit on the chamber floor in protest. Insults were exchanged, and on January 4, 1809, Clay challenged Marshall to a duel.

The duel took place on January 19, 1809, in the vicinity of the mouth of Silver Creek where it joins the Ohio River. United States District Attorney Joseph Daveiss, who filed the first charges against Aaron Burr in 1806, provided the pistols. Both men were given three shots. Clay grazed Marshall across the stomach on the first shot, and Marshall grazed Clay's thigh on the third shot. Henry Clay insisted on the two men taking a fourth shot, but Marshall declined due to Clay's injury, considering the matter settled.

Today, the Loop Island Wetlands are much quieter. A large lagoon sits at the site, serving as a home for many types of aquatic plants, wildlife, and waterfowl. There is also an abandoned trestle spanning Silver Creek that links New Albany and Clarksville. Despite the tannery's historical wastewater discharges into the wetlands, the water and the woodlands surrounding it are safe to explore, and the site is well worth an afternoon spent exploring.

5.4 Right onto E Main Street

5.7 Left onto E 18th Street

East 18th Street leads through an earthen levee to a trailhead for the Ohio River Greenway. To the left, the greenway skirts the northern edge of the Loop Island Wetlands before ending at the trestle mentioned earlier. To the right, the greenway leads toward downtown New Albany and becomes Floyd Street, and later, Water Street. The route continues right, onto Floyd Street.

5.9 Right onto Floyd Street

The Ohio River Greenway continues west toward downtown New Albany as Floyd Street. Vehicular traffic can access this portion of the greenway trail, so be aware of vehicles here, especially as you come around curves in the road where your line of sight is limited.

6.1 Continue onto E Water Street

Floyd Street soon becomes Water Street as it continues toward downtown New Albany. There are spectacular views of the river through this area, particularly as the road passes underneath the Kentucky & Indiana bridge that links New Albany to Louisville's Portland neighborhood. Just to the left is Sand Island, situated just west of Shippingport Island at the lower side of the Falls of the Ohio.

The bridge, referred to as the K&I Bridge by locals, opened in 1886. The bridge featured two wagon lanes in addition to a single gauge track, allowing wagons to cross the river by bridge

Kentucky & Indiana (K&I) Bridge

rather than the traditional ferry. With the popularity of the automobile in the 20th century, the bridge began carrying cars and pedestrian traffic across the river as well.

In 1979, an overweight truck caused a portion of the steel roadway to collapse, and the bridge's owner banned vehicular traffic on the bridge. Over the ensuing years, there have been multiple attempts to force the bridge to reopen to vehicular traffic, but these efforts have been largely unsuccessful. The last major effort to allow traffic over the bridge came in 2011 with the temporary closure of the Sherman Minton Bridge on Interstate 64, but these efforts were also unsuccessful.

New Albany's concrete floodwall, like those surrounding most of the cities that lie along the Ohio River, soon appears along the left side of the road. As the floodwall curves northward slightly, there is a separate bike path that begins along the left side of the road. Bicycles may use the bike path or remain on Water Street.

As Water Street descends a small hill toward the New Albany riverfront, E 6th Street merges with Water Street as it descends from the top of the levee. There is a stop sign on both streets to control traffic, but be wary of vehicles descending the hill from 6th Street that may not stop as required.

7.0 Right onto E 6th Street

The road climbs a short but somewhat steep hill as it climbs the levee and then crosses a set of railroad tracks. It comes to an end shortly afterward at its intersection with Main Street.

7.2 Right onto E Main Street

Main Street is a divided road, with a shared use lane next to the median and a parking lane on the right. Like Spring Street, Main Street is a major artery that links downtown New Albany to Clarksville and Jeffersonville. Although overloaded, heavy trucks and speeding vehicles were once a major problem on Main Street, the recent addition of the median and shared use lane has greatly calmed traffic through the area and has encouraged alternative modes of transportation in the area.

Main Street passes through New Albany's historic district, which is often referred to as Mansion Row. There are many beautiful old homes lining both sides of the street, and this area is easily the highlight of the tour. At the corner of E 6th and E Main Streets is the Sloan-Bicknell-Paris house, built in 1854 for Dr. John Sloan. Today, the historic home has been converted into an inn known as the Admiral Bicknell Inn, named for the husband of Dr. Sloan's daughter Ann.

To the west, just beyond this route, are two important historic sites in New Albany. The most prominent one, Town Clock Church, is visible from the corner of 6th and Main. The Greek Revival style church, built in 1852, was a major stop on the Underground Railroad for escaped slaves seeking freedom to the north. Like many of the sites on the Underground Railroad, freedom seekers traveled mostly by night and hid in tunnels and cellars, or in the homes and businesses of abolitionists that assisted them on their journeys. The church is still operating today as the Second Baptist Church, and a preservationist group is working with the church to restore the building and the tunnel underneath Main Street to preserve this important piece of our national heritage for future generations.

A little farther west of Town Clock Church is the Scribner house, located at the corner of Main and State Streets. The house is a Federal style home that was

Sloan-Bicknell-Paris House

built between 1813 and 1814 by Joel Scribner, one of New Albany's founders. The Daughters of the American Revolution now owns the home and gives tours every other Saturday between May and September. An open house is held every May and December as well.

On the right side of Main Street between 9th and 10th Streets is the Culbertson Mansion. This historic home was once the home of William S. Culbertson, the wealthiest man in the state of Indiana at the time. The 20,000 square foot Empire-style mansion was built between 1867 and 1869 for about $120,000. The architect spared no expense, including hand-painted ceilings and walls, elaborate frescoes, hand-carved details, and crystal chandeliers.

The home passed to his widow upon his death in 1892. She later auctioned the home to John McDonald. After McDonald's death, his

Culbertson Mansion

daughter sold it to the American Legion, who turned the building into a meeting space. By the 1960s, the home had fallen into serious disrepair. It was purchased in 1964 by a local preservationist organization, and in 1976 the mansion became an Indiana State Museum Historic Site. The home was restored in 1980, and efforts to restore the home to its original grandeur are still ongoing. Tours of the home are given between April and December. The home is also a popular Halloween haunted house on weekends in October.

East of Vincennes Street, the median and the shared use lane disappear as the road passes through an industrial area. The route then doubles back, returning the way it came along Main Street, Silver Street, and Market Street.

8.5 Left onto Silver Street

8.6 Right onto E Market Street

8.7 Left onto Cost Avenue

8.8 Right onto IN-62/E Spring Street

The route continues to return the same way it headed into New Albany, traveling along IN-62/Spring Street. A median appears in the middle of the road that prevents left turns directly onto Providence Way. However, there is an exit ramp from Spring Street that leads back to Providence Way. The ramp is steep and sharply curved, which will likely require braking to avoid building up too much speed.

9.1 Right onto Providence Way via exit ramp

At the bottom of the ramp, the route continues to the right onto Providence Way. From this point, the route continues back to the ride start site at the Ohio River Greenway trailhead.

9.3 Right to continue onto Providence Way

10.0 Right onto Lewis and Clark Parkway

10.3 Continue onto McCullough Pike

10.7 Left onto Emery Crossing

11.7 Continue onto Jackson Street

11.8 Continue onto Harrison Avenue

11.9 Right to continue onto Harrison Avenue

12.0 Left onto Ohio River Greenway

13.7 Left into parking lot

Louisville skyline from Clarksville's Ashland Park

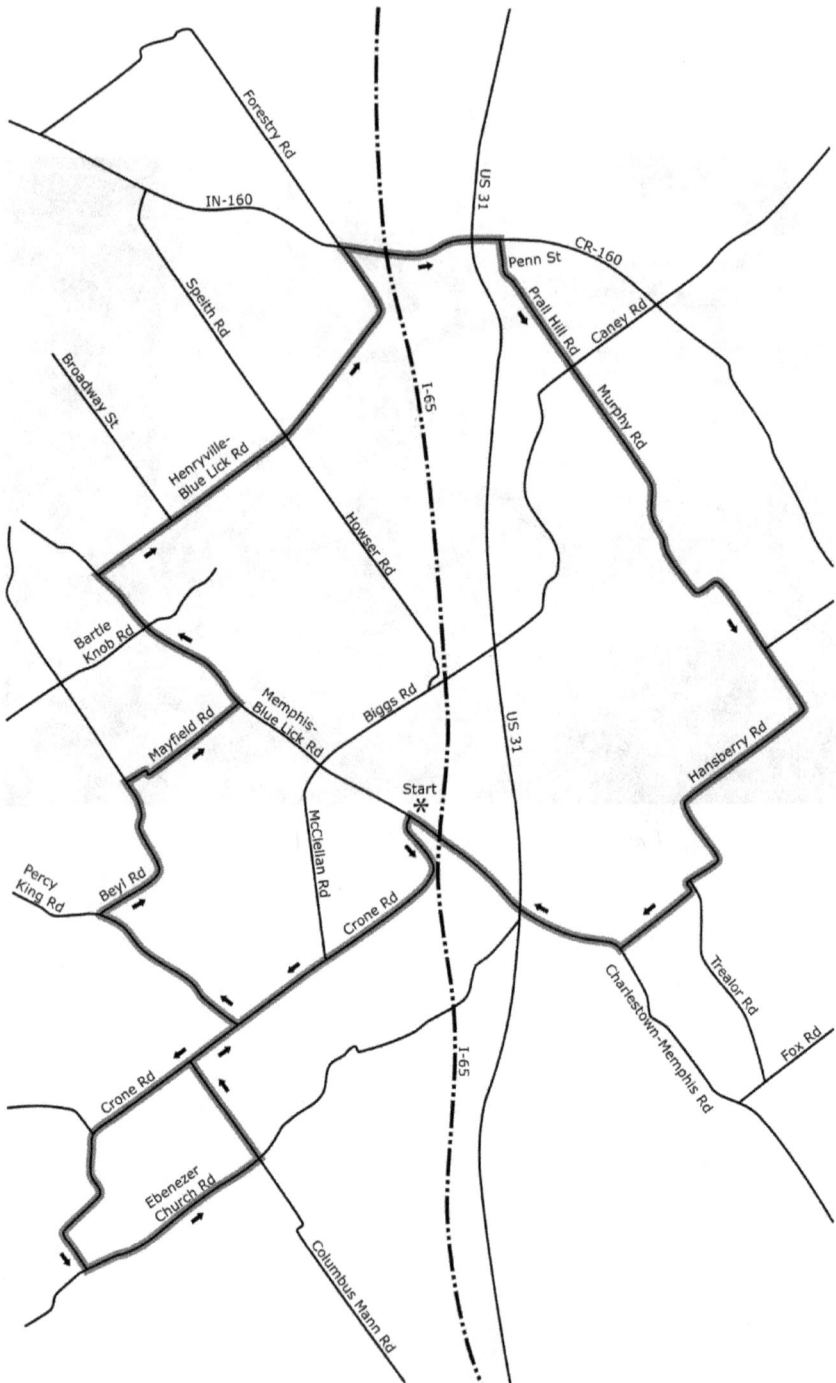

25 MEMPHIS AND HENRYVILLE

Distance: 21.3 miles

Difficulty: Moderate, with a few minor hills. Mostly rural roads with little traffic except for minor congestion near Interstate 65 and some fast-moving traffic on IN-160.

Points of Interest: Memphis, Blue Lick, and Henryville, Indiana

Indiana's Clark County lies directly north of Louisville, across the Ohio River. In addition to the city of Jeffersonville and the town of Clarksville, which are the county's major population centers, Clark County is also home to many other smaller, rural communities like Memphis, Henryville, Sellersburg, and Borden, all of which lie farther north. There are many rural roads in northern Clark County that wind their way through fertile farmland and the tall hills of the Ohio River Valley that make this area terrific for cycling.

Clark County was created by Indiana Territorial Governor William Henry Harrison on February 3, 1801. At the time, the county was comprised primarily of large tracts of land granted to General George Rogers Clark and many of his soldiers for service during the U.S. Revolutionary War. The first county seat was Springville, but it was later moved to Jeffersonville, and then to Charlestown. Charlestown would serve as the county seat until 1873 when it was moved back to Jeffersonville, where it remains today.

Between 1810 and 1869, Clark County grew quickly, Many small towns and settlements sprung up across the landscape, and the county was reorganized into twelve townships. Abundant, high-quality limestone in the area led to lime production, particularly in the Utica area. Along the river in Jeffersonville and New Albany, the area's vast forests supplied abundant, high-quality lumber that nurtured the area's shipbuilding industry. Industries thrived, and Clark County's residents prospered.

By the 1850s, the railroad industry had established a presence in the area, with lines running from Jeffersonville to Columbus, Madison, and Indianapolis. In 1852, the town of Sellersburg was established along the railroad's right-of-way, and it soon became a major manufacturing center in the area. With the increase in commerce, other towns began to develop along the railroad in northern Clark County, including the town of Henryville. By the onset of the U.S. Civil War, Clark County was booming, with a substantial industrial economy in addition to the numerous farms taking advantage of the rich alluvial soil on the north side of the Ohio River.

After the U.S. Civil War, Clark County's industrial base continued to develop and diversity. In 1866, the Falls City Cement Company began manufacturing cement near Sellersburg. By the end of the 19th century, multiple facilities were producing high quality cement, crowding out the lime industry in the Utica area.

Clark County has also witnessed many changes throughout the 20th century. Spurred by the suburban exodus following World War II and the plentiful jobs created by the many industrial parks constructed in the 1960s and 1970s, Clark County's population exploded, rising from around 30,000 in 1940 to nearly 100,000 by the turn of the 21st century. But even with this major population increase, many areas of Clark County, particularly in the northern portion, are still very rural and quiet.

This tour begins and ends near the town of Memphis, which is located along U.S. Highway 31 near Interstate 65 in northern Clark County. Memphis is a small town with a population of 700 that developed along the railroad line between Clarksville and Columbus, Indiana, about 70 miles to the north. The town was founded in 1854 and was named for Memphis, Tennessee, from where its first settlers arrived.

The route winds its way through the rural roads between Memphis and Henryville, which is located a few miles to the north. Henryville, like Memphis, was founded in the 1850s along the railroad line running between Clarksville and Columbus. Originally called Morristown, the town's name was changed to Henryville in 1853 to honor Colonel Henry Ferguson, formerly of the Pennsylvania militia. Today, the town has a population of about 1,900 residents. Indiana's beautiful Clark State Forest lies just to the north of town.

Henryville and Memphis were hit by a massive EF-4 tornado on March 2, 2012. The massive tornado cleared a 50-mile pathway through the area, killing 3 people and destroying many homes, businesses, and churches. The tornado also destroyed Henryville Elementary School and Henryville Junior/Senior High School. Damage from this tornado can still be seen throughout the area.

The tour departs Memphis from the parking lot of either of the two large truck stops that lie on either side of Interstate 65 at the Memphis Road exit. The truck stop is a short 20 minute drive from downtown Louisville. Plenty of parking is available at either site, and the truck stops are a convenient place to buy snacks or fill water bottles before or after an afternoon of cycling. Distances on the route are measured from the truck stop west of the expressway.

The hills of Clark Memorial Forest on the outskirts of Henryville

Route Directions – Memphis and Henryville

0.0 Right onto Memphis-Blue Lick Road
0.1 Left onto Crone Road
3.0 Left to continue onto Crone Road
4.0 Left onto Ebenezer Church Road
5.2 Left onto Columbus Mann Road
5.9 Right onto Crone Road
6.3 Left onto Beyl Road
8.4 Right onto Mayfield Road
9.2 Left onto Memphis-Blue Lick Road
10.4 Right onto Henryville-Blue Lick Road
13.2 Right onto IN-160
14.0 Continue onto CR-160
14.2 Right onto Pennsylvania Street
14.5 Continue onto Prall Hill road
15.1 Continue onto Murphy Road
17.4 Continue onto Hansberry Road
19.9 Right onto Memphis-Charlestown Road
20.6 Continue onto Memphis-Blue Lick Road
21.3 Right into parking lot

Route Description – Memphis and Henryville

0.0 Right onto Memphis-Blue Lick Road

Exiting the parking lot can be an exercise in frustration, especially during the afternoon rush hour. Be aware of traffic coming from the other side of the Interstate, which is cresting a small hill that blocks the line of sight and may be traveling well above the speed limit. There may also be drivers entering and exiting the parking lot who may not be looking in the direction of the turn. The easiest way to exit the lot is to head for truck entrance at the western edge of the lot, well away from the turning cars.

The next turn is almost diagonally across the road from the parking lot where the route begins. Cyclists should be wary of vehicles at the end of Crone Road when making the turn here because impatient drivers may not necessarily pay attention to oncoming traffic.

0.1 Left onto Crone Road

The traffic on Crone Road lightens significantly. Crone Road crests a small hill, then curves around to the east and runs parallel to Interstate 65 before veering off to the southwest. The road climbs and descends a series of small hills as it continues toward the larger hills in the distance. The road soon comes to a three-way stop at the top of a small hill. The route turns left at the intersection, continuing along Crone Road.

3.0 Left to continue onto Crone Road

This section of the road was recently repaved and is much smoother than the previous portion. The road continues to twist and turn as it descends a small hill and ends at Ebenezer Church Road. There is a swampy wooded area on the right side of the road at the corner. After heavy rains, there may be water over the road in this location.

4.0 Left onto Ebenezer Church Road

Ebenezer Church Road heads back to the northeast. The next turn on the route is onto Columbus Mann Road. There is a cemetery on the left side of the road that marks the intersection.

5.2 Left onto Columbus Mann Road

5.9 Right onto Crone Road

The route retraces itself along Crone Road, heading northeast. There is a short, swift descent immediately prior to the next turn on the route, onto Beyl Road.

6.3 Left onto Beyl Road

The pavement on Beyl Road has become rough in places over the past few seasons, and there are many patches and potholes that must be avoided. At the 7.2-mile mark, Beyl road turns sharply to the right and ascends a short hill. At the curve, the road continues ahead as Percy King Road and comes to a dead end at the edge of Clark State Forest.

8.4 Right onto Mayfield Road

9.2 Left onto Memphis-Blue Lick Road

Memphis-Blue Lick Road leads west through scenic Indiana farmland, heading toward the unincorporated town of Blue Lick. Blue Lick once had a post office, but it was closed in the early 20th century. The town's unusual name originates from nearby Blue Lick Creek, which was named for the exposed slate in the creek bed.

Memphis-Blue Lick Road

Blue Lick Road ends just past a cluster of homes where it becomes Pixley Knob Road. If you're up for a more challenging ride, Pixley Knob Road makes a long, slow, gentle climb, then turns much steeper as it then leads through Clark State Forest and up Pixley Knob about 4 miles to the west of Blue Lick.

10.4 Right onto Henryville-Blue Lick Road

Henryville-Blue Lick Road branches off to the right and heads north toward the town of Henryville. Around the 6.7-mile mark, near the road's end, there is a cemetery on the left side of the road as it curves very sharply to the left. There is a small road straight ahead leading into the cemetery, so it will be necessary to pay close attention to the road. The road ends at the very busy IN-160.

13.2 Right onto IN-160

IN-160 carries a large amount of fast traffic. Luckily, vehicles must slow down due to the Interstate 65 interchange and the town of Henryville, which lies just on the eastern side of the expressway. Be very wary of cars entering and exiting Interstate 65 when cresting the hill. After passing the top of the hill, traffic eases somewhat.

On the right side of the road there is a historical marker commemorating Colonel Harland Sanders, the founder of Kentucky Fried Chicken. Sanders was born in 1890 in a small house a few miles to the east of this location. His father died in 1895, and Sanders was forced to help care for his many siblings at a very early age, where he perfected his cooking skills. His mother later remarried and moved the family to Greenwood, Indiana, near Indianapolis. Sanders did not get along well with his stepfather, and after dropping out of school in the 7th grade in 1903 he went to work in Indianapolis. In 1906, he moved in with an uncle in New Albany and found work as a streetcar conductor.

Sanders soon enlisted in the U.S. Army, falsifying his date of birth, and was honorably discharged in 1907. After leaving the Army, he worked a series of jobs in Alabama, Tennessee, and Illinois, and eventually earned a law degree. He practiced law for a short time in Arkansas, but his law career was cut short after a courtroom brawl with a client. Between 1909 and 1930, Sanders worked a series of odd jobs in Indiana and Kentucky but seldom remained at any one job for more than a year or two.

In 1930, Shell Oil offered Sanders a service station in North Corbin, Kentucky. During his time running the service station, Sanders perfected his already well-developed cooking skills, offering various chicken dishes, country ham, and other southern foods to his customers. His fame and reputation grew, and by 1935, he was commissioned as a Kentucky Colonel by Governor Ruby Laffoon. By 1940, he had refined his "secret recipe" and had developed a method of cooking fried chicken in a pressure cooker that was much faster than conventional pan frying.

In 1952, Sanders franchised his Kentucky Fried Chicken restaurant to Pete Harman in South Salt Lake, Utah. Harman experienced phenomenal success with it. Soon, more franchises opened, and Kentucky Fried Chicken became a national phenomenon. By 1964, Sanders' age forced him to sell his company to investors John Y. Brown, Jr. and Jack Massey, who then developed the chain into one of the largest fast-food companies in the world. Sanders continued to serve as a brand ambassador for many years afterward, traveling across the country and all over the world, and starring in the company's television and radio advertisements.

The road soon makes a swift descent leading to a four-way stop at the road's intersection with U.S. Highway 31/Ferguson Street. IN-160 ends at this intersection, becoming County Road 160 as it continues straight ahead.

14.0 Continue onto CR-160

County Road 160 heads down a slight hill and crosses a set of railroad tracks before leading out of the town of Henryville. Just beyond the railroad tracks, the route continues to the right onto Pennsylvania Street.

Downtown Henryville

14.2 Right onto Pennsylvania Street

Pennsylvania Street leads through the historic district of Henryville. There is an old railroad depot, a few historic homes, and an old grocery store. The street ends at the edge of town, where it becomes Prall Hill Road.

14.5 Continue onto Prall Hill road

Prall Hill road leads very quickly to the first climb of the route. Fortunately, it is not extremely tall, only 60 feet in elevation. Although it is a little steep near the end, climbing gears generally are not necessary. At the top of the hill, it comes to a four-way stop with Caney Road. The route continues straight ahead, onto Murphy Road.

15.1 Continue onto Murphy Road

Murphy Road continues through rural northern Clark County, climbing and descending a series of small hills. Around the 9.5-mile mark, the road begins to climb in elevation again, rising about 100 feet in elevation over the next mile. The road ends and becomes Hansberry Road just past the 17.4-mile mark.

17.4 Continue onto Hansberry Road

Hansberry Road continues winding and twisting through the scenic farmland of northern Clark County. Around the 13-mile mark, the road curves sharply to the left just past its intersection with Trealor Road, and then begins a swift descent. The hill is quite treacherous, dropping more than 100 feet in elevation as it descends through two sharp curves before

Scenery on Hansberry Road

flattening out. The road ends at Memphis-Charlestown Road about a half-mile past the end of the descent.

19.9 Right onto Memphis-Charlestown Road

Memphis-Charlestown Road leads back through the town of Memphis. Luckily, the road is nicely shaded through town, giving much-needed relief during the hot summer months. The road crosses U.S. Highway 31 again and then climbs a small hill as it leads back under Interstate 65 toward the start site. Again, caution should be employed in dealing with traffic entering and exiting Interstate 65.

20.6 Continue onto Memphis-Blue Lick Road

21.3 Right into parking lot

BIBLIOGRAPHY

21st Century Parks. (n.d.). Retrieved December 13, 2017, from
https://www.theparklands.org/21st-century-parks.html

About Locust Grove. (n.d.). Retrieved December 13, 2017, from
http://locustgrove.org/learn/about/

About Waverly Hills. (n.d.). Retrieved December 13, 2017, from
https://www.therealwaverlyhills.com/about

About Frederick Law Olmstead Parks. (n.d.). Retrieved December 13, 2017,
from http://www.olmstedparks.org/about/

Abraham Lincoln (captain). (2017, November 24). Retrieved December 13,
2017, from https://en.wikipedia.org/wiki/Abraham_Lincoln_(captain)

A Brief History - About UofL. (n.d.). Retrieved December 13, 2017, from
http://louisville.edu/about/history

Anchorage History. (n.d.). Retrieved December 13, 2017, from
http://www.cityofanchorage.org/history.htm

Annie Fellows Johnston – a Short Biography. (2017, November 09).
Retrieved December 13, 2017, from http://littlecolonel.com/author

Audubon Park, Kentucky. (2017, December 07). Retrieved December 13,
2017, from https://en.wikipedia.org/wiki/Audubon_Park,_Kentucky

Beargrass Creek (Kentucky). (2017, July 16). Retrieved December 13, 2017,
from https://en.wikipedia.org/wiki/Beargrass_Creek_(Kentucky)

Bellarmine University. (2017, December 13). Retrieved December 13, 2017, from https://en.wikipedia.org/wiki/Bellarmine_University

Belle of Louisville. (2017, November 22). Retrieved December 13, 2017, from https://en.wikipedia.org/wiki/Belle_of_Louisville

Berrytown, Louisville. (2017, December 05). Retrieved December 13, 2017, from https://en.wikipedia.org/wiki/Berrytown,_Louisville

Bloody Monday. (2017, July 21). Retrieved December 13, 2017, from https://en.wikipedia.org/wiki/Bloody_Monday

Bowdan, A. (2017, October 04). Toxic gases found under Riverside Gardens homes. Retrieved December 13, 2017, from http://www.wlky.com/article/toxic-gases-found-under-riverside-gardens-homes-1/3753364

Butchertown, Louisville. (2017, December 05). Retrieved December 13, 2017, from https://en.wikipedia.org/wiki/Butchertown,_Louisville

Campisano, Deborah. (n.d.). Pennsylvania Run Memorial Park – A Short History. Retrieved December 13, 2017, from http://kykinfolk.com/jefferson/cems2/PennRun/pennrunhistory.html

Cemeteries. (2015, December 15). Retrieved December 13, 2017, from https://louisvilleky.gov/government/parks/cemeteries

Central Park, Louisville. (2017, November 11). Retrieved December 13, 2017, from https://en.wikipedia.org/wiki/Central_Park,_Louisville

Clark County Indiana History. (n.d.). Retrieved December 13, 2017, from http://www.co.clark.in.us/index.php/about-clark-county-indiana/clark-county-indiana-history

Community Pride. (n.d.). Retrieved December 13, 2017, from http://www.cityofwindyhills.com/

Conrad-Caldwell House. (n.d.). Retrieved December 13, 2017, from https://conrad-caldwell.org/brief-history/

Construction on new cemetery for the poor begins next month. (2009, July 24). Retrieved December 13, 2017, from http://www.wdrb.com/story/10788232/construction-on-new-cemetery-for-the-poor-begins-next-month

Courier-Journal (Ed.). (1989). *A Place in Time: The Story of Louisville's Neighborhoods*. Louisville: The Courier-Journal.

Darr, Savannah. (2015, October 08). The Dark Past of Eastern Cemetery in Louisville, Kentucky. Retrieved December 13, 2017, from https://www.atlasobscura.com/places/eastern-cemetery

duPont Manual High School – History. (n.d.). Retrieved December 13, 2017, from http://www.dupontmanual.com/history.html#content

East Market District, Louisville. (2017, December 05). Retrieved December 13, 2017, from https://en.wikipedia.org/wiki/East_Market_District,_Louisville

Eclipse Park (Louisville). (n.d.). Retrieved December 13, 2017, from https://sabr.org/bioproj/park/cf040064

Fern Creek, Louisville. (2017, December 06). Retrieved December 13, 2017, from https://en.wikipedia.org/wiki/Fern_Creek,_Louisville

Fisherville, Louisville. (2017, December 05). Retrieved December 13, 2017, from https://en.wikipedia.org/wiki/Fisherville,_Louisville

Freedom Park. (n.d.). Retrieved December 13, 2017, from https://louisville.edu/freedompark

Kleber, J. E. (2015). *The Encyclopedia of Louisville*. Lexington: The University Press of Kentucky.

Gene Snyder. (2017, November 15). Retrieved December 13, 2017, from https://en.wikipedia.org/wiki/Gene_Snyder

German Reformed Presbyterian Church Cemetery. (2009, April 19). Retrieved December 13, 2017, from http://unusualkentucky.blogspot.com/2009/04/german-reformed-presbyterian-church.html

Germantown, Louisville. (2017, December 05). Retrieved December 13, 2017, from https://en.wikipedia.org/wiki/Germantown,_Louisville

Grundhauser, E. (2014, October 24). Pope Lick Trestle Bridge. Retrieved December 13, 2017, from https://www.atlasobscura.com/places/pope-lick-trestle-bridge

Hayden, J. (2012, April 05). The Evolution of Butchertown. Retrieved December 13, 2017, from https://www.joehaydenrealtor.com/blog/the-evolution-of-butchertown/

Heart of Germantown and Schnitzelburg remains despite their growing popularity. (2017, February 09). Retrieved December 13, 2017, from https://insiderlouisville.com/business/real-estate/heart-of-germantown-schnitzelburg-neighborhoods-remain-despite-their-growing-popularity/

Henryville, Indiana. (2017, December 11). Retrieved December 13, 2017, from https://en.wikipedia.org/wiki/Henryville,_Indiana

Highland Park, Louisville. (2017, December 05). Retrieved December 13, 2017, from https://en.wikipedia.org/wiki/Highland_Park,_Louisville

Highland Park - Louisville, Kentucky - Gone But Not Forgotten - Tribupedia. (n.d.). Retrieved December 13, 2017, from http://tribupedia.com/tribute/highland-park-louisville-ky-gone-but-not-forgotten/

Historic New Albany. (n.d.). Retrieved December 13, 2017, from http://www.historicnewalbany.com/default.asp?q_areaprimaryid=4

Historic Portland Louisville, Kentucky. (n.d.). Retrieved December 13, 2017, from http://www.portlandlouisville.com/#historic-portland

History – Belknap Neighborhood Association. (n.d.). Retrieved December 13, 2017, from https://www.belknapneighborhood.org/history/

History – City of Audubon Park, Kentucky. (n.d.). Retrieved December 13, 2017, from http://www.audubonparkky.org/history.html

History.com Staff. (2009). John C. Breckinridge. Retrieved December 13, 2017, from http://www.history.com/topics/john-c-breckinridge

History of Jeffersontown. (n.d.). Retrieved December 13, 2017, from
https://www.jeffersontownky.com/561/History-of-Jeffersontown

History of Louisville, Kentucky. (2017, December 13). Retrieved December
13, 2017, from
https://en.wikipedia.org/wiki/History_of_Louisville,_Kentucky

History of Middletown Kentucky. (n.d.). Retrieved December 13, 2017,
from https://cityofmiddletownky.org/history/

History of Prospect. (n.d.). Retrieved December 13, 2017, from
http://prospectky.us/residents/history-of-prospect/

History of the Highlands of Louisville, KY USA. (n.d.). Retrieved
December 13, 2017, from
http://www.thehighlandsoflouisville.com/ScrapbookHistory.php

Holland, H. (2014, July 08). Look Back | Death of Zachary Taylor solved.
Retrieved December 13, 2017, from https://www.courier-
journal.com/story/news/history/river-city-retro/2014/07/08/zachary-
taylor-death-solved/12363933/

Honoring a Forgotten Chapter in Kentucky's Civil War History. (2015,
August 11). Retrieved December 13, 2017, from
https://www.ket.org/promos/kentucky/honoring-a-forgotten-chapter-
in-kentuckys-civil-war-history/

Indiana Limestone. (2017, December 13). Retrieved December 13, 2017,
from https://en.wikipedia.org/wiki/Indiana_Limestone

Indian Hills, Kentucky. (2017, December 06). Retrieved December 13,
2017, from https://en.wikipedia.org/wiki/Indian_Hills,_Kentucky

Jefferson Memorial Forest. (2017, September 19). Retrieved December 13,
2017, from https://en.wikipedia.org/wiki/Jefferson_Memorial_Forest

Jeffersontown, Kentucky. (2017, December 09). Retrieved December 13,
2017, from https://en.wikipedia.org/wiki/Jeffersontown,_Kentucky

Jeffersonville, Indiana. (2017, December 13). Retrieved December 13, 2017,
from https://en.wikipedia.org/wiki/Jeffersonville,_Indiana

John H. Buschemeyer. (2017, September 26). Retrieved December 13, 2017, from https://en.wikipedia.org/wiki/John_H._Buschemeyer

Lake Dreamland, Louisville. (2017, December 05). Retrieved December 13, 2017, from https://en.wikipedia.org/wiki/Lake_Dreamland,_Louisville

Lincoln Institute (Kentucky). (2017, November 22). Retrieved December 13, 2017, from https://en.wikipedia.org/wiki/Lincoln_Institute_(Kentucky)

LMHS School History. (n.d.). Retrieved December 13, 2017, from https://schools.jefferson.kyschools.us/high/male/pages/schoolhistory.html

Long Run massacre. (2017, October 13). Retrieved December 13, 2017, from https://en.wikipedia.org/wiki/Long_Run_massacre

Louisville and Nashville Railroad. (2017, December 11). Retrieved December 13, 2017, from https://en.wikipedia.org/wiki/Louisville_and_Nashville_Railroad

Louisville and Portland Canal. (2017, December 02). Retrieved December 13, 2017, from https://en.wikipedia.org/wiki/Louisville_and_Portland_Canal

Louisville Colonels. (2017, December 12). Retrieved December 13, 2017, from https://en.wikipedia.org/wiki/Louisville_Colonels

Louisville Colonels (1882-1899). (n.d.). Retrieved December 13, 2017, from http://sportsecyclopedia.com/nl/louisville/colonels.html

Louisville Loop. (n.d.). Retrieved December 13, 2017, from https://www.theparklands.org/Parks/Beckley-Creek-Park/10/Louisville-Loop

Louisville, Kentucky. (2017, December 13). Retrieved December 13, 2017, from https://en.wikipedia.org/wiki/Louisville,_Kentucky

Louisville Memorial Auditorium – About Us. (n.d.). Retrieved December 13, 2017, from http://www.louisvillememorialauditorium.com/aboutUs.aspx

Louisville's Southern Exposition. (n.d.). Retrieved December 13, 2017, from http://filsonhistorical.org/galleries/louisvilles-southern-exposition/

Mann's Lick. (2017, October 21). Retrieved December 13, 2017, from https://en.wikipedia.org/wiki/Mann%27s_Lick

Memphis, Indiana. (2017, December 06). Retrieved December 13, 2017, from https://en.wikipedia.org/wiki/Memphis,_Indiana

McDonogh, P. (2015, October 17). Beechmont thrives in south Louisville. Retrieved December 13, 2017, from https://www.courier-journal.com/story/news/local/communities/2015/10/15/beechmont-thrives-south-louisville/73378010/

McDonogh, P. (2015, November 13). Lake Dreamland faces share of tough realities. Retrieved December 13, 2017, from https://www.courier-journal.com/story/news/local/neighborhoods/2015/11/12/along-edge-lake-dreamland/75056066/

Moffitt, M. (2016, April 27). Ghost hunter searching for 'Pope Lick Monster' atop trestle killed by train. Retrieved December 13, 2017, from http://www.sfgate.com/weird/article/Ghost-hunter-searching-for-Pope-Lick-Monster-7379120.php.

Muhammad Ali. (2017, November 07). Retrieved December 13, 2017, from https://www.biography.com/people/muhammad-ali-9181165

Muhammad Ali. (2017, December 11). Retrieved December 13, 2017, from https://en.wikipedia.org/wiki/Muhammad_Ali\

Newburg, Louisville. (2017, December 13). Retrieved December 13, 2017, from https://en.wikipedia.org/wiki/Newburg,_Louisville

Novelly, T. (2017, August 14). Cherokee Triangle statue of Confederate officer vandalized following Charlottesville violence. Retrieved December 13, 2017, from https://www.courier-journal.com/story/news/local/2017/08/13/cherokee-triangle-statue-confederate-officer-vandalized-following-charlottesville-violence/563012001/

Nulu. (2015, November 22). Retrieved December 13, 2017, from http://new2lou.com/neighborhoods/nulu/

Okolona, Louisville. (2017, December 06). Retrieved December 13, 2017, from https://en.wikipedia.org/wiki/Okolona,_Louisville

Old Louisville. (2017, December 05). Retrieved December 13, 2017, from https://en.wikipedia.org/wiki/Old_Louisville

Original Highlands, Louisville. (2017, December 05). Retrieved December 13, 2017, from https://en.wikipedia.org/wiki/Original_Highlands,_Louisville

Our History – City of St. Matthews. (n.d.). Retrieved December 13, 2017, from http://www.stmatthewsky.gov/our-history/

Our History – Louisville Slugger. (2016, March 30). Retrieved December 13, 2017, from http://www.slugger.com/en-us/our-history

Parks. (n.d.). Retrieved December 13, 2017, from https://www.theparklands.org/parks.html

Penile, Louisville. (2017, December 05). Retrieved December 13, 2017, from https://en.wikipedia.org/wiki/Penile,_Louisville

Peterson, E. (2014, October 14). Riverside Gardens: A Former Resort Community Besieged By Pollution. Retrieved December 13, 2017, from http://wfpl.org/riverside-gardens-former-resort-community-besieged-pollution/

Pewee Valley, Kentucky. (2017, December 07). Retrieved December 13, 2017, from https://en.wikipedia.org/wiki/Pewee_Valley,_Kentucky

Pope Lick Monster. (2017, November 13). Retrieved December 13, 2017, from https://en.wikipedia.org/wiki/Pope_Lick_Monster

Poplar Level, Louisville. (2017, December 05). Retrieved December 13, 2017, from https://en.wikipedia.org/wiki/Poplar_Level,_Louisville

Portland, Louisville. (2017, December 05). Retrieved December 13, 2017, from https://en.wikipedia.org/wiki/Portland,_Louisville

Prospect, Kentucky. (2017, December 06). Retrieved December 13, 2017, from https://en.wikipedia.org/wiki/Prospect,_Kentucky.

Regions of the Loop. (2016, October 03). Retrieved December 13, 2017, from https://louisvilleky.gov/government/louisville-loop/regions-loop

Riverside, the Farnsley-Moremen Landing. (n.d.). Retrieved December 13, 2017, from http://www.riverside-landing.org/the-history/

Rubbertown: The Birthplace of Neoprene Manufacturing. (n.d.). Retrieved December 13, 2017, from http://www.rubbercal.com/sheet-rubber/rubbertown-neoprene-birthplace/

Rubbertown, Louisville. (2017, December 05). Retrieved December 13, 2017, from https://en.wikipedia.org/wiki/Rubbertown,_Louisville

Russell, Louisville. (2017, December 05). Retrieved December 13, 2017, from https://en.wikipedia.org/wiki/Russell,_Louisville

Schnitzelburg, Louisville. (2017, December 05). Retrieved December 13, 2017, from https://en.wikipedia.org/wiki/Schnitzelburg,_Louisville

Shelby Park, Louisville. (2017, December 05). Retrieved December 13, 2017, from https://en.wikipedia.org/wiki/Shelby_Park,_Louisville

Shippingport, Kentucky. (2017, November 06). Retrieved December 13, 2017, from https://en.wikipedia.org/wiki/Shippingport,_Kentucky

Shively, Kentucky. (2017, December 09). Retrieved December 13, 2017, from https://en.wikipedia.org/wiki/Shively,_Kentucky

Simmons College. (2017, December 04). Retrieved December 13, 2017, from https://en.wikipedia.org/wiki/Simmons_College

Smoketown, Louisville. (2017, December 05). Retrieved December 13, 2017, from https://en.wikipedia.org/wiki/Smoketown,_Louisville

Spalding University. (2017, November 27). Retrieved December 13, 2017, from https://en.wikipedia.org/wiki/Spalding_University

St. Andrew Cemetery. (n.d.). Retrieved December 13, 2017, from http://stpaulparishlouisvilleky.org/cemetery.php

Stitzel-Weller Distillery. (2017, November 03). Retrieved December 13, 2017, from https://en.wikipedia.org/wiki/Stitzel-Weller_Distillery

St. Joseph, Louisville. (2017, December 05). Retrieved December 13, 2017, from https://en.wikipedia.org/wiki/St._Joseph,_Louisville

St. Martin of Tours Catholic Church (Louisville, Kentucky). (2017, October 06). Retrieved December 13, 2017, from https://en.wikipedia.org/wiki/St._Martin_of_Tours_Catholic_Church_(Louisville,_Kentucky)

St. Matthews, Kentucky. (2017, December 05). Retrieved December 13, 2017, from https://en.wikipedia.org/wiki/St._Matthews,_Kentucky

The Courier-Journal. (2017, November 22). Retrieved December 13, 2017, from https://en.wikipedia.org/wiki/The_Courier-Journal

The History of Churchill Downs. (n.d.). Retrieved December 13, 2017, from https://www.churchilldowns.com/about/churchill-downs/history/

The Highlands, Louisville. (2017, December 05). Retrieved December 13, 2017, from https://en.wikipedia.org/wiki/The_Highlands,_Louisville

The Howard Saga. (n.d.). Retrieved December 13, 2017, from http://www.howardsteamboatmuseum.org/16-2/

The Monument in Historic Eastwood. (n.d.). Retrieved December 13, 2017, from http://eastwoodvillagecouncil.com/History/history.html

Town History – the Town of Clarksville, Indiana. (n.d.). Retrieved December 13, 2017, from http://www.townofclarksville.com/history.php

Two Centuries of Stout House History Come Full Circle. (n.d.). Retrieved December 13, 2017, from https://www.theparklands.org/Blog/245/Two-Centuries-of-Stout-House-History-Come-Full-Circle

University of Louisville. (2017, December 13). Retrieved December 13, 2017, from https://en.wikipedia.org/wiki/University_of_Louisville

Unusual Kentucky: Floyd's Defeat Mass Grave. (2010, April 14). Retrieved December 13, 2017, from http://unusualkentucky.blogspot.com/2010/04/floyds-defeat-mass-grave.htm.

Vanover, K. (2017, May 29). Confederate monument moved from UofL campus rededicated in Brandenburg. Retrieved December 13, 2017, from http://www.wave3.com/story/35539568/confederate-monument-moved-from-uofl-campus-rededicated-in-brandenburg

Wilder Park, Louisville. (2017, December 05). Retrieved December 13, 2017, from https://en.wikipedia.org/wiki/Wilder_Park,_Louisville

Zachary Taylor House. (2017, November 22). Retrieved December 13, 2017, from https://en.wikipedia.org/wiki/Zachary_Taylor_House

Zachary Taylor National Cemetery. (2017, November 16). Retrieved December 13, 2017, from https://en.wikipedia.org/wiki/Zachary_Taylor_National_Cemetery

Louisville skyline over the Ohio River

Michael W. Thompson

APPENDIX
BIKE RIDES IN THE LOUISVILLE AREA

April

Redbud Ride – London, KY
http://www.redbudride.com

Kentucky Derby Festival Tour de Lou
https://discover.kdf.org/tour-de-lou/

May

Harmonie Hundred – New Harmony, IN
http://harmoniehundred.com

Horsey Hundred – Georgetown, KY
http://horseyhundred.com

June

Bike Morehead – Morehead, KY

Limestone Cycling Tour – Maysville, KY
http://www.limestonecyclingleague.com/r2r/

July

BAM! Bike Around Mayfield – Mayfield, KY
https://www.facebook.com/BAM-Kiwanis-Century-Ride-491408877593699/

Round Barn Ride – Brownstown, IN
http://www.brownstownexchangeclub.org/5.html

August

Le Tour de Pork – Corydon, IN
http://tourdeporkride.com

RACK – Ride Across Kentucky – Paducah, KY
http://bikeworldky.com

The Bourbon and Bluegrass Century – Owensboro, KY
https://www.facebook.com/bourbonbluegrasscentury/

September

Hub City Tour – Elizabethtown, KY
http://hubcitytourky.com

Old Kentucky Home Bicycle Tour – Louisville, KY
http://okht.org

Misaligned Minds Bike Tour – Paducah, KY
http://bikeworldky.com

Bourbon Country Burn – Lexington, KY
http://bourboncountryburn.com

October

Trail of Tears Century Ride – Grand Rivers, KY
http://woodnwave.com

Red River Rally – Slade, KY
http://bgcycling.net

ABOUT THE AUTHOR

Michael W. Thompson was born and raised in Paducah, Kentucky, and resided in Louisville from 1989-1994 and 2011-2016. He holds a Bachelor's in Zoology and Chemistry from the University of Louisville and Ph.D. in Biochemistry from the University of Kentucky. A strong advocate for outdoor recreation, he has been an avid cyclist, runner, and triathlete for many years. Dr. Thompson is currently employed as a Professor of Zoology and Biology at Laramie County Community College in Cheyenne, Wyoming.

www.ingramcontent.com/pod-product-compliance
Lightning Source LLC
Chambersburg PA
CBHW062146080426
42734CB00010B/1586